Britain and Europe

Series Editor: Keith Robbins

Britain and Europe

Britain and Europe
1789–2005

KEITH ROBBINS
Vice-Chancellor Emeritus, University of Wales, Lampeter

Hodder Arnold
A MEMBER OF THE HODDER HEADLINE GROUP

First published in Great Britain in 2005 by
Hodder Education, a member of the Hodder Headline Group,
338 Euston Road, London NW1 3BH

www.hoddereducation.com

Distributed in the United States of America by
Oxford University Press Inc.
198 Madison Avenue, New York, NY10016

The advice and information in this book are believed to be true and
accurate at the date of going to press, but neither the author nor the publisher
can accept any legal responsibility or liability for any errors or omissions.

British Library Cataloguing in Publication Data
A catalogue record for this book is available from the British Library

Library of Congress Cataloging-in-Publication Data
A catalog record for this book is available from the Library of Congress

ISBN-10: 0-340-57786-X
ISBN-13: 978-0-340-57786-8

1 2 3 4 5 6 7 8 9 10

Typeset in 10/12 Sabon by Phoenix Photosetting, Chatham, Kent
Printed and bound in Malta by Gutenberg Press

What do you think about this book? Or any other
Hodder Education title? Please send your comments to
the feedback section on www.hoddereducation.com.

Contents

Norman Davies

Peter Ludlow

Robin Mountfield

'History' at Magdalen College, Oxford, 1958–61

Same questions? Different answers?

List of maps

General editor's preface

Years, decades, centuries, millennia come and go, but Britain's relationship with its European neighbours remains consistently complicated and, on occasion, acutely divisive. It forms the stuff of contemporary political arguments both in 'Britain' and 'Europe', debate that is sometimes strident and ill-informed.

The heat may perhaps be excused on the grounds that there are issues of personal, national and continental identity at stake, about which people have strong feelings. The ignorance, however, is not excusable. Whatever views may be taken about contemporary issues and options, here is a relationship that can only properly be understood if it is examined in the *longue durée*. That is what this series aims to do.

It becomes evident, however, that in regard to both 'Britain' and 'Europe' we are not dealing with fixed entities standing over and against each other through the millennia. What may be held to constitute 'Britain' and what 'Europe' changes through time. The present is no exception. In a context of political devolution how Britain and Britishness is defined becomes increasingly problematic as new patterns of relationship across 'the Isles' emerge. And what are perceived to be new patterns turn out on closer examination to be reassertions and redefinitions of old identities or structures. So it is also with 'Europe'. The issue of 'enlargement' of the current European Union brings up old problems in a new form. Where does 'Europe' begin and end? At long last, to take but one example, the Turkish Republic has been accepted as a candidate for membership, but in earlier centuries, for some, Europe stopped where the Ottoman Empire began, an outlook that can still linger, with violent consequences, in the Balkans.

In effect, therefore, the series will probe and chart the shifting of boundaries – boundaries in the mind and boundaries on a map. Where Britain 'belongs', in any era, depends upon a multiplicity of factors, themselves varying in importance from century to century: upon ethnicity, language, law, government, religion, trade, warfare, to name only some. Whether, in particular periods, the islands were indeed 'isolated' depends in turn not only on what they themselves thought or wanted to believe but also upon the patterns prevailing in 'Europe' and what might be thought to constitute the 'mainstream' of its development. The historians in this series are well aware that they are not dealing with a simple one-to-one relationship. They are not committed to a common didactic agenda or rigid formula. Different periods require different assessments of the appropriate balance to be struck in tackling the ingredients of insularity on the one hand and continental commonality on the other. Propinquity has itself necessarily brought the communities of Britain into closer contact, in peace and war, with some continental countries rather than with others and caused it to have established (fluctuating) affinities and enmities, but the connection is not confined to immediate neighbours. Beneath the inter-state level, different sections of society have had different sorts of relationship, sometimes in conflict and sometimes in cooperation, across Europe both at the state and non-state levels, which have varied in content and intensity over time. And what has been happening in the 'wider world' has in turn affected and sometimes determined how both 'Britain' and the countries of 'Europe' have perceived and conducted themselves.

The study of a relationship (just like the living of one) is one of the most difficult but also the most rewarding of tasks. There is, however, no single title for this series that really does justice to what is being attempted. To speak of 'Britain and Europe' does indeed risk carrying the imputation that Britain is not 'part of' Europe. To speak of 'Britain in Europe' or even of 'Europe in Britain' have their difficulties and advantages. In short, in the event, there is something for everybody!

The difficulty, though perhaps also the urgency of the task, is compounded for historians by the circumstances of history teaching and learning in schools and universities in the United Kingdom where, very largely, 'British History' and 'European History' have been studied and written about by different people who have disclaimed significant knowledge of the other or have only studied a particular period of the one that has been different from the period in the other. The extent to which 'British history' is really a singular issue and the extent it is a particular manifestation of 'European history' is rarely tackled head on at any level. This series attempts to provide just that bridge over troubled waters that present European circumstances require. It is, however, for readers to decide for themselves what bridge into the future the past does indeed provide.

Keith Robbins
University of Wales, Lampeter

Acknowledgements

Authors are often asked how long it has taken to write a particular book. In this case, the answer might be nearly half a century. A.J.P. Taylor's *The Struggle for Mastery in Europe 1848–1918* first appeared in 1954. I was given a copy as a school history prize in 1957. One year later, I found myself an undergraduate pupil of Mr Taylor's at Magdalen College, Oxford. The 'struggle' for 'Europe' both before 1848 and after 1918 has been my underlying academic preoccupation as a university teacher and writer. The dedication marks my regard for undergraduate friends, products of the same stable, each of whom has also subsequently wrestled, in different spheres, with 'Britain and Europe'.

The present volume, however, is not another exercise in classic 'diplomatic history'. The formal relations between states naturally loom large in this account but the reader is often directed elsewhere for detailed exposition of particular issues. The attempt is made here, rather, to unpick the assumptions, spoken and unspoken, that were being made, at different periods, both about what Britain was and what Europe was, by 'policy-makers', 'opinion formers' and 'the general public' – by no means all drawn from a restricted sphere of political 'decision-makers'. The subject matter of such an enquiry could be all-embracing, but considerations of space mean that not all of its aspects have been embraced to the same extent. Thus while, at certain points, religious, literary, cultural and economic issues are all touched on, each such topic could be the subject of individual monograph treatment in the context of the overall theme of the book.

In acknowledging my debt to the writings of other historians, I recognize the role that historians have themselves had in shaping 'Britain' and 'Europe' over the modern centuries with which this book is concerned. Location and perception are frequently intertwined, though not so frequently acknowledged at the outset. Both the current 'United Kingdom' and the current 'Europe' are very different, and exist in a very different global context, from the world in which my Oxford tutor wrote in the early 1950s.

It is recognized, too, that no account of 'Britain and Europe' can ignore 'Britain and the United States' and indeed Britain's massive global inter-penetration as 'the other side of the coin'. Even so, while such non-European alignments, whether regarded as competing or complementary, are given some attention, this remains a book with a European focus. It is not, however, 'tract for the times'. It places issues in both a lengthier and more comprehensive framework than is common in what passes for con-temporary 'debate' about 'Britain and Europe', but has no desire to impose a 'blueprint for the future'. In any event, the future of 'Europe' is even more opaque than it appeared when this book was completed in the early months of 2005. We then mooted the possibility that the proposed European Constitution might be rejected in another member state before the United Kingdom voted. A 'European crisis' has arrived and with it a 'pause for reflection'. There could be worse ways of using it than in studying history.

After 1970, although 'English', by upbringing, education and 'ethnic-ity', I in fact held professorial appointments in UK universities outside England. I have participated in conferences of historians that, over the years, have taken me to many, indeed to most, European countries (not only in the 'major' countries and including Russia) on a regular basis. I received the Sir Anthony de Rothschild Award from the Winston Churchill Memorial Trust in 1990, which enabled me to travel widely throughout western and central Europe at a time of dramatic change. I have been a participant in the periodic Franco-British conferences established under the auspices of the French and British governments, and have regularly taken part in the proceedings of the Prince Albert Society/*Prinz Albert Gesellschaft* in Coburg, Germany. I have served on the academic advisory boards of the German Historical Institute in London and the *Institut für Zeitgeschichte* in Munich. Such roles have enabled me, in many conversa-tions with fellow historians and others, to understand how Britain's 'Europeanness' (or lack of it) appears in the eyes of distinguished German colleagues. I have attended meetings of 'Endeavour', the consultative gath-ering established by the British and Irish governments, and chair the International Advisory Board of the Academy for Irish Cultural Heritages of the University of Ulster. I engaged, with other European colleagues, in amicable debate with the late Jean-Baptiste Duroselle as his *Europe: A History of its Peoples* (1990) unfolded. I am a participant in the current European Science Foundation Humanities Programme on 'Representations of the Past: The Writing of National Histories in Europe'. Short academic visits to China, North America and Australia over the past decade have also given me an opportunity to discover how 'Britain and Europe' has been envisaged in distant locations.

The lengthy intellectual gestation of this book was not supposed to have required a lengthy period of writing. For 12 years, however, until 2003, I was a vice-chancellor, with the inevitable curtailment of available time. Such a role, though, gave access to other circles in Europe and the

Commonwealth with rather different perceptions and questions about Britain and Europe than those that have worried the sometimes incestuous world of historians. It also brought me, from 1995–2001, as senior vice-chancellor of the University of Wales, an interesting vantage point from which to observe the operation of devolution within the United Kingdom.

I am grateful to Christopher Wheeler, with whom the idea of the series in which this volume takes its place was devised when he was at Arnold, and his successors as editors and staff at Hodder Arnold, for their patience and encouragement throughout.

Prologue: setting the agenda

This final volume in a series devoted to exploring the relationship between Britain and Europe in its multi-faceted complexity inherits the conceptual difficulties that other authors have wrestled with in previous volumes. However, the closer it comes to the present, it also has to deal with issues scarcely hinted at in earlier centuries. Each volume has had to take account of the fact that what is entailed by 'Britain' and 'Europe' is rarely static. How we think about the one, and then the other, shifts through the centuries, sometimes with dramatic consequences. The series, therefore, has not posited a continuous and coherent 'story of Britain' (does that extend over 1000 years or 2000 years?) juxtaposed against an equally seamless 'story of Europe'. There are senses in which 'the story of Britain' cannot be properly understood unless it is seen as an aspect of the 'story of Europe', just as the 'story of Europe' cannot be written as though Britain had no part in it. Yet both 'stories' do not only exist in relation to each other. That there is an extra-European dimension to the 'story of Britain' is undeniable and there have been times when, in different ways, that dimension may have seemed more important than 'Europe'. Likewise, there have been times when Britain would only have appeared peripheral to the 'story of Europe'. No attempt to grapple with a relationship can neglect the swings, now one way now the other, that seem evident when the matter is viewed in the *longue durée*.

The novelty confronting this author, however, is the fact that at the beginning of the twenty-first century 'British history', as it has been conceived (and taught) over the previous two centuries is coming to an end – indeed, from some points of view may already be said to have come to an end. On the one hand, the 'United Kingdom', in this new century, now contains a plurality of constitutional arrangements. The unity of the state is expressed through the United Kingdom Parliament at Westminster but alongside it sit legislatures that give form to the revarnished identities of Scotland (with its parliament), Wales (with its assembly) and Northern Ireland (also with an assembly, which precariously provides for 'British' and

'Irish' identities in a still unstable context). Only England has no specific legislature of its own. It is manifest that such a 'Britain', with its devolved institutions – which may yet evolve further – embodies understandings of insular relationships that are substantially different from those that prevailed over the preceding three centuries. On the other hand, since the United Kingdom's membership of the European Economic Community in 1973 (and that body's subsequent loss of the word 'Economic' and then the replacement of 'Community' by 'Union', together with its further and still incomplete expansion in membership) the implications of this step have been the subject of constant public debate (in which an appeal to 'History' has not been absent). The fear has frequently been expressed that Britain would be reduced to a 'mere province' in a European 'superstate'. Such a step has been seen as 'the end of British history'. A variety of perspectives currently exist. For some, a process of continuing 'integration' of Britain in Europe is desirable and probably, at this juncture, irreversible. For others, the present level of integration is the limit of acceptability and might take the form, for example, of resisting the adoption of the euro as Britain's currency. Another camp, however, finds the present European Union unacceptable from a British perspective and would wish to have 'repatriated' some powers that have already been ceded by the British state or withdraw completely from the European Union. This debate has already lasted for decades and its detailed consideration will have a place at the end of this book. Our general purpose, however, is to place current arguments, however they are resolved, in a historical context extending over the period of some 200 years that began when the French Revolution of 1789 appeared to usher in the prospect of a 'New Europe' and concludes with another 'New Europe'.

There is a fundamental issue that must be faced squarely at the outset. Is this a book that is concerned with Britain/the British Isles *in* Europe or Britain/the British Isles *and* Europe? To think primarily in terms of the former is to suggest that whatever 'Europe' might be thought to be, the British Isles are as much a part of it as, for example, Portugal or Poland. No doubt, there are peculiar features in the history of Britain/the British Isles, but so there are in the history of all countries. On the other hand, there are sufficient commonalities to make it feasible to think that Europe does have some meaning and that it is not fanciful to speak of 'European civilization'. Precisely how that civilization can be defined, however, is another matter and the subject of many volumes. Historians cannot but be aware of the role they have played either in highlighting 'national characters' or in orchestrating 'Europe'. It is perhaps impossible to eradicate personal predilections in estimating where the balance lies, at any given moment, between what is shared and what is distinctive. The assumption of this book is that Britain is *in* Europe providing it is understood that this does not imply any bland uniformity. Such unity as the history of Europe possesses may be said to lie paradoxically in the way in which the *Sonderweg* (Special Path) of all its states and nations somehow, up to a point, comes together. This may mean that there is no template that lays down what 'Europe' is and what constitutes its 'core' or a 'heart', either in terms of culture or belief. Its location, geographically or spiritually, shifts from country to country as circumstances change. In this respect, the part Britain has played in the history of Europe is in principle no different from that played by any other state. The history of Europe, in the period covered by this book, may suggest a common European civilization, but if so, it is a history plagued by recurrent bouts of 'civil war' between shifting alliances of its member states. In the twentieth century, it was in Europe that two 'world wars' began. Whatever may be said about cultural connections, commercial patterns, common Christianity (if fragmented and perhaps increasingly formal), parallel ideologies, and a host of other 'networks', personal or institutional, what has actually physically brought Britain *into* Europe has been war. No battles have been fought on British soil – though war from the air came in the twentieth century. In contrast, most other European countries have experienced invasion by another European country and an occupation of long or short duration. British troops have fought *in* Europe and indeed, from the late eighteenth century to the middle of the twentieth century (before the advent of mass tourism), first-hand experience of 'Europe' came predominantly to members of the armed services who found themselves in one era largely fighting against France and in another largely against Germany.

It may be said, therefore, that this degree of detachment from what has been a common European experience has produced, or perhaps preserved, along with other considerations, a degree of psychological detachment when confronted by enthusiasm for 'building Europe' as a hoped-for means to remove the scars of battle from the European landscape. And, of course, the capacity to remain detached to this extent stemmed directly from insularity and the naval supremacy that preserved it for most of the period. It might therefore be thought that it is in fact necessary to think rather of Britain *and* Europe. To do so would give due weight to the fact that while indeed a group of islands could not be entire in themselves, to adapt John Donne, neither could they be 'part of the whole' as other countries inhabiting a continuous land mass could be. The British *Sonderweg*, on this reading, was exceptionally special (!) in the extent to which it was geographically determined. The British, when they thought about 'Europe' (insofar as they did), or visited across the 'English Channel' were most commonly, either mentally or in person, going *to* Europe, not thereby moving around *in* Europe. The task for the historian, if this is the case, might be to emphasize Britain's sturdy and endemic suspicion of 'Europe' in any form. Such a mindset has seen the country belligerently engaged against the hegemonic ambitions of any one country or individual to create a 'new Europe' in their own image, or peacefully scorning or sabotaging such attempts as have been made to forge some kind of 'European Union' that has entailed, or may have to entail, the acceptance of (or fabrication of) a 'European identity' above and beyond existing states and nations.

How difficult it is, then, to deal over a period of time with *in* and *and*: no title can possibly include both words. The adoption of *in*, however, does not mean that the matter is settled. There is no intention to foreclose debate and coerce the reader from the outset. It is clear, in this volume, as in its predecessors, that there have been times when Britain has been more *in* than it has been on other occasions. The matters with which the book is concerned cannot be resolved by a simple 'yes' or 'no', 'in' or 'out', even though there have been occasions when British governments have had to make that choice. However, while inter-state relations – the official conduct of foreign policy and the pattern of diplomacy – must remain prominent in any consideration of 'Britain in Europe', the aim is to range more widely. Foreign policy does not, however, exist in a vacuum, however much the 'actors', for most of this period, did inhabit a socially sealed universe and were, to some degree, detached from vulgar xenophobia welling up beneath them. And crowned heads could still suppose, or pretend, that they did speak to other crowned heads as members of an extended family, if not invariably a happy one. What is mentioned in despatches, as diplomats feed into the formulation of the official British mind about 'Europe', and its inter-state relations, has to be set alongside looser trans-national relationships of uncertain significance (in terms of policy or attitude) engaged in by 'non-state actors'. The range, intention and depth of these relationships change over time. Direct contacts may confirm or undermine deeply entrenched stereotypes. New channels of communication open up and new 'opinion formers' emerge. In the period covered by this book, we move through various press 'revolutions' into the age of radio, the cinema and television, which collectively bombard the reader, listener or viewer with 'images of the foreigner', images that in turn depend upon particular self-images. As also, Britain moves, at a measured pace, from oligarchic government to democratic government, the relationship between policy and image becomes ever more complex. The issue of 'democratic control' of foreign policy becomes important. Who determines the 'national interest'? There is, therefore, an intention to look both at 'inter-state' relations and what might be called British participation in the 'Great Game' of European power-politics, on the one hand, and the complex set of perceptions and prejudices present in 'inter-national' relations widely, though not comprehensively, conceived. The relationship between these two levels never admits of any easy generalization. How far, even with the latter-day appearance of opinion polls, it is possible to determine 'representative' opinions remains problematic.

Such explicit open-mindedness about Britain *in/and* Europe runs counter to deep-seated traditions regarding the way in which history is taught, at all levels, in Britain. This author, like many others, was taught both at school and university, in a tradition in his youth that firmly separated 'British' and 'European' history. Different books, teachers, syllabi and examinations dealt with these different topics. The extent to which the one had any bearing on the other scarcely came up for discussion. Though there has been some change in this respect over recent decades, it has not been fundamentally eroded. This historiographical apartheid is in itself a significant cultural fact, relevant to the subject matter of this book. There remain very few books that attempt in any sustained fashion to bridge this chasm (or rather Channel) but, to put it pompously, such an exploration is pedagogically necessary at the beginning of a new century of British/European history. Bridges, of course, sometimes collapse under the weight they are made to bear, or are blown up by warring parties, so the task is not without hazards.

There is, however, a further trap to be avoided. The present may suggest new and perhaps unparalleled developments for 'Britain in Europe' as the European Union enlarges and new structures are devised. Such contemporary possibilities should not lead to a facile dismissal of those attitudes that, both in the past and present, do not relish this prospect and look to 'locate' Britain within some alternative conceptual framework, perhaps primarily an Atlantic or 'Anglo-Saxon' one. It would be foolish, while necessarily concentrating on Britain looking east, to ignore the extent to which, both in past and present, it has continued to look west and to possess a 'special relationship' with the United States and to be part of 'the English-speaking world'. It might be argued that an *inland* question applies also to the British relationship with the United States. Throughout the period, notwithstanding sharp differences on particular issues and even a war, there have always been elements in British society and government that have felt 'closer' to 'the Americans' than to 'the Europeans' and have acted accordingly. Yet, the United States is of course a nation of immigrants in which are to be found communities that, in different waves, have been drawn from all over Europe. In the past, some of these incomers have been 'economic migrants' seeking greater prosperity, but others have been political refugees seeking a safer life in the 'land of the free', away from the seemingly endless cycles of European conflict. Even so, that land, in its formative and enduring notions, drew heavily on ideas and structures that were 'European' ('good' as opposed to 'bad') and in a sense, in its dominant cultures, can therefore itself be seen as a kind of extension of Europe. The degree to which Britain has constituted and still constitutes a bridge between 'America' and 'Europe' cannot ignore the complex European pedigrees of America.

It is, of course, a contemporary commonplace that we now live in a global age when no nation-state, or indeed any institution, can be effectively autonomous. Economic, political, technological and cultural developments glide across boundaries and render the dykes erected in the past against 'the outside world' almost useless. This contemporary porousness may indeed lead us to wonder whether the nation-state has ever been 'master of its own destiny' to the extent that national historiographies across Europe have frequently taken to be axiomatic. On the other hand, we should be careful to avoid adopting uncritically what Professor J.G.A. Pocock has referred to as the unspoken premise of some contemporary historiography – namely that national sovereignty and history never existed, never should have existed, or are at the point of disappearing for ever (and a good thing too).

1

Eve of revolution

The matter of Britain

How should we attempt to define what kind of country the 'kingdom of Great Britain' was in the late eighteenth century, a kingdom whose monarch was also king of Ireland? Certainly, what gave its dominant English element considerable pride and self-confidence, was a sense of the precocious development of 'England'. England could boast of its consolidation as a state within the same boundaries at an earlier date than any other country in contemporary Europe. Other volumes in this series have considered or will elaborate on the nature of that state in earlier centuries and on the relationships of the peoples of the 'British Isles' with each other and with 'the continent'. This author has explored the complex development of 'Britain' elsewhere in a single volume. There is, therefore, no call here for an elaborate initial introduction that explains how the past appeared to the late-eighteenth-century present.

Even so, it is necessary to stress that the kind of 'kingdom of Great Britain' that existed in 1789 had existed merely since 1707, which year had seen the full union, on specific terms, of England and Scotland. Admittedly, the accession to the throne of England in 1603 of James VI of Scotland as James I had produced a union of Crowns, but England and Scotland remained separate countries with their own parliaments. As 'king of Great Britain', it is true, James VI/I had entertained certain notions of what 'Great Britain' could become, but his ideas met resistance both in Scotland and England. It was only after 1707, therefore, that the formal terms of union were agreed. Under the new arrangements, Scotland had lost its own parliament and gained instead some representation in the House of Commons at Westminster. There was no comprehensive reordering of a 'British' polity. Scottish elements were tacked on to an English polity that remained intact. However, Scotland retained its own legal, educational and ecclesiastical systems. In 1715 and 1745, Jacobite rebellions, launched in Scotland (though by no means with universal support there) had threatened the stability of the new Hanoverian monarchy, but had been defeated. If, in the latter case, there had been a simultaneous French invasion, as the Young Pretender had hoped for, the outcome might have been very different. The repressive measures in the Scottish Highlands, which followed the defeat at Culloden in 1746, seemed to have achieved their objective four decades later. New Britain had bedded down as a state. Scotland was effectively 'managed' and the possibility that there might again be European (French) involvement in British dynastic struggles was removed. There had of course been, since 1714, a different kind of European involvement in the British monarchy – when the Crown had gone to the elector of Hanover. It was only the third George, on the throne in 1789, who could persuasively claim to be a 'true Briton'. In Scotland itself the new tranquillity assisted in the dawn of the 'Age of Enlightenment', though strictly speaking that age had several distinct phases. Edinburgh, but not only Edinburgh, acquired a reputation as a 'hotbed of genius' – in the persons of such men as David Hume, John Millar, Adam Ferguson, William Robertson and Adam Smith. Moreover, this was not just a reputation gained in Britain. The impact of their writing can be traced across Europe. Robertson's historical works were translated into the main European languages, as were Smith's.[1] The latter spent a period in France and was familiar with the work of the French *philosophes*. Adam Ferguson, who travelled widely in Europe and corresponded with d'Holbach and met Voltaire, was read with particular enthusiasm in Germany. His *Essay on the History of Civil Society* was published in English in 1767 and translated into German only a year later. His *History of the Progress and Termination of the Roman Republic* (1783) was a volume that, perhaps a little surprisingly, nourished the soul of Johann George Hamann on his deathbed.[2] The Royal Society of Edinburgh was founded in 1783, and Edinburgh became the only city in Britain that possessed both an active scientific society and a university. In 1789 Thomas Jefferson wrote that, so far as science was concerned, 'no place in the world can pretend to competition with Edinburgh'.[3] Moreover, it was an academy that was perhaps closer in tone and spirit to bodies that existed or were being created in Germany and elsewhere than with anything that existed in England. In a sense, therefore, at least for a time, the intellectual firepower of the British state came from north of the border. The 'strong tendency to abstract argument quite unknown in England', which Bagehot detected in the nineteenth century had been discerned earlier, not least by the abstract arguers themselves.[4]

The novelty (though also the apparent stability) of this British state needs some emphasis given the concerns of this book. In 1789 it was as a single entity that 'Great Britain' operated vis-à-vis 'Europe'. In previous centuries, however, Scotland had managed its own external relations – most conspicuously with the Baltic region, with the Netherlands and with France. These relations had involved trade and war and had entailed a multiplicity of cultural and religious links. The ability to involve France – somewhat problematically – vis-à-vis England had been crucial, on occasion, in maintaining Scottish independence. Naturally, in the new state, the conduct of a

'Scottish foreign policy' had become impossible, but previous contacts did not expire completely. The new dispensation had its commercial gains and losses. The customary trade of Scotland's east-coast ports with northern Europe was restricted by British legislation designed to protect English concerns. On the other hand, west-coast Scotland had been able legally – as opposed to clandestinely – to have access to England's North American empire. It has been calculated that, by the late 1760s, the Glasgow 'tobacco lords' had been able to secure half of the total tobacco production of what were then the British American colonies. Given its location, it was natural for Scotland to feel more 'northern European' than England did, but it was not exempt from that commercial tug between a westward and an eastward orientation evident in England. It was in London, however, that the formal foreign policy of Britain was made and where particular Scottish interest-groups had to try to make their cases. It is scarcely possible to discern something that one might call a distinctively Scottish input into British policy. By every measure, Scotland was the junior partner.

The union of 1707 has long been spoken of as being between 'England' and 'Scotland'. So it seemed to most contemporaries. It would have seemed odd to have made any reference to 'Wales' as the third territorial leg of this state. The union between England and Wales, which had been consolidated in the 1530s, was normally thought to have been consummated to such a point that, in any formal sense, it had ceased to exist as a political entity. Princes of Wales, as eldest sons of the king, did not preside over their principality while they waited to ascend the throne in any fashion that gave it political or constitutional coherence. They did not visit. In 1789, not only was that union much earlier, but the antecedent history of Wales could scarcely be compared with the antecedent history of Scotland. Wales had not possessed what might be called the institutional scaffolding that gave substance to Scottish identity in 1707 and that survived the demise of statehood. It had nothing to compare with the urban cultures of Scotland. It had no university. It had no capital city. It was in London that Welshmen who wished to become prominent made their way. They had developed, in mid-century, a network of societies for mutual support and cultural activities.[5] It was in the Old King's Tavern in Soho in 1781 that the 'Ancient Order of the Druids' was revived.[6] What Wales still possessed in substantial measure was a language and a cultural heritage to go with it, albeit one subordinated within an administrative structure that was English-speaking. It was this fact that gave Wales an identity that was otherwise not apparent if one restricted oneself to the consideration of constitutional or political arrangements or supposed that there was an identifiable Welsh 'presence' in Europe. Indeed, it was to the Allegheny mountains rather than the Alps that Welshmen lifted up their eyes. In mid-century, there were sufficient readers of Welsh in Pennsylvania to justify the publication of Welsh books for their benefit.[7] America certainly loomed large but R.J.W. Evans points out the extent to which modern identity formation among the Welsh proceeded in parallel at this time with developments on the eastern peripheries of Europe. He instances the external activities of patriots in foreign cities (for London read Vienna or St Petersburg) and the tendency to forge medieval credentials if they were not genuinely available. In the second half of the eighteenth century nearly 2000 book titles in Welsh appeared – a figure equalled only by Hungarian among the languages of south-eastern Europe.[8]

There was, therefore, a degree of diversity, some of which was 'hidden', behind the formal structures of the British state. Different pasts were being accommodated over time, it appeared, without undue difficulty in the interests of a common British present and future. It was, however, a state in which England dominated. Indeed the fact that Great Britain did now exist had only come about after centuries of pressure and persuasion, in varying proportions, emanating from London and from the English (though quite who 'the English' were, in relation to their past, was scarcely clear). England's early dominance had been pressed home by military and economic superiority. It had a larger population. Notwithstanding occasional outbursts of anti-Scottish sentiment in the capital and the supposition that Scotsmen in London were 'on the make' they occupied an increasingly prominent place in various spheres of metropolitan life – though no full study of Scots 'south of the border' yet exists. It was in London that the British Parliament met and it was to the capital that aspirants for work, wealth or office came from the 'peripheral' regions/nations.

The matter of Ireland

'Great Britain' was one thing, 'Ireland' was another. Strictly speaking, therefore, any study of Britain and Europe should not also incorporate Ireland. Yet to exclude Ireland is unsatisfactory. The problem is that no terminology exists – unless one resorts to excluding any qualifying adjective and speaking only of 'the Isles' or alternatively of the 'Atlantic Archipelago' – which enables one to write neutrally about 'Britain and Ireland' as an entity, and in some senses it was an entity.[9] In mid-century the Irish Parliament in Dublin (itself restricted to Protestant membership) was dependent upon the Westminster Parliament, which could legislate for Ireland and which retained control of the foreign policy of 'the Isles'. By the 1780s, however, 'patriot' pressure mounted in Ireland for the removal of the shackles that the 1720 Declaratory Act and Poynings' Law (a fifteenth-century statute that required prior approval of Irish legislation) placed upon Irish legislative capacity. In 1782 the Declaratory Act was repealed and Poynings' Law amended. Irish bills could no longer be altered at Westminster. However, these steps left Ireland's constitutional position somewhat in limbo. It had an autonomous status (albeit in the hands of its religious minority) in a way that Scotland no longer possessed but it was also clearly subordinate to Great Britain. Dublin was a fine Georgian city and could claim to pip

Edinburgh as the 'second city' of the British Isles. It was there that Handel's *Messiah* had first been performed in 1742. It has been argued that at mid-century Ireland was 'more settled and more prosperous than it had ever been before'.[10] Dublin's aristocracy lived in a world that was part-Irish and part-British (or perhaps we should say part-English). 'Grattan's Parliament' was dominated by an Ascendancy that certainly had a sense of being Irish, but that was also 'English' in culture and by association. There remained an intimate connection between the course of politics at Westminster and in Dublin. Ascendancy politicians sought 'English civil rights' in Ireland. Their country was a free commonwealth, though annexed to the British Crown, which had a separate and distinct government, though one after the same model as England. What being a free commonwealth meant, particularly with regard to economic and commercial matters, could be a subject of endless debate. The Regency Crisis of 1788–89 (occasioned by George III's incapacity) produced different reactions in the two parliaments. It highlighted once more the ambiguous aspects of the relationship between Great Britain and Ireland. There was, however, a certain artificiality about Irish politics, since the 'real' Catholic Ireland took no formal part. 'When we speak of Ireland', John Fitzgibbon, earl of Clare, had declared in 1789, 'it is a melancholy truth that we do not speak of the great body of the people'.[11] The religious question, as it manifested itself in Ireland, was unusual in European terms for, after the mid-seventeenth-century Treaty of Westphalia, territories were either pretty homogenously Catholic or pretty homogeneously Catholic. Ireland was all mixed up. Toby Barnard has recently investigated how Irish Protestants (and Catholics) dressed, ate, drank and entertained in this period with a view to assessing the extent of dependence or independence from British mores. Whether the Protestant elite could maintain its position was becoming problematic. Barnard has concluded that while their possessions and patterns of consumption do suggest that there was something of a 'contested relationship' between Ireland, Britain and Europe, there is little to suggest that they owned or consumed with the set purpose of establishing a particular identity.[12]

Mention of 'Europe' as the third element in this 'contested relationship' is important. The obvious point is that Ireland was a separate island in the archipelago. As has been seen in earlier volumes, Ireland, with its always exploitable cocktail of domestic discontents, offered mainland European states a backdoor entry to discomfort England. Spain had used this opportunity in the sixteenth century. A century earlier, in 1689–90, it was on Irish soil that James II (who controlled Ireland) and William of Orange, the Dutchman who had gained the English throne, fought their battles. The 'European' dimensions of their encounter are illustrated by the fact that James had substantial French forces with him and William's army contained a mixture of nationalities. The outcome certainly ensured the subordination of Ireland, with severe further restrictions on Catholic rights, but the war in Ireland was not so much a war between England and Ireland as the last throw in a European contest between a Dutch *Stadholder* who had become an English king and Louis XIV of France. Despite what had happened in 1690, there remained the possibility that at some future juncture Ireland might call France in aid against England in altered circumstances. The 'Wild Geese', Irish Jacobites, followed James into exile in France – some 40,000 Irishmen were to serve in the French army in the period up to the 1745 rebellion. Only 30 years earlier, in 1760, French forces briefly captured Carrickfergus in County Antrim. It might be thought that these were pinpricks rather than steps that posed a serious challenge to the British–Irish status quo. Even so, it seemed possible that there would be a perpetual European dimension to the 'Irish Question'.

The matter of England

It may seem odd to conclude this brief assessment of the 'ingredients' of the British Isles with an even briefer comment on England. England, after all, was the powerhouse of the state and it might seem more appropriate to devote more space to the 'core' rather than the various 'peripheries'. Yet precisely because Englishmen were inclined, on the whole, to assume that 'England' spoke for 'Britain' they were rarely inclined to wrestle with that dual identity that existed, to whatever degree, in the non-English territories of the British Isles. The inhabitants of these territories were all, in some form or other, accommodating themselves to the rhythms and requirements of a political culture that had its heart in London. Since the political unions of Britain had been accomplished by grafting some elements onto English structures rather than by any comprehensive establishment of 'British' structures (something that might have entailed, for example, the relocation of the British Parliament to York) Englishmen in localities scarcely noted that they had become British. 'Englishness' was certainly something to which an appeal could be made. In the 1760s the radical John Wilkes had raised the awful spectre of a Scottish takeover. 'John Bull' made his political debut as the epitome of the plain-speaking Englishman, adamantine in his opposition to taxation and resolute in defence of liberty (liberty was apparently something not properly understood by foreigners). The antiquity of England could not be gainsaid. The English Parliament, even though it was now the British Parliament, was the embodiment of the English nation. That nation did indeed possess its 'county communities' but its polity was not cluttered up with the regional estates and differences of tax regimes that remained commonplace on the mainland. As a German scholar has put it, an Englishman, for generations, had felt no need 'to clutch at myths and a mere vision of his country's unity: these sentiments could be bodied forth in a self-confident account of his country's political institutions'.[13] There was a certain pride in the fact that England had not gone as far as continental monarchies in the direction of absolutism. The English Crown did not keep a large standing army. Royal officialdom under its direct control was relatively modest. English distinctiveness, in these and other respects, seemed clear to contemporaries. In these circumstances, there was little cause for English writers to agonize over England: it was simply there and always would be. The lack of any real challenge to this assumption may explain why English nationalism, at this juncture, was rather low-key. Indeed, one commentator on the late eighteenth century wonders whether 'a separate sense of "English" national identity existed, as opposed to a series of local perspectives and cultural concerns'.[14] 'Europeans' almost universally still thought about and wrote to 'England' not to Britain, and the English were not such pedants as to feel it necessary to correct them.

The matter of Europe

If, below a certain level, the British Isles was a patchwork of multiple identities so, a fortiori, was 'Europe'. At the end of the eighteenth century, it was as protean and kaleidoscopic a continent as it had always been. Indeed, how and why this tapering promontory of Asia (as it might appear from an eastern perspective) was a continent at all had been and remained a subject of controversy. If – and perhaps a big if – Europe began in the Ural mountains, its extension westwards moved through a mosaic of terrains and climates before it climaxed in a medley of arms and peninsulae jutting out into the Atlantic Ocean, and then there were those British Isles. But of course most inhabitants of Britain did not think of Europe beginning in the Ural mountains, though the continent might conceivably end there. Topographically, ethnically, ecclesiastically and linguistically it was extraordinarily diverse. The nature of European civilization, the degree to which Europe was coextensive with Christendom, the reasons for its bewildering dynamism, both destructive and cooperative, have naturally engaged the attention of historians over many centuries. This book does not attempt to compete with them. We might, however, make one simple observation. A great deal depends on where historians are situated when they write on this subject and whether they look east or east, north or south in search of Europe. Part of the stimulation to be derived from Norman Davies's *Europe: A History* lies in his introductory discussion with its awareness not only of the rich variety of Europe's past but also of 'the rich variety of prisms through which it can be viewed'. He himself has self-consciously made an attempt to 'counteract the bias of "Eurocentrism" and "Western civilization"' and to give equitable coverage to all parts of the European peninsula.[15] It is evident that although a Lancastrian semi-Welshman writing in Oxford, Davies's insights owe much to his own prolonged immersion in the study of Polish history. Some very useful texts in English – for instance, *The Making of Modern Europe* and *The Old European Order* – skirt around the problems. In the former case, Geoffrey Treasure sees, by 1780, the emergence of a 'European man'

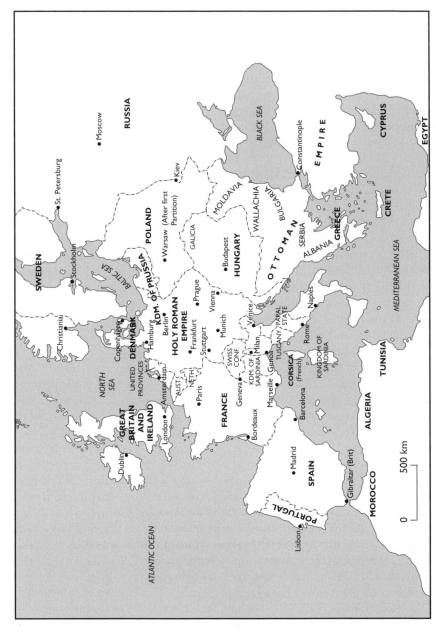

1. Europe in 1780

who was recognizably modern. It is evident, however, that whoever this 'European man' is, he is to be found sitting in the capitals of one of the major powers. Treasure confesses, though with reluctance, that he has left out those peoples – he instances Belgians, Swiss, the inhabitants of the smaller German and Italian states, and of the Balkan lands under the Turks – who did not count for much in diplomacy or war.[16] In the latter case, William Doyle writes admirably on various themes but simply takes it for granted that we all know what Europe is and who Europeans are.[17] More recently, in a comparative social history of the European enlightenment, Thomas Munck has chosen to focus on north-western and northern Europe. He has given good reasons for doing so (which do not include the fact that he is a Dane writing in Glasgow) but concedes that 'important parts of Europe have been given less prominence here than they might deserve'.[18] One could give other examples of the difficulty of perspective encountered by historians of Europe writing in languages other than English.[19] One could go on indefinitely. Perhaps, as Davies suggests, the problem of national bias, whether conscious or unconscious, 'will only disappear when historians and educators cease to regard history as a vehicle for state politics'.[20] It does not altogether look as though this condition has yet been reached.[21]

Whatever view is precisely taken about 'Europe', it must be obvious from the foregoing discussion that 'Britain' and 'Europe' did not constitute a static one-to-one relationship. Europe was itself a world of states, large and small, at different stages of development, with a medley of constitutional structures. Within those states were nations, or embryonic nations. Literacy rates varied widely. It was a continent seemingly constantly on the verge of upheaval, whose history was punctuated at regular intervals by war. Earlier in the eighteenth century it had seen wars of the Spanish, Polish and Austrian succession, to name only some of the conflicts. In the Seven Years' War (1756–63) European states (Britain among them) had turned a European into a global struggle for supremacy. In these wars, often devoid of the spice added to later conflicts by professions of ideology, erstwhile partners sometimes changed sides as their situations seemed to demand. There was little sense of the interest of a state being fixed in a permanent alignment. It was indeed the case that the interests of 'Europe' could sometimes be claimed by belligerents as a reason for their participation in a particular conflict but the appeal of this transcendent notion was frail. It could, when equated with Christendom, be used against the Turk. By 1789, however, unlike the position roughly a century earlier when Vienna had been threatened, the Ottoman threat to 'Europe' was largely a thing of the past. Its disappearance reduced or eliminated the necessity for some kind of European/Christian solidarity.

The aspiration to give 'equitable coverage' to all parts of the European peninsula is an admirable objective in any attempt to write a history of Europe. If, however, the objective is to write a history of Britain in its relationship with Europe what constitutes 'equitable coverage' becomes problematic. While all parts of Europe may have some relationship with each other, and the whole constitute the sum of the parts, it is evident that not all the parts have the same degree or kind of relationship with each other. Britain, as was the case with other states in Europe, was not on intimate terms with all comers. British relationships continued to be dictated by geography and by the complex deposit of past alliances and alignments. Insularity remained of central significance. So long as sea power was adequately maintained, an invasion of England was unlikely. Naval power, therefore, was paramount. Sailors were national heroes. No other major European power was an island, or rather a collection of islands. Such a geopolitical situation necessarily gave Britain a degree of detachment from mainland struggles. Britain normally had a greater degree of freedom than mainland states possessed in deciding whether or not to become involved in a European war. Britain did not have 'neighbours' in quite the same way as European states had neighbours. It was unlikely that a European war would be fought out on the British mainland but it was likely that British troops would be required to fight on the European mainland. In the first decade of the eighteenth century, Marlborough had found himself fighting in central as well as western Europe. European war, however, was always politically contentious in Britain. There was an increasing temptation to use Britain's waxing economic and financial strength to support the armies of other continental states in the pursuit of outcomes that would be beneficial to British interests. In 1742 a British monarch (George II) commanded a mixed army (he did have some British troops) in the battle of Dettingen against the Austrians and Bavarians. He was the last British king to exercise such a command. Somewhat complicatedly, of course, this fighting king was also elector of Hanover (as his father had also been). It was possible to distinguish between his roles but, nevertheless, British governments could not altogether detach themselves from a rather unexpected and not altogether welcome connection with the politics of northern Germany.

The nature of British relationships stemmed from the fact that it had clearly become a 'Great Power' if, from mainland perspectives, a rather odd, fickle and perhaps perfidious one. Unlike other European Great Powers, for whom the acquisition of additional territory remained an adequate pretext for going to war and a supposedly sure way of acquiring fresh wealth and strength, the British coveted no European territory, though it was recognized that this was not because, as a matter of principle, they did not covet territory. The reacquisition of Calais, lost in 1558, did not feature as an objective. Gibraltar, acquired from Spain in 1704, did not represent the first step towards British Iberian hegemony but was rather a bonus for a naval power from the point of view of Mediterranean access. Also, unlike the constitutional position among the other Great Powers, the British Parliament was apt to have views about foreign policy, as well as a degree of control over finance that could frustrate belligerently inclined monarchs or ministers if a case was not adequately made. In addition, as will be considered shortly, that status (although not subject to formal identification) derived, paradoxically perhaps, from the fact of its extra-European connections and possessions. It was the combination of these factors that made Britain somewhat untrustworthy, though trust was not generally liberally exhibited in the system as a whole.

In so far as the European state system was all-embracing, Britain had formal relationships and informal connections with courts and chancelleries across Europe, but the primary relationships were with the 'club' of Great Powers – which had come to mean, by this juncture, France, Austria, Russia and Prussia. In so far as it was these powers that 'carried weight', Treasure is right to focus an account on the 'drivers' of the system. Other states featured – the Dutch Republic, Sweden or Spain, for example – but theirs was a subordinate role. These hierarchies and rankings were reflected elaborately in the titles of the respective diplomatic representatives and were the subject of great sensitivity. Whereas today, states, great and small, give and receive ambassadors, that rank was reserved for the representatives of a select number. Other states had to make do with envoys, ministers plenipotentiary, mere ministers or even secretaries. The system of diplomacy had by this juncture reached a considerable degree of sophistication and formality. Diplomats had acquired immunity to enable them to carry out their duties, which ranged from formal attendance at court functions, as representatives of their monarchs, to information gathering of a distinctly inquisitive kind. Not all courts were equally stimulating.

Britain certainly had an assured position in this European diplomatic world. It was an aristocratic one, though aristocratic diplomats representing other European powers sometimes felt that British aristocrats were not quite up to the mark and, indeed, not all British representatives, strictly speaking, were aristocrats.[22] It was, however, France that set the diplomatic pace in terms both of the training of its representatives and the abundance of them. In London, as compared with its counterpart in Paris, the Foreign Office was a modest little enterprise. French became the language of diplomacy – for correspondence, negotiations and treaties. After 1740, for example, Prussian diplomats used French and, in the later eighteenth century Austrians preferred to do so.[23] Its pre-eminent use in diplomacy, of course, was only one aspect of French cultural hegemony in these decades. The French language – stiffened for more than a century by the vigilance of the *Academie Française* (1635) was the instrument of civilized correspondence and communication across the continent. A *salon* offered the highest form of life and even petty princes eagerly built their somewhat more modest versions of Versailles. In all probability, one can attribute to eighteenth-century French *philosophes* a division of Europe into 'western' and 'eastern' – the 'backwardness' of the latter being self-evident. The English language, and whatever culture it supported, could scarcely compete with French hegemony and, officially, made little attempt to do so, perhaps suspecting, correctly as it was to turn out, that a reaction against it would set in and their peripheral brogue make some headway in Europe.[24]

It is generally argued that by this juncture – a century or so after the Treaty of Westphalia (1648) – religion had ceased to be important in determining the political alignments of the continent. Even so, in a more general sense, the eighteenth-century royal link with Protestant Hanover confirmed the perception in southern and eastern Europe that Britain was a Protestant northern European state. Protestantism did remain a badge of Britishness. Although, in the various territories of the kingdom, Protestantism had taken a variety of competing forms – and that variety was without parallel on the mainland – a common fear and suspicion of Catholicism remained. State religion – the European pattern – remained entrenched in England/Wales, Ireland and Scotland, though dissenters received increasing toleration. The sense that Britain was a haven for Protestant refugees from less tolerant European states lingered. After the revocation of the Edict of Nantes in 1685 French Huguenot refugees had fled across the Channel and settled in Britain and Ireland, forming a not insignificant British subculture. The Church of Scotland occupied a clear place in the European Reformed/Calvinist world. The Church of England, however, could not clearly be located anywhere; while it thought of itself as Protestant, European Lutheran or Calvinist Churches did not quite know what that meant. The oddness of the Church of England had been demonstrated earlier in the century when William Wake, Archbishop of Canterbury, had laboured, though in vain, for intercommunion with the Gallican Church (the Catholic Church in France), a body that was indubitably Catholic but rather grudgingly papal. The new religious movements in England/Wales in mid-century – various forms of Methodism – were not merely insular phenomena. There was a 'great awakening' across Europe (and America) that transcended frontiers and established institutional structures.[25] Tracts and homilies were eagerly translated from English in pietist circles on the mainland. The inherited ecclesiastical disagreements of the western and central European past had not disappeared but a new 'spirit of toleration' was discernible. In 1787, the French 'Edict of Tolerance' substantially restored to French Protestants what they had lost in 1685. There was, however, little disposition in Britain – outside a small Catholic minority – to tolerate the notion that the Papacy constituted the voice of European Christendom. Quite apart from its imperfections from a Protestant standpoint, there was a very limited awareness of an Orthodoxy that existed to the east of Rome and that might vitiate its claims. Greek Orthodox priests even turned up in Oxford and it was supposed, though to no avail, that they might have a college there. Such exceptional connections apart, the world of Orthodox Europe was substantially remote, alien and (necessarily in the south-east because of Ottoman rule) 'closed'. Geography mattered.

By the same token, it was France that presented itself most strongly and immediately to the British consciousness. It was possible to sail from east-coast ports in England and Scotland to Scandinavia, the Baltic and the Low Countries, but it was France that was, literally, the first port of call for most English travellers. Propinquity, however, had never guaranteed mutual sympathy: indeed, it could entail quite the reverse. The cultural dominance of France has already been referred to, but it was the possibility, indeed the probability, of political and military dominance that was the more immediate anxiety. In so far as nations define themselves by their knowledge or image of other nations with whom they come into contact, the British, at this juncture, defined themselves against the French. A writer in the 1730s had discerned in the French a 'civil, quick and active sort of people' though 'extremely given to talking, especially those of the Female Sex'. As a generalization, there was a disposition to see in Frenchmen, at least of a certain sort, a tendency to foppery and insincerity. When that was turned into *politesse*, however, it had an appeal to English gentlemen. Undergraduates at Christ Church, Oxford, were reported in 1773 as being 'quite frenchified' – some of them had risked spending an entire summer in France. Dr Johnson, who paid an unsuccessful visit in 1775 saw no sign of the country's much-vaunted culinary skills. He declared French meals to be 'gross'.[26]

It is difficult to decide how much weight should be placed upon such individual impressions. Expressions of admiration for almost all things French can be set alongside them. Nevertheless, it is not difficult to see why there was always an underlying 'edge' in Franco-British relations in the eighteenth century (though it is sometimes forgotten that whole decades passed without war). When we look at the states of Europe in the later eighteenth century France and Britain stood out as compact and coherent national states even though there was more diversity in their populations than there first appeared. France, to British eyes, was a country as Britain was a country – in a way that 'Germany' or 'Italy' were not. A British traveller in the 1780s, it has been observed, could roam across northern Europe for 1000 miles, from Ostend through something that was called the Holy Roman Empire of the German Nation, although that imposing title would have had little impact in everyday terms. What would have been more immediately evident were the bewildering variety of currencies and measures in a multiplicity of ecclesiastical principalities, free cities, kingdoms, electorates, duchies and the estates of imperial free barons. Moreover, in addition to the rule over Hanover exercised by the British king as elector – though at a distance, for no British monarch (in the eighteenth century) visited his electorate after 1755 – the traveller would find that there were, additionally, German territories, ruled by the monarchs of Denmark, Sweden and Russia.[27] This was as strange in its way as were the heights of the beds that were often encountered by such travellers, beds that gave real meaning to the term 'climb into bed'. The medley of states that was Italy was no less curious, though the beds were not quite so taxing.[28]

France was a real country by comparison. However, not only was it substantially larger but, with a population of more than 26 million in 1791, it contained some three times the population of Britain at that date. Taken in the round, with their rivalry in Europe, India and North America over decades it was tempting to suppose that Britain and France were 'natural enemies' to a degree that could not be said about Britain's relations with any other European state. Pitt, however, thought it prudent in 1787 to reproach his countrymen for supposing that any nation could be unalterably the enemy of another. In any case, there appeared to be good reason to suppose that Britain was not inferior to France in every respect. Certain French visitors, Voltaire included, praised the way in which the British seemed to have found a way of curtailing the power of kings – although Anglophobia rather than Anglophilia was probably the more widespread sentiment in France.[29]

Visitors from other countries also paid Britain a visit in order to discover at first hand how this insular constitutional paradise worked. In 1785, for example, the Danzig-born Johann Wilhelm von Archenholtz, who spent 10 years in England, admiringly summed up what he saw as the five fundamental achievements of the British: freedom of the press, *Habeas Corpus*, public tribunals, jury trials and parliamentary representation. Later, in Hamburg, he edited journals in both German and English, which contributed further to that city's already strong British commercial links. Archenholtz was by no means the only German traveller to penetrate to the British Isles. Indeed, from 1750 the numbers swelled, contributing to what has been described as a mood of 'Anglomania'.[30] The University of Göttingen, within the electorate of Hanover, founded in 1737, became what has been identified as the principal agency for the entry of British ideas and influences into Germany in the later eighteenth century.

On the whole, we may risk the generalization that while British travellers found much to interest them in the sights they saw and the people they met, they assumed that foreigners would find more to admire in Britain than they would be called upon to admire abroad. So many outsiders, Paul Langford has noted, thought the English, as a breed, strangely uninterested in others. Away up in the Baltic, the philosopher Kant concluded that the English did not so much despise or dislike other nations as simply ignore them. Their own merits and virtues were so obvious that there was no call to explain them to others. In all of this, however, one must be careful not to fall into that characterization of nations that most travellers at one time or another felt obliged to make. A Russian advanced the thesis that the Englishman triumphed in parliament and the exchange, the German in his study, the Frenchman in the theatre. Put together, these national vocations, it might seem, produced the curiosity that was Europe.

The matter of the 'wider world'

On the world stage, however, 'Europe' was not a politically meaningful concept. Globally, rivalry and competition between European states dominated the scene. Very recently, Britain had suffered its heaviest blow. The Treaties of Versailles and Paris – signed in 1783 by France, Britain and Spain, and by Britain and the United States respectively – ratified that Britain had lost its American colonies. The transoceanic British nation had fallen apart in fratricidal conflict – which is one way of viewing what had happened since the American Declaration of Independence of 1776. Wherever the blame was put, it had not proved possible to reconcile the differences that had emerged. Perhaps part of the problem, as various historians have pointed out, was that in fact people in Britain did not sufficiently conceive colonial Americans to be their 'fellow countrymen'. The Americans, if that term can be used to cover all the colonists, had come to feel themselves different. In addition, it might be argued that the war against the rebellious colonists partook of some of the characteristics of a civil war within the English-speaking world as seventeenth-century arguments took fresh life. Considerable sympathy for the rebellious colonists particularly existed among English religious dissenters.[31]

However this dramatic rupture is explained, there was no gainsaying that some kind of British imperial mission, if one imperfectly worked out and inadequately executed, had collapsed ignominiously. Such a disaster could not but have profound implications for the British position as a European power. The American success, of course, had been aided by the assistance of some European powers. In 1778 France had signed a treaty with the Americans and followed it up a few months later by going to war with Britain. From a French perspective, here was an opportunity to exploit Britain's difficulties and regain ground lost in the apparently perennial global conflict with Britain that had last ended with the 1763 Treaty of Paris. From an American perspective, French assistance could mean the difference between defeat and victory – and so it proved. Spain, though apprehensive that her South American colonies would be inspired by the example to their north, was nevertheless lured into the conflict by the prospect of regaining Gibraltar. Other European states – initially Russia, Sweden and Denmark but followed by Prussia, Austria, Naples and Portugal (England's 'oldest ally') – formed a League of Armed Neutrality. Britain's diplomatic isolation in Europe was complete. The eventual outcome brought what Lord Grenville later recalled as a deep despondency 'in the sacrifice of that immense territory'. Verdicts in Europe were damning. 'Farewell to the esteem and riches of England,' wrote Emperor Joseph II of Austria to his brother, Grand Duke Leopold of Tuscany, who agreed that, 'This great power, which held France in balance, [is] fallen entirely and forever; all respect and force lost, ... descended to the status of a second-rank power, like Sweden or Denmark'.[32]

In fact, disastrous though matters seemed, the peace settlement of 1783 still left Britain with some elements of empire. Canada remained, as did certain islands in the Caribbean. Gibraltar had not been given up. The positions in India had not been lost – the East India Company held sway in

Bengal. There were prospects in the Antipodes – much interest had been generated by the Pacific voyages of James Cook between 1768 and 1779. Also, notwithstanding the pervasive pessimism, there was a school of thought which felt that these colonial settlements had diverged from the type of empire that Britain should be seeking. It was a maritime empire that would be most profitable, one that would facilitate British worldwide trade. A second and perhaps more sensible British Empire might be possible.

There was also some comfort to be drawn from the fact that despite 'victory' France was not in a position to humiliate a defeated Britain in the way some had supposed inevitable. The war had placed a severe strain on the French Treasury. Additionally, some French officers who had fought in America had been impressed by American ideals. The Marquis de Lafayette did not forget his American friends when they came to Paris. Although the rights the Americans claimed had often been couched within the conventions of British political thought, there was a strong 'universalist' streak, which found expression in the Declaration of Independence. No one sympathized with these aspirations more passionately than Tom Paine, the Englishman who threw in his lot with the rebels. 'Freedom hath been hunted round the globe,' Paine declared, 'Asia and Africa have long expelled her – Europe regards her like a stranger, and England hath given her warning to depart. O! receive the fugitive, and prepare in time an asylum for mankind.' And so, in the year 1789, it was in France that just such an asylum was being prepared. France was to witness a revolution that not only produced an unimaginable upheaval in that country – it was an event that was to change for decades, perhaps centuries, how Britain related to the European mainland.

|2|

Revolution and war,
1789–1802

Fallout from France

The outbreak of revolution in Paris in 1789 was an event of European significance. On 14 July the Paris crowd stormed the Bastille, a step later interpreted as a symbolic blow for liberty and still celebrated as such in contemporary France. It set a lasting political agenda for the continent and provided either inspiration or anxiety in country after country. The Bolshevik revolution of 1917 had a similar impact in the twentieth century. It posed particular problems in Britain. Taken together, the American Revolution and the French Revolution perhaps suggested that the days of Britain's own *ancien régime* were numbered. In a sermon in November 1789, for example, the Welsh-born radical Richard Price detected the ardour for liberty catching and spreading. He glimpsed what he called a general amendment in human affairs. The dominion of kings would be replaced by the dominion of laws, and the dominion of priests would give way to the dominion of reason and conscience. It was time for the world's oppressors to tremble.[1]

His reference to 'the world' was not accidental. An era was perhaps dawning in which humanity as a whole would escape the shackles of superstition and slavery and regain those fundamental rights that, allegedly, had been forfeited at some rather unspecific point in the past. In Birmingham, Joseph Priestley felt certain that, when revolutionary France had established itself, the time would come near when wars would cease to the ends of the earth, and the kingdoms of this world would become the kingdoms of God and his Christ.[2]

If it was indeed the case, in Europe at least, that 'the people' were now panting for liberty then the new creation might render redundant, in due course, the peculiarities of individual European countries. If government was now to rest upon 'rights of man', rights that were, potentially at least, universal, then those aspects of existing governments, constitutional structures and social hierarchies that arose out of the specific historical experiences of individual peoples would fade. The rigorous application of 'reason' and 'conscience' in matters of politics would bring about a new order in which it would become superfluous to suppose that there would be 'British' or 'French' systems. The Declaration of the Rights of Man adopted in Paris in August 1789 by the National Assembly included Articles that specifically addressed particular French abuses and grievances; but such ameliorations derived their authority from the initial Articles, which asserted that men were born and remained free and equal in rights. Those rights were to liberty, property and security. Resistance to oppression was legitimized. The third Article declared that all sovereignty rested essentially in the nation. In France itself, over the subsequent months, the implications of these claims began to be worked out – among them the creation of a new system of local administration (the 'departments') and a civil constitution of the clergy, which provided for the selection of priests by district electoral assemblies and which terminated papal jurisdiction in France. Here, apparently, was a model being worked out that could create a reasonable order in Europe as a whole.

Even so, however wide in Europe the application of these principles might be, it was in France and for France that they were in fact being applied – though no doubt in the first instance. 'History' was beginning again and Paris, in a sense, was only leading the way. The reverberations spread far and wide throughout the European continent. The extent to which what was happening was 'supranational' was emphasized by the accolade 'French citizen' bestowed on such foreigners as the Englishmen Joseph Priestley and Jeremy Bentham, the Swiss Johann Heinrich Pestalozzi, the Pole Tadeusz Kosciuszko, the Dutchman Cornelius de Pauw, and the Americans George Washington and James Madison, among others. Such recognition gave substance to the contention that this was a truly epoch-making revolution – before the term 'epoch-making' became debased by overuse.

Indeed, for a time, some historians detected an 'Atlantic-European' revolutionary mood in the last decades of the eighteenth century.[3] It has also been argued that the continent as a whole, not just France, was ripe for revolution. That it broke out in Paris merely reflected the fact that the *ancien régime* there happened to be more decrepit and detested than elsewhere – but that was only a matter of degree. Certainly, in looking for signs of revolution it would be unwise to focus exclusively on France. There was unrest, to some degree or other, across the continent. 'French patriots' made their appearance, sometimes wearing the tricolour cockade, in towns as widely separated as Hamburg and Bologna. 'Liberty trees' were planted in Württemberg. German writers and poets, for the most part, greeted the news from Paris with that joy that Schiller had anticipated in 1785 when he composed his *An die Freude* (destined, with the musical assistance of Beethoven, to become, some 200 years later, the anthem of the European

Union). The Dutch Patriot movement had tried to limit the power of the House of Orange but had been crushed by Prussian military intervention.[4] In the east of Europe, in Poland-Lithuania, in May 1791, a new constitution was promulgated that supposedly transformed overnight the 'commonwealth of two nations', with a population that contained some eight or nine million illiterate serfs, into a modern constitutional state that embodied enlightened principles. Arriving at Calais in July 1790, at the beginning of a European tour the 20-year-old William Wordsworth found France 'standing on the top of golden hours' – perhaps this would be true for all Europe.

Indeed, in towns and villages across the continent, pent-up local grievances came to a head and gained, for a time at least, a new frame of political reference. It is not difficult to identify this sentiment in favour of change, but any more detailed assessment of its continental strength would have to stress, once more, that 'Europe' remained a patchwork of states at different stages of development on the path to 'modernity'. It would be absurd to suppose that the politics of Portugal or Russia would follow precisely the same path. In almost all countries, however, it could be argued that the core concern revolved around monarchy: either its preservation (but within constitutional restraints that prevented 'despotism') or its abolition (on the grounds that it bred corruption and tyranny). To be sure, this was not a new debate, but how precisely 'constitution' and 'monarchy' should be juxtaposed gained fresh urgency from the sense that there were profound and imperfectly understood forces of change that were shaking the foundations of old Europe. It is not surprising, therefore, that in elite circles throughout the continent there was something of a 'commonwealth of ideas' where these matters were discussed and debated. Nor is it surprising to find that the movement of ideas tended to be from west to east in Europe: it was the east that was 'backwards' and had to 'catch up'. In Russia, Catherine the Great had corresponded with Voltaire in search of enlightenment – her country being regarded, from a western perspective, as distinctly despotic. We read that one in four books published in Russian between the 1760s and 1800 was translated from the French and that by this latter date many educated Russians could read French and German in the original.[5] It seemed axiomatic that France, the leading state in Europe, would determine the continent's fate. Certainly, the language of change, throughout Europe, would be French.[6]

The 'French Revolution' was of course not one single event. Argument continues as to whether the bloody violence through which it was to pass was inherent from the outset.[7] Historians have long wrestled with the interpretation of its specific causes, its course and its consequences. Debate has followed debate as individual writers over subsequent centuries have emphasized variously the importance of economic, sociological or psychological factors in the great crisis that engulfed France at this time. Naturally, however, it has been in France itself that the Revolution has been most fiercely 'owned' or 'rejected'. 'It is really between 1789 and 1799', one

French historian writes, 'that the two big French political families were born, and established the grounds for the confrontation which was to be theirs for the following two centuries.'[8]

British reflections

What was to be true of France, however, was also to be true, to greater or lesser extent, of all the countries of Europe as they 'domesticated' the revolution's significance. In the case of Britain, the fact that revolution had occurred in France constituted a particular difficulty. However much the revolutionary principles did possess general applicability, their origins and working out were indisputably French. So, as reflection on the revolution took place in Britain at various levels, ideology, national self-perception and national self-interest mingled in a confusing manner as its import was assessed. Given the extent to which France and Britain had been in conflict earlier in the eighteenth century, it could hardly be otherwise. In the mid-century decades, as Horace Walpole put it, the elder Pitt had seemed determined that 'his administration should decide which alone should exist as a nation, Britain or France'.[9] While that was a very western European perception, it did reflect the belief that one or other of those nations would hold the ring in Europe. Decades later, perhaps that was still the question. In his last speech in the House of Lords, before his death in 1778, Pitt had looked back with satisfaction to a time when Britain had been 'the terror of the world'. His own ambition had been to be 'the most illustrious man of the first country in Europe' (a continent he had penetrated as a young man, studying in Utrecht and subsequently travelling in France and Switzerland).[10] Did his son (who had left England only once, to spend two months in France in 1783) have the same ambition now that he was prime minister, and what did it mean for Britain to be 'the first country in Europe'?

The initial phase of the revolution, which gave France a constitutional monarchy, by that very fact rendered obsolete that contrast between France as 'absolute' monarchy (as exemplified by Louis XIV) on the one hand and Britain as 'constitutional' monarchy on the other. It was possible, therefore, for some British commentators to interpret events in France as a 'catching up' process. Such an interpretation was no doubt somewhat patronizing but, if it was the correct one, the outcome had to be welcomed. Charles James Fox, then the opposition Whig leader, went so far as to describe the fall of the Bastille as the greatest and best event to have happened in the history of the world. Unsurprisingly, Pitt was more measured but, after the Bastille fell, he was willing to assure France of his continuing desire to cultivate the friendship and harmony that he believed to subsist between the two countries. Initial British commentary was by no means invariably critical of developments in France. Some observers expressed gratification that in their constitutional arrangements Britain and France were coming closer together in a manner that promised well for the future peace and prosperity of Europe. The duke of Dorset, for example, reported from Paris to the duke of Leeds in July 1789 that 'the greatest Revolution that we know anything of' had been effected, comparatively speaking, with the loss of very few lives. France henceforward was to be considered 'a free Country' with a limited monarchy and the nobility reduced to a level with the rest of the nation.[11] Nevertheless, as the new institutions in France established themselves, it became apparent that they could not simply be regarded as admiring imitations of the House of Commons: the changes in France between 1789 and 1792 presupposed the existence of 'rights' not recognized as such in Britain.

It was at this point that the divisions of opinion within Britain became evident. Whereas the movement for parliamentary reform, still basing its aspirations on the rights of 'free-born Englishmen' rather than on some universal doctrine, had spluttered ineffectively in the 1780s, it now had a new opportunity. For Major John Cartwright, of the Society for Constitutional Information, the French were not only asserting their own rights but they were advancing the general liberties of mankind. It was absurd, he thought, to suppose that the British Constitution was ideal. There was plenty of scope to advance British liberties and the 'climate of the times' suggested that a move forward could be made. But how far? What was the 'British system'?

George III had been king since 1760. Glorying in the name of Briton, as he famously did on his accession, he was indubitably a British king (but one who, rather regretfully, but inevitably, took a German Protestant princess as his wife). Renouncing 'the name of Englishman' and using Briton still rankled with 'Junius' in his letters to the press a decade later. George appointed his ministers, though they had to possess a parliamentary majority if they were to govern. His power, however, or at least the way he chose to exercise it, lay in 'blocking men and measures he disapproved of'. As a monarch, Linda Colley continues, George did not attempt to shape policy in the manner of a Frederick the Great of Prussia or Joseph II of Austria. In so far as Britain shared in the 'royal resurgence' evident in European states in the later eighteenth century, it did so distinctively by seeking to enhance the popularity rather than the performance of the monarch. By the end of the century, rather unexpectedly, George was 'popular'. Colley further detects a shift in royal aesthetics from the cosmopolitan to the glorification of Britain's real and mythic history.[12] The king, even if he 'did not much care for Europe', certainly took his place in its dynastic network with a proper concern for status. It was to be deeply shocking when the 'Corsican tyrant' or 'French usurper' should presume to address him, much later, in 1804, as 'Monsieur mon frère'.[13] He had no personal wish to strut in the courts of Europe. He was not even solid about the Rock. In 1782, for example, he wrote privately that he wished he could be 'rid of Gibraltar and to have as much possession in the West Indies as possible'.[14] Nonetheless, as elector of

Hanover, he was a European figure. In that distant capacity he was not subject to the constraints he experienced at Westminster.[15] However, he did not share George II's love of Hanover and he did not choose to go there in person. Indeed, he scarcely went anywhere, that is, apart from Weymouth.[16]

Parliament contained the two chambers of the Lords (hereditary peers and bishops) and the Commons. The latter consisted of 558 elected members chosen by some 250,000 adult males. This electorate was divided into constituencies, some of which differed vastly in size and composition. Some electors were called upon to vote only infrequently since, for candidates, elections were expensive and to be avoided if possible. The king's principal or prime minister (Pitt the Younger at the time of the revolution) had only a limited number of personal supporters but could rely upon the 'Party of the Crown' and a group of independent MPs to provide him with the necessary majority. It has been pointed out that in the age of the French Revolution there was no diminution in aristocratic power. Between 1783 and 1812, only 12 out of 52 cabinet ministers were commoners and only seven of them remained commoners. British government, in short, was a curious mixture of monarchy and oligarchy. 'Parties' were essential to the system but their coherence rested as much upon allegiance to a particular individual as to a clear 'platform' or 'programme'. The MP without party could still be a significant player, though diminishingly so. The Whigs, dominant under the first two Georges, were now in some disarray, split between factions largely on the question of 'reform'. To what extent, therefore, was Britain too now vulnerable to revolution? Would it need to become more 'French'?

Historians have discussed the mood of Britain at this time at some length, but have reached different conclusions. Some accounts have portrayed a country seething with discontent and ripe for revolution. Others, on the contrary, have failed to find any disaffection on a scale sufficient to suggest revolution's imminence. Detailed analysis certainly brings out the complexity of the situation, but historians continue to differ about the extent to which the revolutionary impulse was restrained by repression – or whether it was ever significantly present in the first place.[17] It must be stressed, too, that opinion concerning France was not static but fluctuated as events unfolded – not surprisingly, people changed their minds. Some initial enthusiasts for 'following France' moderated their enthusiasm as they digested the implications of the flight of the French royal family to Varennes in June 1791.

In November 1790 Edmund Burke published his *Reflections on the Revolution in France* – a French translation was in progress at least a week before the publication of the English edition. It was a work that sold 30,000 copies in its first two years and elicited over 100 rejoinders and over 200 works in support.[18] Burke set his face against universal panaceas. An Irishman himself, but one whose career had been made in England, he stressed rather the particular rights and duties that Englishmen had been fortunate enough to inherit. He distrusted the assumption that society could be turned upside down and still retain what he regarded as the values of civilization. And, within a few years, what had initially appeared to be hyperbolic exaggeration on his part came to be regarded as prophetic insight. On the other side of the argument, Thomas Paine's *The Rights of Man*, the second part of which was published in February 1792, probably sold approaching 200,000 copies and presented a very different future. Its objectives, however, antagonized conservative Whigs and, although enthusiasm for reform in Britain remained in certain quarters, alterations tended to be advocated pragmatically without reference to 'extreme' radical ideology. Supporters of Charles James Fox, some 50 Whigs, maintained a passionate, but ineffective, defence of 'liberty' in opposition to the 'coalition of politicians' assembled by Pitt, which saw itself as managing the 'national interest' at a time of crisis.

Warlike solutions

Over a longer time span, the debate thus joined raised issues about human nature and identity, issues that had profound implications for 'Britain', for 'Europe' and for 'Britain in Europe'. Was it the case, as the Scottish philosopher and historian David Hume wrote, that 'Mankind are so much the same, in all times and places, that history informs us of nothing new in this particular. Its chief use is only to discover the constant and uniform principles of human nature'. If that was so, perhaps all that was required, whether in Britain, in Europe or the world, was 'an exact and reasoned account' of those institutions that best conformed to the innate constitution of this universal man'. The contrary position was that there were no such uniform principles. Human nature was always contingent. One did not meet 'Man', but only Englishmen, Frenchmen or Spaniards, or whatever – and it was meeting males that was held to be significant. From Montesquieu onwards, there had been increasing speculation about the causes of the differences between societies that travellers could not fail to notice. Montesquieu had stressed the effects of climate and environment in determining the character of particular peoples and countries. In these circumstances it was a touch premature for a set of gentlemen, in May 1790 in Paris, to divest themselves of their 'national' identity and proclaim themselves to be 'Britons, by birth, but by sentiment and principle, Universal Patriots'.[19]

This led on, however, to a further debate. Some commentators attempted to deal with the diversity they still encountered by arguing that there were deep underlying 'primary' similarities possessed by all peoples. Such 'local differences' as remained observable should be regarded only as 'secondary'. Even if this solution were thought plausible, however, there was ample scope for disagreement when it came to identifying what was 'primary' and what was 'secondary' with regard to human nature.

There was nothing surprising in the conclusion drawn by most contemporaries that war would be the final arbiter between nations and states. 'Human nature' seemed to suggest that it would always be so. The states of Europe in mid-century exhibited what F.H. Hinsley identified as 'a kind of schizophrenia, the outcome of their urge to expand and their need to be careful'.[20] All was in flux. Dynastic principles were giving way to 'pure power' considerations and a premium came to be placed on the internal efficiency of states. It was a matter of debate at the time whether there was any underlying international order in 'Europe'. There were variations, from Voltaire onwards, on the theme that Europe was a kind of great republic, but one divided into several states. These states allegedly all had the same principle of public law and politics, unknown in the other parts of the world.[21] It was largely accepted, however, that the near-equality between several leading states in Europe at this juncture had rendered impossible the idea of a 'universal monarchy'.

In reality, however, despite some aspirations to the contrary, it was increasingly difficult to treat the entire continent of Europe as any kind of single community. The wars that had been taking place between Russia and the Ottoman Empire raised again the question of the boundary of this supposed 'single community'. Russia had annexed the Crimea in 1783 (a step that the weakened Ottomans, with their French supporters distracted by America, did not contest). In addition, it was difficult to 'think European' when there was rarely a moment when a war of some kind was not taking place, or was being threatened, between European states. There was, for example, a short war in which Sweden attempted to take advantage of Russian campaigns from 1788 to 1790, although it ended with a peace that preserved the pre-war status quo. Prussia appeared to some observers to be perpetually on the prowl. Austria, on the other hand, seemed constantly worried by the prospect of war. The carve-up of Poland started in 1772 and was to be completed in two further operations in 1793 and 1795. Poland's own internal revolution was destroyed by foreign force. Horace Walpole had sardonically observed at the time of Poland's first partition that a British fleet could not easily sail to Warsaw. It was not to be the last time when it was to become apparent that Britain did not possess the capacity to intervene militarily in east-central Europe, and exercise a major role there, even if sometimes it wished to do so. Britain could not prevent Poland disappearing from the map as an independent state – though of course, in the future, 'Poland' was to reappear in various territorial habitats.[22] The only benefit, a dubious one, that followed from the partition of Poland was the equilibrium allegedly established between Russia, Prussia and Austria – with the implications this held for Europe as a whole.

In the north-eastern corner of Europe, the Baltic, rather far away from the disdainful English, the philosopher Immanuel Kant meditated in Königsberg on the 'international problem' as it existed in his time. He published his *Thoughts on Perpetual Peace* in 1795. He saw no easy solution, arguing both that a peaceable federation of nations was impossible but also, nevertheless, that individuals should try to establish one: an intriguing philosophical position that scholars, though not statesmen, have delighted to explore ever since. Kant firmly asserted, however, that no state could simply be acquired by another state through inheritance, exchange, purchase or gift (something that had often happened in the past in Europe). State legitimacy, he argued, derived from the consent of the governed – however that consent was established. It was an assertion, though, that did not seem to have much bearing when one considered the fate of Poland. Even so, it is possible, at the end of the eighteenth century, to detect an increasing unwillingness in some European societies, or at least among certain elements within them, simply to acquiesce in what has been called 'a fatalistic acceptance of war'.[23] Europe, indeed the world, should aspire to a better future, one in which endemic conflict, which had characterized much of Europe's history, would be banished.

British interests and the passage to war

In Britain, the aspiration to be 'the terror of the world', to repeat the elder Pitt's apparently laudable ambition, had by no means disappeared. A 'terrorist' state can hardly have qualms about the use of force to sustain itself. In a century that had seen ample conflict, a further round at the end of the eighteenth century scarcely seemed a novelty requiring specific justification. Even so, after Britain had again gone to war, there were those who argued that it might at least be *Inconsistent with the Doctrine and Example of Jesus Christ*, to quote the title of one 1796 tract. In 1793 a Brighton preacher had offended militia members of his congregation by preaching a sermon in which, according to his own account, he had merely 'endeavoured to divest *war* of those assumed splendors, and that appearance of gaiety and happiness, which do not belong to it, but which seduce the unthinking to view it as a PASTIME'. He was greeted by chanting officers who shouted 'out with the Democrat – no Democrats'.[24]

War, therefore, whether or not it was conceived as a pastime, brought fresh dilemmas for Britain and had certainly not been something planned for since 1789. However, the new Habsburg emperor, Francis II, rejected an ultimatum from the French Legislative Assembly requiring him to renounce every treaty it considered to be directed against the sovereignty, independence and safety of the French nation.[25] In April 1792 the assembly declared war in defence of a free people against the 'unjust aggression of a king' – and Pitt and Grenville (a prime minister's son, foreign secretary 1791–1801) do seem to have blamed Austria and Prussia for war. The government had no wish to intervene on the continent and had not taken significant steps to prepare to do so: 'salt water entrenchment' seemed a better bet. Until this point, the ministers seem to have thought war unlikely. Grenville himself had no direct foreign experience – if an earlier period in Dublin Castle as chief secretary does not qualify. At Eton and Oxford his academic world was classical. He had demonstrated a considerable lucidity in Greek and Latin composition. In a later period of retirement, he published editions of the *Iliad* and the *Odyssey* at his own expense. He read the Greek New Testament and classical poets. French and English history books, mainly concerning the seventeenth century, received some attention.[26] However, no overarching view of Europe emerged. It has been suggested that the Foreign Office did little more than monitor events in Europe for much of that year – during which the Anglo-Prussian alliance had collapsed.[27] Britain did not initially join in supporting Prussia, Austria and Piedmont in the ensuing struggle against France. Grenville himself had embarked upon a protracted honeymoon. The commander of these allies, the duke of Brunswick, had declared that his armies were intervening in France to suppress anarchy and restore the royal authority of the king of France. Months later, for its part, the assembly declared that the French armies were offering fraternity and assistance to all peoples who wished to assert their liberty. In August, Brunswick's troops invaded France and initially seemed to make good progress, but this was not sustained. By October, victorious French forces had regained ground. Even in November 1792, Grenville's 'tableau for Europe' for the coming year envisaged that 'we shall do nothing', which he supposed would also be the view of Russia and other small European states.[28]

These developments, however, did place the political nation in Britain in a quandary – particularly since the general assumption had been that a German army would indeed succeed in occupying Paris, a step that, in turn, would have given British diplomacy a mediating role in the subsequent negotiations. The collapse of the French constitutional monarchy brought additional complication. If there was fear in Britain aroused by events on the European mainland, it was still fear of 'France' rather than fear of 'revolution' that predominated – though the September massacres caused a certain outrage and alarm, and had resulted in an influx of French refugees. In his horrific depiction, the cartoonist Gillray illustrated how revolutionary freedom had allowed the French *sans-culottes* to turn from consuming frogs and *soupe maigre*, as he supposed was their wont, to cannibalism. Other cartoonists graphically portrayed anarchy running amok in France.[29] In face of 'the power and ambition of France', there was official anxiety for Holland, and for the Austrian Netherlands (where a short-lived revolt had put a country called 'Belgium' on the political agenda). Such anxieties were constant and of course had a long pedigree. The 'threat to the Channel ports' could be readily drummed up – though Charles James Fox, for one, did not believe that there was any such threat.

Yet, even if there was, it still seemed precipitate for Britain to risk war. In the previous spring, the British cabinet had had to conclude, embarrassingly, that the political nation would not back the British ultimatum that had been delivered to Russia to compel it to withdraw from a captured

Turkish fortress. It was clearly not sensible to deliver an ultimatum that could not be followed up for domestic reasons. Yet, while British ministers did not relish a war, French success in the Austrian Netherlands came to make it seem more likely. Even so, it was important that France should appear as the aggressor – an objective largely achieved in the war of words that culminated in the French declaration of war on Britain in February 1793. It has been noted, however, that 'this last and greatest chapter of the secular Anglo-French struggle' began, on the British side, with a curious insouciance concerning its possible consequences.[30]

It was not easy, initially, for British ministers to state what was at issue.[31] In the previous year, Pitt had told the House of Commons that he looked forward to the day when France, one of the most brilliant powers in Europe, as he put it, would enjoy just that kind of liberty he venerated and the valuable existence of which it was his duty, as an Englishman, peculiarly to cherish. Such a noble veneration of liberty on Pitt's part, however, did not unduly interfere with his domestic suppression of opposite views in the years ahead. Sedition and treason trials in England and Scotland restrained the reform societies. Public meetings were 'gagged'. Habeas corpus was suspended. Such bodies as the United Englishmen and the United Irishmen were to find themselves outlawed. There could be no truck, apparently, with treason and the threat that it posed to the old England of roast beef and brown ale. It was not altogether certain, however, that the states that would be Pitt's partners in the First Coalition of 1793 – Austria, Prussia, Britain, the Netherlands and Spain – cherished liberty, as he conceived it, to the same degree.

Various 'principles' certainly jostled awkwardly together at this time. Until this point, ministers maintained that Britain was anxious only to keep good relations with other European governments. How they conducted their internal affairs was not its business. But did this still obtain? If it did not, was Britain now committed to 'cleansing' France of the stench of Jacobinism. Such a clean-up, it was supposed, would undoubtedly be facilitated by the revival of religion in France and the restoration of the *ancien régime*? In short, was there a firm ideological objective at the heart of the war? If so, in what would be sure to be coalition warfare, would the inevitable corollary be that Britain would be firmly in the camp of 'reaction'? John Bowles, who was to emerge as one of the most prominent 'loyalist' pamphleteers, had no doubt. Only by going to war could Britain avoid its metamorphosis into a 'department' of the French republic. War, he emphasized, was 'the PALLADIUM of CIVILIZED SOCIETY'.[32]

In these as yet unresolved questions about the purpose of the war lay a conflict between national self-image and the harsh demands of European power-politics. In his famous budget speech of February 1792 Pitt tried to set out what it was that formed and upheld the national character. He formulated it as being liberty with law. It raised a barrier equally firm against the encroachments of power, and the violence of popular commotions. It afforded property its 'just security'. It produced the exertion of genius and labour. That was the greatness of Britain. The extent of Pitt's commercial emphasis stands out in these remarks and testifies to another reason why British politicians were reluctant to intervene. Britain had certainly demonstrated throughout the eighteenth century that it was not averse to fighting in particular circumstances, yet it was not at heart a military power. The absence of a major standing army – and the 'militarism' that was a feature of those continental countries that were more frequently exposed to conflict – had been perceived externally as a defining characteristic of Britain. The jurist Sir William Blackstone had famously described regular forces of the Crown as 'temporary excrescences bred out of the distemper of the State, and not as any part of the permanent and perpetual laws of the Kingdom'.[33] In 1792, the British army consisted of fewer than 45,000 men, two-thirds of whom were manning garrisons overseas. Any declaration of war would therefore entail a rapid increase in numbers – obtained by press-ganging if need be. The county militias of England and Wales, under the control of the country gentry, could furnish men in an emergency but they were of dubious quality. Militia units were not liable for duty outside the country without consent. Suggestions that the British army needed to become more 'professional' (for example, by the establishment of a Royal Military Academy) were rejected. Its officers were drawn from the lesser aristocracy and gentry who, in turn, communicated with 'other ranks' through non-commissioned officers. Its structure reflected the class structure of Britain. The 'other ranks' arrived by various routes. We read that, of four regiments recruiting before sailing for India in 1787, two had to fill up with 'prisoners from Gloucester gaol, dismissed seamen and even out-pensioners from Chelsea Hospital'.[34] Recruits obtained from the continent – at a price – were probably better value. Any attempt to achieve 'continental efficiency' in matters military was regarded with mingled scorn and apprehension. The British believed that they possessed a small army but a very good one – and that there was a relationship between these two things. As Michael Howard points out, 'If the British had had to create an army on a continental scale, they would have had to take the continental model very much more seriously; which would, in turn, have had far-reaching implications for the structure of their own society.'[35] It still did not appear that Britain wanted to be part of that kind of Europe.

British 'highmindedness' in this respect was in large measure a reflection of the prevailing belief in the primary importance, for an insular state, of maritime predominance – and in this area there was work to be done. The triumphs of the Royal Navy in the Seven Years War, 1756–63, had been followed by humiliation during the American War of Independence. Between 1778 and 1783 the French Navy had seized much of Britain's rich West Indian empire. It was time to regain pre-eminence in the Caribbean.[36] Over the next decade, an extensive programme of naval rearmament was undertaken so that, when war did occur, Britain could reasonably expect that the

Royal Navy would do its duty – and it was hoped that the negative impact of the revolution on the effective officering of the French Navy would assist it in its task.

It had been Pitt's assumption, in the speech referred to above, that France's internal difficulties would remove a threat to Britain which that country might otherwise present – and which she had been perceived to present over past decades.[37] A year before going to war with France, therefore, he had reduced the estimates for the armed forces and, like other European statesmen of the time, he had been inclined to believe that French power was in decline. While that might have been true in 1789, a new situation was now developing. Universal conscription for military service was introduced in France in August 1793 and, in due course, produced the massive formations of the revolutionary armies (some 75 per cent of France's pre-Revolutionary officer corps had emigrated). The armies of other states, it seemed, if they were to fight effectively, had no option but to imitate them, while at the same time seeking to prevent the revolutionary fervour that, initially at least, inspired the French revolutionary armies, from infecting their own.

Not surprisingly, if the initiating states could have known what would be the consequences of their actions, they might have hesitated before engaging in war. In his classic interpretation of foreign policy, *Britain in Europe, 1789–1914*, significantly first published in 1937 when Britain's involvement in another European war appeared highly possible, Professor R.W. Seton-Watson stressed what he called 'the extreme forbearance, not to say reluctance' with which British statesmen entered the military arena, coming as it did after following 'a period of unquestioned eagerness for peace and reconciliation with their old enemy'. To him, the behaviour of government ministers in the late 1790s provided 'a key to British psychology'. Ministers showed in their conduct that a blend of hesitation, detachment and ignorance did not necessarily spell 'degeneracy'. The very men who showed such extreme reluctance to go to war nevertheless developed a stubborn staying power and simply refused to accept failure.[38] So, why did they take the 'fateful plunge'?

One answer might be to say that overweening French ambition left them in the end with no alternative. But that in turn leaves the question of French motives open to speculation. The classic answer provided by the nineteenth-century French historian Albert Sorel was that revolutionary France was determined to follow Louis XIV and Henri IV in seeking France's 'natural frontiers'. It has been suggested, however, that the idea of 'natural frontiers' was itself a revolutionary development rather than an elaboration of France's traditional policy. Paul Schroeder argues that such a formula, in any case, served to obscure rather than to clarify objectives: confusion and disagreement persisted after the 'natural frontiers' had in fact been attained. The root cause of the conflict lay not in the pursuit of 'natural frontiers' per se but in what he calls 'security through hegemony in Western Europe, acquired by French control over the smaller states from the Low Countries through western Germany, Switzerland, and northern Italy to Spain'.[39] Such a 'protective glacis' would make both the revolution and the state secure.

From a British perspective, however, 'almost automatically', according to 'balance of power' principles, such a French objective seemed aggressive and dangerous. Britain had to resist such aspirations not only in her own interests but to prevent the whole of Europe becoming completely subordinate to France. Yet, viewed from Paris, it was both natural and proper that Europe's leading state should possess that kind of influence over Europe. It was, rather, the British attempt to prevent her from exercising such influence that was 'unnatural'. Such contrary perceptions between states are not unusual in international relations. Both causes evoked strong emotions. In this case, a duel was subsumed within a struggle for mastery, at least over western Europe. France wanted to have that security around it to give it the upper hand in its dealings with Britain – precisely why Britain wished to prevent such security. Pitt declared in his war speech of 15 February 1793 that, unless the French 'system' was checked, it would threaten 'the tranquility of this country, the security of its allies, the good order of every European Government, and the happiness of the whole human race', but Schroeder is surely right to argue that neither Britain nor France entered the war with any concept of what might constitute a lasting peace throughout the continent. Both countries used 'Europe' for their own ends without giving any serious consideration to the good order of Europe as a whole. Thus, when the prospect of peacemaking occasionally surfaced in the years of belligerency it was never a peace for 'Europe' that was envisaged but merely one that purported to enhance the position, from the perspectives of those who controlled their policies, of either France or Britain in Europe.

That is not to say, however, that there was no wider reflection at the time. Edward Gibbon, who reflected long on empires, accepted that it was the duty of a patriot 'to prefer and promote the exclusive interest and glory of his native country', but a philosopher might consider Europe 'as one great republic, whose various inhabitants have attained almost the same level of politeness and cultivation'. The balance of power would continue to fluctuate and the prosperity of the British and neighbouring kingdoms might alternately be exalted or depressed, but such 'partial events' could not essentially injure 'our general state of happiness, the system of arts, and manners, which so advantageously distinguish, above the rest of mankind, the Europeans and their colonies'.[40] There was no doubt, however, that it was patriots rather than philosophers that determined policy.

The long war: first phase

The ensuing struggle was to last until March 1802 – though even at the time the 'Peace of Amiens' concluded at that point seemed more like a pause in hostilities rather than a termination that was likely to endure. By the time the allies entered Paris in July 1815, the war against France represented the longest continuous period of English/British military engagement since the wars of Elizabethan England with Spain. In its initial phase, it could be interpreted as a struggle between 'Europe', on the one hand, and the French Revolution on the other, in which Britain would be hardly likely to play the leading military role. The First Coalition – consisting of Prussia, Austria, Holland, Naples, Spain, Portugal and, nominally, Russia – did, however, owe a good deal in its initial organization to British diplomatic efforts. Agreement between these states was always difficult and British diplomatic activity remained very important. Although a British force was initially present in the Low Countries as a sign of British commitment, the force had to be withdrawn in 1795, with heavy losses. It ransacked its way to Hanover. Otherwise, the way Britain went to war was to pay for German mercenaries and subsidize the king of Sardinia. Its direct contribution would come as a result of its efforts against the French in the West Indies, though the immediate value of this activity to the European was not always apparent in Berlin or Vienna. This coalition did not last long in the face of French military success. Prussia, followed by Spain and smaller German states, deserted, leaving only Austria, Britain and Sardinia to fight France (and the allies France began to acquire). The main French attack was then directed against Austria, both in southern Germany and Italy. Sardinia was forced to make peace. The Austrian position in Italy became hopeless. The Peace of Campo Formio (October 1797), which took Austria out of the war, signified the effective end of the First Coalition.

French expansion continued with vigour under the command, in the peninsula, of a 27-year-old, newly promoted general, Napoleon (no longer Buonaparte but newly a proper Frenchman as Bonaparte) who proceeded to remodel its political geography. In the Italian peninsula, as elsewhere (the Batavian and Helvetic republics), it was clear that the revolution was indeed for export and would result in substantial change. Britain was now the only major state engaged in war with France and, in these circumstances, it was difficult to see how French dominance could be challenged. It was clear that a traditional naval and colonial emphasis on Britain's part would not reverse it. The possibility of a French invasion of Britain could not altogether be discounted and, in the first half of 1797, naval mutinies at Spithead and the Nore caused serious alarm at Westminster, only partially relieved by victories over the Spanish and Dutch fleets (now in alliance with France). Exploration of peace terms revealed that they would be humiliating.

Moreover, in mid-1798, a rather different challenge presented itself. Napoleon, (possibly seeing himself as a latter-day Alexander the Great) at the head of a so-called 'Army of the Orient' set off for Egypt (an Ottoman dependency), occupying Malta on the way. Perhaps it seemed a better bet than trying to occupy England. Whether the expedition was seriously intended to threaten the British position in India remains contentious, but its initial military success in July in Egypt was alarming enough. The tables were turned, however, by Nelson's destruction of the French fleet at Aboukir Bay on 1 August. Britain had a new naval hero. Even so, first in Syria and then in Egypt, Napoleon remained menacing until he set off back to France in August, arriving there in October 1799. Two years later, the French occupation came to an end as the weakened French forces were compelled to evacuate by an Anglo-Egyptian expeditionary force. An extraordinary episode came to an end with the British dictating terms.

The expedition had also played its part in facilitating the creation of some kind of fresh coalition against France in Europe. The new Russian tsar, Paul, happened to have formed an enthusiasm for the Knights of St John of Jerusalem in Malta – he had been elected their grand master in 1798. The island had been held by this order from 1530 until the French conquest of 1798. The tsar, who had a personal obsession with medieval chivalry, supposed that, stiffened by Russian nobility, the dormant crusading zeal of this extraordinary survival from an earlier era of European history might now be directed against French infidelity. Subsidized by Britain, Russian forces might be a substantial element in the equation. Coalition-building proved as complicated as previously. The 'Second Coalition', which was at war with France by the spring of 1799 (chiefly Britain, Austria, Russia and the Ottoman Empire), was fragile from the outset (the involvement of the Ottoman Empire stemmed directly from the Egyptian situation). Whether Prussia or Austria constituted a better partner for Britain has been a constant talking point. British historians, at least of an earlier generation, surveying the bickering of politicians in Vienna and St Petersburg, have expressed dismay at the rigid attitudes held by the two emperors, supported by their unscrupulous ministers. Continental courts, it seems, were unaccountably failing to notice that, in Pitt's words, Britain was in a position 'to animate the public spirit of Europe, to revive its dismayed energy and to give a turn to the political aspect of the world favourable to the cause of humanity'. Such words had a hollow ring when the fortunes of the coalition in 1799 are considered. A planned invasion of France from Switzerland had to be aborted. The unlikely combination of British and Russian forces operating in the Netherlands failed to make an impact. The Russians and the Austrians finally fell out and the former withdrew from the coalition. A little earlier, the British unwillingness to let the Russians share in the garrisoning of the newly recaptured Malta did not seem fully consonant with the common espousal of the 'cause of humanity'. At the end of 1799, at the height of his power and prestige, Pitt had avowed that 'one campaign, if our Confederacy *can any how* be kept together, will secure all we can wish'. The following months demonstrated that such complete success remained elusive – though Napoleon, in power after his November coup, knew that the French position was far from comfortable (the Austrians, with Russian help, had cleared the French from Italy). Pitt, declining to treat with 'this last adventurer in the lottery of revolutions', did not wish to enter into peace negotiations.

But what was it that Britain did wish? Britain had, as Schroeder puts it, 'a set of war aims distinctly narrower and less European than those of any other great power'. Territorially, the focus of British concern remained, in order of importance, France and the Low Countries, the Iberian Peninsula, the Baltic, the Mediterranean and the Near East (the latter three paramountly reflecting commercial concerns). Extra-European concerns, for Britain, rivalled European. The matters that dominated the discourse of central European diplomacy – Poland, Italy, the Balkans, Germany – featured chiefly for Britain in their bearing on the war with France. Schroeder further argues that it is misplaced, at this juncture, to ask whether British policy 'centred' on Europe or the British Empire. The position is even more basic. Britain simply had no concept of Europe and did not understand other states when they occasionally claimed that they did have such a concept. Here lay the importance of cultivating Russia – it was, in some vital respects, 'a half-European, half-world power' like Britain itself.[41]

Austria, having been defeated by Napoleon at Marengo in June 1800, and having suffered later reverses, concluded peace by the Treaty of Lunéville in February 1801. The Habsburg position in Belgium and Italy was undermined, and there were other unpalatable outcomes for Vienna. Even so, the Austrian Empire remained a sort of great power, still a key element in the European structure. The reality therefore was that Britain had been 'abandoned by everybody, allies and all' as Lord Hawkesbury, the new foreign secretary put it. There was little option but to enter into peace negotiations. Eventually, after earlier preliminaries, the Peace of Amiens was signed in March 1802. In the interval, there had been difficult moments. For example, it had looked as though there might have been a Franco-Russian *rapprochement*, with all that would mean for Britain. In the event, the assassination of Tsar Paul in March 1801 made such a development unlikely, at least for the moment. It was the issue of the rights of neutral states at sea that had brought Britain into conflict in the Baltic. States there, affected by the forthright British stand on this matter, had formed, with Russian support, an 'armed neutrality'. However, Nelson's defeat of the Danish fleet off Copenhagen warded off the prospect of lasting damage to British commercial interests in the Baltic.

The treaty-making of these years, even at the time, was widely perceived to be little more than a hiatus in the fighting. It was a new government in Britain, under Addington, that concluded the peace after many months of bickering over detail – Pitt having resigned over the question of Catholic emancipation. The return of all the British overseas conquests, with the exception of Trinidad and Ceylon, seemed to many contemporaries to be a high price to pay for peace. Malta, in theory, was to be neutralized under a Neapolitan suzerainty – a somewhat unknown quantity in the circumstances. It seemed clear, however, that Britain needed at least a pause in

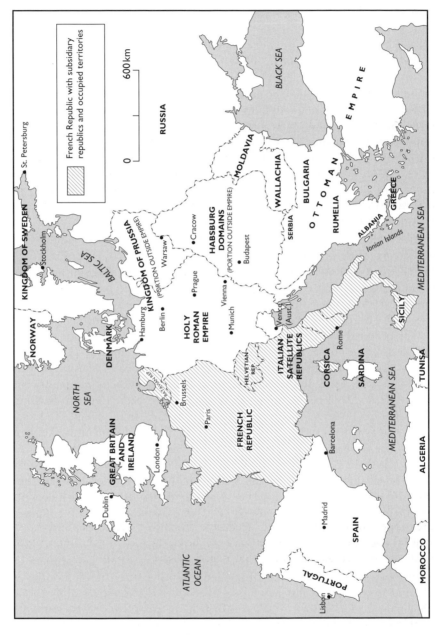

2. Europe in 1801, after the Treaty of Lunéville

order to regain financial and economic equilibrium – overseas trade had been severely damaged in the war – quite apart from any other consideration. No doubt the income tax, introduced for the first time in 1799, was accepted merely as a temporary expedient, but it was scarcely greeted with enthusiasm.

It was easy to identify the broad basis that made the Peace of Amiens feasible – French domination of western Europe and British maritime supremacy, coupled with predominance in India. Russia could be said to have been allowed a free hand in eastern Europe. However, although this could be presented as a reasonable set of spheres of predominance, it was far from clear that it would create a lasting settlement. Whether it would in fact do so might not depend entirely on the principals involved, but on the extent to which the other great and small states were willing to accept the position of France. At some point, Britain might again be encouraged to take an active European role if French predominance actually came to threaten their own survival. It might be, however, that they would be prepared to accept that France should 'lead' Europe against the insular maritime predator that was Britain. It was not the first time, nor was it to be the last, that Britain's position in relation to Europe could be thought about in these terms. It was clear in the aftermath of its conclusion both that the Peace of Amiens left Napoleon with considerable scope to exploit its provisions and that Britain could be accused of treaty violation if it responded determinedly to such exploitation. For the moment, however, a kind of peace had returned.

Boundaries: maps and minds

Gibbon suspected that it was from outside that the common European civilization that he posited might be threatened. Rulers and diplomats seemed simply obsessed with the actions and ambitions of their European peers. He warned, however, that unknown dangers might arise 'from some obscure people, scarcely visible in the map of the world'. There is no evidence, however, that British diplomats sought anxiously to identify this unknown phenomenon. It was in 1793 that Lord Macartney visited China, a country that was certainly visible on such a map, as Britain's first ambassador. To outward appearance China could seem the greatest, wealthiest and most powerful country in the world. It was not, however, perceived to constitute a challenge or a threat of a kind that might cause European states to 'think continental'. Indeed, by the time of Gibbon's death a year later, it was not from some obscure people that a threat to European civilization might appear. That civilization was threatened from within. The British envoy at Constantinople was told to warn Ottoman ministers, no less, that a government – if that was what it could be called – had arisen in Paris that aimed at 'nothing less than the subversion of all the established religions and forms of government in the whole world'.[42] Here, apparently, was a new

phenomenon that could render obsolete the long confrontation between
'Christian Europe' and the Islamic Ottoman Empire.

The question of 'frontiers', whether 'natural' or otherwise, in this extraordinary new circumstance, took on fresh significance in trying to identify
friend and foe. What did a boundary now mean? The assumptions about the
nature of states, which had long underpinned the old European territorial
order, now looked under threat. There was a certain irony in the fact that at
the end of the eighteenth century mapping was itself becoming both a more
scientific and a more widespread activity. Professor Black has drawn attention to the complexities involved at this juncture in trying to 'represent'
names, places and spaces authentically and authoritatively – as states and
peoples, sometimes in unison, sometimes in contestation, sought to claim
what was 'theirs'. The very nature of this activity encouraged the identification of 'strangers' and 'brothers'. Was there such a thing as a 'natural frontier'? The war was to bring dramatic changes in the political map of Europe.
The revolution increasingly replaced the old jurisdictional-territorial criteria
when it came to drawing up frontiers both within and outside France. A
regime that invented a new calendar and unit of measurement could scarcely
rest content with the jumbled and seemingly haphazard boundaries of the
past. It was time to construct a rational basis for the existence of states and
reconsider 'nations'.[43]

The judicial, financial and linguistic homogeneity of Britain contrasted
with the diversity that existed within many European states at this juncture,
although it was not quite as great as an English political elite, scarcely con-
versant with the cultural complexity of Britain, supposed. There was, however, by contrast with the mainland of Europe, little territorial 'tidying up'
to do in 'the Isles' – although whether 'Monmouthshire' lay in Wales (itself
an uncertain entity and scarcely recognized) or England, and whether
Berwick-on-Tweed lay in Scotland or England, could cause modest local
excitement. It is significant that anxiety about a possible French invasion led
to the establishment of the Ordnance Survey. In the 1790s its task was to
ensure that no place in Great Britain was without a name. It was an operation that went some way towards stamping an English standardization on
the place names of Britain and thereby perhaps creating an illusion of British
homogeneity.[44]

On the European mainland, however, various territorial 'peculiars' were
still very apparent at the time of the French onslaught on the continent. The
process of pacification at the end of wars had come increasingly to be
accompanied by an attempt at precise mapping of boundaries and frontiers
from the mid-eighteenth century onwards. Diplomats came to rely and insist
upon maps in treaty negotiations. Delineating boundaries between Austria
and the Ottoman Empire (where Europe ended?) proved particularly contentious precisely because the relationship between physical space and
sacred space (Muslims and Christians) in any territory escaped easy delin-
eation in mixed communities on the eastern periphery of Europe. In this

process of mapping in Germany and central Europe ancient jurisdictions came to seem increasingly anomalous and anachronistic in the new era of change and rationalization.[45] It was not yet certain, however, what this zeal to categorize space really signified in terms of 'ownership' in the perceptions of the inhabitants of particular territories. Only the final outcome of the war would determine whether the new spatial configurations would solidify and produce a 'new Europe' based on enduring 'principles' that would replace the ramshackle inheritance from the past, or whether the old administrative and constitutional structures would be revived.

Mapping, however precise, could not capture the authentic springs of community. It was evident that some radical spirits at the time deduced the principles of democracy and popular sovereignty from the principles of rationality and universality they espoused – though that was itself not an invariable conclusion. If it was indeed the case that the revolution had destroyed the *ancien régime*, a new community had to take its place. Such a community could only be formed by real consent and real will. In the past, it was argued, there never had been true communities in Europe because previous communities had been moulded from above and were not 'natural'. Now, however, men were no longer born simply to give allegiance to monarchs who were supposedly endowed with authority by God – monarchs, moreover, who were themselves frequently 'alien'. Communities in Europe would henceforth be 'made', not 'given'. Past allegiances, it was argued, should offer no guide to the future. New sentiments of solidarity would have to be invented or perhaps discovered.

Moreover, such a challenge was being issued when Europe was far from stable. In itself, population growth struck at the existing social order. The population of Europe accelerated from the middle of the eighteenth century. A continent that in 1750 contained 130 million inhabitants, had doubled its population by 1800. Disease, famine and war, which had maintained the demographic balance for centuries, no longer did so effectively. The surge in population density was unparalleled. People migrated into the increasingly swollen cities of the continent – Paris, Madrid, Naples among them. In central and eastern Europe, where uncultivated land could still be opened up, rulers invited substantial German settlement – in the Banat or the Volga region, for example. Movements on such a scale, within the apparently firm framework that dynastic empires provided, did not seem initially to raise issues of identity. That situation was to change.

In France, at the time of the revolution 'it had seemed natural to define the nation as a political community in which the sovereignty once possessed by the crown had devolved'. In a sense, anyone who refused to pledge allegiance to this newly established nation ceased to be French – and any non-French person might perhaps become French by giving such allegiance. In reality the correspondence between community, nation and state was not in fact complete in France. Barère, charged by the convention to study the question of language, had no time for Breton, Alsatian, Occitan, Basque or

Corsican languages. These were languages, it was argued, used by priests to peddle superstition. French opened the way to 'la philosophie' and should be insisted upon universally – though 'pure' French was probably spoken in no more than 15 of the 83 departments. Even so, France could appear more homogeneous than almost any other part of mainland Europe. It was increasingly asserted in 'Germany' that what constituted a nation was not a political bond but a common language and the cultural identity that accompanied it. Johann Gottfried Herder, for example, imagined the world as a vast garden in which the nations had grown up like so many different plants. They developed in their own individual way. Peoples had their own ways of feeling and understanding. That was where future life lay. He happened to be on holiday in Rome in the summer of 1789 and found the city depressing. At St Peter's, the outward ceremony and the voice of the *castrati* depressed him. Rome was a city of the dead.[46] There had to be a new form of future.

Schulze argues that the increasingly widespread belief that poets and singers, drawing on legends and folk songs, were much closer to 'the people' than their rulers or civil servants 'was one of the comforting ideas by which the nations of Central and Eastern Europe compensated for their backwardness compared with the nation states of the West, and by which they affirmed their cultural identity'. At this juncture, therefore, two views of the nation – what he calls the subjective, political view of the French Revolution and the objective cultural view of German Romanticism – intermingled and interacted. It did appear to be the case that when so much was changing, the identification of the individual with the nation simplified complex social and international relationships and provided a firm anchor for loyalty.[47]

Locating 'Great Britain and Ireland'

Such comments form a background against which to consider what became, in July 1800, the United Kingdom of Great Britain and Ireland (passing into law in January 1801). Since 1782, 'Grattan's Parliament' in Dublin operated under a constitution the effect of which was to give the Irish Parliament (exclusively Protestant) greater autonomy from Westminster, though the various measures of Catholic relief passed by the parliament had London origins. Events in France, for many decades if not centuries, had significance for Ireland itself and for Irish–British relations. There was a perennial London fear that Ireland could offer a continental power a 'back door' into Britain – and indeed from late 1793 Ireland was of distinct interest in Paris as a means of destabilizing Britain. It was in this context that Theobald Wolfe Tone, a young Protestant lawyer, had in 1791 founded the Society of United Irishmen in Belfast.[48] The idea of an Irish republic had an appeal in a certain section of the Protestant population, which supposed that men of their own kind would dominate a population that was four-fifths Roman

Catholic. Grievances of the largely Catholic 'lower orders' sprang from issues relating to land. In turn, playing on Protestant anxieties, the Orange Order was founded in 1795. It vied with the Catholic Defenders, whose purpose is self-evident. There was almost constant talk of insurrection and contacts were established with Paris. Wolfe Tone had produced a memorandum for French agents in 1794 in which he made it clear that Ireland was a conquered, oppressed and insulted country in which the name of England and her power was 'universally odious' except among those who had a personal interest in its maintenance.[49] Bad weather prevented a French expedition – some 15,000 soldiers – landing in Bantry Bay in December 1796. What would have happened had it landed can be only a matter of speculation. However, it may reasonably be surmised that such a force, if supported by localized rebellions, would have stretched the capacity of the Irish state.[50] The largely Protestant yeomanry was able to undermine the United Irishmen's organization but it is now generally agreed that the methods used to suppress revolutionary elements alienated the Catholic rural population. Eventually, a rebellion did take place in Wexford in August/September 1798 – some 50,000 turned out – but it failed, partly again because French support was both too late and too limited. It was also the case, however, that the political ambitions of the United Irishmen did not unite all Irishmen: north/south and Protestant/Catholic differences were very apparent. Wolfe Tone committed suicide while awaiting execution.

The British government, however, had received a fright. There was a direct line from the rebellion of the United Irishmen to the Act of Union. From a British perspective, it was necessary to strengthen the ties between Britain and Ireland. Pressure and bribery were applied to dissolve the Irish Parliament and instead to establish Irish representation at Westminster (100 seats in the Commons and a small number of Irish peers). Ireland retained its own legal system. Commercial and financial changes were envisaged that would create a free-trade area between the two countries. Irish Catholics expected that they would be given the right to sit at Westminster but, in the event, that did not happen swiftly.

This hastily constructed incorporation, facilitated by judicious bribery, had important and not altogether perceived consequences for 'Britain in Europe'. Union might indeed significantly reduce the opportunities for French or other European intervention in Ireland, with whatever beneficial knock-on consequences that might have for Britain's security. On the other hand, it was by no means clear that Ireland would become as integrated an element within the United Kingdom as Scotland seemed to have become since that Act of Union of 1707. It had not escaped attention, indeed, that Scotsmen had carved for themselves prominent mercantile, administrative and military positions, and had already transformed what had been an English Empire into a British one.[51] For a start, no transcendent name for the new entity was available. 'Great Britain' had embraced 'England' and 'Scotland'. Ireland, however, did not join the other territories that existed within 'Great Britain'. The new state became 'Great Britain and Ireland'. On the other hand, though this was indeed the state's title, no one seriously supposed that the government in London was other than 'British' and that the balance of insular power lay in London and not Dublin. Indeed it was common for the British government to be perceived as 'English' and to be referred to as such. Ireland was a substantially Catholic country, but it also had a significant, though regionally skewed, Protestant population. Britain, by contrast, saw itself as a Protestant country (in a variety of denominations, some territorially concentrated). Moreover, it was a country that had not yet fully 'emancipated' its own very small Catholic population. In so far as Irish roads inescapably led to Rome, there was, as a consequence of Union, a new context within which London governments had to deal with the longest-reigning 'dynasty' in Europe – that of the popes, who were themselves caught up at this juncture in the great European crisis.

One further evident difference was that Ireland showed few signs of being other than a rural and agrarian country with 'peasant' inhabitants in substantial numbers. There was doubt whether, by this stage, 'peasants' any longer existed in Britain, or at least in England. Moreover, Ireland already showed for decades an unusually high rate of marital fertility, one of the explanations for its extraordinarily high percentage rate of population growth since the mid-eighteenth century – and the potential use of Irish manpower, once statutory impediments had been removed, in the British army had not escaped notice. Finally, there was the Irish language, which further identified Ireland as 'different', though that language was manifestly in crisis. Whether Ireland would escape from its quasi-colonial state – in which the parallels, social, cultural and economic, with central and eastern Europe stand out – into a partnership of parity, within a reconfigured United Kingdom that could be both 'British' and 'Irish', remained to be seen. Certainly, the Irish Act of Union, created a United Kingdom of Great Britain and Ireland whose texture was more 'European' in its cultural and religious complexity and, to a degree, its ethnic heterogeneity, than was appreciated or perhaps desired in the capital of a country still more often than not referred to as 'England'.

Questions of culture

The 'culture' of Britain/Ireland, using that word generously, in its relation to issues of political identity was problematic at the end of the eighteenth century, and particularly when viewed in a European context. Cultural and literary historians have wrestled with a concept such as 'Romanticism' and agonized over the extent to which we may speak meaningfully of a pan-European set of ideas and feelings. The interest of the Welsh stonemason and bard extraordinary Iolo Morganwg in proverbs and gnomic verse in the 1790s, to take but one example, is very similar to that of the German

Johann Gottfried Herder.[52] It can be claimed that Iolo 'absorbed all the varied ideas of European and English Romanticism, and adopted them for the Welsh people'.[53] Edmund Burke wrote boldly in 1796 that 'No European can be a complete exile in any part of Europe'. Even so, while a 'climate of the age' can be said to exist across Europe it expressed itself in sometimes explicitly 'national' terms. In reality, many Europeans, perhaps most, could not avoid being partial exiles if they ventured beyond their native cultural environment. In that spirit, English literary culture was already being characterized on the continent as that of a people resistant to the language of theory. Shakespeare was the Titan and his genius lay precisely in the extent to which his characterization, in all its variety, irritated those who sought in 'theory' certain common principles and general truths. Translations by Wieland and Schlegel, in the middle and late eighteenth century, were, however, to make Shakespeare the third 'German' classic author after Goethe and Schiller. He could often be seen in German culture, however, as a 'beautiful monster'.[54] In any event, the English had no intention to lose their grip on him. His memorial, installed in Poet's corner in Westminster Abbey, was erected in 1740–41 at a moment of intense national anxiety. Over subsequent decades, Shakespeare's status as national icon was enhanced.[55]

It was undoubtedly the case, however, that France remained 'the largest cultural entity' and 'England' was in no position to challenge that hegemony within Europe. Earlier in the eighteenth century, knowledge of English among elites had been limited but, by 1800, as a result of changes in school and university curricula, English had probably established itself on the continent, though still second to French, as the most commonly learnt living non-mother tongue. Viewed from a suitable distance, the Isles could appear as beacons of liberty. And with liberty went a certain notion of English culture as being essentially wild and intriguingly undisciplined. One only had to look at 'English gardens' adopted in Germany and elsewhere to draw a comparison with France. There was a certain pride that the vitality of English culture did derive, in part at least, from the mode of its production and circulation. It has been noted that whereas both in France and Germany, eighteenth-century culture and knowledge was still associated with the patronage of princes or of the aristocracy, in England by mid-century patronage from those sources was of negligible importance for literature. While the other countries had academies and universities in greater profusion, they had nothing to compare with the English network of booksellers and distributors, with their reviews and magazines. Indeed, to make a more general point, England might be said to have worked as a country through its networks. The point forcibly struck Arthur Young, journeying in France in July 1789. A country in which men were 'puffing themselves off for the First Nation in Europe' demonstrated, he thought, extraordinary backwardness in everything that pertained to passing on intelligence internally.[56]

'Germany', however, was the 'land of ideas' and only if ideas generated there could be mastered and assimilated could Britain perhaps compete in the European cultural marketplace. There had been an interest in German drama in the 1780s and 1790s but it has been judged to be short-lived and was replaced by negative ideas about 'German literature'. By 1800, reviewers were complaining of the 'trash' they encountered, and wrote unfavourable notices of plays by Kotzebue and Schiller. Teutonic poetry, Francis Jeffrey wrote in the *Monthly Review* in 1802, either astonished by its boldness and sublimity or engaged by its familiarity and plainness. Jeffrey specialized in denouncing any 'doctrines' he could identify as being 'of German origin'.[57] It was in these years, however, after a visit to Germany (with inadequate linguistic equipment), that Samuel Taylor Coleridge decided he had to engage seriously with the writings of Immanuel Kant. A few years later, he felt a need to remind himself of the danger of falling into unfair generalizations about the character of German or any other literature. It remained self-evident, however, that there was such a thing as the genius of a nation. Even though Coleridge had crossed the German Ocean in search of one such genius, to be followed later by other seekers after enlightenment, what the genius of the continent was to be, as the nineteenth century began, would lie with the military and, so it would seem, with the extraordinary Corsican immigrant/soldier Napoleon Bonaparte, who had himself crossed many boundaries before becoming, in the summer of 1802 'consul-for-life' of the French Republic. The Peace of Amiens, which he signed, would be unlikely to endure.

|3|

Britain and Napoleon's Europe

Napoleon

The fate of Europe (and of Britain) still appeared to lie with the 32-year-old Napoleon, proclaimed consul for life in August 1802. A clear majority of the French electorate, as it was then constituted, had voted in favour of this step. Not to do so, propaganda had been suggesting, was to support chaos. Earlier in the year, the Concordat with the Papacy, the details of which had been published in April, further consolidated Bonaparte's position. It would substantially assist in the neutralization of counter-revolutionary forces, both inside and outside France. Had he been a Jew, it was cynically observed, Napoleon would have rebuilt the Temple of Solomon. Catholicism was restored as 'the religion of the great majority of citizens', but the principle of religious toleration – which applied to Protestants and Jews – was maintained.[1] The clergy became salaried employees of the state, though a declaration, rather than oath, of loyalty was deemed sufficient for them to swear. Napoleon forced the pope to deprive the counter-revolutionary bishops of their jurisdiction. The process of nominating new bishops, though theoretically agreed, was to prove contentious in practice. The significance of this accommodation was, of course, primarily in France itself (shortly to be extended by annexing Piedmont) but it might have wider utility. The acquiescence of the clergy in Belgium or northern Italy could facilitate the consolidation of French power in these territories.[2]

More generally, however, the 'reconciliation', which was apparently being achieved, was a further indication of the regime's willingness to accommodate – on its own terms. Napoleon both assimilated and distorted the legacy of the revolution. Plebiscitary consultation gave an appearance of democracy, but Napoleon's imperial coronation in Notre Dame in Paris in December 1804 presented another image. The imperial eagle clearly replaced the red Phrygian bonnet in the symbolism of the regime. The singing of the Marseillaise was henceforth largely avoided, though the

anthem still had resonance with the people. For Talleyrand, erstwhile revolutionary and republican, Napoleon as 'temporary sovereign' offered the
best chance of re-establishing an acceptable monarchy in France without
having to worry about the House of Bourbon. Napoleon alone, and the
institutions he established, could offer France a way out of the misfortunes
of the previous decade.[3] The word image is used advisedly. Portraits carried
messages. Painted by Gérard, in his coronation robes Napoleon could
almost have been mistaken for the Roman Emperor Augustus.
Alternatively, astride a white horse, Bonaparte was portrayed as an individual genius. A cult of his personality was in the making. One historian had
gone so far as to suggest that Napoleon was the first ruler 'to elevate propaganda into a weapon of war'.[4] The regulation of the press drew tighter. 'The
truth', Napoleon himself once remarked 'is not half so important as what
people think to be true'.[5]

The truth concerning this dynamic bastard regime in France indeed mattered less in Britain than what British observers and politicians thought or
wanted to be true.[6] With the return of peace, some travellers did make
forays into France. A group of peers, MPs, artists and writers, for example,
was particularly keen to see the treasures Napoleon had accumulated from
across Europe and now generously put on display in the Louvre. The young
J.M.W. Turner, one of the party, filled page after page of his sketchbook in
his excitement. More generally, however, anxiety about Napoleon had not
abated. The extent to which commentary focused on this one man is
remarkable. It has been noted, with reference to a Cruikshank cartoon of
1803, that while his stereotypes of 'Holland' and 'Spain' remained constant,
'France' had changed and had come to be symbolized in the person of
Napoleon.[7] James Gillray caricatured him as 'Little Boney', a puny creature
in comparison with 'John Bull'.[8] Opinion divided broadly on party lines.
Tories, who were largely in office, thought that little could be said in his
favour. He was an uncouth upstart adventurer, the heir to the lawlessness
and militarism of the Jacobins. It was as military tyrant that he was depicted
in William Burdon's *The Conduct and Character of Napoleon Bonaparte*
(1804). There was, however, an element of sympathy, in some radical quarters, for the extent to which his regime opened up careers for men of talent
on a scale believed not to be the case in Britain. The pedagogue Dr Samuel
Parr was in 1807 to take the generous view, though privately, that
Napoleon had 'done more towards the practice of sound morality, the
advancement of true learning, and the establishment of rational Piety than
all the prices and potentates have done from the creation of the world to the
present time'.[9] William Hazlitt continued to express an admiration for
Napoleon that was to find its fullest expression, years later, in a laudatory
biography.[10] Such voices, however, were in the minority. If contemporaries
had had formally to consider 'Napoleon: For and Against', the predominant
verdict would not have been in doubt. It was only after Waterloo that a
popular cult of Napoleon emerged.[11]

Invasion and intervention?

The appraisal of Napoleon's character and conduct was, of course, not simply an academic exercise. Opinions hardened in an enveloping atmosphere of crisis. Invasion, massacre and desolation seemed imminent. Bonaparte and other 'French frog-eaters' would find fierce resistance if they should land; fear of invasion has been quite simply identified as the reason why men were prepared to volunteer for service. Britain did not enjoy idyllic social harmony but discontent was not on a scale to suggest that a successful French invasion would remedy those social problems.[12] The knowledge that Bonaparte had an 'Army of England' encamped at Boulogne from 1803 stiffened 'patriotic' resolve. Whatever had been the case in the revolutionary wars, it looked now as though 'the people' could be trusted. Some women from Neath in South Wales pleaded with the prime minister to be allowed light pikes so that they could learn exercises – exercises that could subsequently come in useful. Women in the town had been 'used to hard labour all the days of their lifes, such as working in coal-pits, on the high-roads, tilling the ground, etc.'. They emphasized that they were 'serious' in their proposal.[13] They would fight.[14] It would be only a matter of time before conflict was renewed and the nation would be 'one'. Volunteer strength in Britain and Ireland remained at over 300,000 in 1804–06. Among the political elite, there had always been those who had been opposed to the Peace of Amiens and who had felt it had been madness to throw away, as they regarded it, conquests that could be of future strategic importance, or at least useful bargaining counters.[15] George III's continued use of his title 'King of France' was perhaps a little fanciful, but was this the moment to give it up – as he was induced to do? French aspirations appeared undiminished. A new fleet was busily being created. Even part of South Australia was optimistically claimed as *Terre Napoléon* in April 1802. Moreover, the return of peace had not been accompanied by the resumption of unimpeded commerce, with the benefits that were expected to flow from it: British merchants were barred from ports in France, the Low Countries and Italy. The peace was indeed only 'experimental'. The foreign secretary, Lord Hawkesbury, instructed his emissary to Paris, Lord Whitworth, that the king would never forego 'his right of interfering in the affairs of the Continent on every occasion in which the interests of his dominions, or those of Europe in general' might appear to require it.[16] It was indeed Britain, somewhat to Napoleon's surprise, that presented an ultimatum and, on 18 May 1803, began the war again. 'Not for the last time in their history', as one historian has grandly portrayed it, 'the British mobilized their fleet and went to war against a European dictatorship'.[17] Napoleon rewarded this assertion of George III's royal 'right' by immediately overrunning Hanover.

Even so, in resuming hostilities, it was by no means clear what the interests of the king's dominions were, or what those of 'Europe in general' were, let alone whether they coincided. The proposition that Britain did have a 'right' to interfere in the affairs of the continent remained axiomatic, but some politicians at the highest level questioned what that right might actually entail. Hawkesbury, for example, in trying to estimate how Britain and France stood vis-à-vis each other, argued that France, over the recent past, had suffered 'an incalculable loss of wealth', while if 'the real increase to the substantial power of Great Britain' was considered it would be found 'in proportion to the Continental increase of France'. There is a hint, here, that Britain's economic strength insulated it from the convulsions of Europe, and perhaps, to take it even further, what went on there was not, after all, of such crucial importance.[18] Hawkesbury seemed to assume, however, that British commerce would not be subjected to crippling disadvantages in Europe. Not so, retorted William Windham, 'the competition will not be left to its natural course. This game will not be fairly played.' British intervention would be necessary to ensure that the laws of the market would operate freely. Addington, the prime minister, for his part attempted to rebut the notion that commercial pursuits were incompatible 'with high sentiments of honour and national glory'. Britain was a splendid instance of a commercial and wealthy country that could preserve its advantages over other states by uniting military excellence with its superior wealth.[19] This emphasis on safeguarding British commercial interests as a fundamental aspect of British policy was scarcely new, but it was being given additional emphasis.[20]

Special pursuits

The very fact that such a matter was debated, however, was itself a recognition that there was something special about Britain. It was on an imperial basis that the finances of the British state had been consolidated. Britain, at a high military cost, had held on to the valuable West Indian trade with Europe. Without the West Indian trade the British could not have sustained their credit on the London financial markets. It has been argued that Britain was about a century ahead of France in evolving modern financial institutions. Confidence in sterling had allowed Britain to leave the gold standard and adopt emergency measures in 1797.[21] Moreover, it was not just in the consolidation of the remains of the first British Empire that British interests were extended. The most striking feature of these years, under Richard Wellesley, Lord Mornington and his successors, was the affirmation of British rule in India. The East India Company was breaking out of the limited enclave of Bengal and the wars against the Marathas (1803–05) constituted a major further phase in the expansion of control, an expansion that at times seemed a response to existing administrative and financial difficulties and could end up by compounding them. There was no gainsaying that this was rule based on conquest. Indian rulers, accustomed to giving allegiance to Mughal rulers would, instead, give it to British authority and, eventually, to the British monarch. Here, and on a smaller scale, elsewhere in Asia, lay an embryonic major empire. In ways that were foreseen and unforeseen there was to be a 'civilizing' impact, but the viability of British rule rested, to a degree at any rate, on moulding existing structures to suit British needs. The future that was to be British India could not clearly be seen in May 1803, and could not determine policy, but developments in the subcontinent were very much in the minds of the mercantile and political elite of the capital.

It was not only its Indian extension (which now dwarfed the French presence in the subcontinent) that made the new United Kingdom stand out among European powers. The grand tour of the English *milord* was matched, in the late eighteenth century, by merchants and nobles from almost all European states, who were anxious to view extraordinary pieces of machinery in Britain – the steam engine, the spinning wheel and the coke-using furnace.[22] Their interest was not academic. Spinning machinery was smuggled out and it was not unknown for British artisans to be virtually kidnapped. The Cockerill family sought its fortune in machine-building in various European countries and it was not alone in so doing.[23] The country differed in important aspects from the socio-economic pattern that still prevailed in most European states. In the last quarter of the eighteenth century, between seven, and in some countries more than nine, out of every ten persons, lived on the land, nearly all of whom derived their living from agriculture.[24] The actual circumstances of this 'peasantry' deteriorated as one moved eastwards. The social structure was divided into orders, with a hierarchy of privileges and obligations. In England, by contrast, it has been estimated that in 1801 the proportion of the total occupied population engaged in agriculture, forestry and fishing was 35.9 per cent. Those who were employed produced more – English productivity per head in agriculture was massively better than the continental figure. It is also suggested that nutritional levels were probably higher in England than elsewhere. The scale of urban growth, too, set it apart from the continental pattern. It has been calculated that during the second half of the eighteenth century 70 per cent of the rise in the overall population living in towns in Europe as a whole is accounted for by the growth of English towns – a process that, in turn, saw the emergence of major centres like Manchester (little more than a village in the 1780s) and Birmingham. Many county towns, hitherto well known in English history, lost their prominence. Despite these changes, however, it would still be true to call England a pre-industrial society.[25] The term 'Industrial Revolution' tends now to be suspect, and emphasis is placed rather upon a process of change that accelerated at particular points but that must be seen over the *longue durée*. In Scotland, however, it is argued that there truly was an Industrial and Agricultural Revolution of a dramatic kind in these decades.[26] Taken as a whole, Britain had a pattern of development that goes a long way to explaining why the country appeared to be capable of punching above its demographic weight. A country's ability to buy troops from elsewhere, either as allies or mercenaries, could be as important as its own manpower resources. Even so, for contemporaries, it remained the case that, just across the Channel, France had the largest population in western Europe. Boney might be little but France was decidedly big. What purpose and expectation was there in going to war again?

Continental conflict

It had naturally rankled that Napoleon had continued to exploit opportunities open to him both in Europe and elsewhere. The fate of Malta was always a source of conflict. The island's future opened up haggling opportunities for both Britain and France. The presence of the Knights of St John, perpetually on the brink of reformation as they were, added an exotic ingredient to negotiations. Developments in 'Germany' were of more long-term significance. Napoleon already ruled west of the Rhine and his pressure had helped to ensure the abolition, at the Diet of Ratisbon in 1803, of nearly all of the old imperial free cities and the domains of the prelates. Princes and electors were the compliant beneficiaries. He buttressed the Helvetic Confederation as its 'mediator'. His ambitions seemed to British ministers to be limitless. Napoleon would be master of Europe.

But what did such an expression mean? Napoleon certainly thought and acted as the real Frenchman he had become. He was not swept along by a consuming vision of a political Europe that would emerge somehow from its existing independent states, all of which would acknowledge a hitherto elusive but perhaps plausible European identity. As Paul Schroeder has put it, he ruled Italy and sought to take over Spain in exactly the same spirit as he ruled Egypt. He had 'no underlying purpose at all' for what he did.[27] It was left to others in Napoleon's entourage to endeavour to offer a more coherent alternative to the apparently limitless and mindless expansion on which he had embarked. Talleyrand, for example, sought in October 1805 to base the empire in a durable international system on the basis of an accord between France and Austria, which posited Russia as a common enemy.[28] However, although there was indeed a sense in which the 'integration' of Europe was being achieved, it is the case that Napoleon's empire could not become a potentially durable form of European international politics. Such an interpretation, however, does not lead to the conclusion that the Napoleonic impact was merely superficial and transitory. Individual case studies bring out the transforming capacity of the French presence even though it did not necessarily have precisely the same consequences.[29] Whether successful (in its own terms) in particular instances or not, Napoleonic government beyond French frontiers has been interpreted as a deliberate French policy of 'cultural imperialism'. Any 'European worldview' emanating from Paris at this time, even if it aspired to be more than a

'French world-view', was being formulated in a very French way.[30]

It was, however, easier for English cartoonists to caricature the 'imperial tyrant' and his wicked ambitions than for ministers to explain how he might be resisted or defeated. In 1803 the possibility of invasion was indeed real.[31] For his part, among more directly relevant military preparations, Napoleon thoughtfully arranged for the Bayeux Tapestry to be transported around France as an encouraging, if distant, reminder of a previous successful invasion. It was impossible in London to ignore the fact that hundreds of flat-bottomed boats in Boulogne and other French and North Sea ports were merely awaiting orders before they set sail across the Channel. The army they would carry was personally attached to Napoleon. It would therefore be an imperial enterprise. He was also careful to ensure that it did not consist only of Frenchmen and thus let it be known, should anyone suspect otherwise, that France would be acting in an interest greater than her own, perhaps even for 'Europe'.

Sometimes, retrospectively, it has been suggested that Napoleon was conducting an elaborate feint (and it was to Napoleon's advantage, when no invasion occurred, to encourage such an explanation). However, the scale of his preparations, among other considerations, counts against such an interpretation.[32] If he could successfully have invaded between 1803 and the date in August 1805 when he accepted that war with Austria, and probably Russia, was inevitable, he would have done so. The British countermeasures, particularly fortifying the coasts, nonetheless took deterrent shape as the months passed. George III was hopeful that Weymouth would be protected by one of those smart Martello towers. What would have happened if Napoleon had invaded can only be speculated upon. The king took the opportunity to inform the bishop of Worcester that should the enemy approach too near to Windsor he was proposing to send the queen and his daughters to lodge in his episcopal palace, safely across the Severn. It would not be too inconvenient for his lordship since a proper servant and furniture for their accommodation would accompany them. Some other British observers, perhaps including the prime minister, in their optimistic moments, envisaged Frenchmen in their thousands dead on the beaches of southern England. Others, if they had known that in March 1804 Napoleon was suggesting that it would only take a favourable wind to plant the imperial eagle on the Tower of London, might have been inclined to agree with his assessment. It is also possible to suspect that an invasion, even if it had taken place, would have been a disaster for Napoleon. Rather than simply a matter of planting eagles, he might have been bogged down on the beaches. The troops so detained – and perhaps stranded – would not have been at his disposal for his continental campaigns and success in them might have eluded him.

Addington, despite his many qualities as prime minister, did not seem, at this precise juncture, to be able to provide sufficient inspiration. Pitt, physically not robust, nevertheless emerged, in his capacity as lord warden of the

Cinque Ports, to head 3000 local volunteers – and perhaps the country. It was only in May 1804, however, that support for Addington ebbed away, and he eventually became 'the man for the hour'. His freedom of action, once back in office, was limited by parliamentary circumstances and his own health, but he brought an offensive spirit to the conduct of affairs. Whether there could be a real offensive was another question. Efforts to expand the regular army took time – it took almost two years to raise 13,000 men. A total of some 150,000 British and foreign regular soldiers in January 1804 grew to just under 200,000 three years later – during which time, of course, casualties had been sustained. Some half a million men, 3 to 4 per cent of Britain's population, were directly involved in military service on land. Napoleon, in 1805, had 310,000 front-line troops.[33] It was difficult, if not impossible, to conceive that Britain would 'defeat' Napoleon.

Trafalgar

This reality again raised the question of the war's purpose. Now that Britain had begun it again, it was necessary to ensure, so far as possible, that there would be no invasion and British independence maintained. Whether that could be done would depend upon naval supremacy. Despite strenuous efforts, manpower shortages could be serious and, despite a superiority in ships of the line and frigates there was always an underlying anxiety that Napoleon had the resources to eliminate it. Perhaps British seamanship, superior gunnery and the ability of the commanders – this was the great age of Howe, Cornwallis, Collingwood, St Vincent and Nelson – would carry the day. The decision by Spain in December 1804 to side with Napoleon perhaps gave an opportunity for a combined Franco-Spanish fleet to break the British hegemony. It was this threat that Nelson effectively removed by the victory over that fleet at Trafalgar in October 1805 as it came out of Cadiz. That stunning success lingered long in national myth and memory. A century later, the poet Henry Newbolt published *The Year of Trafalgar*, a piece of serious historical discussion of the tactics involved, but that also contained 26 poems about the battle, six by Newbolt himself. A decade earlier, he had gained a wide public with *Admirals All*, which, beginning with Effingham and Grenville, culminated in 'Nelson's peerless name'. The vivid portrayal of the achievements of *The Island Race* (1898) reinforced a national image. Newbolt reflected a little later with pride on the fact that soldiers across the globe recited his verse around their camp fires, ministers quoted him in the Commons and bishops recited him in sermons in St Paul's before the new king and queen.[34] The maintenance of naval supremacy had a resonance once again in the early twentieth century. Newbolt's friend, Sir Edward Grey, who was to become foreign secretary in the centenary year of Trafalgar, had written to him two years earlier stating that he had come to think that 'Germany is our worst enemy & our gravest danger'. He wanted

Britain 'to have closer relations, if possible, with France & Russia ...'
– something that was to be achieved in 1904 and 1907.[35]

In 1804, Pitt also needed closer relations with other powers, if possible,
if his worst enemy was ever to be defeated. Before he died in January 1806
the victory of Trafalgar could be said to have given Britain a certain security
but, when viewed in the context of what was happening on the continent, it
could hardly be said to presage the defeat of Napoleon. Responding to a
description of himself as 'the Saviour of Europe' he had replied in
November 1805 that Europe was not to be saved by any single man.
'England had saved herself by her exertions, and will, I trust, save Europe by
her example'. But what did 'saving Europe' mean? Was it really the case that
Britain had at length come to focus on the fate of the continent and would
desist from expansion elsewhere? It has indeed been noted that, in contrast
to his policies in the 1790s Pitt made no attempt to conquer Caribbean
islands (though a force was prepared in the summer of 1805). However, an
expeditionary force of over 6000 men was sent to capture the Cape of Good
Hope from the Dutch, which was successfully achieved in January 1806.[36]
The lure of South America – in a war with Spain – also proved difficult for
the British to resist. The example that Britain provided did not necessarily
seem the shortest way to save Europe.

Coalition warfare

Aware that victory could be won only on land, Pitt had swiftly embarked on
a series of initiatives to form a Third Coalition, though the fortunes of the
first two hardly suggested that its formation would provide a straightforward basis for victory. It was no easy matter to persuade the courts of
Vienna, Berlin or St Petersburg that they should resume fighting simply
because Britain had decided to do so. There was irritation that British ministers seemed to have that opinion. In Vienna, it was correctly perceived that
Austria was in no condition, either militarily or financially, to fight
Napoleon. His actions in Germany had been observed with anxiety and his
assumption of the imperial title upset Emperor Francis even more than it did
George III. If Austrian neutrality can therefore be loosely labelled 'anti-
French', Prussian neutrality at this juncture can similarly be broadly charac-
terized as 'pro-French'. Neither power had any particular reason to be
'pro-British' and each, suspicious of the other, sought to mend fences with
Russia. The stance taken in St Petersburg would indeed be decisive.

Alexander I succeeded his vicious and murdered father Paul in 1801 with
a modest declaration that he wished to see peace established not only in
Russia but in the whole world. He wanted nothing for himself, merely to
contribute to the peace of Europe. The eighteenth-century partitions had
now given Austria, Russia and Prussia shared frontiers. The acquisition of
the Grand Duchy of Lithuania, in particular, meant that Russia had

extended her borders 'into the heart of Europe' – wherever that precisely was. On the other hand, the conquest of the Caucasus began in 1801 with the annexation of Georgia. No more than George III, however, did he know this Europe at first hand, never having travelled abroad. His knowledge of other countries came from study and friendship with non-Russians (Poles) or from young Russians.[37] It was a cultural milieu in which French remained dominant. Of course, peace would suit his huge and diverse empire, whose development, though by no means even, seemed encouraging. His first foreign minister thought it best for Russia to remain detached from European affairs and concentrate on internal matters. One historian has identified a fivefold increase in Russian national income between *c.*1720 and *c.*1807, which put Russia alongside Britain 'at the very top of the national-income league table'.[38] In his *Letters of a Russian Traveller* (1790s), the Russian historian Nikolai Karamzin took the view that Russians had caught up with Germans, Frenchmen and Englishmen 'in several years'.[39] The contribution from England and Scotland to the economic development of Russia in the eighteenth century had not been insignificant. Trade between Britain and Russia had become important to both countries.[40] While that had indeed been the case, the two countries were at loggerheads on the question of 'armed neutrality'. A hostile British fleet was in the Baltic. Alexander speedily reached an understanding, and trade between the two countries resumed. The theories of Adam Smith had considerable appeal among young men in his circle. However, Alexander was not suffering from exclusive Anglophilia (or Scotophilia). France was assured that, as friends, the two countries would put a stop to the 'little disagreements of the continent".[41] And, captivated by the charm of his wife, Alexander struck up what he believed to be a special relationship with Frederick William III of Prussia. Plans for perpetual peace in Europe were canvassed by Prince Czartoryski, Alexander's assistant foreign minister (and a Pole), which envisaged the countries of Europe provided with solid constitutions that reflected their needs and stage of development. Poland would re-emerge under the protection of the tsar. Alexander appeared to concur. While a constitution for Russia itself might be premature, a start could be made (in 1803) in providing one in the Ionian islands in the Adriatic, an erstwhile Venetian territory under Russian occupation after the expulsion of the French in 1799. In addition, the tsar in the same year endeavoured to act as arbiter between France and Britain, offering the suggestion that, among other gestures, France might care to surrender dominance in Germany, Switzerland, Holland and the Italian peninsula. Napoleon declined. Alexander then fully shared the disgust of the mature courts of Europe on hearing the news of Napoleon's coronation. He was apprehensive about the growth of French influence in the eastern Mediterranean, being persuaded that the destiny of the Ottoman Empire was a matter for Russia alone, and persuaded the Turkish sultan to express equal abhorrence.

It was in these circumstances that an elaborate and protracted

British–Russian diplomatic quadrille began. 'Grand designs' for the future of Europe had entered into Russian thinking, particularly via Czartoryski. They mingled idealism about a 'new order' together with a desire to see the extension of Russian influence, and the notion, in effect, that Britain and Russia should oversee a revamped Reich and exercise a joint European hegemony. Britain was certainly not uninterested in the latter. It was, however, particularly interested in Russian soldiers. What the tsar was keen on was substantial financial subsidy. If the British were still not willing or able to provide their own men they would have to pay even more than they had done habitually in the past. Together – supposing they could be together – Austria, Prussia and Russia might yet deter Napoleon from marching eastwards without having to accept the British war agenda. Russia was no more enamoured of British penetration in the eastern Mediterranean than were the French. Proud of his protectorship of the Knights of St John, he wanted the British out of Malta. Eventually, after much haggling, a British–Russian treaty was concluded in April 1805 and ratified in the following July. Earlier, in January, a letter to the Russian ambassador, almost certainly prepared by Pitt personally, had expressed satisfaction that the two countries shared a common view concerning 'the deliverance of Europe'. It was asserted, in three points, that countries that had been subjugated by France since the beginning of the revolution would be rescued and France reduced to its former limits, and there would also be an 'arrangement' with regard to such territories in order to constitute a more effective barrier against future French encroachments. Further, a general system of public law should be established in Europe.[42] In May and June, Napoleon had taken the throne of what was now called the 'kingdom of Italy' and annexed Genoa to France. These actions both clinched the British–Russian alliance and assisted Austria in deciding to join it. Sweden and Naples also joined. Prussia, however, remained neutral, as did most of the smaller German states. Baden, Bavaria and Württemberg joined Napoleon. The Third Coalition had at length been formed. It was an arrangement whereby

> two dominant states, alike half-European and half-world powers, each supposing itself invulnerable, each ignorant of Europe's conditions and needs and armed only with crude notions of possible solutions, proposed to impose upon Europe a settlement they had concocted while making Europe in the main pay and fight for it.[43]

The long maturation of the Third Coalition was followed by a swift demonstration of its frailty. In mid-October 1805 Napoleon, in a brilliant strike, surrounded the main Austrian army in Bavaria and forced it to surrender at Ulm. His cavalry entered an undefended Vienna a month later, while his main army pursued the retreating Austro-Russian forces and inflicted a crushing defeat at Austerlitz on 2 December. Austria withdrew from the coalition and, at a price, signed the Treaty of Pressburg on 26 December. Austria lost Venetia and the Dalmatian coast to France and ceded territory to the southern German states of Baden, Bavaria and Württemberg, the latter two blossoming as fully fledged kingdoms, not to mention the payment of indemnities. A few months later, Napoleon consolidated his alternative monarchical system by setting up his brothers as kings of Naples and Holland, though the former still had to cope with revolting peasants in Calabria and the British, protecting the fleeing King Ferdinand, installed in Sicily. The Napoleonic Empire now threatened to become universal. Earlier in the month, Prussia had deemed it prudent to confirm that it was not hostile to Napoleon and, as a reward, was ceded Hanover, which Napoleon had been occupying, and gave it a coveted supremacy in north Germany. In return, however, it had itself to guarantee the territories of France, the Ottoman Empire, Italy and the south German states. All of this placed Trafalgar in a different perspective. Alexander was left to contemplate the gap between aspiration and achievement. The hegemonic ambitions of the two policemen of Europe now looked absurdly pretentious. The very survival of Austria as a Great Power, long suspected, suddenly looked real. Sensible states in the heart of Europe feared the worst and hoped for the best by accommodating themselves to the new order. It is small wonder, then, that when the 'Saviour of Europe' died in January 1806 he was not a happy man.

In the 'Ministry of all the Talents' that followed, Charles James Fox supposed that he might 'manage' a peace and then retire but when, in September, he sadly succumbed to the punitive cures of Georgian medicine it had eluded him. It has been observed, however, that in the course of the negotiations Britain had appeared implicitly to be prepared to consider a three-way division of 'the world' in which she would enjoy naval and colonial supremacy, with a presence in the Mediterranean. Russia would be supreme in northern and eastern Europe and the Near East. France would control western, southern and central Europe.[44] The fact was, however, that such an arrangement was not reached.

In October, Napoleon attacked Prussia and inflicted heavy defeats at Jena and Auerstädt. Alexander felt obliged to offer Prussia support, and a series of encounters with the French took place before the decisive battle of Friedland in June 1807 convinced the tsar that he would have to settle with Napoleon. His expectations that there might have been a British military diversion had been disappointed. The *grande armée*, for the moment, carried all before it, though the Russian army was not broken. The two men met at Tilsit, on the borders between the Polish lands of Prussia and Russia in late June. Frederick William of Prussia, who had been harboured by Alexander, was excluded as the pair proceeded to a settlement that deprived Prussia of one-third of her territory and almost half her population. Alexander, who allegedly began the conversation by stating that he hated the English as much as Napoleon did, was rewarded for this declaration by modest loss of territory. He was, in effect, the junior partner but convinced himself, with customary facility, that the resulting pattern was good for Europe as a whole.

Such developments placed Britain in even greater difficulty, but also raised fundamental questions. Initial assumptions in 1803–04 had been that the resumed war would require the traditional pattern of subsidy for allies and the enlisting of suitable troops, if they could be found, on the continent. Experience suggested that the scale of such support never seemed to satisfy, but manpower was forthcoming. Pitt wrote to Lord Harrowby, foreign secretary in November 1804, urging an increase in the Hanoverian corps and, more surprisingly, the formation of an Albanian corps.[45] Some 17,000 foreigners served in the British army's formations in January 1804 (a figure that was to treble by 1813 and constitute between a sixth and a seventh of its total strength).[46] If Britain was to demonstrate that it could be a serious player, in military terms, then a presence of some kind might be necessary. It also presumed, however, that the only way this could be resolved would be if war were fought *à outrance*. But could Britain commit both the men and the money?

There was indeed some continental activity. The presence of 5000 British troops in Sicily was the residue of an unsuccessful British–Russian move on Naples. In northern Europe, there was some passing hope that British forces might regain control of Hanover and, further expectation, in the autumn of 1805, that a British, Russian and Swedish force would set about conquering Holland. Britain did assemble roughly 25,000 troops in Hanover by the early days of 1806. In the event, the force was not able to play the anticipated role but it was evacuated safely. This episode served, subsequently, to lead governments after 1807 to resist the notion that Britain's military policy should be subordinated, as they saw it, to the demands of actual or potential alliance partners.[47] There was indeed a lack of direction in policy. It did not help that foreign secretaries followed each other in unusually rapid succession. The indecisiveness and parsimony of British governments, as the tsar perceived them, did not lead him to see the British constitution as one to be emulated. It was the case, indeed, that British politicians continued to behave as though there were more things in life than foreign policy, and disagreed with each other accordingly. The health of the king was a further complication. Important as these considerations are, however, the conduct of British policy still reflected the reality that Britain was 'only marginally a European country'. Napoleon was indeed aggressive but, so it has been argued, 'Britain's insularity, ignorance of Europe, and indifference to its needs' had been prominent among the causes of the absence and impossibility of peace.[48]

Europeans on the margin

An island state can scarcely be blamed for its location. Britain's outreach was indeed continuing to extend beyond the bounds of the continent in ways that gave it distinctive perspectives. Ignorance of Europe, however, is a bold statement. It implies that the British 'decision-making elite' differed from its peers in other countries who had abundant knowledge of 'Europe' or perhaps, somehow, knew that they were 'Europeans' in their bones. Naturally, too, the exponents of the foreign policies of Great Powers tended to assume that there was something especially important about the Great Powers, who in turn tended to assume that they carried the weight of Europe on their imperial shoulders. It was an education in Latin and Greek that the British governing class tended to receive and, while this did not provide instant briefings on contemporary developments, it was at least a not insignificant European heritage. New critical reviews, such as the *Edinburgh Review* (1802) and the *Critical Review* (1809), which themselves set a new European genre, gave substantial coverage to continental political and cultural developments. British diplomats stationed throughout Europe were not conspicuously defective, in comparison with their counterparts, in obtaining the kind of information about their countries of residence that was deemed appropriate for the conduct of inter-state business. They all moved in an aristocratic milieu with common understandings of what it was and was not important to know. Aspiring young British politicians at least recognized that a knowledge of French, the language of diplomacy, was necessary, though it was in The Hague that George Canning spent months after coming down from Oxford in 1791 seeking to master the language. His travels in the Low Countries brought him into contact with 'most noisome and unwholesome smells' of a kind from which he had evidently hitherto been insulated.[49]

The British, in short, were not 'marginally European', they were 'Europeans of the margin', a geographical condition they endured alongside other Europeans, north, south and east. The perceptions that flowed from their vantage point were no doubt partial and self-interested, but in that they were not exceptional. European states, for obvious reasons, made it their business to be well briefed about their immediate neighbours and only secondly about other parts of the continent. It is difficult to identify any contemporary European state that was significantly more well informed than Great Britain about the totality of Europe. The concept of marginality implies the existence of a commonly and continentally acknowledged core to Europe. There was, however, no such single 'centre' exercising a constant hegemony – political, cultural, economic and military. The 'heart of Europe', restricting oneself to geography in a rough sense, might be taken to lie midway between Russia and Britain (if both are allowed to be European), but it was just that region, stretching from southern Denmark to 'Italy', which at this juncture seemed to lack enduring state structures within boundaries, that had some 'logic'. At this juncture, in other words, the future of this 'non-marginal' Europe was itself too uncertain to enable it to determine what the future of Europe should or should not be. Napoleon ensured that state structures, titles and territories were in flux. Marginal Europe – that is to say Britain – remained by contrast maddeningly and idiosyncratically self-absorbed and self-confident. It had a parliament that, amid the crises of 1809, took two months to consider corruption charges against the duke of York and to examine his relations with his mistress. While continuing to lament British tunnel vision, inability to appreciate the concerns of others, failure to understand long-term effects or systemic consequences in international politics – a not inconsiderable list of disadvantages – Professor Schroeder reluctantly came to the conclusion that 'remaining British' in fighting Napoleon may well have outweighed these disadvantages.[50]

A new continental system?

One further development in the heart of Europe should be noted. The Holy Roman Empire (of the German nation), which still purported to offer a continuity with the Roman Empire, staggered to an end on 6 August 1806. Francis II of Austria laid down the crown – a corollary of the decision of south and south-western German states, on the formation of the Confederation of the Rhine, to withdraw. It ended after 1006 years (when Charlemagne 'inherited' it at his coronation in 800), but left the stage with a whimper rather than a bang (Goethe affected to find its demise less interesting than an argument in which his coachman was at the time engaged). Even so, within the territory it embraced, it 'left something behind that was as old as the Reich itself: its myth'. The Germans, whoever they precisely were, had some sort of special mission that was European if not universal in character.[51] At the point of dissolution, however, it was very unclear what, if anything, this would entail for the Europe of the immediate future. It could not be said, however, that the Holy Roman Empire had excited much interest on the part either of British scholars or politicians. Even fewer supposed that the idea of empire it embodied had any relevance for international order. It was not until the 1860s that the young James Bryce published a masterly distillation of what the medieval Holy Roman Empire had been.[52]

Taken in the round, therefore, Europe could not itself determine what Europe 'needed'. Only from outside could a disinterested assessment of its needs be put forward – and neither the nervous sultan of Turkey, nor the president of the infant United States nor the remote emperor of old China offered their services.

In such a context, therefore, the task before Britain seemed clear. Negatively, it had to survive the impact of the 'continental system/blockade' and, positively, it could seek ways in which Napoleon could not only be withstood but also be defeated. Napoleon's hand was undoubtedly strong. In population terms, the Europe he controlled was roughly half of the continent's population of 167 million (including Russia). The Berlin decree of November 1806 (itself the consolidation of steps that were already being taken to isolate Britain) declared that the British Isles were in a state of blockade – months earlier Britain had itself declared a naval blockade along the French coast. British goods and ships were to be regarded as lawful prizes. British subjects within the French zone of control were to be made prisoners of war. Both sides, thereafter, tried to stiffen their respective policies. Napoleon steadily enforced compliance on the subject states and sought to bring neutral states into line. Denmark sided with France in September 1807 and in the same year Portugal was forced to close its ports to British goods: in both instances, as will be noted, Britain had intervened. Historians generally agree that the blockade, when it was monitored effectively, did have an impact on British exports, particularly during the first half of 1808, the autumn of 1810 and the summer of 1812. Even so, the ingenuity of British manufacturers and merchants was considerable, and lessened the impact of the ban. Smugglers on Britain's behalf were effective in places as far apart as Heligoland in the North Sea and Salonika in the Aegean. New markets were also found in the Americas. As a grand strategy, therefore, the system did not achieve its objective of crippling Britain. It has been pointed out that almost half of the money Britain spent in financing foreign coalitions against France from 1793 to 1815 was spent in the last five years of the period. Britain's superiority in commerce, industry and finance had not been dislodged. There was a further reason for the disappointing dividend the system yielded Napoleon. The portrayal of France as guardian of a common 'continental' interest had met with some success. There was indeed a considerable fear of British goods that could be tapped and turned into a more general dislike of Britain. The system, for example, offered great opportunities for Belgian coal and textile production – to the extent that the Belgian departments have been described as the 'engine-room of the Napoleonic Empire'.[53] Indeed, it can be speculated that if the subject and allied states had been offered genuine reciprocity of trade in the huge imperial market then an overwhelming mobilization of 'Europe' against Britain might have resulted and proved fatal to British independence.[54] It was, however, not on offer. And, as time passed, the extent to which, in particular instances, the blockaders rather than the blockaded were damaged commercially, could not be disguised. The port of Hamburg, for example, was seriously disrupted. In France itself, despite ingenious efforts, the port of Bordeaux stagnated. Strasbourg, on the other hand, enjoyed economic expansion.[55] It was a contrast that illustrates the extent to which, nationally, France was 'looking east' as the Atlantic and Caribbean were closed off. The British maritime blockade deprived France of important supplies of colonial goods. And, not able to stop the smuggling, Napoleon was forced to start selling some exceptional licences to trade so that the state might at least gain some financial benefit. No more than in other respects, however, was the Napoleonic system a genuine partnership between equals. The perceived interests of France were paramount and were not to be challenged.[56] Indeed, the sporadic efforts to make the system more watertight had resulted in a further French annexation – in 1810–11 as far north as the Baltic. Following a Russian attack, King Gustav IV of Sweden was deposed and replaced by the French marshal, Bernadotte. On paper at least, Sweden was forced to join the system. Even so, while the Continental blockade should not be dismissed as of no serious consequence for Britain, it did not do what it was designed to do. Britain was not throttled into submission by means other than directly military (though, perhaps ironically, it was the fact that grain continued to be imported from the continent that saved Britain from starvation in 1811).

The continental system did not break Britain but neither did its relative failure defeat Napoleon. Only war could do that and there was a defiant, even reckless, mood in London. George Canning, foreign secretary in 1807 (until 1809), epitomized a new ruthlessness. He had authorized the bombardment of Copenhagen and the seizure of the Danish fleet in the summer of 1807. The British had been here before. In 1801, putting a telescope to his blind eye, Nelson had circumvented an order to withdraw in a bloody engagement that inflicted heavy losses on the Danish fleet. Politically, it resulted in the dissolution of the league of armed neutrality of Denmark, Sweden, Russia and Prussia. In 1807, the aim of the attack had been to prevent Denmark from moving into the French orbit and a consequential closing of British access to the Baltic. Denmark did so move, and indeed came strongly to support the continental system (but a British fleet, annually despatched, was able more or less successfully, to protect British trade in the Baltic). However, even if the political objective had not been achieved by the bombardment, a pre-emptive strike of this kind demonstrated that international law would be treated with some indifference in a struggle for survival. Indeed, if only the fleet and army had got back in time, Canning would have liked 'another Copenhagen', whose purpose would have been to 'persuade' the Portuguese similarly that they should not succumb to Napoleonic pressure. In the event, while Portugal was likewise also coerced into the system, the royal family and navy, under convoy of a British squadron, set sail for Brazil. Here was respect, of a kind, for Britain's oldest ally. The foreign secretary was not deterred even by the knowledge that George III considered 'Copenhagen' to be a very immoral act. The fact was that the British were so generally loathed that all-out maritime war could not alienate further. That being the case, it was better to be ruthless and win.[57] Castlereagh, the secretary for war, who was to fight Canning in a duel on Putney Heath, shared this offensive spirit. It has been argued that he did 'more than any other man since the Seven Years War to enable Britain to fulfil the role of a great power in a continental war'.[58] Events in Spain were to provide the opportunity for military involvement for which they had been waiting.

Britain in Iberia

Late in 1807 and in the early months of 1808 Napoleon sent French troops into Spain on the pretext of a joint operation to subdue Portugal. He was dissatisfied with Spanish participation in the continental system as he had been with the Spanish navy. It seemed desirable to establish another satellite kingdom. His brother Jerome, seasoned as a monarch in Naples, was transferred to his new kingdom in May 1808. Supporters of the deposed Ferdinand VII rose in revolt in a crisis that rapidly took the form of a popular uprising, and irregular forces won a victory over French forces in July. Subsequent operations by French forces, however, showed that this success was misleading. Even so, there was enough life in the Spanish revolt to provide an arena for British military intervention. Emissaries from the Spanish provinces of Asturias, Galicia and even Andalusia landed at Falmouth in June to issue an invitation. It was at this same Cornish port that Don Manuel Alvarez Espriella allegedly landed, bent on writing a series of letters to his Spanish compatriots to try to explain England to them. The author was in fact Robert Southey.[59] One initial British reaction – to ship out to the rebels Spanish arms that had been kept in the Tower of London after they had been captured in another Spanish incident in 1588 – was perhaps of limited value. Canning told the House of Commons that any nation of Europe that was determined to oppose France became instantly Britain's 'essential ally'. Use of the word 'nation' was not an accident: although it was not advisable to delve into its meaning too deeply, it could safely be used in a context where the rulers were French or French-buttressed. This was not going to be a matter of doing a deal with another unsatisfactory monarch. In giving him the orders that were to see him landing with 15,000 men in Portugal in early August 1808, Castlereagh told Wellesley (Wellington) that the absolute evacuation of the peninsula by the troops of France was the only basis upon which the Spanish nation should treat or lay down their arms. This would not be a matter of occupying Lisbon or securing Cadiz, it would be the beginning of a grand strategy. Every British heart, according to William Wilberforce, was full of schemes and sympathies for the poor Spaniards.[60] For its part, however, the British government was contemplating schemes that envisaged acceptance of the at least partial independence of Spain's South American colonies. It was better that this should happen than that they should be controlled by a France that, in turn, controlled Spain. However, despite the extent to which Wellesley's expedition in 1808–09 represented a considered concentration of British force, it was not the kind of success that had been hoped for – Wellesley himself was for a time superseded in his command, only to resume in 1809. Sir John Moore had succeeded in saving the Spanish and Portuguese forces from complete defeat but his death at La Coruna in January 1809, after the disastrous winter retreat, brought the effort to an end. British forces withdrew. Portugal, however, remained secure and Castlereagh concluded that a fresh British presence would stiffen the Portuguese forces and make French subjugation of Portugal very costly in men and resources. It was to be left to the youthful Palmerston, who spoke in the Commons for Castlereagh's successor, Lord Bathurst, to continue with the military reorganization, which Castlereagh had begun, in order to make a return to the peninsula possible. The 'poor Spaniards' though, as things turned out, had not been greatly aided, but their time might yet come.

There was, however, initially, encouragement in the extent to which tying down French troops in Spain encouraged fresh thinking in other European capitals. A reorganized Austrian army – though not matched by a refilled treasury – led to the Habsburg decision to declare war on France in April 1809. It proved a solitary fiasco. The only serious attempt at support came from the British attempt to destroy the French naval base on the island of Walcheren at the mouth of the Scheldt. It was a large-scale effort but it was a disaster with heavy losses. Politicians hastened to place the blame elsewhere. The sober reality was that a month after war was declared Napoleon was in Vienna. By July, an armistice had been signed. The peace settlement of Schönbrunn in October saw Austria lose her share of the Polish partition, her strip of Dalmatian coast, and territory to Bavaria. The Austrian army was restricted in size and an indemnity fixed. Emperor Francis, however, kept his throne and, in theory at least, remained distinct from the subject kingdoms supplied by Napoleon with their monarchs. The new Austrian chancellor, Metternich, however, had few illusions in 1809. He expressed the view that Europe would soon undergo total reform. Spain would be subjugated. The Ottomans would be driven beyond the Bosphorus. The great empire would stretch from the Baltic to the Black Sea. Russia, in a few months, would be confined to Asia. Napoleon's long-standing plan would have succeeded. He would be the ruler of Europe. In such a situation, all that Vienna could do was to become a compliant collaborator in the triumphant French system and might, perhaps, through diplomacy, seem a more reliable ally than Russia. After divorcing Josephine, Napoleon married the Austrian emperor's eldest daughter in the spring of 1810. Perhaps the first step in collaboration had been taken.

In these circumstances, it seemed exaggerated, to say the least, to identify Wellington in 1809 as a key figure in frustrating the ambitions that Metternich identified. Increasingly, however, Wellington came to be seen in that role in Britain. Initially, while Wellington was very aware of Napoleon the reverse was not true. After the victory Wellington gained at Talavera in July 1809, however, Napoleon came to see him as a significant threat.[61] There are, indeed, certain extraordinary coincidences about the two men, starting with their birth in the same year, 1769. The military fate of France was in the hands of a Corsican and the military fate of Britain in the hands of a Dublin-born Protestant Irishman (though one who asserted that 'just because one is born in a stable didn't make one a horse').[62] They were both soldier-politicians, admittedly, at this stage at different levels (Wellington had become an MP in 1806 and was chief secretary for Ireland when he embarked on the five-year campaign in the peninsula). Their first-hand knowledge of their own countries was limited. Only in 1810 did Napoleon spend a whole year in France and between 1805 and 1814 spent only 900 days out of a possible 3500 in Paris.[63] Wellington, a 'sepoy general' as Napoleon condescendingly supposed, served in India from 1797 to 1805 – but he had learnt French in Brussels, and in 1786 had been at the Academy of Equitation in Angers. Napoleon had no comparable English experience.

After his victory at Talavera, Wellington was forced to retreat. Napoleon sent heavy reinforcements in 1810 with the objective of pushing the British out of the peninsula.[64] In the winter of 1810/11, Wellington held the French at the lines of Torres Vedras near Lisbon. At a heavy price, they withdrew back to the Spanish/Portuguese frontier in the spring of 1811, but battles, skirmishes and sieges, to and fro, continued. It was only in the following year that Wellington was in a position to make a sustained offensive in Spain. Retreating French forces were caught at Salamanca (July) and Madrid was taken in mid-August. The situation, however, remained complicated and setbacks ensued, though they did not endanger the superiority that was being established and then conspicuously demonstrated with the triumph of Vittoria in June 1813. Large numbers of troops had come to be deployed by both sides. There were some 100,000 British troops and some three times that number of French. It could no longer be said that British interventions into continental warfare were invariably short-lived, ill-judged and unsuccessful. The financial cost had been considerable but it had been borne. Wellington's success can largely be explained by his skill in ensuring that the full weight of the French armies was not deployed against him at any one time. The defeats constituted the first serious setback that Napoleon had sustained. Britain, for the moment at least, had become a serious military player – as was noted elsewhere. There remained, however, some ambiguity about the British presence. Wellington's success could not have been obtained without the support of Spanish and Portuguese forces, regular and irregular. He had been appointed commander-in-chief of the Spanish armies.[65] On first arriving in the peninsula, he had prudently brought with him both a Portuguese grammar book and a Spanish prayer book. There was no doubt that Wellington saw himself in charge. The conduct of his British troops, on occasion, showed little sign, in their own sometimes dire circumstances, of great sympathy for 'poor Spaniards'. The memoirs of British soldiers who fought in the peninsula naturally focused directly on their military experiences rather than on 'Britain and Spain'. The chaplain of brigade to the British expedition, a talented water-colour artist, did reflect in words and pictures on the scenes he encountered. Englishmen had never been seen before in these Portuguese villages and their attire attracted great attention. The chaplain was gratified to be able to explain to a Portuguese friar, who had doubted the matter, that English clergymen held a belief in Jesus Christ. Later, in Salamanca, he was somewhat scathing about the Spanish people. Their glorious efforts in the cause of freedom had rightly been a subject of astonishment to all Europe, he wrote, but they appeared 'to have been caused by an ebullition of their native valour rather than from any definite object of producing a reform in their Government' and the moment the French armies were subdued they appeared 'to have sunk into their original languor'.[66] Southey's Iberian visits produced in him a hatred of the popular Roman Catholicism he encountered there, and that was not simply because of the smell of the friars. Catholicism was 'naked nonsense'.[67] In short, Iberian ways of life and belief did not greatly attract British observers at this time. Iberians had simply to be put up with in the interests of defeating the French.

Meeting at Waterloo

In 1814, with victories at Orthez (February) and Toulouse (April) Wellington was able to take the struggle to French soil. Napoleon abdicated and retired to Elba. Wellington was created a duke and became British ambassador in Paris. Napoleon made his final bid for power when he landed on the French mainland on 1 March 1815, proceeded to Paris and again became ruler of France. On 18 June, after distinctly difficult moments, Wellington defeated Napoleon at Waterloo in Belgium. It was as a British prisoner that Napoleon ended his days on the island of St Helena in the South Atlantic.[68]

Such a succinct account might tend to the simple conclusion that Britain had defeated Napoleon. However, just as the victory at Waterloo could not have been gained without the participation of Blücher's Prussian forces, so the defeat of Napoleon had been achieved by developments that the British could neither initiate nor control. Their role had latterly become highly significant, but it was not decisive. The unravelling of Napoleon's empire began in June 1812 when he invaded Russia. His occupation of Moscow in mid-September, however, did not lead the tsar to sue for peace. Russia was a big country in which to retreat. A horribly harassed, humiliated and depleted army struggled back to Poland at the end of 1812. In March 1813 Prussia formally entered the war in alliance with Russia. A Fourth Coalition – Russia, Prussia, Britain, Sweden, Spain and Portugal – was in existence by the summer. The fact that he was now having to fight seriously on two fronts sapped Napoleon's resources. The very large subsidies Britain provided – largely to Russia, Prussia and Sweden – were of vital importance. And not only subsidies – a million muskets made their way to the eastern powers in 1813. After much wavering, Austria declared war on France in August 1813, though it did not formally join the Fourth Coalition. Russo-Prussian plans for the future caused much apprehension in Vienna. The coalition armies, with clear numerical superiority, produced a decisive victory at Leipzig (the 'Battle of the Nations') in October 1813 and by the end of the year Napoleon had retreated across the Rhine – though not in disarray. Peace proposals conveyed by Napoleon to his father-in-law eventually came to nothing. The allied armies made careful progress thereafter, despite the small-scale victories that Napoleon gained. Paris was captured at the end of March. The emperor, which he still was, took possession of his Mediterranean island in May. Apart from his final fling, the extraordinary adventure was over.

Even in 1813 Napoleon had still hoped, with some reason, that the underlying tensions between the powers now arraigned against him would once again surface and some settlement be reached that would preserve him in power in Paris. His analysis was correct in so far as the achievement of a consensus among the victorious powers concerning the future of Europe had not yet been achieved. It fell to Castlereagh, foreign secretary since March 1812, to shape the British contribution to that process. (Its detail will be given further consideration in the next chapter.) What was already clear in 1812–14, however, was that the British role would be a major one. How that hand was played, however, depended on underlying assumptions, spoken and unspoken. There remained certain key elements. Military participation in the peninsula, and then beyond, had certainly brought about changed perceptions, both within and without, about the kind of country Britain was becoming. Unlike all the other major participants, however, it had not witnessed on its own soil such major battles as had occurred elsewhere in Europe over the preceding years – battles that had left strong emotional legacies. That escape remained of psychological significance. While British troops had indeed experienced 'the foreign', they had not ranged across the continent in the manner of their French counterparts. The British fleet was very much at home in the Baltic but the land mass of east-central Europe was unknown territory. War had cut off the continent and a new generation of Britons had largely been deprived of the experience of 'cultural tourism' that its parent had taken for granted. It was Castlereagh himself who founded the Travellers' Club in 1814 specifically to encourage the exchange of ideas between British and foreign gentlemen.[69] Simultaneously, therefore, for more than a decade, Britain had become both more inward-looking by force of circumstance, but also more participatory by virtue of its manifest financial, naval and even military power. Its engagement beyond its islands, however, had not been restricted to Europe. It had even been possible, in 1812, to engage in a short further war with the United States, although this could in a sense be regarded as an extension of the European conflict in so far as it arose out of British counter-measures to the continental system. There was no disposition to abandon colonial activity, even if it could no longer quite be said that Britain's only real interest lay in colonial acquisitions. As a polity, the United Kingdom had survived the strains of a decade of war with considerable success. Robert Emmet's 1803 'rising' in Ireland had caused great alarm at the time but it had not been repeated.[70] Much of the manpower in the 'British' army was Irish and indeed Irish

Catholic – perhaps as much as 50 per cent by 1815.[71] As an Irishman, however, Castlereagh knew what a double-edged weapon a British endorsement of 'nationality' as the basis of states might be.[72] The United Kingdom, however, had been directed by men unpersuaded of the benefits of parliamentary reform. What was British was best. It was certainly the view held by the Duke of Wellington, British ambassador in France and commander-in-chief of the British occupying forces in France. It was in such a context that the congress of Vienna first assembled on 1 October 1814 to determine the future of Europe.

|4|

*Making a European peace,
1814–1830*

Ending war

The Napoleonic Wars were unprecedented in scale and intensity.[1] Hundreds of thousands of men had struggled across the continent, backwards and forwards, to end up in hitherto strange destinations: Frenchmen at the Moscow River and Cossacks in Paris. It was not visions of a 'common European home', however, that struck them in consequence. Encounters en route with new languages and landscapes made soldiers more aware of differences than commonalities. The wars had disrupted the familiar institutions of society and they struggled to regain their shape. The customary structures of political organization in Europe – empires, kingdoms, principalities, duchies – were still there, but they no longer seemed preordained. It would clearly be no easy task to produce a peace that would endure. That peace was indeed a desirable objective was, for the moment, generally accepted. Yet it would be a mistake to suppose that the sight of slaughter and suffering on the field of battle had totally transformed the outlook of policy-makers. Territorial acquisition followed by successful assimilation was still usually thought likely to be a sure way in which a country could gain new wealth. It could still be worth fighting for. In war, as the German philosopher Hegel reflected, the strength of a state was tested. War could not be regarded as an absolute evil. Just as the sea would become foul if there were no winds, so nations would be corrupted by prolonged peace.[2] The Great Powers had passed the test – some more easily than others – and now wanted a period of peace, but they neither supposed nor indeed desired that henceforth Europe would be perpetually becalmed. The settlement they reached did in fact prove durable and it was only in 1830 that there was significant change. The process presented the United Kingdom with a major role in the re-ordering of Europe. It will become apparent, however, that its participation in sustaining that new order was ambivalent, both with regard to particular features and to the general assumptions that underpinned it.

Settling the Great Powers

The peacemakers did not suppose that the new settlement would be the product of consultation or be subject to popular ratification. Nor was it the case that all states, not to mention all peoples, would play their full part. The basis of peace would be decided by the Great Powers. In 1814–15, 'Europe' meant victorious Austria, Britain, Prussia and Russia (a fact they happily confirmed between themselves). The mere fact of a shared victory, however, did not erase mutual suspicions, divergent aspirations or geopolitical realities. The scale of the recent conflict did suggest that there was some need to 'think European' but each Great Power had its own version of what that meant.

All the Great Powers of 1814–15 were equal, but some of them were more equal than others. The United Kingdom and the Russian Empire, at the extremities, remained the 'hegemons'. Over both Prussia and Austria hovered the question of 'Germany'. The difficulty of achieving an equilibrium in Europe was therefore complicated by the search for a secondary equilibrium specifically in relation to the German question. The construction and crumbling of coalitions against France had demonstrated that the interests and aspirations of Austria, Prussia and Russia, in particular, were only precariously compatible. France, though defeated, remained a Great Power and, whether or not it now directly participated in the construction of the new order, its importance could not be ignored. Calculations of power were vitally important in the pursuit of peace.

Alongside assessments of power, however, always an imprecise business, ran more ideological questions. Should a settlement have an 'organizing principle'? If so, should it be 'legitimacy'? There was to be no more eloquent exponent of this concept than Talleyrand, the French foreign minister. His career had taught him how to adapt the term to circumstances. Countries annexed to France, he argued, had never really been lost by their sovereigns – unless formally signed away – and should simply be restored to them. Such governments, and he spoke of governments rather than of monarchies, rested on their acceptance by all other states and a majority of the populations concerned.[3] The latter notion, however, was not acceptable to Metternich, the Austrian foreign minister. Such statesmen, though for the last time, still believed themselves in a position to devise a 'rational' arrangement for Europe. It was not their business to deal with the peculiar animosities to be found among the masses, or to be overly concerned about the impact of particular conclusions on those individually affected by them.

Empires and nations: placing the United Kingdom

Ranged against such abstract reflection was the emotional appeal of the 'nation'. Defining a 'nation', however, raised many difficulties. The Russian and Austrian Empires, in particular, were 'multinational' (though there was little agreement about how many 'nations' existed within their borders). If there were any general acceptance of the notion that states should be based on nations, and that a nation might substantially be defined by use of a particular language, there would be no future for these empires – and indeed, though less obviously, for the political coherence of any state in existence in 1814–15 – if the state order of Europe was to be based on 'nation-states'. It was not, therefore, in the interest of the Great Powers, and perhaps more generally, to give explicit recognition to 'nationality' as some kind of fundamental principle, or at least only to do so where it coincided with the restoration of a legitimate monarch. Such a stance, however, might entail repression of the poets, priests, preachers or philosophers in different parts of Europe who supposed that they were expressing the soul of their peoples, peoples longing for communal coherence in an uprooted world. Such repression would bring its own instability, but autocratic sovereigns might order it with equanimity.

These issues were not without relevance to the United Kingdom. It was a Great Power but the others realized that it had peculiar features that, given their assumptions, made it awkward to deal with. It stood out as being the state in which royal power was limited to a greater extent than existed elsewhere in Europe, even in the other parliamentary monarchies of its northwestern corner.[4] The Prince Regent was not an autocrat. It was not an empire, if to be an empire meant to rule over vast contiguous territory, though there had been suggestions in the past, particularly at the time of the Anglo-Scottish Union, that it might be thought of as an empire. The anonymous author of *The Queen an Empress and her Three Kingdoms One Empire* (1706), for example, suggested that the monarch should reside in London but be supported by a pan-insular nobility. His or her sons, where available, should be styled princes of the British Empire and reside respectively in England, Scotland and Ireland.[5] However, if it was not an empire, neither was it a straightforwardly homogeneous 'national' state. The United Kingdom of the early nineteenth century operated domestically in different ways for different functions and with different outcomes. The absence of a comprehensive legal framework to encompass its arrangements seemed particularly puzzling to continental observers.

From one angle, therefore, its linguistic, ecclesiastical and ethnic diversity suggested that the country was not in fact so different from the empires of central and eastern Europe where such diversity also obtained. From another angle, however, even with Ireland in the Union, a fuzzy 'Britishness' provided an acceptable integrating concept, perhaps acceptable because rather unspecific, which gave the United Kingdom a sense of unity lacking in the eastern European empires. In 1815, in the aftermath of war, the United Kingdom appeared stable and able to manage such tension between diversity and uniformity as existed. The passage of the Catholic Emancipation (Relief) Act in 1829 was of particular importance in this respect. The emasculation of the Protestant character of the British state was still not complete but, despite fierce opposition in the House of Commons, an important step had been taken in the religious and cultural configuration of the state. Catholics could now sit in parliament and became eligible for all public offices except regent, lord lieutenant and lord chancellor. The monarch, however, could neither be a Catholic nor marry one. The repeal of the Test and Corporations Act at this time removed the legislation that had excluded Protestant non-conformists from public office. It remained the case, however, that the Church of England and the Church of Ireland were 'established'.

The issue of 'Catholic emancipation' had naturally been most important in the Irish context. Daniel O'Connell, whose Catholic Association had been founded in 1823, had mobilized 'public opinion' in dramatic and novel fashion. Peel and Wellington, previously hostile, had brought in the measure following O'Connell's electoral success in County Clare. Was 'repeal' of the Union, whatever that meant, now to become the issue? A return to the previous status quo was scarcely conceivable, but how a future British/Irish relationship would be structured was obscure. In his own person, O'Connell illustrated the ambiguities of the British/Irish/European relationship at this juncture. His first language was Irish but he dismissed its importance. Scion of gentry, he had been educated in France and brought to his Catholicism a 'liberalism' not notably present in Irish clergy. His opposition to slavery used language that could have fallen from the lips of English evangelical abolitionists (Britain had declared the slave trade illegal in 1807 and had insisted on the inclusion of an anti-slave-trade clause in the peace negotiations of 1814–15 – a zeal not shared in France). He dabbled in the rather un-Catholic theories of Bentham and Godwin and, for a spell, found London not uncongenial. He was a master of the mysteries of both Irish and English law. The complexities in O'Connell's own make-up were matched in many areas of British-Irish life. The government of Ireland had not been fully integrated with that of Britain and had its own mysteries. Free trade between the two islands did not come until 1824, with separate currencies persisting for a further two years. Excise duties and taxation could be sharply at variance.[6] Involvement in the entity of 'the British Isles' certainly did not exclude the distinct European network that Irish people had built up through emigration and exile, military service, commerce and study over a long period.[7] Geographically further from 'the heart of Europe' than Britain, the identification of its majority with 'Catholic Europe' paradoxically brought it culturally close. Such a reality meant necessarily that United Kingdom governments had to pay more attention to the Vatican that they might otherwise have been disposed to do. It also meant, however, that the Protestant minority (which included a small but articulate Huguenot element) saw little that was attractive in such a Europe.

The territories of Great Britain did not appear to pose quite so many questions. Sir Walter Scott, who sprang to fame at this juncture, exemplified the paradoxes of Britain. In his person, Scotland produced a national novelist whose work was speedily and enthusiastically read across Europe. A sort of 'cult of Scotland' emerged in consequence. His historical novels, beginning with *Waverley* (1814) and *Guy Mannering* (1815), explored the turning points in Scotland's past. The dislocations with which they dealt perhaps had stronger continental than English parallels, particularly in so far as they concerned the clash of cultures' resulting movement of 'marginal' populations, *pauvres* montagnards, into lowland cities.[8] Not that Scott was a Scot who sought to place Scotland in 'Europe' in contradistinction to locating it in 'Britain'. Married to the daughter of a French royalist family, he rejoiced in the 'British' victory at Waterloo. He eagerly visited the battlefield and Wellington was his hero.[9]

'Wales' stood in a different position from either Ireland or Scotland. Constitutionally, it was invisible and its Prince knew little about it. When he became Prince Regent, his Welsh appearance was limited to a visit, before sailing to Ireland, to the marquess of Anglesey, the bones of one of whose legs His Royal Highness was to search for, in tears, but in vain, on the battlefield of Waterloo some months later. As king, however, George IV was persuaded by an English bishop of St Davids that Wales needed a college, and he produced £1000 to help establish one at Lampeter. The spoken language of the majority in Wales was still Welsh but the language of the state was English. The disjunctures this produced in its social, religious and cultural life made Wales very different from England, notwithstanding its apparently complete integration. Its experience of living within the shadow of a dominant culture corresponds to that of peoples in central Europe, in their case in the shadow of German culture.[10]

Even one further diverse element might have been added to the United Kingdom if a great collector of specimens had had his way. The president of the Royal Society, Sir Joseph Banks, famous traveller in the South Seas, wrote to an Icelander in 1807 that 'No one who looks upon the map of Europe can doubt that Iceland ... ought to be part of the British Empire'. It seems, however, that Iceland that proved to be an island too far.[11]

It was an indication of the importance attached to insular unity at this time that George IV went on his travels in his United Kingdom – not something his Hanoverian predecessors had ever been tempted to do. Ireland came first. George IV crossed the Irish Sea in a steamboat on his fifty-ninth birthday in August 1821 and was delighted by the hundreds of carriages and thousands of gentlemen on horseback who escorted him on his entry into Dublin. A year later, in an event choreographed by Sir Walter Scott and painted by Sir David Wilkie, George IV appeared in Edinburgh as a kilted Highlander. The United Kingdom, in short, was certainly not to be equated with 'England', but continental observers who continued to write about 'England' were not wrong to identify England as its hub and 'driver'.

As its ruler, and therefore on his own account, George also visited the electorate of Hanover, which had been restored to him, in 1821.

Castlereagh, however, came with him. He was warmly received, though perhaps George's German was now spoken with an English tinge. His constitutional position in Hanover as elector was different from his position in the United Kingdom as king. His role in Hanover gave him a personal entrée into European politics, a reality that sometimes irritated his British ministers.

It was a German, the philosopher Hegel – as he brooded in Berlin in these decades over European, indeed over world developments – who thought he had discovered some fundamental truths about this island kingdom. The English, he noted, knew, as a rule, how history should be written, and in itself this was revelatory. Like the French, they shared the attitudes of a common culture. The Germans, by contrast, were still struggling to find out how to write history. Englishmen had a past heritage that lived on in their memory and gave them a sense of identity. 'If he is asked,' Hegel wrote, 'any Englishman will say of himself and his fellow citizens that it is they who rule the East Indies and the oceans of the world, who dominate world trade, who have a parliament and trial by jury, etc.' That an Englishman should apparently first think of the sea when asked the question came as no surprise. Hegel believed that the sea always gave rise to a particular way of life. Those who sailed to earn their livelihood and wealth must earn them by hazardous means. The sea itself was limitless and was not conducive to the kind of life that characterized inland cities and regions.[12] The reach of British merchants and their trading companies was indeed universal and showed no sign of diminishing.[13] It is perhaps not surprising, therefore, that the royal countenance 'glowed with pleasure' as he heard the singing of 'Rule Britannia' at a banquet in his honour in Trinity College, Dublin, in 1821.[14] He had not similarly glowed when receiving the Catholic hierarchy and only a considerable imbibing of alcohol had fortified him for that experience.

Castlereagh and the projection of Britain

It was while he was in his northern kingdom in 1822 that the king heard that Viscount Castlereagh, still his foreign secretary, had killed himself. The personal reasons behind this act remain a matter for speculation, but the cumulative strain of managing the policy of such an ambivalent country wore Castlereagh out. There was also an element of personal ambivalence that is not without relevance to the situation in which he found himself. He was the 'British' foreign secretary at this pivotal point in British/European history but he was as much a latecomer as a Briton as Metternich was as an Austrian. He had come to England for the first time as a 17 year old when he went to St John's College, Cambridge, in 1786. Born in Dublin, he had been to school in Armagh. His lineage was not anciently aristocratic. His Ulsterman father, another Robert Stewart, had married the daughter of an English peer, and had been ennobled in the peerage of Ireland only in 1789.

By 1816 he had become marquess of Londonderry and, after the Union, sat in the House of Lords as an Irish representative peer. Father remained a Presbyterian all his life and his family, neither then nor later, disdained the world of business. Judicious marriage brought the later Londonderrys considerable coal deposits in the north-east of England and they did not despise them. Such a background neither constituted 'the typical education of the British landed aristocracy' nor one that would have been accepted as 'aristocratic' in more exacting continental circles.[15] Indeed, Liverpool's cabinet, in which he served, attested to the variety to be found within the British ruling elite. In the case of most of the ministers it had only been recently that their families had made social progress, often in the service of the state.[16] As a man, Castlereagh lacked the vivacious charm thought characteristic of aristocrats. Apparently oblivious to status, he established his household in modest Viennese accommodation. Singing hymns in his drawing room on Sundays, with harmonium accompaniment, seemed to Metternich to be a drole activity for a foreign secretary. Castlereagh himself was not a business man but he brought to diplomacy the calculations of a commercial kingdom. He subsequently stated in its defence that the Congress had been convened 'for great practical purposes' not for the discussion of moral principles.

Battling to victory

Russia, Prussia and Austria had agreed their war aims against France, in the Treaty of Teplitz. Castlereagh sketched his own initial position to British ambassadors in a despatch of 18 September 1813. His own underlying aspirations, at this stage, were very much in line with the views Pitt had identified in 1805 (and which Castlereagh had then helped to draft). Certain pledges were held to be inviolable, but other objectives were merely desirable. The confederacy that had now been assembled was to be considered 'as the union of nearly the whole of Europe' against the ambition of an individual. Castlereagh argued that it was different from former confederacies, not only in the number of powers involved, but in what he called its 'national character'. The sovereigns now had the prevailing sentiment of their subjects with them. It was vital, whether in war or negotiation, that the allies should keep together. This required that they should agree on certain fixed principles and common binding instruments.[17]

Despite the victory of the eastern allies, at great cost, in the Leipzig 'Battle of the Nations' in the middle of October (during which battle Castlereagh's despatch was at length received) it was nevertheless clear that Austria and Prussia might be tempted by a settlement with Napoleon that would ignore British interests. It would be no easy task to achieve the broad objectives the foreign secretary outlined. There was a real danger that Napoleon could persuade the continental powers that it was Britain that stood in the way of an acceptable settlement. In writing to 'ambassadors', however, it would be wrong to suppose that British interests in Europe were clarified and prosecuted by a cadre of career professionals. The diplomatic world was in disarray. Although there were some 'back channels' that could be used, in the immediately preceding years Britain had not even had diplomatic relations with Russia, Prussia, Austria (where the last British ambassador had been murdered) and Sweden. The ambassadors to Russia and Prussia selected in 1812–13 were soldiers not renowned for their diplomatic finesse – Lord Cathcart and Castlereagh's half-brother, Sir Charles Stewart – as they proved in their relations with each other in their common peripatetic lives as they journeyed with the allied headquarters. The arrival of another general offering his assistance – Sir Robert Wilson, unlike the others, an Englishman and also somewhat 'out of area' since, in theory at least, he was British military adviser to the Ottoman Empire – further complicated matters.[18] Castlereagh sent out young Lord Aberdeen, an architectural enthusiast, as ambassador to Vienna. At the time, Aberdeen was more authoritative on the topography of Troy, having reviewed a major book on this subject, than he was on that of central Europe, through which he found himself travelling.[19] En route, his carriage overturned on several occasions. This ill-assorted trio of ambassadors frequently adopted the standpoints of the courts to which they were accredited. They saw little wisdom in their colleagues. In any event, their despatches not infrequently referred to matters that had been settled by the time they reached London. It was in these circumstances, somewhat to the chagrin of Aberdeen, that the foreign secretary decided to come in person. The Austrian *Grande Armée* proceeded through south-western Germany to the French/Swiss border at Basle and it was there that Castlereagh arrived on 18 January. He had the considerable benefit of drawing up his own instructions.

The fluctuating military situation still determined the diplomatic outcomes. After weeks of negotiation in February/March, Napoleon rejected terms that were at length advanced by the allies. Castlereagh suspected that he would be stoned if he had returned with a settlement that kept Napoleon in office, so strongly was 'no peace with Bonaparte' proclaimed at home. However, the foreign secretary's personal stature grew steadily as he mediated between the allies. It had become clear that Britain would not be content with a marginal role. It is not an exaggeration to say that it was his sustained pressure that turned the existing coalition into a 'grand alliance' when Britain, Russia and Prussia signed the Treaty of Chaumont on 1 March. The powers agreed not to make a separate peace with Napoleonic France. Perhaps even more significant was an agreement that the alliance should remain in existence for 20 years to counter any possible French revival. Castlereagh appeared to be committing a large British force for such a contingency. He approved substantial British subsidies to lubricate the arrangements. The allied military progress was now rapid on several fronts. Bordeaux was handed over to Wellington and it was gratifying to the British that it was there that the return of the Bourbons was proclaimed. Only the British among the allies had been pressing for a Bourbon restoration. Paris fell on 31 March. It was the Russian tsar, at the head of what was then the largest army in Europe, who marched his troops into the city. East had come very far west. Since he alone of the allied leaders was in the French capital he was determined to make a major impression. It seems that he had only one enemy in France, and that man was about to board a ship for Elba. Alexander stated that he had come to bring peace and commerce, but he also brought with him spiritual insights and instructions offered persuasively to him on his journey through Germany by evangelical pietists, both male and female. Assuming, apparently, that he spoke for his allies, he made a start by working out the Treaty of Fontainebleau with Talleyrand, which accorded the departing emperor, and his family, substantial pensions (from French funds) in recognition of their services to Europe. It looked to be leniency of an impressive order.

Afflicted by gout at an awkward moment, but freshly fortified with the Order of the Garter and the good wishes of the prince regent, Louis XVIII left his agreeable residence in Buckinghamshire and boarded the British royal yacht, *Royal Sovereign*, to return to France as king. He entered his capital on 3 May 1814. A 'charter' set out the basis of this restoration, though it was later made clear that this constitution had been one that the monarch had graciously ceded rather than one that resulted from sovereignty being vested in the people. Even so, while Louis's long exile in Britain had not convinced him that the British constitution was ideal even for the British, his knowledge of British institutions arguably helped to resign him to the introduction of a broadly comparable system in France. In the circumstances, some compromise political settlement was inevitable.[20] Even so, the French people (and the army in particular) appeared still to revere Napoleon, a fact that Louis thought best to ignore.

The Treaty of Paris and the world beyond

Although a married renegade bishop was not in principle a congenial prospect to him, Louis had little alternative but to entrust the negotiations with the victorious allies to Napoleon's foreign minister, Talleyrand. The resulting Treaty of Paris was concluded with them on 30 May 1814. Castlereagh, with Aberdeen in attendance, had joined in these negotiations over six weeks. Aberdeen had come to be struck by 'the goodness, the bonhomie, the honesty' of all ranks of Germans with whom he had latterly come into contact. By contrast, on encountering them again, he found the French to be 'a vile and despicable people'.[21] At the level of direct contact, if Aberdeen's reaction is taken to be typical, the restoration of peace would not in itself turn the two peoples into amiable neighbours. Certainly, the thousands of French prisoners who were returned from England treasured no happy memories of their grim incarcerations on Dartmoor and else-where.[22] It was hard for them to swallow the notion that the British had somehow 'liberated' their country.

The foreign secretary's objective, however, was to agree a settlement with France that would safeguard Britain's interests but not be so draconian that it would lead France to seek to overthrow it. The restored kingdom would retain the boundary of 1792 (rather than that of 1789) and France renounced territorial claims in Europe outside it. An independent Switzerland should govern itself. 'Italy', beyond the limits of the territories that were to revert to Austria, was to be composed of sovereign states. There were to be no reparations and no actions against individuals because of their conduct or political opinions during the years of belligerency. Prussian sug-gestions that France might be partitioned were discounted. It should remain a major state. Metternich hoped that it would counter-balance Russia.

From a British perspective, however, it was important that France should be ringed by effective states, most particularly in the Low Countries where Britain had always claimed particular interests. It seemed timely to create in the Netherlands a unitary rather than a federal state so as to provide an effective defensive bulwark. The departure of Austria would mean that, for the first time in centuries, the Bourbon and Habsburg dynasties would no longer confront each other in western Europe. Northern and southern Netherlanders came together under the Orange dynasty in a new Kingdom of the Netherlands. It was important to secure the Scheldt from French influence. Britain was in a position to insist on such an arrangement, but its role was not merely a matter of power. The British monarchy was some-thing of a model (though by no means exactly copied) as the Netherlands departed from its previous 'estates' system. Only after the state was estab-lished, however, did the government begin seriously to address the issues of language and history that might make this 'nationality' rather fractious.[23] The 'German question', however, remained for the future. The German Confederation, consisting of 39 states and cities, had a federal diet (at Frankfurt) that was little more than a forum for discussion. Neither Prussia nor Austria could dominate. The rulers of Denmark, Britain and the Netherlands were members as heads of the houses of Schleswig, Hanover and Luxembourg. The political order in 'Germany' was therefore linked with that of Europe. Indeed, the arrangement has been seen as 'a last attempt to prevent Germany from becoming a compact power at the cen-ter'.[24] Heligoland, a small island near the mouth of the River Elbe, became a British North Sea naval base, but scarcely gave Britain a commanding position in German affairs. British missions, however, were confirmed or established in all the larger kingdoms of the confederation, and to the diet, with responsibilities that also extended to the minor states. No single 'view' of Germany as a whole predictably emerged from the individuals who carried out their reporting responsibilities, but there was an awareness that the structures might not endure.[25] Finally, to the south-east of France, the kingdom of Sardinia (the island of Sardinia, together with Savoy, Nice, Genoa and Piedmont) was another small state that was strengthened. In both of these instances, security concerns were paramount, though Castlereagh was somewhat sceptical about 'strategic boundaries'. He wrote in April that real defence and security arose from the fact an aggressor would know that he was 'declaring war on all those interested in maintaining things as they are'.[26]

The world beyond Europe had also to be settled. The British, however, had no intention of restoring to France, the Netherlands and Denmark all the colonial territories that had been captured at one stage or another – Malta, the Cape, Mauritius, Tobago, St Lucia and part of Guyana. They made it very plain by such retention that colonial supremacy was now theirs. As a mild gesture, however, other French territories in the Caribbean were returned, as were the Dutch East Indies. A further restriction on French territory in India, together with the earlier acquisition of Ceylon [Sri Lanka] in 1802, confirmed the importance of the subcontinent for Britain. 'A free though conquering people' thus found itself in a paradoxical position, easily open to a charge of hypocrisy, as it too pursued a policy of annexation.[27] It is not the case, however, that British imperialism threatened the peace of Europe. As Professor Schroeder argues, 'the way the British ran their formal and informal overseas empire clearly contributed to stability, at least in Europe'.[28] Britain's naval power, on balance, benefited the commerce of Europe as a whole in guarding the most important sea lanes. It was not used, in the immediately succeeding decades, to monopolize overseas expansion. For example, while the British certainly did not welcome the French conquest of Algiers in July 1830, they did not stop it.

In 1815, Britain's revamped 'empire' was a ramshackle affair. A collection of the dominions of the British crown, it had no legal identity. There were no 'provinces', there was no representation of the 'colonies' at Westminster, there was no ecclesiastical uniformity. Expansion overseas, however, was scarcely an un-European activity. It was what the states of Europe's maritime littoral had been doing for centuries. To be engaged creating some kind of 'Europe beyond Europe' was a very European thing to be doing. At this particular time, it was simply that the British were clearly operating overseas more comprehensively and, it seemed, more successfully, than anybody else. It could be claimed that their empire was not of the Napoleonic kind.

Even so, when they criticized Napoleonic imperialism in Europe, it could not be because the British had a rooted objection to all forms of empire. They too engaged in 'empire building'. Whether 'directly' or 'indirectly', the British already controlled very different types of society. Their presence necessarily had an effect on the values and cultures of the subordinated peoples. In India, for example, the East India Company hovered uneasily between Anglicization on the one hand and, on the other, the recognition of

'Oriental difference'. Nor, as will be seen, was the nature of dominion an issue for the British solely in distant continents.

The Vienna settlement: matters for negotiation

The Treaty of Paris, in its treatment of the Low Countries and 'Italy', demonstrated what Great Powers, when in agreement, could do to smaller entities. Prussian claims on Saxony and Russian claims on the duchy of Warsaw, however, touched directly on the relations between the Great Powers themselves. Prussia's desire to annex Saxony was strongly resisted by Austria. In the event, after much negotiation, Prussia was allowed to take the Rhineland and was thus, for the first time, given a stake in western Europe. It was assumed that Prussia would strongly oppose any future French expansion. Bound up with both issues was the question of the future of 'Germany'. Would there be an 'independent centre' in Europe? Prussia was to sprawl from the Baltic to the French border. Castlereagh hoped that these matters would be largely settled at the London conference that was scheduled to follow the discussions in Paris, but was alarmed lest Alexander would prove 'the sole feature for admiration' on his visit. However, despite the attendance of Frederick William III of Prussia and Metternich (representing his emperor), plus sundry generals, it was in fact the tsar who excited enthusiasm in England – except in quarters where it mattered. The University of Oxford bestowed honorary degrees on the royal visitors and on Metternich. The Corporation of London paid an elaborate tribute. However, Alexander infuriated the prince regent by upstaging him before the London crowds and bowing to his estranged wife. British politicians were irritated that a foreign visitor should trespass on a local sport by such conduct. He upset ministers by consorting with opposition politicians. That 'Europe' had come to London was gratifying, but there was also irritation at the vanity that foreigners manifestly displayed. Even Oxford was surprised by the speed with which General Blücher became drunk. In short, the London conversations did not produce the results that Castlereagh had hoped for.

It was already highly unusual that a foreign secretary should have been present in person on the continent for so long (Castlereagh had previously, in his early twenties, spent a short time in France and Belgium, without admiration for the impact of the French Revolution). He had no doubt that his own presence in Vienna would be central to success and left his prime minister in no uncertainty on that score. It could not be said, however, that a journey to the heart of Europe was either swift or comfortable. The turnpikes of England were not known there. It was supposed to be a brief Congress that would confirm what had already been decided. In fact, it was to take nine months. The extent to which the cabinet could exercise control, however, was limited by the fact that it took between 10 and 12 days for a courier to get to Vienna. It was with difficulty that Castlereagh insisted over the coming months that there was a vital continuing British interest in the totality of the European settlement. He was repeatedly told that it would be impossible for Britain to become involved in hostilities arising out of any matters under discussion. Britain, he had no doubt, had to play a role in European questions of the first magnitude.

The delegations assembled in Vienna in September 1814, somewhat in dribs and drabs, and it was only in November that the Congress really got going.[29] The Austrian capital was a city of some 250,000 inhabitants. Its population was only around a fifth of Europe's largest city, by far, at this time – London. Nevertheless, for geographical, if for no other, reasons, Vienna could properly claim to be the appropriate location to decide the future of Europe. Emperor Francis I was anxious to demonstrate, by his sumptuous hospitality, that Austria, at its heart, had a pivotal role to play. Settling the great issues of the moment was so much more enjoyable if accompanied by balls, ballets and banquets. The handsome town residences of Austria's great families found eager new occupants – Talleyrand, for example, moved effortlessly into the Kaunitz Palace. In the vast Hofburg, the emperor entertained the tsar of Russia, four kings, two crown princes, three grand duchesses and an ample supply of minor German royalties, together with princely families and diplomatic representatives in hundreds from across the continent. An expenditure of 30 million florints seemed a reasonable outlay. Here was the perfect combination – an Austrian city in which one spoke French. Moreover, behind the monarchs, and sometimes not very far behind them, stood experienced ministers and advisers who knew the variety that was Europe at first hand. Metternich, born in the Rhineland and raised in Brussels, was more at home speaking French than German. At his elbow, however, was von Gentz, student of Kant in Königsberg, translator of Edmund Burke, creator of political journalism in the German-speaking world and student of international statecraft. In the entourage of the Russian tsar were a German, a Pole, a Swiss, an Alsatian, a Greek and a Sardinian. The pope sent Cardinal Consalvi. The sultan sent his *Chargé d'Affaires* in Vienna, who happened to be a Greek. Friedrich Ludwig Jahn, father of German patriotic gymnastics, wearing what was assumed to be distinctly German attire, was to be seen in the city. The ever-hopeful Knights of St John of Malta were represented. The Polish national hero and general, Tadeusz Kosciuszko, was present in order to urge, though with no chance of success, the reconstitution of Poland.

The absence of a British monarch from Vienna was fortuitous, but also illustrated political reality. Russian, Austrian and Prussian rulers made their own decisions on the spot because they had no doubt where power and authority lay. Their prerogatives were sacrosanct. State policy and a wider enthusiasm might on occasion coincide, as in Prussia in 1813, but such a coincidence was not in any of these states a necessary condition of policy-making. Alone among the Great Powers, Castlereagh was beholden to parliament in relation to a final settlement, though, in particulars, what that meant was obscure. It would have seemed absurd to him to suppose that the zig-zagging course of British diplomacy could have been subjected to sustained scrutiny as it proceeded. He knew, however, doubling as leader of the House of Commons, that in due course he would have to defend his vision of Britain in Europe there.

Given what had already been agreed, which largely met Britain's particular objectives, prolonged involvement in matters beyond the Rhine did not appeal to the prime minister and other colleagues. The 'less Britain had to do with [Poland] ... the better' Liverpool wrote to Castlereagh on 14 October 1814. The foreign secretary, while accepting that the frontiers of central and eastern Europe – which had been left unresolved by Russia, Austria and Prussia in 1813 – did not directly affect Britain, was particularly apprehensive about Russia. The tsar had written to Kosciuszko in May to say that he hoped to effect the regeneration of the Polish nation. That turned out to mean a separate kingdom of Poland but with himself as king. It would also mean that Prussia would give up its Polish territory. Compensation would come by its acquisition of Saxony, whose king had failed to detect the way the wind was blowing and had stood by Napoleon at the Battle of Leipzig. Such an outcome did not appeal to the Austrians for obvious reasons. They suspected that in practice Russia would subvert the constitution, which Alexander proclaimed he had a moral duty to give to the Poles. It was the territorial extension of Russian influence that chiefly concerned Castlereagh since he did not relish being put in a position whereby he appeared to be vetoing a constitution for Poland. His role as a go-between, particularly in trying to reconcile the differences between Austria and Prussia, was of great importance, but in early December he was warning the prime minister of total stagnation and sudden war. Talleyrand, on the watch for opportunities to reinsert the voice of France, spoke strongly for the survival of Saxony under its 'legitimate' monarch. It seemed, later that month, that Prussia was treating a refusal to recognize annexation of Saxony as tantamount to a declaration of war. Without referring back to the cabinet, Castlereagh concluded a defensive secret treaty with Austria and France in January 1815. With Britain and Austria now making it clear that France was to be a full partner, Prussia backed down. Even so, there remained much hard bargaining both on the territory that Prussia was to acquire while still leaving Saxony independent (eventually about two-fifths) and what Russia would cede from the erstwhile duchy of Warsaw to Prussia and Austria. Although in reality the kingdom of Poland was subordinated to Russia, the constitution, on paper at least, gave Poles considerable scope. There were, of course, many smaller territorial issues to be haggled over – whether Salzburg should be Austrian or Bavarian, for example – but with the great issue resolved, Castlereagh returned to London in February 1815, to be succeeded by Wellington.

The return of Napoleon brought the Great Powers together again after the friction caused by the Polish/Saxon issue. On 25 March, Britain, Prussia, Russia and Austria renewed their alliance (and included France – in what was to be a war against the French army). The Congress resolved remaining matters with despatch and concluded its work before the actual fighting with Napoleon began. Although, of course, he was defeated, the 'Hundred Days' had exposed the frailty of the Bourbon restoration. Castlereagh arrived in Paris to try to teach Louis XVIII how to make a better job of monarchy. Although France had to pay for the renewed Napoleonic episode by having to accept its 1790, as opposed to its 1792 frontiers, by having to pay an indemnity of 700 million francs and by having to accept an army of occupation until the payment had been made, there were British voices that clamoured for more severe measures. Once again, Castlereagh, supported by Wellington, stood for moderation. To attempt to partition France would have been a recipe for instability and perhaps further attempted revolution. Pursuit of the mirage of absolute security would be likely to destroy what it sought to accomplish.[30] Their British view prevailed. It was not in British interests for France to be turned into a permanently dissatisfied power. The Second Peace of Paris, 20 November 1815, confirmed the final act of the Congress of Vienna of 9 June and at last brought the protracted process of peacemaking to an end. The treaties were accepted by the House of Commons (by 240 votes to 77) in February 1816. What had been achieved was satisfactory from a British perspective. The continental Great Powers had acknowledged British (and Russian) hegemony in their respective spheres but expected that it would be exercised 'in a tolerable way'. Similarly, the smaller powers had tacitly accepted a general Great Power hegemony, so long as their independence and rights were guaranteed.[31]

There were, however, British critics who loathed Great Power behaviour. In April 1815, the transfer of Genoa to the kingdom of Sardinia 'in concurrence with the wishes of the principal Powers of Europe', had angered the Whig, Sir James Mackintosh. In the House of Commons he launched into a wider assault on the peacemaking. He was appalled at the way in which the 'Confederacy of Kings' had arrogated to itself the right to regulate a considerable portion of Europe. Something unacceptable was being raised 'on the ruins of that ancient system of national independence and balanced power which gradually raised the nations of Europe to the first rank of the human race'. He further instanced the way in which, by detaching Norway from Denmark and linking it to Sweden, the Congress had presumed that it had the power to make nations. That was impossible. Nations could not be made by the application of laws. Their whole spirit and principles arose from their character.[32] It is worth examining his particular illustration in a little more detail for the light it throws both on Britain and on Scandinavia at this juncture.

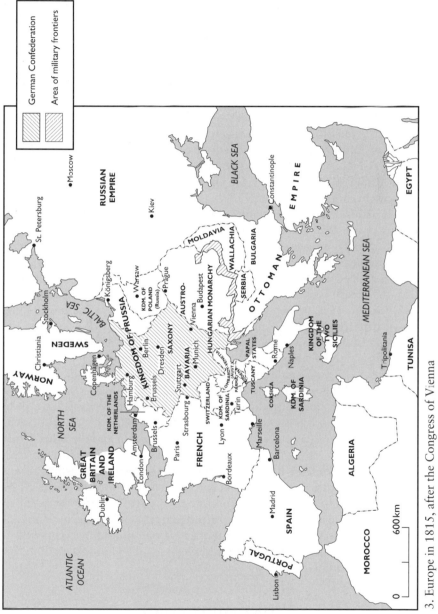

German Confederation

Area of military frontiers

3. Europe in 1815, after the Congress of Vienna

Sorting northern Europe

The specific 'marriage' of which Sir James complained was indeed forced. Northern Europe was indeed at the receiving end. The detachment of Finland from Sweden (and its incorporation as a grand duchy in Russia together with the Swedish departure from Pomerania) and the placing of Norway within Sweden rather than within Denmark was indeed arranged from outside.[33] However, it was not quite a matter of transferring one clear-cut nation to another, nor was the British relationship with these countries simply that of an external bully. Despite their continuing enmities and differences, the states of 'Scandinavia' were also conscious, to some degree, that together (possibly to the exclusion of the Finns) they constituted a special part of Europe. When they were 'out of area' this was particularly the case. It was Hans Christian Andersen, no less, planning Christmas celebrations in Rome in 1833, who wrote that in that city 'Swedes, Norwegians and Danes become one nation'.[34]

The British role in the reduction of Denmark from a not unimportant second-rank power to a definitely minor one could not be denied. And a British fleet had 'persuaded' the Norwegians that their place in the Swedish state was inevitable. This was 'Great Power' behaviour, exercised in what the British perceived to be an historic sphere of influence (as, a millennium earlier, the British Isles had been a sphere of Nordic conquest and influence). There was, however, more to the relationship than power. There was some sense of affinity, not least spiritually, between the British Isles and the Nordic lands. John Bunyan's *Pilgrim's Progress* (translated into Swedish from German and Dutch copies) was a standard item in pious Swedish households.[35] To be 'Scandinavian' was a bit like being 'British'. Both concepts embraced unity and diversity in puzzling and protean combinations. The 'British Isles' and 'Scandinavia' did not occupy the same European 'space', but they both possessed and indeed cultivated, a degree of detachment from its supposed centres.[36] In short, while Britain and the other Great Powers did not impose a Scandinavian settlement that universally satisfied, neither was it fundamentally unacceptable. If further adjustment was required in the future, it would be likely to be achieved without violence. Be that as it may, the Mackintosh perspective on the settlement constituted an influential critique and became more rather than less influential in Britain as time passed. Its logical conclusion was that Europe should be composed of 'natural' nation-states. What that would mean for the United Kingdom this Anglicized Scotsman did not say.

Perpetuating peace

Whether this particular configuration of northern Europe would 'stick' was only part of the more general problem of durability. Bringing the world back to peaceful habits, as Castlereagh put it, would require patience and commitment. Europe remained in a state of uneasiness and fermentation. All the peacemakers asked themselves how the settlement could be made to stick. In Article VI of the November treaty the four Great Powers agreed to renew their meetings at fixed periods 'for the purpose of consulting upon their common interests' and to consider what measures might be salutary 'for the repose and prosperity of nations and the maintenance of the peace of Europe'. The suggestion was Castlereagh's. It arose directly out of his long and unique experience of personal diplomacy over the recent past. It was something of an afterthought, but was to result in an attempt to govern Europe by conference.

Tsar Alexander had a different approach. His predecessors had not made a habit of attending Quaker meetings, but that is what he did in London. One Friend, Stephen Grellet, had earnest conversation with him on spiritual matters and recorded that the tsar held his hand and responded thus (speaking English): 'These, your words, are a sweet cordial to my soul, they will long remain engraven on my heart'.[37] Grellet – himself a former Frenchman – was able to persuade the emperor of Russia and the king of Prussia (the prince regent was said not to be able to sign without a counter-signature, and the pope declined) to agree to a document that came to be known as the Holy Alliance. It spoke of 'reciprocal service' and 'bonds of true and indissoluble fraternity', which linked the signatories. They and their peoples formed part of 'the Christian world' and acknowledged no other sovereign than Him to whom alone power belonged.[38] Castlereagh, suspecting that the tsar's mind was not sound, would have none of 'this piece of sublime mysticism and nonsense'.[39] Metternich dismissed it as a 'loud sounding nothing'. It has frequently been dismissed ever since by diplomatic historians as 'merely a vague and romantic piece of sentiment'.[40] Sir Harry Hinsley rightly observed, however, that the Holy Alliance 'was not the brain-child of an eccentric Tsar' but only the most extreme of attempts to escape from balance of power doctrines as they had operated in the eighteenth century.[41] Paul Schroeder argues that no international settlement can be expected 'to create the wider societal and cultural conditions necessary to make it durable'.[42] It was that 'moral deficit' that Alexander was seeking to address.

In attempting to do so, the tsar was certainly moving beyond the sphere of formal international relations but he had tapped into a pan-European religious current, though one that was impatient with established ecclesiastical boundaries and structures. Evangelical networks had transcended state boundaries for decades and continued vigorously to do so.[43] It was the British and Foreign Bible Society (1804) that established depots in many places across northern Europe from the Baltic to the Franco-German border between 1812 and 1817. It was a Clydesider who was assisting the Swedish Bible Society.[44] At another level, the pope was back in the Vatican, having seen off revolution.[45] Perhaps the rationalist spirit of the Enlightenment had reached a dead end. Here, after all, were three Christian sovereigns –

Protestant, Catholic and Orthodox – proclaiming that Europe was a Christian family. It was time to make a fresh start – and in 1817, as a first step, the Prussian king hammered Lutherans and Calvinists in his domains into one united church. In Britain, evangelical optimism expressed itself in the foundation of the Peace Society, a body that took a different view of war from Hegel. The Holy Alliance, and its assorted hangers-on, remote from the Courts of Power though they were, looked for a new kind of perpetual peace.

The idea either of a 'congress system' or a 'Holy Alliance', however, caused difficulties domestically. Castlereagh might be 'thinking of Europe' but he was in a lonely position in doing so. Alexander was now regarded with suspicion. William Cobbett, in a 'Letter to Lord Castlereagh' in April 1815, thought that the whole country had gone 'military-mad' and now seemed to have a conceit of itself as a greater military than naval power. The fleet, however, was the defence 'which reason and nature so clearly point out to us'. Whereas, in his view, continental connections had formerly been anxiously guarded against, they were now being eagerly sought. The people looked for relief from the long-endured burdens of the war, not for a continuing engagement with continental problems. The foreign secretary was urged to 'disclaim all connection with a continent where we never can have power without the ruin of this island'. The country would have peace and prosperity in consequence and be as great as France.[46]

Such opinions were not confined to outsiders. As the years passed, his cabinet colleagues sought to restrain Castlereagh as the 'allied reunions' assembled in Aachen (1818), Troppau (1820) and Laibach (1821). At the first, the remaining issues regarding France were settled without substantial difficulty and France was re-admitted to the 'Great Power Club'. Castlereagh was satisfied that there was little danger of a Franco-Russian alliance. He was, however, already concerned by the way in which Russia, in particular, saw the powers of Europe being bound together in a league that guaranteed the existing order of things in thrones as well as in territories.[47] Challenges to thrones were already brewing in Spain, Portugal, Piedmont and Naples, but no British government could commit itself to a general doctrine of collective intervention in the internal affairs of other countries (if countries with particular interests chose to do so, perhaps Austria in Naples, that was a matter for them). For Castlereagh, the infraction of treaties was one thing, the suppression of internal convulsions another. He did not attend the Troppau Congress (sending his half-brother instead). Britain stood firm against the 'protocol' drawn up by Metternich, which authorized united intervention if international order and stability were threatened. In Spain, neither the obtuse obstinacy of the king nor the wild plans of revolutionaries appealed to him. Britain was the last government in Europe that could be expected to commit itself in advance on any question of abstract character. When any actual danger menaced the system of Europe the country would be found in its place but it would not 'act upon abstract and speculative principles of precaution'.[48] Britain withdrew from the Congress at Laibach and by the middle of April 1821 the Austrians had suppressed revolution in both Naples and Piedmont. At Verona, after Castlereagh's death, Britain withdrew on hearing of Alexander's willingness to assist the French in suppressing the Spanish revolt – the French sent an army into Spain in April 1823. Although there were further conferences in St Petersburg in 1824/25, there was no British representation. The Congress 'system' had lasted a decade and Canning, Castlereagh's successor, emphatically had no wish to revive it. It was time to revive independent action – 'for Europe ... now and then to read England'. In the quarrels of the day, Britain should not seek to bolster despotism nor engage in a 'wild crusade' to impose her own system upon Europe. Its role was to stand 'neutral not only between contending nations, but between conflicting principles'. Whig attacks on the sovereigns of the three eastern powers were fierce. Mackintosh referred to them as 'imperial commissioners for exercising the office of dictator of Europe'. Lord John Russell, in a book published in 1824, called them opponents of 'the glorious cause of humanity, of civilization, of science, of freedom, of every thing that dignified and adorned our common nature'.[49]

Bringing back 'Balkan Europe'?

At the Congress of Verona, reiterating that it was not possible any more 'to have an English, French, Russian, Prussian or Austrian policy' but only a general European one, Tsar Alexander asked rhetorically 'What need have I of augmenting my empire?'[50] Whether he needed to or not, however, the perception elsewhere was that Russia was bent on further expansion. The arena was the Balkans. The peninsula remained under Ottoman control, as it had been since the fifteenth century. The threat that Ottoman forces had posed to 'Europe' did not lie so very far in the past. In 1683 Vienna had been under siege from Ottoman forces, a siege lifted by an international army under a Polish king. In the decades that followed, Turkish forces were pushed back, first from Hungary (which came under Habsburg control) and then further south. A century later, although formally represented, there could be no suggestion, from either side, that the sultan would be an appropriate person to participate in the decisions on the future of Europe that were made in Vienna in 1815. Certainly he did not seem an appropriate person to endorse the theology of the Holy Alliance. While the focus of the peacemakers in 1815 was elsewhere, Vienna itself was a keenly aware of Balkan developments. It was there in 1797 that the first Greek-language newspaper was published. It was, perhaps, only a matter of time before the Ottoman Empire would be rolled back throughout the Balkans. But what would that mean? It was already apparent, from a British perspective, that the region would not be left to its own rather sanguinary devices. At one level, it was in the Balkans that the boundary was to be found between 'Christian Europe' and the world of Islam – wherever, at any particular point, it might be drawn. At another, it was likely to see conflict between Catholicism and Orthodoxy as representatives of that 'Christian Europe'. Austria and Russia would be Great Powers anxious to be portrayed as Catholic and Orthodox respectively, whatever other ambitions they might have. It was already apparent that the historical claims of Balkan peoples to particular territories no longer matched the actual distribution of populations. Moreover, there had been significant conversions to Islam. Add to this the complexities produced by geography and embedded structures of Ottoman administration, and only one descriptive word seemed to fit: a mixture.[51] The relationship between 'Europe', the Balkans and the Ottoman Empire took a new and dangerous form. The Serbs and the Greeks set the question alight.

A major Serb rebellion against Ottoman rule had begun in 1804, though killing was not restricted to Turkish targets over the next decade. The deadly feud between two Serb families complicated the position. However, in the decade after 1815 the Serb prince, Milan Obrenović, was able to gain more autonomy, though still under Ottoman suzerainty. Turkey still retained Albania, Bosnia and Hercegovina, Macedonia and the Sandjak of Novi-Bazar (which separated Serbia from Montenegro) in the west/north-west, but by 1830 Serbia had a degree of independence. It was, however, not the Serb cause that excited most enthusiasm in Britain. It was the hope that the 'Greeks' could be resurrected that stirred distant imaginations.

It was not easy to say who Greeks were, what language they spoke or should speak or where they lived.[52] Answers were many and various. Classical antiquity might excite scholars in Oxford and Cambridge, Glasgow and Edinburgh, but did not excite 'Greeks'. In so far as a Greek past was being rediscovered it was a Byzantine one. The Ottoman Empire had attracted British aristocrats of varying proclivities. Lord Elgin had arrived as British ambassador to the Porte at the turn of the century. The Foreign Office had surprisingly declined his suggestion that he be provided with funds to enable him to act as collector and patron of the arts. Undeterred, Elgin succumbed to the antiquarian fever that led him to the Parthenon and the acquisition of the 'Marbles'. Lord Byron, who had himself been in Greece in 1809–10 castigated Elgin as the taker of 'the last poor plunder from a bleeding land'.[53] At least 22 ships had been required before the last pieces reached England in 1815. Elgin saw himself as a great benefactor and rescuer. It was fitting that England was safeguarding the classical past of Europe. The Greeks of Athens did not seem to have much connection with the age of Pericles. Ottoman rule had isolated the scattered Greek world from the great historical movements of 'Europe', but some Greeks had carved for themselves a particular role within it. The Orthodox Church remained intensely conservative and isolated. It could still be argued in the 1790s that the sun revolved around the earth. The

Vatican was a threat, not an ally. Conversely, the Catholic minority had at times found a modest shield in the Porte. A cultural renaissance was evident in the 1810s. In March 1821 a Greek with a commission in the Russian army, raised a revolt against the Turks in the Danubian principalities of Moldavia and Wallachia. The tsar, though proud to constitute himself protector of the Greek Orthodox faith would not help. It was against the principle enunciated at Troppau. That revolt was put down, as was one in the Morea shortly afterwards. A bloody struggle began. News of massacres reached western Europe and excited phil-Hellenes who imagined, at least until some of them arrived in support, that the resistance fighters were likenesses of the classical heroes they admitted. Diplomatic relations between Russia and the Ottoman Empire were broken off and it was left to the British ambassador to try to make progress in negotiations with a view to alleviating the position of the Greeks and reducing Turkish forces.

It is scarcely surprising that the British did not intuitively feel at home in this region of Europe, if indeed that was what it was. Yet, after 1815, they were on site. In the Adriatic, the demise in 1797 of the Serenissima Republic of Venice, and then the defeat of France, left a vacuum that the British were to fill. The new 'United States of the Ionian islands' (Corfu, Cephalonia, Zante, Santa Maura, Ithaka, Cerigo and Paxos) was placed under the protection of the British Crown. A British lord high commissioner was to oversee the drafting of a constitution. The reality, throughout the islands, was that the British were in control, whatever the formal degree of autonomy they were allowed. The British found it difficult to categorize the islanders, who seemed morally degenerate, as either oriental or occidental, 'European' or 'non-European'.[54] British administrators or soldiers did not feel drawn to the culture they found. The desire of some islanders to go across to the mainland to fight for 'Greece' was a problem. Canning was still anxious to maintain a neutral stance but recognized the Greeks as belligerents in March 1823. Lord Byron mobilized support in London and arrived in person at Missolonghi in January 1824.[55] He died fighting 'freedom's battle' in April, though in fact from malaria. A cross given him by an Italian Capuchin in Athens to assist him in his fight against 'the infidels' proved to be of no avail.[56] Bitter fighting continued over the following years, with British volunteer officers playing important roles in organizing Greek land and sea forces.[57] Despite mutual suspicions, Britain, Russia and France agreed on a position on autonomy for Greece, but it did not prove acceptable to the sultan. The Ottoman fleet was destroyed by the British at Navarino in October 1827, and Russia declared war on the Ottomans in the following spring. The war was concluded by the Treaty of Adrianople in September 1829, by which time Greece was recognized as an independent state – and given a guarantee by Britain, France and Russia in 1830. A Bavarian prince was elected as the first King of the Hellenes in 1832. A major breach in the Ottoman control of the Balkans had been made and British policy had steered an uneasy course between 'liberation' and anxiety about Russian intentions.

Greece, by geography – whatever territory it was deemed to cover – was both a Balkan and a Mediterranean country. It might even be thought to have an Asian dimension – it was in Smyrna (Izmir) that Korais, the Paris-based 'purifier' of the language, had been born. Britain had become involved because it was a Mediterranean power. If 'Europe' had a southern boundary, it was Britain that now patrolled it. Direct control extended from Gibraltar through Malta to the Ionian islands in the Adriatic. Here were Catholic and Orthodox cultures whose ethos was certainly not that of Protestant northern Europe. These small insular or peninsular societies had long been used to domination from outside. Sicilians, though now restored to their ruler as a part of the kingdom of Naples and Sicily, had been benefiting from a British military presence and from the belief of Lord William Bentinck, the British minister, that they would gain from a new form of constitutional government.[58] In these locations, as elsewhere, the British were the latest in a long line of foreign occupiers, but it looked as though they would stay for a long time. In Malta, the governor set the island on an educational course – a quite unanticipated one – that would make Malta in 2004 the fourth member state of the European Union to have English as one of its official languages. For the moment, however, whatever its own complicated past amounted to, Malta was firmly anchored in a 'British Mediterranean'.

Capital projecting

There was, therefore, looking at its place in European affairs as a whole, no doubt that the United Kingdom had 'arrived'. Yet there remained ambiguity about what it entailed and how that status should best be 'projected'. There was no palace in London to be compared with those of Vienna. Architects saw their opportunity. Within a few years, Sir John Soane proposed a vast residence in Hyde Park, while Joseph Michael Gandy wished to place his proposal in Regent's Park. In the event, on becoming king, George IV decided to transform Buckingham House into a suitable royal palace, and work began in 1825. The British, clearly, were 'coming' but the full architectural expression of their transformed international status was still to be achieved.

Similarly, with the capital itself. London, of course, had not been without monuments and public sculpture but did not quite reach continental standards of ostentation. There was a view that this should be changed. It was time to build monuments to commemorate great national heroes. Wood, in his *Essay on National and Sepulchral Monuments* (1808), argued that from the most remote antiquity to the 'polished nations of Europe' sepulchral monuments had been a way of marking admiration for the illustrious dead.

Nelson swiftly achieved his column, but the illustrious living (namely Wellington), had to wait for his memorial. The soldier also fell behind the admiral in the allocation of London streets named in his honour. But there was more fundamental capital image-making to be done. The prince regent had already shown his expensive enthusiasm for building and John Nash was on hand to lay out Regent Street (commenced in 1813) and create a new garden suburb in Regent's Park. The prince's palace at Brighton was taking exotic shape – the eclectic use of Chinese and Indian elements showed that no mere European models would suffice. Arches were needed for London – notably that at Constitution Hill and the Marble Arch – and were to be decorated with sculptural celebrations of Britain's military victories. The Hanoverian dynasty would receive due commemorative attention. Wellington still had to wait and had to be satisfied with the naming and opening of Waterloo Bridge in 1817, to the sound of a 292-gun salute – appropriately the number of French canon captured at Waterloo. George IV (as, at last, the prince regent became in 1820) was set upon a path of public building in the capital, which would ensure, as a contemporary wrote, that 'England will continue to be the 1st country and London the first city of the world'. It is noteworthy that merely to become the first city of Europe would not be enough.[59] London had hitherto got by without a university to sit beside more ancient but more 'provincial' foundations, but since Berlin had achieved one in 1810 even that might have to change.

It was not only London within the United Kingdom, however, that looked to monumental embellishment on a European scale. Although not without controversy, commemoration of victory was set in hand in a Dublin still anxious, despite the new lack of a parliamentary focus, to demonstrate that it was a capital city. Nelson's pillar was erected in Sackville Street in October 1809, the anniversary of Trafalgar. It was, however, a statue, according to *The Irish Magazine* that 'records the glory of a mistress and the transformation of our senate into a discount office'. In 1813, noblemen and gentlemen convened a meeting to establish a fund to erect a monument to 'the extraordinary achievements of their heroic countryman' – Wellington. A foundation stone was laid in 1817 but the statue was not to be completed until 1861.[60]

There was also an increasing consciousness that England lagged behind in the presentation of art. There was no National Gallery. In French eyes, such an absence was merely a reflection of the fact that the English lagged behind not only in their presentation but in art itself. It appeared on the other side of the Channel that English painting had really only begun in the eighteenth century. That was perhaps a reflection of climate, for the British Isles lacked sun. Painting ships and beaches had much to commend it, but was somewhat limited when viewed in a European context. English patrons of art lacked the intellectual sophistication of their European counterparts, or so it was claimed. They were too fond of portraits of their families, their dogs and their horses. Smarting under such observations, there was a determination in London to emerge from the foggy obscurity of the English artistic past and establish a National Gallery that could hold up its head in Europe. In the meantime, Dulwich Gallery opened in 1814 to house a collection of European paintings that had originally been acquired by a dealer for the king of Poland, but that monarch had abdicated before they reached him. Thus did a London public begin to become more intimately acquainted with the art of Europe.

Beneath this fervid cultural rebranding, however, there remained an underlying British political suspicion of display and an indifference to the taunt of 'barbarism' sometimes levelled against their civilization. 'Foreign countries might indulge in frippery,' declared the radical Joseph Hume, 'but England ought to pride herself on her plainness and simplicity'.[61] It partly stemmed from a reviving evangelical austerity that had an iconoclastic tendency. It also stemmed from the self-image of a 'commercial people', suspicious of the higher realms of aesthetics (though this did not stop the British from entering into the art market with a vengeance). Each people had its character. French and German visitors in the 1820s, penetrating the island once again, concluded (perhaps with surprise and dismay) that 'England' had become the 'centre of civilization', it being farther advanced there 'than in any country on the Continent'.[62] Simply to ape the *beau monde* of Europe, as assembled in Vienna, would therefore be to fall into the trap of mistaking show for substance. Britain might not shine in the politics of culture but its feet were on the ground.

The condition of the ground, however, gave cause for concern. Peace in the short term brought with it distress and disaffection. The 'bloody practices which have attended the French Revolution' suddenly seemed a real possibility in England. The political consciousness of the lower orders had become a reality with which governments now had to deal. Economic recovery blunted its impact but even so it was doubtful whether the old assumptions about the nature of the British constitution could be sustained indefinitely. Aristocratic government was under threat. The 'July revolution' in France in 1830, which brought Louis Philippe to the throne, was perhaps a portent. In such circumstances, 'reform' of some kind seemed necessary, but only within limited parameters. It was ministers rather than 'the people' who should determine where British interests really lay. It was best to 'rectify' anomalies in the existing electoral system rather than to embark on comprehensive change in its basis. That would still be the British way. It remained to be seen whether pragmatic adjustment could maintain the position of that elite that had shaped Britain's European stance in 1815 and thereafter. It was already difficult, however, to believe that this British way would constitute an ideal for either European liberals or conservatives (for different reasons) to wish to imitate it. For Liberals, it was the 1831 constitution of the new Belgium, with its clear definitions of parliamentarianism, that excited admiration for their juridical clarity. For Hegel, indeed, the common law tradition in England stood in the way of rational legislation.

Although there were some signs that Britain was catching up with the *Zeitgeist*, the fundamental recasting of provisions that had been carried out 'in the civilized states of the Continent' had not taken place.[63]

Whether as laggard or leader in the constitutional stakes, the United Kingdom clearly took its place in a continental community of ideas and institutions. Conservatives and Liberals alike in Britain agreed with Sir James Mackintosh that Europe was in the first rank of the human race – though they tended to place southern Catholic states at the bottom of the continental league table. Lord John Russell was by no means alone in seeing China and India as decayed civilizations unable to withstand contact with Europe.[64] Africa offered no competition. There was, however, enormous promise in the 'new world' of North and South America. Hegel reflected growing interest when he wrote in 1826–27 that America was 'the world of the future', for it was still in the process of growth. European emigrants had brought the benefits of European culture there without the accompanying disadvantages.[65] And, of course, no European state was closer to the United States than the United Kingdom, and no European state was more dominant in South America, as independence was gained from Spain and Portugal, than the United Kingdom.[66] In November 1822 foreign secretary Canning had expressed to Wellington the opinion that 'the American questions are out of all proportion more important to us than the European'.[67] It was not an observation that any other European foreign secretary could have made. Balancing the old world and the new was on its way to becoming the British way of life.

5

Revolution, c.1830–c.1850

1848: the revolutionary moment

Beginning in January 1848 with a revolution in Palermo, Sicily, the European continent, with certain exceptions, was swept thereafter by political excitement. Constitutions were granted in unlikely places – Tuscany, Naples and even the papal states. In France, the government of Louis Philippe was overthrown in late February, to be followed by the provisional government of the second republic. Then the Habsburg Empire was in disarray. Metternich resigned, the imperial court fled to Innsbruck and a constituent assembly appeared. A pan-Slav congress met in Prague and proposed a changed status for Slavs within the monarchy. It issued a manifesto calling for a European congress of nations. Free nations, it was claimed, would more easily come to agreement than paid diplomats. The Hungarian diet, meeting in Bratislava (Pressburg), thought that Hungary should be for Magyars. In the territories of 'Germany' the black, red and gold flag of the national movement was widely displayed and 'March demands' were made and conceded. In Berlin, King Frederick William IV, faced by a revolt, promised a new constitution. In May a German national assembly convened in Frankfurt to produce a new constitution and elect a national government. The Austrians were swept out of Lombardy and the Veneto. Piedmont declared war on Austria, and was joined by Tuscany and the 'Kingdom of the Two Sicilies'. By the end of November the pope had fled to Gaeta, in Neapolitan territory, and a Roman republic was proclaimed. These were the heady days in which, it appeared, Europe was to be transformed: 'the springtime of peoples'. Yet, as rapidly as the old order had collapsed in these and other instances, so, within some 18 months, it had been patched up once again. It was, admittedly, a different landscape but scarcely more congenial to the 'forces of change'. A new emperor and chancellor reinvigorated the Habsburg Empire. The various Italian and the Hungarian insurrections were militarily defeated. The king of Prussia, smelling the stench of revolution attaching to the offer of the crown of a united Germany made by the Frankfurt Parliament, declined it. The surprising outcome in France was the election in December 1848 of Louis Napoleon as president of the second republic.

Historians, ever since, have sought to disentangle the particular and the general in their consideration of these events. Few would dispute that there was a 'revolutionary moment', perhaps the last expression of romantic optimism, that was 'European', but, on close examination, each revolution had its own distinctive features and each outcome hinged upon a particular combination of circumstances. It soon became clear that there was no fundamental unity within the 'forces of change', once initial euphoria evaporated. Solidarity splintered once specific proposals for social or political change had to be confronted. As arguments in Prague, Frankfurt or Budapest illustrated only too clearly, an appeal to 'nationhood' revealed profound disagreement. While it was true, both in 'Germany' and in 'Italy', that things would never be likely to be the same again, the nature of a 'unity' that might be found remained elusive and internally contentious.[1]

The United Kingdom, not unexpectedly, stood in an ambiguous position in relation to the specific developments of 1848–49 and the pressures for political and social change that lay behind them.[2] Either immediately, or a little later, it proved the place of exile for participants, on one side or the other, in the drama that had taken place. Prince Metternich, former Austrian chancellor, and his wife acquired a house in Richmond.[3] Mazzini, inspirer of 'Young Italy' and hero of the defeated Roman republic, was installed by Jane Carlyle in lodgings over a post office in Chelsea, smoking cheap Swiss cigars, reading Byron and looking after his tame canaries.[4] He also formed a European Central Democratic Committee designed to foster unity between the different exile communities. Karl Marx, now also settled, with many other Germans, in London, was scathing about the 'platitudinous paradise' of Mazzini's 'cosmopolitan-neo-catholic-ideological manifestos'.[5] No doubt he supposed that the same observation could not be made about the *Communist Manifesto* that had appeared in Paris in 1848. The Carlyles had befriended Mazzini in his earlier period of London residence (1837–43) and they perhaps a little upset his conviction that there was no liking in England for transcendentalism or big indeterminate generalizations of the kind in which he engaged. It was also in London that he had discovered, in the person of organ-boys, the existence of an Italian working-class. Many years later, somewhat grudgingly, he admitted that England had become 'a kind of second country'.[6]

There were arrivals of a different kind. François Guizot, historian, education minister after 1833, and prime minister of France after 1840, with whom British ministers had had many tussles, settled down in South Kensington. Palmerston asked him to dinner and Greville noted that such was their cordiality they 'would have shaken each other's arms off'.[7] Guizot had a considerable acquaintance with Englishmen. One of them, Nassau

Senior, had been accustomed to spending the legal vacations travelling on the continent and also numbered Alexis de Toqueville and Adolphe Thiers among his friends.[8] Louis Philippe, lately king of the French, with his whiskers shaved off and wearing goggles, had escaped from Le Havre armed with a British passport in the imaginative name of Mr William Smith – Charles X, whom he had replaced in 1830, had also fled to England 18 years earlier. He moved to the Isle of Wight where one of his kindly 'neighbours' had helpfully suggested that he be anonymously helped financially. Queen Victoria did not like to see monarchs in distress. Only four years earlier, on a state visit to Windsor Castle, he had been the first French monarch to set foot in Britain since Jean II after the Battle of Poitiers, and the latter had not come voluntarily. As always, while events elsewhere in Europe had been followed in the United Kingdom, officially and unofficially, it had been events in France that had excited the greatest concern. It is argued, at the conclusion of a comprehensive study, that it was not fear of a European war that preoccupied the political class, but rather possible repercussions within the United Kingdom itself.[9]

There were indeed reasons for concern. A question mark was placed against its institutions. In the event, however, despite initial alarm, the structure held. The British monarchy, safely in female hands since 1837, was not seriously threatened. The Reform Act of 1832 had apparently given sufficient legitimacy to its parliamentary institutions. The 'British Way' resumed its exemplary position as news of the turmoil abroad came to hand. Yet there was also an awareness that many of the forces that had erupted elsewhere were also present within the United Kingdom. In April, there was the prospect of a Chartist march on the Houses of Parliament after an assembly on Kennington Common.[10] The Duke of Wellington made formidable defensive preparations. Anticipating trouble, the prime minister, Lord John Russell, put Blue Books to good use by blocking his windows with them, but their effectiveness was not put to the test. Nor were the skills of a French special constable, Prince Louis Napoleon Bonaparte, required. His performance as 'visiting knight' at the celebrated mediaeval tournament held on the earl of Eglinton's estate in Scotland in 1839 had earlier shown his mettle. It does not appear, though, that his visored helmet was to hand in Trafalgar Square where he stood waiting for action. The queen, from the security of the Isle of Wight, expressed the hope that 'the bright and glorious Example of this Country' would be 'a check to the wild notions and wicked example set by France'. Was Europe once again to be led astray by French 'wildness'? Lamartine of the Académie française, the most renowned poet of the age, and therefore an obvious choice as foreign minister in the new French provisional government, saw the need to issue a 'Manifesto to Europe', which stated that while France would not recognize the frontiers, or any of the other provisions, of the Treaty of Vienna it wished to live in peace with all nations. History was not going to repeat itself, but who could be certain?

In South Kensington, Guizot, erstwhile translator of Gibbon, now free of political responsibility, could turn again to the question of European civilization. In 1826 he had published his *L'Histoire de la Révolution d'Angleterre*, the greatest event, he stated, which Europe had to narrate, previous to the French Revolution. He had a profound sense, as he had put it in an inaugural lecture in Paris in 1812, that between the different nations that had emerged from the ruins of the Roman Empire, relations had subsequently so multiplied that an actual unity had resulted. In lectures given at the Sorbonne in 1828–30 he had wrestled with the relationship between 'English' and European civilization. He rejected the notion that the English people had existed 'in a kind of moral isolation analogous to its material situation'. He concluded that 'Considered in their entirety, the continent and England have traversed the same grand phases of civilization: events have, in either, followed the same course, and the same causes have led to the same effects'. English history, however, had an outstanding characteristic – 'never has any ancient element completely perished; never has any new element wholly triumphed, or any special principle attained to an exclusive preponderance'. National good sense had formed itself more rapidly there than elsewhere. He could not but be struck by a twofold fact about English character – 'on the one hand with the soundness of its good sense and its practical ability; on the other, with its lack of general ideas, and its disdain for theoretical questions'.[11] The paradoxical unity of European civilization lay in its lack of uniformity. It was a varied, confused and stormy history. In ancient times, all societies had seemed cast in the same mould, but modern Europe presented examples of all systems, all experiments in social organization, pure and mixed monarchies, theocracies, republics all thriving simultaneously. Notwithstanding their diversity, they all had a certain family likeness that it was impossible to mistake. It was the perception of a Protestant from Nîmes, devoted to German culture, English literature and, ultimately, to a Russian princess. Here was a man whose father had been guillotined in the year II and whose fellow Protestants had been massacred by ultraroyalists in 1815. There had to be a reasonable middle way for France and for Europe. He looked to history as a means of binding people together by their awareness of a shared past.[12] In 1848, at the moment of exile and political failure, it was not certain that either his hosts or the new revolutionaries had identified it.[13] Was the notion of 'family likeness' simply the kind of deception to which a French liberal historian reading the *Edinburgh Review* was too easily prone? There were grounds for supposing that the 'grand phase' of European civilization that was under way was, in the short term at least, producing economic, social and political changes that accentuated differences rather than similarities. In any case, since the English apparently disdained theoretical questions, they were unlikely to be found speculating about 'Europe'. The City of London engaged in speculations of another kind.

Ministers and their Europe

It was a Whig government, under Lord John Russell, in office since 1846, that faced this European turmoil. It was not a bourgeois administration. His colleagues, almost without exception, were peers. It was a ministry that relied for its majority on a motley crew of Whigs, Irish and Radicals. The foreign secretary, Viscount Palmerston, who as an Irish peer sat in the Commons, had first held that office in the government formed by Earl Grey in November 1830. That prime minister had kept a very watchful eye (Grey resigned in 1834) over his conduct. By 1848, however, he was a substantial but endlessly controversial figure in his own right. Consideration of formal British foreign policy in this chapter must focus on him. This continuity of aristocratic composition and, to a large extent, of ethos over these decades again conveyed stability. The formulation of British foreign policy remained in the hands of an elite. Conventions and assumptions about Britain and Europe tended to be passed down within family groupings and preclude any simple identification of 'party' foreign policy. The foreign secretaries between 1830 and 1848 – Palmerston, Wellington (but only very briefly in 1834–35) and Aberdeen (1841–46) – had all been involved, in one way or another, in the high politics of war and peace leading to the 1815 settlement.[14] That was the era in which they had formed their perceptions of Europe and how Britain related to it. Lord John himself, son of a duke, was born in 1792 and elected to the Commons for the first time in 1813, while still under age. He led his party from 1835 to 1855. Early experiences had given him an unusually high personal knowledge both of the United Kingdom and of southern Europe. He spent time in the viceregal lodge in Dublin in 1806, and three years, spasmodically, at the University of Edinburgh. Lord and Lady Holland had invited him to Spain where they were offering wisdom on the subject of British parliamentary institutions.[15] Christmas Eve 1814 found him conversing with Napoleon on Elba in French. The following year, with the war over, he set foot in France. There was, he conceded, a self-confidence about the French that would seem quite unattainable 'to all other Europeans'. Over the following years his travels took him to Brussels, Amsterdam, Frankfurt, Dresden, Vienna, Geneva, Milan and Genoa. Thereafter, he went to France every year, and also frequently to Italy. He had no doubt that he was a European but one who believed that, wherever possible, Europe would benefit from the principles of English Whiggery. After all, on St Helena, even Napoleon had been eager, it seems, to make out what he could from the copies of the *Edinburgh Review* that reached the island.

Palmerston, too, had been taken travelling as a boy.[16] The family reached Paris on 1 August 1792 – not a quiet moment – and young Harry was to be out of the country, largely in Italy, for two years (he retained in later life the Italian he learnt there). The touring party called on Gibbon at Lausanne but the boy was not thereby inspired by the prospect of a scholarly life reflecting on the decline of empires. As a student at Edinburgh (and less so at Cambridge) he had been serious, a deficiency he compensated for later in life. He had become secretary at war in 1809 at the age of 25, and held the post for 19 years (in five successive Tory administrations). It was an illustration of the fluidity of party alignments and personal allegiances that Palmerston, a follower of Canning and a 'moderate' reformer, could emerge without undue difficulty as a Whig. As foreign secretary for all but six years in the period covered by this chapter, he promoted the rise of an empire with a jaunty robustness. He was, however, not insular. He visited France 10 times. His visit in 1815 led to the conclusion that 'without bayonets no man can govern France'. On a visit to the Netherlands in 1823, looking at pictures, he found that his efforts to speak Dutch, dictionary in hand, were defeated by the fact that everybody he met spoke English, though 'really the Dutch language is *too* ridiculous to an English ear'.[17] In the bookshop in The Hague 'nothing was to be seen but English books, Walter Scott, Byron, English Poets, Travels, Philosophy, etc'. In 1844 he travelled through Belgium, Germany and the Austrian Empire, reaching Prague and Berlin. Travelling through Germany, what struck him was 'the slowness of all their proceedings, agricultural, domestic and locomotive – an English population of equal number would draw twice as much out of the soil as these people do'. The country was certainly advancing in civilization, 'but it would take them a hundred years at least to reach the point at which England is arrived in the arts of life'. The habits and manners of living were what they were in England 150 years earlier. From what he saw of manufactures he found nothing 'to inspire any fear for the commercial prosperity of England'.[18] In Berlin he dined with the king of Prussia, met the historian Ranke and claimed to be acquainted with the *History of the Popes* in English translation, though their conversation was on 'eastern affairs'.[19] Although he held strong views on their politics, he never visited either the Balkans or the Iberian peninsula. The job of a foreign secretary was to stay at home – his travels took place when he was out of office – and he worked very hard, if irregularly. He drafted all important despatches himself. The status accorded France, Austria and Russia was reflected in the fact that it was only to these countries (with the addition of Constantinople) that ambassadors, usually aristocrats, were accredited. Palmerston treated these men with respect. Other European states had to be content with ministers, men treated with less respect. The foreign secretary (who himself spoke and wrote French well) took various decisions, small in themselves, but that cumulatively served to indicate that 'England' had arrived. In 1834 he 'remedied' the convention that diplomatic notes from one government to another were written in French. In future, British emissaries abroad were to write officially in English, though they could use another language when writing privately if they so wished. He declined decorations from foreign governments – the British did not need such things. He was quite content that British monarchs, contrary to custom, did not send an envoy to congratulate foreign sovereigns on their accession. Tending to a view of the importance of his own time, the most distinguished of foreign visitors could be kept waiting for their appointments. At dinners, it was said that the Palmerstons always missed the soups. Such traits were personal, but it was an appropriate juncture to cultivate the image of 'the most English minister'. With respect to alliances, he declared that he held 'England' to be 'a power sufficiently strong, to steer her own course, and not to tie herself as an unnecessary appendage to the policy of any other Government'.[20]

Reforming the United Kingdom

At first sight, Palmerston might appear simply to be upholding the conventions in which he had been raised and to be reflecting, in his hauteur, merely the arrogance of his own class. Yet it had been his government, a mixture of Whigs and Canningites, when it came to power in November 1830, that was pledged to reform the parliamentary franchise. Not that Palmerston, unlike Lord John Russell, was in the van. He wanted minimal change, claiming, in a speech in March 1831 that the English people agreed with him. 'They formed a striking contrast to their neighbours on the Continent … who boasted of the newness of their institutions, while the English were proud of the antiquity of theirs'.[21] Cambridge University, which Palmerston initially represented in the Commons, found unpalatable the amount of change that he was nevertheless prepared to countenance. He lost his seat in the March 1831 general election, though an alternative was quickly found. As the crisis proceeded, however, his support for what was on offer became firmer and he set himself against the Tories (he had been a Canningite Tory). The first reformed election under the new franchise in December 1832 was a disaster for the Tories – the opposition held only 185 of the 658 seats. In three-quarters of the constituencies there had been contests, whereas over the previous half-century only some 30 per cent had been contested. The legislature was still dominated by the Whig and Tory aristocracy and gentry. The Reform Act for England and Wales, which resulted in some 18 per cent of adult males being enfranchised, was followed by separate measures for Scotland and Ireland – such different measures necessarily reflected the very different franchise provisions that occurred within the United Kingdom. It was the Scottish electorate that expanded most rapidly (from 4500 to 65,000). The whole thrust of the legislation had been to remove indefensible 'anomalies' in the system as they had accumulated over time. There was no suggestion from within the ministry that the franchise should have been based upon some principle of 'democracy'. Parliament was a place where 'interests' of various kinds should be represented, the greatest interest still being land and agriculture. Palmerston had taken the view that if the bill were passed 'property, rank and respectability would still maintain the same influence in representation – an influence of which he should be the last man to deprive it'. His confidence appeared justified. There was certainly no simple transfer of power to 'the middle class', though among the so-called Radicals, of which there were around 100 MPs, there were certainly men who would not previously have been elected. Nothing in the legislation formally affected the powers of the Crown or of the House of Lords, but it was to be demonstrated that de facto the Commons had been strengthened. The Crown could not sustain a ministry unless it had a clear majority in the Commons. The resulting system was one in which Palmerston could function successfully. The Chartist, George Julian Harney, embarrassed Palmerston in 1847 by standing against him in his Tiverton constituency in 1847, debating against him and 'winning' on a show of hands by the unenfranchised. Palmerston, however, was a man who could live with embarrassment.

The outcome seemed to demonstrate that 'the desire of the people' could succeed by peaceful means. The elections of 1831 took on the character of a plebiscite on the question of reform. The legislation had been framed within Parliament itself by the Whig aristocracy. Tory opponents had, in the end, yielded, though many, like Lord Aberdeen, the previous foreign secretary, thought that the Constitution, as it was now conceived, would not last long. The House of Lords would fall and the authority of the Crown, and perhaps the kingly character itself, would be destined 'to speedy destruction'.[22] Such pessimism contrasted with the official line that what had been achieved constituted a 'once and for all' settlement. The extent to which it had been reached by outside public pressure remains contentious. Was the country close to revolution in 1830–31? Certainly, in 1831, the rejection of a second reform bill led to disturbances in various parts of the country. Bristol was in the hands of rioters for three days and the bishop's palace set alight. The same fate attended the duke of Newcastle's castle in Nottingham. Lord Aberdeen, however, reported that his own character as an anti-reformer had not made him odious in the north of Scotland where, he claimed, the people were opposed to reform. Indeed, lack of interest in voting on the part of those who possessed the franchise resulted in 1826 in a situation in which nobody in Scotland at all voted in the 1826 general election.[23] It was once normal to argue that the French Revolution of 1830, which saw the downfall of the Bourbons (whose return Wellington, now prime minister, had so much encouraged in 1815) had given a stimulus to parliamentary reform in Britain. Doubt was cast on such a correlation but that, in turn, has been questioned. The possibility that London might follow Paris was being widely mentioned in the autumn. Public enthusiasm for the July revolution, it has been concluded, lasted until after the passage of the Reform Act of 1832 and it became commonplace, in subsequent decades, to assert that there was a relationship.[24] It appeared, after the events of 1830–32, that Britain and France (together with the new Belgium) were now setting a pattern of 'reformed' constitutionalism in western Europe, though the franchise was distinctly more restricted in these two countries –

1 per cent of the population in Belgium – than it was in the 'new' Britain.[25] What beneficial consequences might stem from such constitutional correspondence remained to be seen. Prime minister Grey had expressed the view in the House of Lords in November 1830 that 'by the union of the two countries holding their liberties by the same means and by the same principles the peace of Europe will be maintained'.[26]

Interference? Belgium, Poland, Spain and Portugal

The issue of Belgium soon put this dictum to the test. Palmerston was apprehensive that France might seek to extend her northern borders or create a client state, but he was strongly opposed to restoring Dutch authority in the southern provinces (the 'legitimacy' favoured by the conservative powers). It was, perhaps, in this instance as elsewhere, as Paul Schroeder claims, the 'lax, inefficient nature of many regimes' and the inhibitions of monarchs with regard to using force that allowed such rebellions to succeed. French troops had entered the country in order to compel the Dutch to evacuate. Paris again toyed with the idea of partition but gave way when Palmerston warned that war would follow if France did not withdraw troops unconditionally. There was much dispute about control of certain border fortresses. The foreign secretary's stand not only reflected a long-standing British interest in the fate of the Low Countries – it was at a conference in London that these matters were thrashed out. It was also a reflection of the foreign secretary's reluctance to embrace the Francophilia urged on him by certain Whigs. His successful policy had been criticized in the Commons and the country as being pro-Dutch or pro-French – it was neither. Leopold of Saxe-Coburg, a German Lutheran, would make a good Belgian king. However, once the Belgian question was settled in a style that gave Britain the upper hand, Palmerston began to speak publicly of the need for a 'cordial good understanding' with France. The Orleanist government, treated with hostility by the eastern powers, made similar noises. Palmerston was prepared to contemplate force to get his way in establishing a satisfactory Belgian state. Aspects of the Belgian question remained in contention until 1839 when Belgium's independence and neutrality were guaranteed by all the Great Powers.[27]

Rebellions against the established order elsewhere in Europe from about 1830 to 1834 raised more complicated issues in places beyond easy reach. In November 1830, a rumour that the tsar planned to send his Polish army against Belgium sparked an uprising in Poland. It was finally suppressed, by Russian forces, in the following autumn. In consequence, the Polish constitution was suspended and rebels were deprived of their freedom and property. Some 10,000 Poles fled to various parts of western Europe (an equal number were sent to Siberia). Palmerston had expressed the view that Britain had a right to be consulted on the fate of Poland, but it was not one

that he either expected or desired to see accorded by St Petersburg or
Vienna. Envoys from the insurgents received admiration but no encouragement. Lord Holland, Whig doyen, found Palmerston's unwillingness to
sanction any intercourse between the king and the Poles 'idle squeamishness
… if not sheer pusillanimity and imprudence'.[28] After the collapse of Polish
resistance, Prince Czartoryski, who had headed the Warsaw government,
escaped to London. Palmerston received him on several occasions but
offered no solace. Only by going to war could Britain have helped the Poles,
but that would not have been possible. He famously added that burning the
Russian fleet would have been about as effectual as the burning of Moscow.
Czartoryski decided that it would be better to live in Paris.[29] There were,
however, a considerable number of Poles in London,[30] but little unanimity
among them. Parliament awarded them an annual grant of £10,000. The
poet Thomas Campbell organized the Literary Association of the Friends of
Poland, with branches in the big cities, though organization was not his particular forte. Despite Palmerston's frostiness towards Polish pleas, the
events contributed to a shift in his attitude to Russia, although in 1831 he
was still arguing that Russian expansion in the Caucasus added little to the
means of Russia to attack the rest of Europe. A couple of years later, however, he identified Russia, the champion of reaction, as the great threat to
the peace of Europe. It was almost 'a necessary condition of her existence'
that she should encroach upon her neighbours. Britain should therefore be
on its guard. Particularly in the aftermath of the Polish defeat, Russophobia
gathered pace.[31]

Palmerston had declared that the British people would not have counte-
nanced the sending of an army to help Poland. *The Voice of the People*,
organ of John Doherty's Manchester-based National Association for the
Protection of Labour, took a different view. It declared that 'The people will
not stand and see the Poles quietly butchered. Let us see all Europe in a war
before the catastrophe of a national slaughter'.[32] Another Irish Catholic,
Daniel O'Connell, saw the people of Britain, France and Germany ranging
themselves 'with every rational government' and insisting upon justice being
done to Poland.[33] War would not be necessary. The view was frequently
taken in the unstamped press that Britain's cowardly foreign policy was due
to the unreformed state of the House of Commons. It was this linkage with
the reform campaign that helps to explain the prominence 'Poland'
achieved. It was not as though any of the eloquent advocates of her cause
actually knew the country at first hand.

The internal affairs of the Iberian peninsula in the middle 1830s, as had
been the case in the middle 1820s, remained an area of British concern.
Rival claimants to the crowns of Spain and Portugal, of different genders,
struggled for supremacy and tossed constitutions into the contests, with just
sufficient plausibility to enable them to be portrayed as being between reactionary and progressive forces. Britain, France, Spain and Portugal signed a
Quadrilateral Alliance in 1834 and therefore, in European terms, what

Palmerston called a 'Western Confederacy' had been formed. In reality, it was a fragile affair – only partly because of continuing and seemingly endemic Iberian instability. The foreign secretary finely displayed a principled stand for 'free institutions', but chiefly wished to keep the French role to a minimum, a strategy that did not escape notice in Paris where there was a view that Spain was a 'natural' sphere of influence. From 1837 onwards, reaffirmations of the value of the *entente* from both sides of the Channel could not disguise the reality of conflicting standpoints. When King William IV spoke publicly of the French in 1833 as 'the natural enemies of England', it was a sentiment that was widely shared. Even so, it was not in the interests of either side, at this juncture, to make matters worse.

The eastern Mediterranean border zone

The issue that came to require even more attention than the politics of the Iberian peninsula was the future of the Near East. Palmerston had come to accept the view, which he had not always held, that it was as well to bolster the Ottoman Empire as long as possible. The idea that it was a sapless trunk, he wrote, was unadulterated nonsense. If it could have a decade of peace under the joint protection of the five powers, and reorganize its internal system in that time, then it would again become a respectable power. Mehemet Ali, pasha of Egypt, and his adopted son Ibrahim, threatened Constantinople. The sultan concluded a treaty with Russia in July 1833 (Unkiar Skelessi), which brought him support, albeit by making concessions to St Petersburg. Mehemet Ali seemed to Palmerston nothing but an ignorant barbarian, though this was apparently not a condition against the pasha that counted in Paris. The sultan, perhaps a bloodthirsty tyrant rather than just an ignorant barbarian, tried and failed to dislodge the Egyptians from Syria. He died in 1839. The fate of the Ottoman Empire looked precarious under his neurasthenic 16-year-old successor. Palmerston took the line that Mehemet Ali had to be confined to Egypt, but France proved obdurate. The convention for the settlement of the Near East, which he signed with Austria, Prussia and Russia in July 1840, did not include France. It was a British fleet that bombarded Acre in November, leading to Mehemet Ali's acceptance of the offered terms in the following month. In the new circumstances Palmerston now wrote that peace in Europe required a strong barrier against French aggression. 'Western Confederacy' was replaced by amity with the northern courts and Russia was identified as Britain's 'safest ally'. Louis Philippe and his minister Thiers would in fact not be as warlike as they sounded, but it looked again as though the French itch 'to give law to Europe' was reappearing. In the view of some of his cabinet colleagues, the foreign secretary had overstated the position. The following year France did sign, with the other Powers, a Convention that excluded foreign warships from the Dardanelles and Bosphorus (thus negating the special advantage Russia had gained by the Treaty of Unkiar Skelessi).[34] And, if Russia was indeed Britain's 'safest ally', it had not ceased to be, under Nicholas, a despotism, viewed with deep suspicion in many quarters. The most insistent was the Scottish aristocrat, David Urquhart, erstwhile first secretary at the British Embassy in Constantinople until removed by Palmerston. Urquhart was firmly of the belief that the foreign secretary was in Russian pay. The visit of the tsar himself to London in June 1844 infuriated Urquhart and his associates, a fury in no way mitigated by the tsar generously establishing a race at Ascot with an annual prize of £500. The tsar was reassured that Britain's only concern, apparently, was that no government in Egypt was in a position to interfere with British trade and British mails across Egypt.

Palmerston claimed that he had acted in the way he had done because France could not be 'allowed to dictate to the rest of Europe', but that was conventional hyperbole. The interface between 'Europe' and the Near East increasingly raised profound questions that were obscured by such simple assertions. The 'ignorant barbarian' – a tobacco trader from Macedonia who had come to Egypt with an Albanian detachment of the Ottoman forces – might really be a 'European'. French, Italian and Greek communities increased in size and contributed to the country's industrialization under its 'modernizing autocrat'.[35] It might be a British interest – with an eye to India – to cut him down to size, but not much more. Mehemet Ali (an Albanian) was not leading an 'Arab revolt', but who knows in what shape he would have left the 'Arab world' in its relations with 'Europe' had he succeeded? Urquhart, however, had learnt Turkish, and in *Turkey and her Resources* (1833) and *The Spirit of the East* (1838) identified Turkey as an ideal community that should be saved from a rampant Russia. 'England' (and 'Europe') had more to fear from St Petersburg than from Constantinople.[36] Urquhart was at least able to persuade Englishmen that they could benefit from the Turkish baths. He pioneered their introduction to England. He was, of course, eccentric. Edward Lear, balanced author of nonsense verse, Balkan traveller and water-colourist extraordinary, in Constantinople in 1848, was not convinced. He declared that the Turks were a 'semi-barbarous people' who lived with all the evils of the English climate and none of its benefits. He detected 'the absence of *all* we Europeans consider as necessary to existence', therefore Stamboul was at best a 'profitable exile'.[37] So, perhaps it did not matter, and might even be a good thing, if Turkey were brought into 'Europe' under Russian aegis? Paradoxically, however, it was at this juncture that some Russian intellectuals began to turn away from the idea that Russia's political and educational system should be based on French or British models. Russia could not be, should not be, part of Europe if Europe was defined by the values of the 'advanced' West. Chaadev, writing in French in 1829, concluded that Russians did not belong to either the West or the East as they did not have the tradition of either. In the decade 1838–48, 'Slavophiles' sought to identify and strengthen what they regarded as indigenous Russian traditions. The cold and superficial rationality of the West was dismissed and renewed emphasis placed on the insights and values of Orthodox Christianity.[38] For his part, Lear, no longer in Constantinople but on Mount Athos, came to despise all the trappings of Greek Orthodoxy and issued a diatribe against 'muttering, miserable, mutton-hating, man-avoiding, misogynic, merriment-marring, monotoning, many-Mule-making … minced-fish and marmalade masticating Monx'.[39] Palmerston was no doubt right to say that Europe should not be dictated to, but who could say where Europe began and where it ended?

Peel and Aberdeen

Palmerston's tenure of the Foreign Office had been interrupted by the advent of two Conservative administrations. Lord Melbourne's brief Whig administration was brought summarily to an end by his monarch in November 1834. It was in the Hôtel de l'Europe in Rome where, eventually, the Conservative leader, Sir Robert Peel, was tracked down and told that he was to be prime minister. The choice of his hotel should not be taken to indicate any particular enthusiasm on his part. He was in Rome for the shopping. Son of a northern cotton-spinner but himself an Oxford graduate and Staffordshire landowner, his youth had not been spent Grand Touring. After a brilliant Oxford career, at the age of 24 he was chief secretary for Ireland in 1812 and home secretary in the 1820s. It was his decision to change his mind and support Catholic emancipation that split the Tory Party – the pope personally thanked Peel when he paid a courtesy call in 1834. The ministry he formed on his return, however, was only short-lived. In his ministry from 1841–46 it was domestic rather than foreign affairs that absorbed his interest and energy. It was this administration that set the United Kingdom on a free trade course with the reduction or elimination of duties. The failure of the Irish potato crop in 1845 argued strongly for the abolition of the Corn Laws, but Peel could not carry his cabinet with him and the Conservative Party split. In a decade of turmoil, at least retrospectively, Peel was seen to have led an administration that was 'practical' and businesslike – as befitted the country.[40] Listening to Sir Robert in the House of Commons in 1835, the youthful Piedomontese, Camillo Cavour, already an avid reader of Adam Smith and other British economists, and of Byron and Bentham, found a hero whom he might emulate.[41] If only he himself were English, he wrote, he might retain illusions of grandeur and glory. Guizot, turning to biography, called him in 1856 'a man of essentially practical mind, consulting facts at every step, just as the mariner consults the face of heaven'.[42]

Foreign policy under Lord Aberdeen was less strident and assertive than under Palmerston. In Europe there was an attempt to renew the *entente cordiale* with France, which had been wrecked by the events of 1839–40, but it proved impossible. Sometimes, the two foreign ministers, Guizot and

Aberdeen, as time passed, appeared to be the only real advocates. It was generally accepted in British political circles that the 'liberal alliance', on an ideological basis, could not be revived, but it would be possible to establish an atmosphere of cordiality in which disputes could be resolved. It was perceived in practice, however, that Guizot would not, or perhaps could not, deliver on specific issues. The French chamber was predominantly Anglophobe and his options were limited. Aberdeen tried to negotiate his way through a series of disputes, which ranged from Tahiti, the Indian Ocean, the slave trade (which had been abolished throughout the British Empire in 1833) to Greece and, once again, to Iberia (this time, comically and almost explosively, on who should marry the teenage queen of Spain). At root, the 'Spanish marriages' question touched on the contrasting views of what 'partnership' between Britain and France entailed and, absurdly perhaps, came to dominate the foreign policies of both countries. In the end, by 1847, in a chilly atmosphere and after Palmerston's return, Guizot can be said to have triumphed, though it did him little good. It was only in the circumstances of his losing power that Palmerston shook him so warmly by the hand in his dining room in 1848.[43]

The cold diplomatic spat took place in a context in which the British realized, as Sir Charles Wood put it in December 1846, that 'the application of Steam to Ships' was rendering erroneous the old assumption that 'our wooden walls are a complete defence against invasion'. A couple of years earlier, the Prince de Joinville, sailor son of the French king, had published an article suggesting that in the future a French steam fleet could mount powerful raids against the English coast. The Channel, Palmerston declared in the Commons in July 1845, was no longer a barrier. It was now nothing more than a river passable by a steam bridge. A letter from Wellington in January 1847, leaked to the press, suggested that the British army could not adequately resist an invasion force. Decisions taken in this atmosphere included the creation of large fortified breakwaters at Dover and Portland. Experts launched into detailed evaluations of the respective merits of paddle-steamers and screw propulsion.[44] This sense that something fundamental was shifting in the defence of Britain against 'the continent' was paralleled in other spheres. Old assumptions about 'the foreign', 'foreign policy' and Britain were being challenged by different developments whose consequences were unpredictable.

Making fresh tracks

Foreign-policy-making remained a matter for an elite in a system that did not even purport to be democratic.[45] According to critics, it was a conspiracy of the governing classes. Only when that changed fundamentally would a different vision of Britain and Europe emerge. In the meantime, they could only articulate alternative futures through pamphlets and the press.

Probably more newspapers were sold (and circulated) in Britain than in any other European country at this time – sales of London newspapers having risen nearly threefold in 1801–36. 'Liberty of the Press' was a toast to which Whigs frequently drank. After 1824, British governments virtually gave up the idea of press prosecutions (radical journalists, of course, having been their target).[46] Metternich commented, however, that the English government would certainly complain to the French (and vice versa) of the toleration of foreign instigators of rebellion who used the press.[47] The repeal of the newspaper tax or stamp duty came in 1855 (only after that date was it viable to have a daily newspaper published outside London).[48] Meaningful freedom of the press, in mid-century, existed only in Britain, the Low Countries and Scandinavia. The invention of the telegraph in the 1840s made possible the creation of efficient news agencies. Newspapers began to employ regular foreign correspondents. Gradually, therefore, information about 'the foreign' became both more swiftly and more comprehensively available, though the main focus remained domestic. It would be absurd, however, to suppose that the press en bloc was devoted to the dispassionate dissemination of cosmopolitan enlightenment.[49] William Lovett, of the London Working Men's Association, believed that the press in both Britain and France in the 1840s was seeking to fan old animosities into a flame of destructive war. The British press was indeed a factor in the politics of this period and Palmerston, in particular, was assiduous in cultivating certain newspapers.[50] *The Times*, according to Richard Cobden, was 'the most powerful vehicle of public opinion in the world' and, with an average circulation of 38,141 copies per day in 1850, more than doubled the average of its five metropolitan rivals.[51]

There were, however, other major developments that brought 'the foreign' closer.[52] The 'age of mobility' was getting under way. 'Steam and cheap postage', as the Chartist Feargus O'Connor put it, were doing much to produce a situation in which all nations were rushing forwards into one great system of brotherhood. It was now possible to shake hands with America and kiss France (a revealing choice of physical activity?). Travellers in the first three decades of the century were furnished with volumes that gave them necessary information about the sizes, wheels and speeds of various carriages. One such, *The Traveller's Oracle*, devoted the bulk of its pages to travel in the British Isles – it was only a small elite that ventured far into Europe. By 1850, however, extraordinary change was already evident. It was in 1841 that Thomas Cook organized his first cheap excursion.[53] 'Middle-class' travellers began to venture into the unknown Europe in serious numbers (some 50,000 people embarked annually from the British Channel ports in the 1830s).[54] Such 'tourism' was of course facilitated by the transport wonder of the age – the railway. In 1825 Stephenson's Rocket pulled passenger coaches from Stockton to Darlington. Dismissing from their minds Louis XIV's railway of 1714, which ran on rails, used a turntable and was powered by servants pushing with their arms, the railway was perceived by the British as another of their contributions to mankind. By 1850 there were some 10,000 kilometres of railway track in Britain, very nearly as much as the whole of the rest of Europe put together. 'Germany' came next with 6000 and France with 3500 (with very small totals in Belgium and 'Italy'). Travellers could now begin to travel with ease from city to city in Europe. It was, of course, necessary to make the Channel crossing by boat – an experience that in 1843 even the strong stomach of the historian Macaulay found taxing.[55] Baedeker's *Travellers Manual of Conversation* helpfully enabled one to say, in four languages, 'I am very much inclined to vomit'.[56] The Le Havre–Rouen line, sprinkled episcopally by way of benediction at its opening in 1847, was a boon. Palmerston, travelling by train from Leipzig to Berlin in 1844, thought this 'a wonderful acceleration compared with posting'. Travellers were naturally clutching explanatory guidebooks that revealed at least some of the mysteries of the continent. Publishers hastened to provide illustrated accounts that could inspire even those who stayed at home.[57] There was, however, a frankness about what British visitors might encounter. Murray's guide, for example, was anxious to dispel the notion that the south of France was to be conceived as the 'paradise of the troubadours'. The fervid temperament of the people there apparently knew no control or moderation. They were rude in manner, coarse in aspect and harsh in speech. Hasty and headstrong by disposition, they were led, on the slightest pretext, to acts of violence 'unknown in the North'. They seemed to be always about to fight even when merely carrying on an ordinary conversation.[58]

A touch of history

Macaulay probably did not have many guidebooks in his luggage. He had made himself linguistically proficient – he learnt German, as he had learnt Spanish and Portuguese, by beginning with the Bible, which he could read without a dictionary. A spell in Rome had led him, in reviewing Ranke's *History of the Popes* in 1840, to express the view that there never was 'a work of human policy so well deserving of examination as the Roman Catholic Church'.[59] Nevertheless, what really engrossed him was the history of England. His wish to write 'an amusing narrative' resulted in the vastly popular *History of England from the Accession of James II* in five volumes, 140,000 copies being sold in Britain alone. Readers could have little doubt that the history of England and the progress of civilization amounted to the same thing.[60] 'Apologias for the nation-state', and the identification of particular qualities within one's own nation might, of course, be said to be normal across western Europe at this time, though the desire to amuse was not so ubiquitous. Such historiography was matched, in some countries, by an interest in the history of foreign countries that was largely lacking in Britain – no English historian wrote a 'German history', for example, at this time that could be compared with Ranke's *English History*.[61] It would be difficult to find any British writer of this period who was prepared to reflect *à la* Guizot on 'European civilization' and the 'English' part in it. British travellers would therefore be unlikely to be primed to think systematically about 'Britain and Europe'. Such reflections as occurred to them were triggered by specific encounters and experiences. It would be difficult to say what intellectual or cultural reorientations might follow from this invasion, though there were signs that some of the arrivals would be impervious to such considerations. The novelist Thackeray identified the Britons of Ostend as 'for the most part shabby in attire, dingy of linen, lovers of billiards and brandy, and cigars and greasy ordinaries'.[62] There was no doubt, however, that the British were 'coming over' on a scale that showed no sign of diminishing – with impacts both on their hosts and on themselves that could not yet be assessed.[63] Some of them, indeed, so liked what they saw that they stayed, in Paris, Rome or Berlin.[64] The English domestic chaplain to the duke of Cumberland, preaching in Berlin in 1835, expressed his anxiety that 'no adequate provision has been made for the religious wants of that large British population resident in the great cities of Europe'. He was apprehensive 'that foreign accomplishments can be too dearly bought at the expence [*sic*] of those homebred qualities, which, with all the faults of our nation, do still distinguish the *genuine* English character'.[65]

Spreading cities

There were other unsettling 'dislocations', using the word both literally and metaphorically. No one could ignore the 'urban revolution' that was taking place. Robert Vaughan, Congregational minister and professor of history at the new University College, London, published *The Great Age of Cities* in 1843. He attempted to rebut the charge that the great cities were 'the great evil of the age'. He did not dispute that they contained great evils, but anything 'which should diminish everything commercial and civic, so as to place the military and the feudal in its old undisturbed ascendancy, would be a change fraught with more evil than good'.[66] Other writers could find little good in what they saw and yearned for 'Merrie England'. The 1851 census reported an aggregate 'urban' population as narrowly exceeding a 'rural' one for the first time. The Belgian level of urban concentration – the closest comparator – had risen to one person in five, the level Britain had been at in 1801. In the rapidity and extent of her growing population, Great Britain was 'without peer'. There were indeed great cities in Europe but as yet only in Britain could one speak of the urbanization of society.[67] Of course, such a startling if apparently simple fact requires much greater explanation for its true significance to be understood, but there was no escaping that a fundamental realignment of town, city and nation was taking place differently across Britain.[68] Continental Europeans, wondering whether this was also to be their future, came to see for themselves.[69] In 1835 de Tocqueville discovered a civilization that produced miracles but one in which civilized man was turned back almost into a savage. Some 60 or 80 years earlier, wrote the young Friedrich Engels in *The Condition of the Working-Class in England in 1844* (1845) – the book was not translated from German into English until 1892 – England was a country like every other but now, with its capital of two and a half million inhabitants and vast manufacturing cities, it was like no other. It was a 'different nation' from that it had been.[70] Engels' analysis stemmed from his period in England in 1842–44 studying the cotton industry in Manchester. It was that city that was endlessly cited as the prime illustration of this transformation, spoken of with horror or amazement at home and abroad. Its need for untrained labour was 'mainly, if not entirely, supplied by immigrants from Ireland, Wales, Scotland and the English agricultural counties'.[71] Disraeli's 'Coningsby' (1844), who devoted himself for several days 'to the comprehension of Manchester', was forced to conclude that it was 'the most wonderful city of modern times'.[72] It was a city that had come virtually from nowhere. It was a city in England, but was it an English city? The presence of a well-established Armenian community was one reflection of the fact that the Ottoman Empire was taking more Manchester piece goods than all the European countries put together.[73] The German traveller, Johann Kohl noticed Africans, Asiatics and Europeans huddled together in the night asylum against the chilling blasts of an English winter's night. In Disraeli's *Sybil*, published a year later, when Egremont proudly declared that, although they were living in strange times, the queen was nevertheless reigning over 'the greatest nation that ever existed', his interlocutor famously replied that she reigned over two nations between whom there was no intercourse: the rich and the poor. Contemporary writers struggled to find a vocabulary that could encapsulate the relations that obtained in this society undergoing transformation. A world of hierarchy and 'orders' was giving way to one of 'classes'.[74]

New 'addresses'

It is hardly surprising that this rapidly changing scene produced reactions that challenged prevailing assumptions. What if 'class' sentiment subverted assumptions about both 'nation' and 'state'? If England was already, in part at least, 'a different country' and, at some stage in the future, the same transformation would occur throughout Europe, did not another structure have to emerge? An 'Address of the Workmen of Nantes to the English Trades' Unions' appeared in June 1834 in *The Pioneer*, the periodical of the Grand National Consolidated Trades Union, founded in that year under the influence of the anti-capitalist Welshman, Robert Owen. Stating, naturally, that the working classes of all countries were brothers, it suggested that a union between the two trades union organizations would compel a union between England and France, countries in turn that were strong enough 'to play the part of civilizers to all mankind'. Communications should not be stopped by the seas or rivers that marked the boundaries of states. Indeed it was time to put in direct communication with one another London, Paris, Manchester, Lyons, Liverpool, Nantes, Bordeaux, Porto, Lisbon, Madrid, Cadiz, Barcelona and Turin. Although there was then reference to 'all the great centres of industry in the world', that was a rhetorical flourish. It is note-worthy both that no city in 'Germany' or eastern Europe sprang to mind and that the civilizing mission of England and France was not in doubt. The press would be the primary means of such communication but could be sup-plemented, where necessary, by 'the expense of individual correspondence and special messengers'.[75] The response they received was not encouraging. However, this sense that 'the great centres of industry' now shared common experiences and problems that could mark them off from their surrounding national hinterlands was quite widespread. After all, it was not whole coun-tries that were uniformly industrializing but rather particular regions, over-throwing pre-industrial balances of power within them in the process. It was time for this 'new' Europe to align itself against the 'old'.

Over the next decade or so there were elaborations on these themes from various quarters. William Lovett, chief organizer of the London Working Men's Association (LWMA), formed in 1836, claimed that he was the first person to introduce the mode of 'international address' between the work-ing men of different countries. The LWMA addressed 'the working classes of Belgium' and declared the international solidarity of the emerging work-ing-class movements across the continent. In their reply, Flemish workers acknowledged that 'Children of Britain' were forerunners in the struggle to emancipate the working man. They scorned appeals to 'love of country' and knew of no nation 'but the whole world'. Further 'Addresses' to 'the Working Class of Europe' and the 'Working Class of France' followed in subsequent years. The latter, in 1844, called for a 'conference of nations' to settle such disputes as might arise between countries by arbitration, and was explicit in believing that there was 'an identity of interests' between British and French workers. Bronterre O'Brien, at home in French and Italian, vis-itor to France, repeated rich diatribes against the unnatural system of despo-tism and capitalism.[76] It was time for 'the productive classes of all nations' to form their own 'holy alliance'. However, in the years from 1838 to 1842, it is argued that while there were references to European issues in the Chartist press, Europe and European exiles were not of central importance within Chartism as a whole. Chartists felt justified in concentrating upon achieving the 'six points' of the Charter at home because, as Harney put it in 1838, 'The eyes of all Europe were on England ... for if England were made free, every country in Europe would establish the rights of man'.[77] The failure of the great Chartist petition of 1839 suggested that such foreign observers would look in vain. In turn, it led some Chartists to contemplate insurrection and some continental handbooks on street warfare did circulate. When a rising did take place, in Newport in 1839, in which a Polish exile and supposed Russian spy was allegedly involved, British soldiers did not join the insurgents. Regardless of the veracity or otherwise of this involvement, radical Poles, it seemed, were everywhere. They were to be found in all London working-class activities in the early 1840s and the gory fate of Poland was regularly referred to in radical speeches.

It was not only a matter of a Polish presence. While London had not invariably been the most attractive place of exile for those fleeing their own countries under some degree of duress it was safer and seemingly less susceptible to swings of the political pendulum than Paris.[78] The 'fraternization of nations' went on with some vigour, promoted by educational, propagandist and sometimes conspiratorial bodies. One such group, existing in an uneasy relationship with Chartists, were the 'Fraternal Democrats' who printed their motto, 'All Men Are Brethren', in 12 languages. One of the most prominent figures in this world was the remarkable Ernest Jones, born in Berlin, the son of an equerry to the duke of Cumberland, who came to England in 1838 and was to inject a strong emphasis on class. He could speak German to the German Brethren in London, whose numbers were to swell after the disappointments of 1848–49.

Alternative internationalism: Cobden's crusade

A young calico printer (b. 1804), an omnivorous general reader in history, literature and economics, recently and significantly established in Manchester, also had visions. Richard Cobden possessed what he called a 'Bonapartian feeling'. In the early 1830s he spent nearly a year away from England in a period of just over four years. Significantly he visited both the United States and Europe (France, Switzerland, the eastern Mediterranean and 'Germany'). He had earlier travelled in Ireland. America greatly impressed him. Although Europeans tended to patronize it, it seemed likely that it would soon surpass Europe in wealth and power. He scorned the way in which half the educated world in Europe devoted more time to the Lilliputanian states of the ancient world than they did to the modern history of South and North America. It does not appear, however, that his American travel (to New York, Philadelphia, Baltimore, Washington, Pittsburgh for a month) led him to see the United States as alien. 'Boston [is] like an English city – the people like the English,' wrote Cobden. That he should have made such a specific comment testified to the fact that other cities were more undoubtedly 'American'. Cobden's observations may usefully be set alongside those of other visitors around this time.[79] Charles Dickens, for example, in his *American Notes* (1842), saw in many Americans, whom he described as 'restless and locomotive' an 'irresistible desire for change'. Americans were clearly not just transplanted

Englishmen, but on the other hand it was becoming more English, even in New Orleans according to a Scottish traveller, everything that was French, everything that was Spanish was 'being rapidly submerged by the great Anglo-Saxon inundation'.[80] There was a sense, not least linguistically, in which British reactions were different from 'European' but in their reactions to modes of life and manners they tended to be the same. Paradoxes abounded. Despite its size, and the distinctions often drawn between north and south, between merchant and planter societies, de Tocqueville in 1835 believed the whole American nation would one day be assimilated into the civilization of the north. Differences between Maine and Georgia, he supposed, were less than those between Normandy and Brittany. Cobden himself still had many European differences to explore but already felt both that Britain had a distinct mission in the world and that the United States was a beacon of progress.

In two pamphlets, *England, Ireland and America* (1835) and *Russia* (1836?), Cobden set out alternative strategies. In essence, he was suggesting that Britain should make its way in the world through its economic and political progress rather than through military might. It was a mistake to intervene actively in the affairs of Europe. He predicted that the steam engine, at no distant date, would produce moral and physical changes that would surpass the effects of all the wars and conquests known to history. It was England's industrious classes that were influencing the civilization of the whole world and teaching surrounding nations 'the beneficent attachment to peace', though the textile industry in Saxony might soon present a real challenge. It was the government of Prussia, so simple and economical, 'so deeply imbued with justice to all and aiming so constantly to elevate mentally and morally its population', that most impressed. He contrasted it favourably with the flummery of the English constitution, its church-craft, sinecures, armorial hocus-pocus, primogeniture and pageantry. Its educational system meant that people in Prussia did not live in that condition of deep ignorance to be found in the English population. It is interesting to note that, at the same time, Lovett railed against Prussian centralization in education – control over teachers, superintendents, teaching methods and books crushed in embryo all the buddings of freedom. Cobden liked being in a Protestant state and would at least have been in agreement with Lovett that, in contrast to English cities on the sabbath day, it was possible to find rational and enjoyable recreation.[81] He was not enamoured of priestcraft, whether in Ireland, where he had encountered it, or Poland. Where the latter country was concerned, he unusually considered that sympathy for the revolt was misconceived. It had been an enterprise of the Polish aristocracy. Polish peasants were better off under the Russians. In instance after instance his refrain was that Britain was not called upon to preserve the peace and good order of the entire world. Above all, while hostile to the St Petersburg government, it would not be a disaster if the tsar came to rule in Constantinople. Such an outcome would not threaten the security of the rest of Europe. The Russians would be tied down by the task of both subduing and improving the conquered backward territories. The 'balance of power', so beloved of British diplomacy, was 'an undescribed, indescribable, incomprehensible nothing'.[82] On his return from his travels, he threw himself into the campaign of the newly founded Anti-Corn Law League and was elected to the Commons. His 'speaking lieutenant' was the Quaker, John Bright (b. 1811), who had similarly travelled in Ireland, Belgium, 'Germany' and the Levant.[83] The repeal of the Corn Laws in 1846 cannot simply be put down to the work of the League, nevertheless it was a significant achievement for two coming men. They believed that a new era for Britain, Europe and indeed the world, was dawning. With the fall of Peel's government, however, they were faced by the return of a foreign secretary from an earlier era – Lord Palmerston had been in government before Bright had been born – one who showed little disposition to be converted to their way of thinking.

Afforded the means of travelling as their missionary, Cobden now declared himself willing to be 'the first ambassador from the People of this country to the nations of the continent'.[84] The free trade principle, he believed, would change the face of the world and introduce a system of government entirely different from that which prevailed. The desire for large and mighty empires, for gigantic armies and navies, would die away. His extraordinary tour of Europe began in August 1846 and ended in October 1847. This time he was emphatically a celebrity. His first evening in France saw him being received by Louis Philippe and he subsequently had audiences with the kings of Naples, Piedmont and Prussia, and with Pope Pius IX as well as with leading ministers in all the states he visited. After three weeks in Paris he spent three months in Spain, thence to 'Italy' via Mediterranean France. In the summer he travelled through Austria and Saxony to Prussia. He then spent a month in Russia and came back to England via the Hanseatic ports of northern Germany. It was a programme packed with interviews, lectures and banquets – the accolade in the last named going to Hamburg where 700 sat down to dinner. *The Times* described him as 'the undiplomatized but not unacknowledged internuncio of a new economic creed, which his country was the first to profess. He has been received with the respect due to an ambassador, and the reverence which belongs to a discoverer'. It was not altogether clear, however, in continental capitals, that 'free trade' should be greeted with reverence. Was it not merely a means of ensuring British hegemony?[85]

It was more difficult to say what this new European 'celebrity' had achieved. He was very well aware of the extent to which his crusade to extend free trade could be represented as a strategy to extend British domination of the world economy. He stressed that he spoke as an individual without official ties, but this did not altogether convince. He had no patience with the idea that infant industries needed initial protection. Half of him hated meeting the ministers and diplomats he had to meet. Metternich, for example, he dismissed as 'probably the last of those state physicians who, looking only to the symptoms of a nation, content themselves with superficial remedies from day to day'. That sort of order of statesmen would pass away 'because too much light has been shed upon the laboratory of governments, to allow them to impose upon mankind with the old formulas'. Cobden could not fail to notice, however, in some instances, that the banquets that were ostensibly to honour him were in fact being used by their organizers for political purposes of their own. He had set out as a self-conscious 'middle-class man' from Manchester but 'the middle class' of Europe, which he sought to energize, was a very capacious category and by no means straightforwardly attuned to his priorities. 'Liberalism' could mean very different things in different contexts. Whether the *Zollverein*, the customs union that had started in Germany in 1834 under Prussian leadership, constituted, from the British perspective, an encouraging tendency or posed a threat, was not a straightforward issue.[86] There was, too, an arrogant naiveté in his 'economism', his apparent belief that the issues with which 'old diplomacy' dealt, were not issues of any significance. In short, he returned to England impressively armed with facts and figures, and possessing an 'on the ground' knowledge of what was happening in Europe (within which Russia was of course to be included), but with a limited understanding of the extent to which issues of national identity, for the moment, had greater resonance. Mazzini, for example, detested the Cobdenites. 'Your Peace Societies,' he wrote in an open letter to 'the people of England', in 'allowing God's law and Godlike human life to be systematically crushed on the two-thirds of Europe ... seem to me to be the reverse of religious'.[87]

Cobden's underlying assumption, shared by some other writers and activists, was that the peaceful order he so much desired was being obstructed by governments and the vested interests that lay behind them. The predominant emphasis in Britain was upon the role of an enlightened public opinion rather than upon the creation of alternative structures – for example, federations. The 'peace movement' of the 1840s contained diverse strands of opinion, chiefly revolving around the extent to which a commitment to peace was 'absolutist'. The strands were, with difficulty, reconciled. The chief lines of contact and communication, certainly on the part of those with religious convictions, were across the Atlantic. There was ongoing debate on the purpose and nature of arbitration treaties, a Congress of Nations and 'general disarmament'. There was a struggle between 'pacifism' and 'pacificism', as there was between free trade supporters, who believed it a vital ingredient of a peaceful order, and those who saw the issue of free trade as distinct. To a considerable degree, 'Anglo-America' was on one side of these arguments and 'the continent' on the other.[88] The former recognized, however, that if the continent were to be 'conquered' for peace, accommodations in language and objective would have to be made. The Peace Congresses of Brussels (1848), Paris (1849) and Frankfurt (1850) attracted considerable attention, though sometimes only to have them dismissed as 'utopian'. It could not be denied that the British role, both in organization and in participation, was absolutely crucial, and totally overshadowed the 'continental' contribution. At the Paris Congress, for example, where Cobden was one of the star speakers (in French), there were 670 delegates from Britain, 130 from France and Belgium, and only a total of 30 from the rest of Europe.[89]

It was, however, Victor Hugo (b. 1802), poet, dramatist (and son of an army general), who presided at the Paris Congress. He held out a vision of a day when those two immense communities, as he put it – the United States of America and the United States of Europe – would hold hands across the sea. France, Russia, 'Italy', England and 'Germany' would, without losing their distinctive qualities and glorious individuality be blended into a superior unity and constitute a European fraternity. He also airily referred to 'other nations' but, perhaps prudently, did not identify them. Normandy, Brittany, Burgundy and other provinces had been assimilated in France. The same thing would happen within Europe. Hugo's was an expansive aspiration, but not unique. It chimed in with federal proposals of one kind and another emanating from various continental quarters, though chiefly French, over the previous decade or so.[90] Many of them had not been inclined to include Russia, believing that it was destined to form a unity of its own (and, so far as one could see, would remain an autocracy). French Comtist enthusiasts thought that western Europe, which was held to comprise England, Germany, Spain, Italy and especially France, should constitute the initial federation. Ultimately, when all fear had been abolished, France could be divided up into 17 republics. Saint-Simon too had believed that France and England, together stronger than the rest of Europe, should help it reorganize itself.

Such sentiments and proposals were not strongly echoed across the Channel, although Robert Owen emerged in October 1848 to state that Europe 'should, as speedily as practicable, without violence, become one people, with one language and one interest, having one general government'. When that happened there would no longer be talk of Great Britain, France, Germany etc., but only of Europe and Europeans. Owen did not explain by what means one language was to prevail, but 'common sense' would no doubt have suggested that it should be English. A European Congress, consisting of delegates elected in each state by universal suffrage would frame a constitution and a code of laws.[91] Sir Harry Hinsley has highlighted the divergence between continental and 'Anglo-Saxon' opinion. Most European thinkers thought the Anglo-Saxon peace movement too limited and sought the union of Europe as much as, if not more than, they sought peace. There was some suspicion of a free traders' plot to unite Europe before it was reformed and republicanized.[92]

Britain: 'far behind' or 'in front'?

Matthew Arnold, the 25-year-old private secretary to the Whig grandee Lord Lansdowne, Francophile young poet and devotee of George Sand, came to the conclusion in 1848 that England was 'in a certain sense *far behind* the Continent'. Its intellectual isolation, as he conceived it, arose from 'the sheer habitual want of reading and thinking' and too great a faith in England's practical virtues. Many observers, including Sarah Austin, translator of Ranke, were among those who contrasted the organization of intellectual life in Germany with the universities of at least England. (Scotland might be different.) On the other hand, by and large, by not producing so many graduates, England had avoided that 'excess' of educated but perhaps unemployable intellectuals that some historians suppose to be found elsewhere in western Europe.[93] Adopting as his own a thought of Lamartine, young Arnold concluded that '100 years hence the Continent will be a great united Federal Republic, and England, all her colonies gone, in a dull steady decay'.[94] His father, Thomas, the redoubtable Dr Arnold, headmaster of Rugby, had often taken his family across the Channel and had been struck by 'the total isolation of England from the European world'. Conversations he had had led him to conclude, 'We are considered like inhabitants of another planet, feared, perhaps, and respected at many points, but not loved, and in no respect understood or sympathized with'. Englishmen, likewise, little appreciated or wished to imitate the 'intellectual progress' of Europeans. It was a fact, however, or so he thought, that 'England has other destinies than these countries'.[95] It would be 'voluptuous enjoyment', he reflected on Lake Como in 1829, to settle in Italy – something that had perhaps occurred to the British painters and sculptors who made it their home and who were sometimes loath to return to their origins. It was possibly the case, however, that an element of 'voluptuous enjoyment' could be introduced into England.[96] Arnold later reflected that if he had ever been obliged to quit England it would be in Germany that he would settle.

Unlike other Europeans, however, Britons had not been obliged to quit their own country and seek 'a second home' somewhere else in Europe. If they had been, it would have been likely that the majority would have joined Thomas Arnold in Germany. The 'boundless World of Thought' that was Germany leaked steadily into the Victorian mind through Coleridge and Carlyle, and was to be carried on by G.H. Lewes, who embarked on his life of Goethe. 'George Eliot' began learning German in early 1840. In 1846 she published her translation of Strauss's *Leben Jesu (Life of Jesus)*. Published in German in 1835, it was a work that caused enormous debate. Orthodox critics in England and Scotland found it another example of misplaced German rationalism. English churchmen, said Hugh James Rose, in *The State of Protestantism in Germany*, sermons preached in Cambridge, should beware 'that large party of men in Germany who, calling themselves Christians, have shown an anxious desire to get rid of all that is supernatural in Christianity'.[97] Even so, whatever might now be happening in Germany, its Protestantism was what still strongly commended it. 'Who would take the trouble to learn German', Macaulay asked in 1849, 'if it were not for what the Protestant part of Germany has produced?'[98] That was in line with his impartial verdict that Edinburgh, over the previous two centuries, had added more to the sum of human knowledge than the whole of southern Europe. At another level, the German connection was strengthened by the marriage of Queen Victoria to Albert of tiny Saxe-Coburg, a 'pumpernickel state', as the novelist Thackeray called it, though anonymously, in *Punch*, in 1840. 'I shall never cease to be a true German', the departing Prince had written as he left for London. Radical newspapers could not understand why the queen had chosen a German when so many young, generous and handsome Englishmen surrounded her. The Coburgs, according to the *London Dispatch*, were 'alien by birth, alien in principles, alien by education, alien by German prejudices and German predilections to all that is free and just in Britain'.[99] Albert, only 21, sought to overcome these indisputable shortcomings by hunting pheasants and hare with Sir Robert Peel in Windsor Great Park.[100] And, since it had long been apparent that Germany had to supply insular musical requirements, Albert, no mean organist, facilitated a continuing supply. Mendelssohn made no less than 10 visits to Britain in his short life and Queen Victoria accepted a dedication of his 'Scottish' symphony in 1843. Of course, from the standpoint of governments, there were complications arising from the German connections of the royal house (though Queen Victoria had not been able to succeed in Hanover) at a time when the future of 'Germany' in a political sense still remained very unclear. It had been noted from Frankfurt in early 1836 that 'the Customs Union gives the real power in Germany to Prussia' but, on the whole, most British envoys in the German territories did not oppose the idea of Prussia constituting a buffer zone in the middle of Europe. The reality remained that the states that made up the Confederation were very heterogeneous. British foreign secretaries could not do much more than watch and wait for the political Germany of the future. They could not create it.[101]

Whether 'England' was 'far behind' or 'far ahead' of 'the continent', therefore, admitted of no simple answer. Strands of cultural contact and communication pointed in different, sometimes contrary, directions and, however strong the German link at this particular juncture, it was by no means the sole stream. Predictably, however, it was substantially a 'traffic' between the great linguistic/cultural blocs of Europe, mirroring though not necessarily correlating with the diplomacy of the Great Powers: English, French and German, with walk-on parts for Italian or Spanish. That the Russian contribution to the European exchange, in so far as it was made, was not expressed in Russian, literally spoke volumes. Exchange required translation and even when it was entrusted, as it frequently was, to women, who could say whether there was real understanding?[102] Louise Creighton, translating Ranke's *Englische Geschichte*, felt constricted by his wish that it should be very literal. Examples could be multiplied. A famous breakfast took place in London in 1843, christened the 'Babel breakfast', when Ranke and Macaulay, amid a confusion of tongues, could not get through to each other. And, though the 'Great European' world did not acknowledge it, or did not appear to need to acknowledge it, there were other languages and cultures to add to the variety of Europe that, somehow, would have to be accommodated. When Palmerston visited Prague in 1844 he thought he was visiting a German city. Half a century later, he would have found it different.

So it was also the case within the United Kingdom, most notably in respect of Ireland where 'Repeal of the Union' had been an issue in British–Irish politics in the first half of the 1840s before the catastrophe of the famine and the migration of some million people from Ireland in the period 1846–50 added a new and tragic dimension in the relationship between the two islands. The reaction of British governments to this event, to put it no more strongly, constituted a standing reproach when seen from the continent. It usefully undermined infuriating British 'moralism'. Yet 'Young Ireland' in 1848 was a derisory rebellion when contrasted with what other 'Young' movements achieved, however briefly, elsewhere. And Mazzini, apostle of national liberations, did not think the Irish should qualify for such exalted status. It was right that they should protest against any violation of their human dignity, but he did not suppose that a true Irish nationality existed. The Irish could not 'plead for any distinct principle of life or system of legislation, derived from native peculiarities, and contrasting radically with English wants and wishes'.[103] Certainly, involuntarily or voluntarily, the Irish presence became an increasing presence in the life of Britain. In political terms, Chartism attracted a large number of recent immigrants and was sometimes portrayed as an Irish conspiracy. But it was not only in respect of Ireland that diversity was hidden behind the bland use of 'England'. In the 1840s rural west Wales, where the Welsh language was dominant, was sometimes perceived in London to be rebellious and disconcertingly alien. The 'spin' put on the state of Welsh culture and education in the Education Report of 1847 confirmed in Wales that the English were alien. The Cambrian Archaeological Association, founded in 1846, set about the arduous task of trying to discover what Wales really was. And in Scotland, the harmony of Mendelssohn's royal symphony hardly corresponded ill with the discord of that year, 1843. The 'Great Disruption' occurred within the Church of Scotland, reducing it, with profound repercussions in Scottish life, to a minority 'establishment'. Even a Scottish Presbyterian foreign secretary, Lord Aberdeen, was powerless to prevent it. As for the English, it seemed increasingly likely that they were indeed Saxons, perhaps still groaning under a Norman yoke. Matthew Arnold thought that in Ireland the government was trying to uphold a body of 'Saxon landlords' and a 'Saxon Church Establishment'. That left Thomas Carlyle, as a Scot, free to lambast Saxons as drunkards 'lumbering about in pot-bellied equanimity'. Clearly, there were matters here requiring clarification now that there was a real Saxon as the royal consort.[104] In short, in microcosm, the United Kingdom was itself a mirror-image of the Europe of which, in respect both of unity and diversity, it was a part.[105]

Yet there was a difference, perhaps a growing difference. 'Location' in Europe was important, so was the 'balance of power' in Europe but the world was changing. It was Cobden who remarked that 'the Equilibrium of Europe was a phrase of some significance when the whole world was in Europe'.[106] In 1839–42 Britain was fighting the first of the 'Opium Wars' with China and, under the 1842 Treaty of Nanking, was ceded the island of Hong Kong. An Englishman became rajah and governor of Sarawak in November 1841. Two British armies entered Kabul in Afghanistan in late 1842. The first Sikh War began in December 1845. A future for Aeoterea/New Zealand was established under the 1840 Treaty of Waitangi. And there were many other indications of British activity worldwide. Most notably, however, there was the United States, with which, in relation to border disputes with Canada and other matters, British relations were tense. The two countries could even, in 1847, have gone to war again. Europe may have been successfully frozen again after the drama of 1848–49, but in another 'thaw' in the future Britain was even more likely to be conscious that the whole world was not in Europe.

6

More mapwork, c.1850–c.1870

Exam questions

The Foreign Office, in 1871, under pressure from the Treasury and Civil Service Commissioners, produced an examination to assess the capacity of nominated applicants for posts. After all, unlike recruits to the Diplomatic Service, who were understood to have private incomes, these men were to be paid. There were eight compulsory papers – spelling, arithmetic, précis-writing, English composition, French translation, dictation and conversation, Latin, German translation, and a general intelligence test. Further, candidates with a knowledge of Books I to IV of Euclid could shine, though there was also opportunity to be tested on the constitutional history of England. In addition, there was a combined paper on European geography and history (1783–1847). This was more demanding than the qualifying test that had reluctantly been instituted in 1855. That had prudently not involved anything 'of a puzzling character'.[1]

There were, however, a number of matters that might have puzzled the young British minds of 1871 if they reflected – though not, evidently, for examination purposes – on what had been happening since 1847. Their map of that year would now require revision. It was in the Hall of Mirrors at Versailles on 18 January 1871, following the Prussian defeat of France, that the assembled German princes proclaimed King William IV of Prussia German emperor. A deputation from the German federal diet had asked him to take this step a month earlier. The creation of the German Empire, which saw the end of Bavaria and Saxony as independent states (Hanover had been annexed by Prussia in 1866), brought about a profound change in the structure not only of central Europe but, by implication, of Europe as a whole. Not that this empire embraced all of what might be regarded as 'Germany' – the southern boundary of the empire marked no 'national' frontier. Austria, which had been defeated by Prussia in the war of 1866, had been excluded from the German confederation; whatever 'Germany' was to be, it was clear that Austria would not have a significant role in shaping it. After 1867, its hybrid character had become more explicit following the 'compromise' (*Ausgleich*) which established that the Habsburg sovereign ruled in Austria as emperor (*Kaiser*) and in Hungary as king (*König*). 'Dualism' was a complicated structure that identified matters of common concern to both halves of the empire – foreign affairs, military affairs and finance – but which then left competence over all other matters to 'Austria' and 'Hungary', each possessing its own prime minister and government. Quite how this division of responsibility would work in practice was another matter.

The map of the Habsburg Empire had changed in the south, in stages, by the incorporation of Lombardy and Venetia into the new 'kingdom of Italy' whose Piedmontese monarch found himself, unexpectedly, in possession of papal Rome, when Napoleon III was forced by the Franco-Prussian War in 1870 to withdraw his protecting troops. It was time for Rome to become the capital of Italy. These cartographic changes were frequently taken by contemporaries to represent the achievement of German and Italian 'unification'. The history that these changes embodied, however, would require more demanding attention from aspiring Foreign Office men. It was scarcely likely that the assumptions made about Europe in 1850 would hold good after 1871.[2]

One historian has gone so far as to conclude that mid-century 'Britain was scarcely in any sense at all a "European" power'. It would have been impossible, he writes, for Britain, as it then was, to have become part of the continent, as it then was, without changing her social and economic structure and her political nature fundamentally.[3] Our evidence in the preceding chapter has lent some support to that contention, and much in what follows in this chapter confirms it, yet the statement is too blunt. In so far as it holds true, it may do so only if the emphasis is placed on 'power' rather than on 'European'. Whatever role the United Kingdom was playing in the world, whatever extraordinary characteristics possessed by its economy and society, it was still inescapably a part of the unfolding complexity that was Europe itself. It is noteworthy that it was only the geography and history of Europe, and that of no other continent, on which the young would-be Foreign Office men were examined. When the time came, in the late 1850s, to erect an appropriate Foreign Office building, the resulting 'battle of the styles' was a European one. It fell to Disraeli in 1868 to open the Venetian palace that Palmerston had insisted on. The great double staircase and huge reception rooms were another indication of a grandeur that was European, and could not fail to impress. There were, certainly, aspects of the United Kingdom's situation that, in many quarters, suggested self-sufficiency and pointed to a 'special way' (*Sonderweg*) – but that was only one part of the story. In the early 1850s, a sequence of apparently unconnected 'set-pieces' enables us to glimpse how, directly or indirectly, in various modes and at various levels, the United Kingdom 'positioned' itself: the death of the Duke of Wellington (1852), 'the Don Pacifico Affair' (1850), the Great Exhibition

(1851), the 'Papal Aggression' (1851). The mingled confidence and confusion displayed in these episodes provide the background to the stance occupied by Britain in Europe in the two decades that followed.

Saying farewell to Wellington

The death of the Duke of Wellington on 14 September 1852 took the nation by surprise, though *The Times* prudently had his obituary at proof stage. He was 83 and had lived long enough to enable the political antagonisms of 20 years earlier to be largely obliterated. In the opinion of Queen Victoria, England had lost 'the greatest man she ever had'. The prime minister, Lord Derby, wrote to his son to say that the nation would wish to pay 'every tribute of veneration to the greatest man of this age'. It took some time to make appropriate arrangements for the funeral, which took place in St Paul's cathedral. The procession to the cathedral took two hours to pass. Crowds turned out in their hundreds of thousands. Large congregations also assembled in churches up and down the country. No one, other than a sovereign, had ever been buried with comparable magnificence. 'The last great Englishman is low,' wrote Alfred Tennyson. The Dublin *Freeman's Journal*, a nationalist organ, pointed out that the London crowds 'saw in that car the bones of their greatest warrior and statesman; but they ought to have seen more – the remains of an Irishman who had won them an empire'. However, the panels commemorating his victories had still not been inserted, for lack of funds, around the base of his monument in the city of his birth. In sermons and addresses across the United Kingdom there was much reference to 'the end of an era'. Prince Albert, in private correspondence, mourned the decline of 'the Spartan virtues' and lamented the current rule of 'Calico and Cant'. Other correspondents, noting with some apprehension that there was now another Napoleon in charge of France, thought it no bad time to recall the coalition that had defeated his great uncle. The vicar of Leeds, Walter Hook, encouraged his congregation to 'glory in the fact that we are Englishmen, and remember that as Englishmen we are to set an example to the world'. It was, however, the London-based Scottish Presbyterian minister, John Cumming, who stated that Wellington 'had occupied a larger space in our history, in our successes, in all that constitute that beloved thing which we call *country*, than any other man for many a day'.[4] The 'example to the world', or at least to Europe, displayed in the recent past, however, was puzzling in its mixture of pugnacity and peaceful progress.

The little world of Don Pacifico

In June 1850 the House of Commons was asked to confirm that the principles on which the foreign policy of Her Majesty's Government had been regulated had been such as to maintain the honour and dignity of the country, and 'in times of unexampled difficulty', to preserve peace between England and the nations of the world. It was a motion in the name of the Radical, John Arthur Roebuck. The debate was occasioned by the controversy caused by Palmerston's conduct in the 'Don Pacifico' case. In April 1847, a Portuguese Jew (or perhaps he was Spanish), 'Don Pacifico', had his house in Athens pillaged by a mob, possibly an anti-Semitic one, and looked for very substantial compensation. He appealed to Palmerston for help, claiming British citizenship on the grounds of having been born in Gibraltar. The foreign secretary was already vexed with the Greek government for defaulting on an earlier British loan. In addition, a British subject named Finlay had not been compensated for the confiscation of his garden to make way for a new royal palace in Athens – a Scots historian, engaged on a history of Greece from the Roman conquest to the present, was not going to let that pass lightly. King Otto, the Bavarian prince who now ruled Greece as an absolute monarch, was very good both at building palaces and displaying indifference to the financing of them. It was irritating, too, that the Greek government sympathized with rebels in the Ionian islands. Palmerston sent a fleet that would, if necessary, blockade Athens in order to gain compensation for Don Pacifico, a man of doubtful integrity. The upshot was that the Greek government capitulated. 'A slight scrimmage' was how Palmerston described these developments to the cabinet. The other guarantors of Greek independence, however, Russia and France, considered the British reaction excessive and made their displeasure known (the French ambassador was withdrawn from London). In the House of Lords, earlier in June, protectionists and Peelites combined to pass a vote of censure on the government's handling of the Greek affair. It was this result that led to Roebuck being put up to introduce his general motion in the Commons which, in the event, after five nights of speeches, was carried by 310 votes to 264.

There had been some manoeuvring to remove Palmerston from the Foreign Office, a step that would have pleased the queen because the hatred in which he was held 'by all the Governments of Europe', as she put it, was placing the country in serious danger. However, as he sat down amid 'loud and prolonged cheers' Palmerston knew that he had carried the day and was indispensable. A speech that lasted some four hours – a gigantic intellectual and physical effort Gladstone called it – cannot readily be summarized in a few lines. Its conclusion, that as the Roman had held himself free from indignity when he could say *Civis Romanus sum* (I am a Roman citizen) so also 'a British subject, in whatever land he may be, shall feel confident that the watchful eye and the strong arm of England, will protect him against injustice and wrong', exemplified its tone. The only other government speaker, the prime minister, dubbed Palmerston 'the Minister of England'. Relations with the court were patched up and Lord John's government wobbled on. In the event, however, despite his status as hero, Palmerston did not survive long in office. He had let it be known to the French ambassador in London, though not to the British ambassador in Paris, that he approved of Louis Napoleon's coup in Paris in December 1851, an approval of what would be an arbitrary and absolute government that surprised his own admirers. Palmerston's action, whether by design or not, produced a political storm, Lord John required his resignation for this precipitate conduct, a step that relieved the Crown of trying to obtain it. This time Palmerston had stepped out of line once too often. The Austrian chancellor hurriedly arranged a ball in Vienna to celebrate the news. It was widely thought in Britain that his long career was at an end. So it was to prove, as a foreign secretary, but after serving as home secretary, he returned as prime minister in February 1855 in a ministry that lasted three years, and again served in this role from 1859 until his death in 1865. The 'Palmerstonian era' was not yet over.[5]

However much it was occasioned by the specifics of the 'Don Pacifico' affair, Roebuck's motion invited a general review of the conduct of British foreign policy. Palmerston was not reluctant to provide it. The creation of an independent Belgian state had fully and completely succeeded. The Portuguese and, indeed, the Spanish question had been presented as a question between absolute government on the one hand and constitutional government on the other. Britain had taken the proper constitutional side but, professedly, had no desire to exercise a controlling influence. Spain was for the Spaniards. Then came the question of 'Italy', a topic that always excited more eloquence than Belgium. Palmerston contrived to condemn both violent and hot-headed 'revolutionists' and those whose antiquated prejudices prevented the 'timely application of renovating means'. The reference was to the mission undertaken in 1847 by his Edinburgh student friend, Lord Minto, allegedly at the request of the pope. Palmerston denied that Minto had been exciting revolutions and that Britain had then abandoned the victims it had deluded. Despite this robust defence, the foreign secretary's meddling in the peninsula – there had also been de facto encouragement of Sicilian rebels against the King of Naples – had hardly produced a beneficial outcome.[6] Palmerston was having to make the best of a bad job. It was the faithless new president of France, Louis Napoleon, who had restored the pope to Rome and whose troops remained there. It was an action that gave him the support of Catholic France and satisfied his faithful wife. The Sicilian rebels had been suppressed. The old order had been restored, with the additional hazard that a once 'liberal' pope had seen the error of his ways. All of this, however, did not appear to hinder the foreign secretary's triumphant reception.

Distinguished parliamentarians had spoken against him in vain. Sir Robert Peel remonstrated (in what was to be his last speech before the riding accident that killed him) against the mischievous use of diplomacy – his own son was serving in Switzerland, a country, internally riven at this juncture, that had also received Palmerston's attention. Britain should not interfere with the domestic affairs of other countries unless there were circumstances that directly affected its interests. It would be a great mistake to declare in favour of the principle of self-government. Who would construe its basis? How would Britain feel if other powers sought to inculcate the right of self-government among the people of India? Finally, as events seemed to have proved, interference did not work, Cobden spoke in similar and predictable terms. The progress of freedom in Europe depended more upon the maintenance of peace, the spread of commerce and the diffusion of education than upon the labours of cabinets and foreign offices. Gladstone, too, exposed without difficulty and to his satisfaction the absurd excess Palmerston had displayed in the Greek affair. He then advanced a more general critique of British policy under Palmerston. It was right that other countries should know of the 'inestimable blessings' that derived from the 'free and stable form of government' in Britain, but propagandism was wrong. Interference in foreign countries should be 'rare, deliberate, decisive in character and effectual for its end'. The analogy with the Roman citizen was dismissed. He had rights then that were denied to the rest of the world. Surely the foreign secretary did not wish to place his countrymen in that category?

It was a powerful, if verbose, contribution from a man who was only a child when the Vienna settlement had been made. Still only 40, Gladstone had already wrestled with issues of identity, allegiance, belief, structure and power to an extent more normal political colleagues regarded as inordinate. It might be gratuitous and arbitrary to meddle in the internal concerns of other states, but he himself had long been meddling mentally with the question of Europe, and his convictions were still evolving. When he sat down in 1850, few suspected that it would be this awkwardly able but still largely untried young man – within days to be deprived of his political guiding light, Sir Robert Peel – who would be confronting the 'new Europe' of 1870/71 as prime minister of the United Kingdom in the first 'Liberal' government.

The specific issues fastened on during this debate were almost exclusively 'European'. The argument was that Palmerstonian 'meddling' gratuitously offended European states, big and small. Opposition to his policy united men whose opinions were otherwise very diverse. Yet it was difficult to pin the man down. There was no secret about his opposition to any further electoral reform but he could also play to the liberal gallery. Palmerston, by his bullying and bragging, was the Devil's son – a sentiment expressed in German. It is easy to see how this perception could arise on the continent. Yet perhaps his contemporary British critics failed to grasp, as Palmerston had done, that there was a new mood abroad. The Great Powers, having survived 1848/49, were no longer 'satisfied' and perhaps could again risk war to achieve greater influence or territory – and could only do so at the expense of one of their number.[7] In such a circumstance was 'non-interference' an absolute? It would not be long before matters were put to the test.

The Great Exhibition, 1851

The full title of a great display held in Joseph Paxton's Crystal Palace – a vast technological marvel – in Hyde Park in 1851 was the 'Great Exhibition of the Industry of all Nations'. Needless to say, the full title was not commonly used but its formal employment encapsulated a certain ambiguity as to 'ownership'. That it was being held in Britain was testimony to the great industrial and commercial country that Britain was (even if half of the population of England and Wales was still 'rural' in 1851). The extent of its apparent (and acknowledged) pre-eminence can briefly be indicated in various ways. Britain was by far the largest international trader. Its imports (frequently subsequently re-exported) constituted between 30 and 40 per cent of the exports of the rest of the world. Put starkly, Britain was the richest country in the world in the 1850s and, around 1860, it is likely that the per capita incomes of the UK, France and Germany were, respectively, £32.6, £21.1 and £13.3. Gross national income has been estimated at £523.3 million in 1851 and £916.6 million in 1871.[8] Britain excelled in the 'staples' of cotton, coal and iron, and was a formidable exporter. The pattern of that trade is illuminating. In 1860, for example, in comparison with France, the Netherlands and Belgium, more than two-thirds of whose trade was with other European countries, only two-fifths of British trade was European (21 per cent in North America, 15 per cent in Asia, 9 per cent in South America, 6 per cent in Africa, 5 per cent in Australasia).[9] As a percentage of gross national wealth, overseas assets doubled between 1850 and 1870 to reach nearly 12 per cent. In the same period, Europe as a region for UK overseas investment more than halved, falling to 25 per cent in 1870.[10] These and other indicators explain why Britain should host a great exhibition of industry in 1851.

It is important to remember, however, that it was to display the industry of *all* nations and that it was Prince Albert, with his 'great mind', as the queen put it, who had been the domesticated Teutonic driving force behind this great 'peace festival' – the same great mind that tried to push the University of Cambridge in the direction of reform.[11] One half of the Crystal Palace was devoted to the exhibits of Britain and her empire, with the other half reserved for foreign displays – besides Britain only France displayed a colonial possession (Algiers).[12] Albert had had to use his personal connections with foreign monarchs to get their countries to exhibit. How 'Germany' was to be 'represented' raised particular difficulties at this juncture.[13] *The Times*, in October 1849, commenting on the prospect of an exhibition, remarked 'We are an island and want international communication. Our merchants and gentry go abroad upon business or pleasure; but the great bulk of the people know the nearest nation of the continent only by name'. No doubt the six million people who visited the Crystal Palace knew rather more about the continent at the conclusion of their visit. *The Times* also recognized that, despite 'the inexhaustible energy of our race', 'the want of native taste' could only be acquired by communication with those who possessed that precious gift.[14] Perhaps that meant France – just as 'science' and chemistry in particular meant 'Germany'. British students were to be found in Liebig's laboratories at Giessen.[15] If the Great Exhibition, in the area of its concerns, did in the event modify the island to the satisfaction of *The Times* it did not do so simply by becoming 'part of the main'. Through the smog of British industry could be glimpsed not merely a continent that had perhaps been 'cut off' but, according to Albert, 'the Unity of Mankind'.

For the moment at least, London led the way to the future. Its predominance in Europe, with a population of 2,685,000, was even more marked in 1850 than it had been in 1800. Paris, its nearest rival, just topped the million mark. Vienna, St Petersburg, Berlin and Naples fell just short of half a million. Other capitals, Amsterdam, Brussels, Lisbon, Madrid, contained just under or just over a quarter of a million, while Budapest, Stockholm, Copenhagen, Turin and Warsaw did not significantly exceed 100,000. Athens, Belgrade, Christiania (Oslo) and Sofia had yet to reach 50,000. London was truly in a different league.[16]

Paris, however, was unwilling to accept that pre-eminence rested on population alone. Indeed it was the French capital that 'took over' future world's fairs, beginning in 1855.[17] Accompanied by Prince Albert, Queen Victoria came to Paris in that year. It was, however, to see the exposition rather than to receive the crown of France (it had been in 1430 that the last English monarch had come to Paris – and with a crown in mind). Little Bertie had his first, but by no means his last, experience of France. The Palace of Industry could not compare with the Crystal Palace, but the latter, being shunted out to Sydenham, had lost its capital impact. Nearly twice the number of people attending the Great Exhibition of 1851 attended the Paris world's fair of 1867 (at which the number of British exhibits was smaller than the Turkish or Italian).[18] Monarchs and princes, the greatest being the king of Prussia and the tsar of Russia, flocked to Paris.[19] Not without underlying political purpose, Paris 'underwent an unprecedented transformation in its physical and social geography, its economic life and its population', according to the vision of Napoleon III and his agent, Georges Haussmann.[20] Although Brussels, for example, had also been rebuilt on a grandiose scale, the two cities of Europe were undoubtedly London and Paris. In political and economic terms, the former had no doubt that it was supreme, but the latter became '*capitale du plaisir*', to the delight of British visitors (the largest foreign group). In the eyes of one contemporary French writer, Paris had the mission of being 'the entertainer of Europe', attracting 'the European upper-crust' to itself.[21] It was not a fate that London could easily emulate.

Roman returns

Nicholas Wiseman, newly made Cardinal, travelled triumphantly out of the Flaminian Gate of Rome in October 1850 to take up his appointment as archbishop of Westminster on the restoration of the Catholic hierarchy in England and Wales. He proceeded from Florence, Siena and Venice to Vienna (where he was dined by the Austrian emperor). It was an appointment that, according to *The Times*, 'was one of the grossest acts of folly and impertinence which the Court of Rome has ventured to commit since the Crown and people of England threw off its yoke'.[22] In 1845, John Henry Newman had left the Church of England, a step that confirmed, apparently, that 'Tractarianism' led ultimately to a 'Roman' conclusion. James Bryce met Newman in Birmingham 20 years later and wrote, revealingly, that he found him 'still an Englishman more than a R. Catholic'.[23] Lord John Russell, personally preferring 'the Roman Catholic foe to the Tractarian spy', was determined to promote an Ecclesiastical Titles Act, which he asserted to be a step to preserve national independence, not to restrict religious liberty. Both the pope and Wiseman were burned in effigy in some places as Protestant pulpits fulminated against 'papal aggression'. The bill was carried by a massive 'Protestant majority' in 1851.[24]

The 'return of Rome' raised issues that went beyond the theological differences that separated Roman Catholics and Protestants. 'Britain', in aggregate, had long displayed a Protestant face. England (and Wales) had the Church of England as its 'national church'. More than that, it was Protestantism that gave Britain its 'northern' alignment in Europe. Southern Europe had apparently decided that the time was ripe to bring England back to the bosom of Rome (and perhaps that meant the spiritual centre of European civilization). Pleading for more missionaries to join him, the Italian passionist Father Dominic Barberi thought that English influence, energy and might far surpassed that of any other nation and the only thing it lacked to become the finest nation in the world was possession of the Catholic faith.[25] It seemed evident that most Englishmen did not share that view. Even if the Catholic faith did have any virtue, the condition of its 'headquarters' scarcely commended it. An Englishman in Rome, Macaulay had found in December 1838, had an agreeable time but he could think of nothing more insupportable than the position of a layman who was a subject of the pope; a few years earlier young Gladstone had thought there was 'every absurdity involved in the idea of an ecclesiastical sovereign'. The states of the pope he supposed the worst governed in the civilized world.[26] Writing from Rome in December 1847 the later Lord Kimberley became

> more convinced on the extreme errors and superstitions of the Roman Catholic Church every day that I live here and no one who does not come to the headquarters of Roman Catholicism can form a true idea of what it is when thoroughly carried out.[27]

If he had ever wanted to stop himself turning Romanist, Lord Blatchford felt 'Rome is the place I should fix myself in'.[28] The Free Church of Scotland minister in Livorna (Leghorn) – where some 200 Scots were resident – reported home on the gruesome treatment meted out to Italian Protestants in Tuscany and elsewhere. James Bryce, on leaving England for Rome in 1864, thought that he might very possibly turn Catholic there but concluded, after living in the city, that Rome only made Catholics of the weak.[29]

State and church

More was at issue, in these reactions, than the competing claims of Roman Catholics and diverse Protestants to embody authentic Christianity. The 'confessional state' was crumbling fast. In 1851, alongside the decennial census, an attempt was made to count the number of 'attendances' at places of worship on a particular Sunday. It revealed that in England and Wales, taken together, half the population did not worship anywhere. The established church attracted just under a quarter of the population, while the remainder worshipped elsewhere. The Church of England was still substantially larger, and had more even coverage, than the next denomination (the Wesleyan Methodists) but it was with difficulty, though not for want of trying, that it could maintain itself as 'the church of the nation' in such circumstances. And if 'the nation' was taken to be 'British', its religious diversity was now statistically transparent. In Wales, dissent, though itself fragmented, was in a clear majority, and the way was open for challenging the establishment. The prospect of a revived alliance of church and state was having to be abandoned. In Ireland, the position of the Church of Ireland was unacceptable both to Roman Catholics and Presbyterians. In short, in the diverse United Kingdom, it could no longer be expected that Christianity could be reliably conveyed through church establishments that were in some sense arms of the state.[30] Finding it intolerable that a secular court could decide on theological issues (the Gorham baptismal case of 1851) Henry Manning and a number of other leading Anglicans embraced the Roman Catholic Church.

The stresses and strains produced by these dissolving relationships had a profound significance. Although the 1851 religious census was found dispiriting by the British churches, the level of attendance was significantly higher than in parts of continental Europe.[31] It could plausibly be maintained, comparatively speaking, that the United Kingdom was a Christian country. Even so, the markers of allegiance and identity were shifting. While, for many upright Englishmen, to be loyal to the Church of England ran *pari passu* with loyalty to their country, that overlapping allegiance could no longer be automatically assumed and certainly not on the part of the inhabitants of the United Kingdom as a whole. The spheres of religious belief and political allegiance were separating across Europe, if at different speeds, with unpredictable consequences.[32]

Gladstone makes up his European mind

No man tried harder to find firm ground in these shifting sands than William Gladstone. The march of events had compelled him to abandon the intimate relationship he had set out in *The State in its Relations with the Church* (1839). His original Toryism, too, had been gravely damaged. The 'progress of the democratic principle', he had written in March 1844, was becoming 'continually more formidable'. If government, he had also written, was no more than the representative of the people it had no duty to perform other than to reflect the popular will. It had no right to express its own preference for any particular religion, or indeed for religion at all.[33] But if this was so, what, if anything, gave coherence and 'meaning' to 'national' existence? Oscillating between an emphasis on authority and on liberty, Gladstone struggled – even while wrestling with finance in such a demanding post as chancellor of the exchequer (1852–55) – to bring into equilibrium nationalism and internationalism, a splintered 'Christendom' and that 'democratic principle' that would have to be satisfied even if its triumph could dissolve any coherence of value or belief within states.

Earlier, in 1832, visiting the battlefield of Waterloo, he had felt it right that an Englishman's heart should 'beat high with exultation' and this sense of 'national destiny' never left him. Yet it was matched by a 'European sense', steadily fed by reading, correspondence, acquaintance and travel, which made him distinctive. He became fluent in French, German, Greek and Italian.[34] Although he placed the blame for the schism in western Christianity firmly upon Rome, as he wrote on his first visit to St Peter's in 1832, it was there, so he himself noted some years later, that he had experienced 'the first conception of unity in the Church' and had first to have longed for its visible attainment. Such an object appeared hopeless in every human sense, but no less to be desired. So perhaps it also was with the unity of Europe. Being in Italy made one think long term. As James Bryce put it, reflecting on his own visit to Italy in 1864/65, 'one is weighed upon by the notion of time'. Monte Cassino, happily referred to as 'the All Souls of monasteries', spoke of a Europe before 'England' or 'Scotland' existed. Gladstone, too, had a sense that the past, in Italy, was so long and eventful that it became a perpetual present.

The present of 'Italy', however, had to be redeemed. In 1850, visiting Naples, he had seen liberals in prison and returned to write pamphlets against the Neapolitan regime. Infamously, it was 'the negation of God erected into a system of government'. He had earlier immersed himself in Dante.[35] When Gladstone agreed to become chancellor of the exchequer in 1859 he shared an enthusiasm for the Italian cause with his prime minister who, a year later, described unification as 'miraculous as no one in his senses or in his dreams cd [*sic*] have anticipated such continuous success'.[36] Gladstone had a kind of Italian conversation with Garibaldi during the soldier's extraordinarily popular visit to London – his fourth – in April 1864. It is argued that this affair strengthened the government and contributed to the Liberal revival that led to the election victory of 1868 when Gladstone became prime minister.[37] Rome, now as the capital of a 'united' Italy was not something he had expected when he had first visited the city.

Gladstone's southern European attention was not confined to one side of the Aegean. In 1858 we find him in the agitated Ionian islands (reaching there via Brussels, Berlin and Vienna) as high commissioner. Gladstone's desire to familiarize himself with Orthodoxy allegedly led to him being 'obsequious to the half-barbarous priests of Corfu'.[38] His formal task, however, was to identify Ionians of 'station and intelligence' who could be persuaded to resist the immediate allure of *enosis* with Greece and sample the 'peaceable and steady exercise of local liberty', which continuance of British rule could surely provide. Naturally, in the Aegean, his mind also turned to Homer, the object of lifelong study and reflection. Over a period of 45 years, he wrote a series of articles on Homer and no less than five books, one of them consisting of three volumes and containing more than 1700 pages. No other European statesman matched such devotion. In 1886 Gladstone was to record that he was reading the *Iliad* for perhaps the thirtieth time – every time, apparently, more glorious than before.[39] It was not certain, however, that scholarship on this scale greatly assisted the resolution of the contemporary problems that a British prime minister encountered in south-eastern Europe.

Crimean War

The events of 1848/49 had left Russia in an unexpectedly strong position. It was the only great power in continental Europe whose government had not been overthrown. It had assisted the Habsburgs in suppressing revolution in their domains, particularly in Hungary. 'One of the Emperor's distinguished Generals', as Queen Victoria felt obliged to describe the Austrian General Haynau, had played his full part in this process. He received a thrashing from the workers at Barclay's brewery in Southwark when he injudiciously paid a visit there in 1850. It was an expression of a strengthening feeling, at both popular and official levels, that Russia, as the friend of Prussia and the protector of Austria, saw itself as the arbiter of Europe. Russia might still be economically and technologically backward but, on two fronts, its expansion could threaten western Europe on the one hand and the integrity of the Ottoman Empire on the other. Additionally, from a specifically British perspective, there was a supposed threat to India from Russian expansion in Asia. From the perspective of the new ruler of France, causing the northern powers to fall out could offer his country the opportunity to play that major role in Europe that had been denied since 1815. Napoleon backed the claims of Roman monks over Greek Orthodox monks concerning the holy sepulchre and other 'holy places' in Palestine. The tsar wanted his voice to be heard in the matter.

In April 1853 Russia declared its protectorship over the Orthodox Christians within the Ottoman Empire. Exchanges between the powers concerned were further complicated, on the British side, by differences within the coalition government presided over by Aberdeen. In July, having threatened to do so for several months, the tsar occupied the Danubian principalities. In October, the sultan declared war on Russia, although the European Great Powers continued to negotiate.[40] At the end of November, a Russian squadron sank a Turkish fleet – an action denounced by the British government as a violation of the tsar's pledge that Russia would remain on the defensive. The cabinet could not easily decide what to do next – Palmerston briefly resigned, ostensibly in dispute about parliamentary reform, but triumphantly returned. Some thought that a blow against Sebastopol would be 'memorable in Europe' and 'settle the affairs of the East for some time to come'. Others were dubious about the legality of a British presence in the Black Sea. Britain and France then presented (separately) *ultimata* to the tsar requiring Russian withdrawal from the Danubian principalities. He did not think it proper to make any reply. Britain and France, having concluded a formal alliance treaty with the Ottoman government, declared war on 27/28 March 1854. The British objective, declared the foreign secretary, Lord Clarendon, was to secure a peace honourable to Turkey. If Russia were to come into possession of Constantinople she would also subjugate Circassia and Georgia. Graphic pictures were painted of massive Russian power, but privately British ministers could not agree about the kind of settlement to be sought. Palmerston urged substantial territorial adjustments, including the restoration of Finland to Sweden, the re-establishment of a substantial Poland, and the Crimea and Georgia given to Turkey – an outcome, he conceded, that presupposed great defeats of Russia. Even so, Russia would remain an enormous power, but one far less advantageously posted for aggression on her neighbours. Aberdeen thought that such a programme would require another Thirty Years War in Europe. Indeed, it was far from clear how and where Russia was to be attacked. Russian withdrawal from the principalities (which were then occupied by Austrian and Turkish forces) could have led to a negotiated settlement, but there was now a determination, both in London and Paris, to achieve a substantial military success. The Crimea, substantially Muslim and far from the centre of Russian power, would be the place to start. The fighting, however, did not go well, as newspaper correspondents reported in detail. The 'Charge of the Light Brigade' in October 1854 was a tragedy. A prolonged siege of Sebastopol began in November – it was to last until September 1855 – and the conditions in the trenches were appalling.

In these exceptional circumstances, in February 1855 Palmerston, at the age of 70, became prime minister, replacing Aberdeen, who had never been wholeheartedly behind the war. The Commons and the country were looking for an outcome that would make the suffering worthwhile. Yet 'all Europe' had not joined Britain and France – Piedmont, which joined in January 1855, was not quite an equivalent. Austria and Prussia had remained neutral. Vienna was the scene of negotiations, but there was no immediate conclusion. Palmerston's preference was to go on with the war, but French enthusiasm waned. Despite Queen Victoria's warm reception when she visited the *Exposition Universelle* in Paris, there remained a smouldering ambiguity in British–French relations. The capture of Sebastopol in September 1855, achieved more by French than by British arms, led Napoleon to want a settlement. The Austrians were eager to be intermediaries – too eager from the standpoint of London. Palmerston had ultimately to follow the French and Austrian lead.

The location for the negotiations was significant. The British would have preferred a neutral city, perhaps Brussels or Frankfurt. They rejected Vienna. The eventual selection of Paris had a symbolic significance that was not altogether congenial. It did, however, reflect a prevalent view elsewhere in European diplomatic circles that France had been the chief beneficiary from the struggle. Napoleon's mediatory role was thought likely to be crucial. There was satisfaction in Paris that France was again becoming 'the pivot of the diplomacy of the Governments of Europe'.[41] The congress was concluded in a little over a month with the signature of the Treaty of Paris on 30 March 1856. The clause from which Britain drew most satisfaction was the neutralization of the Black Sea (and Russia promised not to establish military or maritime arsenals on the coast). In fact, however, 15 years later, the Franco-Prussian war gave Russia an opportunity substantially to modify these restrictions. The Danubian principalities (Wallachia and Moldavia) gained Bessarabia from Russia and the prospect of a united 'Romania' was opened up – Austria had refused to exchange north Italy for them. The navigation of the Danube was open to all nations.

This settlement scarcely corresponded to the more sweeping territorial changes that Palmerston had envisaged in March 1854. Perhaps only he could have carried the actual outcome with a public opinion that remained in a generally belligerent frame of mind. The pacificist enthusiasms that had been embodied in the peace congresses over the previous half dozen years, had collapsed. The peace movement, at the 1853 Edinburgh Peace Congress, had seen itself as 'becoming an important social power in this country' but the limits of that power had swiftly been made manifest.[42] Cobden and Bright in vain urged non-intervention. Bright considered the danger posed by Russia to be a phantom and British love of civilization a sham. Manchester, however, no longer proved to be a citadel of the peace party.[43] When a general election came in 1857, Cobden, Bright and other leading members of the Manchester School lost their parliamentary seats. Kinglake, the historian of the war, was not alone in blaming the 'peace party' for encouraging the belief that for the future Britain would always be 'tame' in Europe. Bright suffered a complete breakdown in his health and was out of action for some two years.[44] 'Cobdenism', as it had already been labelled, no longer appeared to make inexorable progress. Even so, the debate that had been started did represent one further stage in thinking in Britain about international relations. What had Britain achieved by going to war? What did its outcome mean for 'Europe'?

Unifying disorder?

The most obvious consequence of the war appeared to be that Russia could no longer be the military guarantor of conservatism on the continent though, as was shown in 1863 in putting down another Polish insurrection, it could still contain rebellion within its own sphere. In European terms, one might even speak of Russian 'withdrawal'. The emancipation of the serfs (1861) would, among other things, pave the way for a modern mass army. Although there were changes in the structures of governments in the 1860s, they scarcely amounted to a parliamentary system. In any case, some intellectual voices continued to doubt whether parliamentarianism suited the Russian soul. Pan-Slavists posited a fundamental incompatibility between what they described as the Roman-German and Slavic cultural-historical types. So perhaps, as Danilevskii wrote in 1869, 'Russia' and 'Europe' could not come together.[45]

It was a view echoed in Britain. Europe, for Richard Congreve, one of the 'positivists' writing on the foreign relations of England in 1864/65, was 'The West'. Russia was an eastern not a western power, or more eastern than western. It had not, as a nation, shared in Greco-Roman culture, and that was decisive, whatever the 'western' elements in her court and government (Poland, by virtue of Catholicism had become 'western'). For Congreve, the five Great Powers that together constituted 'western Europe' were France, Italy, Spain, England and Germany (which should be formed from a 'merger' of Austria and Prussia).[46] It was an academic analysis, separate from, but nevertheless congenial to, that popular Russophobia that still lingered. Congreve also excluded Turkey, though he believed it to be more 'western' than Russia, having been far more intimately bound up with the history of Europe. Notwithstanding this assessment, however, British travellers on the perimeter still recognized an 'Oriental city' when they saw one, and certainly when they smelt one.[47] Whether in Salonika, Cairo or Algiers, it seemed, however, that a kind of Europe was extending. It was to Algiers that John Bright went to recuperate from his breakdown. Cobden followed in 1860. Looking down on its bay, however, Frederic Leighton, the painter, (an inveterate traveller round Europe) realized that he was 'in no European land' despite the fact that the lower town had been so completely 'Europeanized' that one might fancy oneself to be at any French seaport town.[48] 'We will never renounce this conquest', Napoleon III had declared of Algiers in 1852. In Egypt work on the Suez Canal, backed by France but opposed by Britain, began in 1859 and it was opened a decade later in the presence of the Empress Eugénie. Was all the Mediterranean littoral becoming 'Europeanized'?

Another positivist writer, Frederic Harrison, concluded that the relationship between 'England' and France constituted the heart of this 'West'. 'Northern' and 'southern' Europe, respectively, looked to them for guidance. Particularly without the 'protector', which Russia had been in 1849,

Austria had already been shown to be vulnerable. The shape of European civilization would only finally be resolved when the 'German question' had been settled, but Harrison was unusual in having no difficulty in recognizing that in 'the system of western Europe' France was 'the centre'. The Parisian press, publicists and jurists could alone be called common to Europe. If politically and morally Europe could be said to be one whole – and he assumed that it could – then the instinct of the greater number pointed for its centre to be Paris. No other country in Europe, his encomium continued, was as wonderfully cohesive and perfectly homogeneous as France. The obvious answer was the union of 'England' and France (which could, of course, include Algiers, with its restorative climate).[49]

Such a proposal, as Harrison recognized, would have been rejected by many if not most of his contemporaries. Whatever might be said – and not infrequently, in various quarters, it was said – about the key relationship of Britain and France, at this particular juncture in European dealings between the two countries could swing alarmingly between amity and hostility. Young George Otto Trevelyan, an eager 'volunteer' at Cambridge, was not impressed by the French liberal society he dined with in Paris in 1862. The French, he thought, had an intense ignorance of everything that was not French. The only English author known around the dinner table was his uncle Macaulay.[50] Even so, looking at a variety of evidence, at one level, it has been concluded that 'by the close of the Second Empire, the two peoples were better informed than at any period in their history about each other's manners, habits and general way of life'.[51] Matthew Arnold, for one, found conversation with a cultivated Frenchman like Saint-Beuve infinitely preferable to an encounter with an English Philistine. It may be, too, that there was a more indulgent attitude, in this period, towards the perceived national idiosyncrasies of both countries. Such careful cultivation of respect, however, could not disguise political divergence and unpredictability – on both sides of the Channel. In 1859 fears of a French invasion gave rise to a volunteer movement in Britain that expanded rapidly over the next few years. Naval rivalry remained strong, though in the later 1860s it had less of a bi-polar character as both countries had to reckon with the growth of navies worldwide. Nevertheless, Palmerston put in hand naval expansion and further dockyard fortification.[52] On the other hand, after protracted exchanges, a commercial treaty to reduce tariffs was signed in January 1860. Cobden, who had a special role in the negotiations, saw such an agreement as 'God's own method of producing an *entente cordiale*'.

Part of the problem lay in the person of Napoleon III. 'Our friend is an odd little chap', Lord Clarendon observed, with massive English condescension. 'It is impossible not to like him'. That was not a universal view. Dickens, for example, thought of him as a 'cold-blooded scoundrel'. Napoleon's regime was frequently portrayed as corrupt and oppressive – and the thought that, in foreign policy, he would seek to emulate his uncle was never far away.[53] For his part, having lived among them in several spells, Napoleon did not dislike the English – though, if he had had any option, he would not necessarily have chosen Chislehurst as a place to die. He thought, however, with good reason, that where Europe was concerned he had the upper hand.

Concerning Italy, cavorting with Cavour, he sent French troops to assist the Piedmontese in May 1859, after Austria had been provoked into attacking Piedmont. Within the space of a year, Italy was 'unified', with the exception of Rome and Venetia, though few could have predicted the actual sequence of events. It was one that was closely followed by British ministers, not least for its bearing on papal sovereignty. Britain emerged as a 'friend of Italy' but throughout showed no disposition to intervene directly on behalf of the Italians.[54] Suspicion of Napoleon remained too strong. Indeed, writing privately to the Prince Consort, the former prime minister, Aberdeen, took the view that Austria was 'fighting the battle of Europe'. It was whimsical, to say the least, he thought, for Britain to join a cry against the bad government of Austria in Italy to the advantage 'of the very power which at this moment we dread more than any in the world'.[55]

France, not Britain, led 'the West' in the continuing re-emergence of a Balkan Europe. Napoleon presided over the transition, in stages, of the Danubian principalities of Moldavia and Wallachia to a 'Romania' equipped in 1866 with a hereditary ruler, a German but with an adequate dash of French blood, recognized by the sultan, although still under his suzerainty. Bucharest could perhaps become another Paris, in a country anxious to establish its 'Roman' credentials. Elsewhere, some French support was also offered to Prince Michael of Serbia, in his periodic clashes with Ottoman forces, by persuading the sultan to dismantle some garrisons. Paris was very aware of the volatility in the region and the potentially competing claims of different peoples. The British involvement remained chiefly with Greece. In 1854–57 Britain and France occupied Piraeus, the port of Athens, to restrain zealots who wanted to take advantage of the Crimean War to enlarge the territory of Greece. Even the attentions of Mr Gladstone had not calmed the Ionian islands. The tactless, childless and still Catholic King Otto was ousted in a coup in 1862. He returned to Bavaria but could be seen in Munich (a city that had allocated a central church to a Greek Orthodox congregation) wearing traditional Greek dress. He was replaced, not by the second son of Queen Victoria, as many Greeks apparently wanted, but by the grandson of the King of Denmark, who became King George of the Hellenes (a title that indicated a claim to the allegiance of all Greeks, many if not most of whom still lived outside Greece) in 1864. He was essentially the British candidate, into whose safe hands the Ionian islands were conveyed. However, he proceeded to marry a Russian grand duchess and name his son Constantine – an obvious indication that his heir would, one day, reign in the capital that shared his name. Britain gave no encouragement when Cretans, proclaiming union with Greece, rose in revolt. In 1870, the murder of a party of kidnapped British aristocrats, on an excursion from Athens to Marathon, by 'brigands' caused a diplomatic crisis and served further to erase lingering phil-Hellenism.[56] Greece remained 'a fit object' for the application of the beneficent protection of 'western Europe', as Congreve put it, but could scarcely be thought to be part of it.[57]

The Polish and Danish questions raised different but analogous issues. Napoleon contemplated intervention to support the 1863 insurrection. His cousin Jerome sent him a memorandum urging that it could provide the prelude to a redrawing of the map of Europe. Eventually, other initiatives having failed, he sent out an invitation in November 1863 to all European rulers to attend a congress in Paris to 'lay the foundations of a general pacification'. It never took place. The upshot was that the Polish insurrection was contained and Russo-French relations were strained. It is not surprising that when war between Denmark on the one hand and Prussia and Austria, backed by Russia, on the other, broke out in 1864 over the claims of the former to the duchies of Schleswig and Holstein, there was no common British/French position. It had become evident that, whatever his particular successes, Napoleon could not effectively play the role of arbiter of Europe.

The stance of Britain was one reason why he could not do so. The cabinet had, with unnecessary bluntness, snubbed his plans for a congress to consider Poland. Lord John Russell, now foreign secretary, had declared earlier that neither the obligations, the honour nor the interests of England required the country to go to war for Poland. In relation to the duchies, he had hinted in July 1863 that if anyone interfered with Danish independence 'it would not be Denmark alone with which they would have to contend'. There was serious talk, a year later, of sending a British fleet to Copenhagen at this time, in support of the Danes (contrary to normal practice), but it was never despatched. An additional complication, from the government's standpoint, given that the constitutional position of the duchies constituted an impenetrable mystery, was the marriage of the prince of Wales to the daughter of the heir-presumptive to the Danish throne. British diplomatic involvement, in short, was intense but to little benefit. There was a fear that Napoleon might attack the Prussian Rhineland and conceivably threaten Belgium. Under the Treaty of Vienna of October 1864 the Danes surrendered the duchies to Prussia and Austria. A year later, still prime minister at the age of 80, Palmerston died. It would not fall to him to handle that dénouement of the 'German question' that could be imminent.

Leaping in the dark

The pervasive unease in British public life in these years, which lies behind the expressed commitment not to intervene directly in the localized wars which now seemed to be becoming prevalent in Europe, stemmed from different sources. The performance of the British army in the Crimean campaign scarcely inspired confidence in its capacity, should it be called upon, to take part in a conflict in Europe. Better not to call upon it for this purpose. There were calls enough worldwide. Even so, at the close of the Congress of Paris, Britain did conclude a secret treaty with France and Austria, which committed it to upholding the integrity of the Ottoman Empire by force. Then the Indian Mutiny of 1857 brought a further shock to assumptions of easy predominance in the subcontinent. There had also been a war against Persia. In the immediately following years, British forces were to be found storming the emperor's summer palace in Beijing as the climax to disputes with China. In the former instances, Napoleon had not exploited Britain's difficulties and, in China, Britain and France worked together. Then a second Maori war broke out in New Zealand. There remained, too, issues concerning the extent of British involvement in the 'responsible government' now being established in British North America and in the Antipodes. The Canadian federation was set up in 1867 and the notion of a 'dominion' established, if somewhat uncertainly.

The crisis of confidence, even within an 'age of equipoise', had other aspects. It was not too difficult to suggest that there was something seriously wrong with British government and administration. Gladstone, who had resigned from the Cabinet during the Crimean War, now referred to the glorious conventions and institutions of the British constitution as a 'heap of absurdities'. Continental theorists, who hitherto had thought that they had understood (and admired) the constitution, failed to grasp that it was really an antiquated muddle. In politics, economics and military affairs, these were indeed 'years distinguished by a multitude of undecided battles and inconclusive contests'.[58] The 'adjustment' of 1832 no longer had the appearance of a full and final settlement. Gladstone's pronouncements in 1864 on electoral reform, although Delphic, had been sufficient for the University of Oxford to feel that he should not represent it in the Commons. The death of Palmerston, the 'unmuzzling' of Gladstone and the oratory of John Bright brought about a climate in which 'reform' was back on the agenda. It fell to Derby's minority Conservative administration, formed in 1866, to produce, by protracted process, the Reform Act of 1867, which increased to some 36 per cent the proportion of adult males enfranchised in England and Wales (separate legislation for Scotland and Ireland followed). It was this electorate that gave the Liberals their clear majority in the general election of 1868 and made Gladstone Liberal prime minister.

Disraeli, now leader of the Conservative Party, had famously described this step as 'a leap in the dark'. There was much contemporary discussion of 'democracy', as though it had arrived. It was an open question whether the political parties would survive in their existing form in the new era that was apparently dawning. And what would it mean for the conduct of foreign policy, still largely formulated and executed within narrow circles? Would this electorate be indifferent to 'foreign' issues? Would its presumed lack of 'culture' solidify an existing insularity in relation to 'Europe'? Would the conventions of aristocratic diplomacy, which in some sense still oiled an increasingly fractious state-system, survive into an era in which there would be likely to be a demand for the 'democratic control' of foreign policy?

Gloomy answers to these questions were not lacking, both from dyspeptic intellectuals and from operators within 'high politics', but there was also optimism in other quarters. If one believed the radical banker and politician, George Grote, Athenian democracy rather than the Roman Empire or the establishment of Christianity was where 'European civilization' began. After decades of work the first volume of his *History of Greece* had appeared in 1846. Grote saw little appealing in kingship. To democracy alone was owed, as he put it, the unparalleled brilliancy and diversity of individual talent that constituted the charm and glory of Greek history. He advocated a Britain (and a Europe) that would epitomize the values of civic humanism. The year after the publication of his history, Grote had dashed across to Switzerland because he saw there, in its troubled condition, the fifteenth century in immediate juxtaposition with the nineteenth, and identified analogies with his own historical investigations.[59] Gladstone, troubled by Grote's republicanism and lack of Christianity, immersed himself in Homer to try to rebut his conclusions.[60] Contemporaries joined in the struggle to find a 'democracy' in the Greek past that might serve as a model for nineteenth-century European civilization, indeed constitute its very essence. More prosaically, fearing that 'more means worse', they sought ways in which 'interests' might be represented. Specific seats might somehow be reserved so as to ensure efficient administration. The university seats could not be relied upon to this end. It did not prove easy, in short, to agree on what democracy in Britain (and Europe) might be. Did Napoleon III's mixture of universal suffrage, plebiscites, authoritarianism and unrepresentative government qualify?

Bismarck, Prussia and Germany

Otto von Bismarck, newly appointed minister-president and foreign minister of Prussia in 1862, took a dim view of British developments. The 1832 Reform Act, he supposed – in 1856 writing to the Prussian juridical expert, Leopold von Gerlach, when representing Prussia at the German Confederation at Frankfurt – had 'deposed' statesmen and aristocrats, and wise direction of British policy had become impossible. Gerlach had visited England in 1844 and 1852 to study its legal institutions, but seems to have supposed that the country was a divine-right monarchy because people cheered 'God save the Queen'. Prussia, Gerlach thought, had no need to adopt representative government, which had only arisen because of peculiar English circumstances.[61] Bismarck suspected that the wisdom embodied in the hereditary principle had been lost and only 'the people', with their bare and passionate egoism and their lack of knowledge of continental

conditions, remained. The English had been a great nation as long as they
had been ruled *despite* their constitution, but it now looked as though constitutionalism was going to be taken *ad absurdum*. His views on the dangers
of public opinion in England had solidified over 20 years. It became his standard doctrine that England's foreign political relationships were more
volatile than in all other states because they depended on elections and their
consequent majorities.[62] The English themselves, however, he had to admit,
were really rather likeable. He had inevitably read Shakespeare, Byron and
Scott in his youth. More dashingly, he had fallen, unsuccessfully, for several
young Englishwomen. More exotically, he considered joining the British
army in India. He paid one visit – to inspect industrial Lancashire.[63] The
business of statecraft, however, could not be determined by such personal
likes and dislikes.

Our consideration of the British reaction to the Danish crisis of 1864 has
already indicated that there was no willingness to contemplate armed intervention. Bluff and bluster was no substitute, as events had demonstrated.
But, quite apart from the question of capacity to intervene, the dramatic rise
of Prussia and the unfolding, in some form, of a unified Germany, did not
arouse any pervasive or fundamental anxiety in government or official circles. It was certainly not strong enough to shift opinion away from established perceptions. Only days before his death, Palmerston was writing that
Prussia was too weak to be independent in her action. He thought it desirable that 'in the aggregate', Germany should be strong 'in order to control
those two ambitious and aggressive powers, France and Russia'. He warned
Russell that the power of Russia would in due time become almost as great
as the old Roman Empire. Germany ought to be strong to resist Russian
aggression, and a strong Prussia was essential to German strength.[64]

Whether Palmerston would have approved of the way Bismarck asserted
Prussian strength over the next five years is another matter.[65] Historians will
continue to debate at length the mixture of strategy and opportunism in the
course Bismarck followed in the years after his death.[66] In March 1866
Prussia inflicted a crushing defeat on its erstwhile partner, Austria, at
Königgrätz. Foreign secretary Clarendon reported to Queen Victoria that it
was the cabinet's view that the country would not tolerate any direct interference in a quarrel with which it had no concern. Neither English honour
nor English interests were involved. He continued to believe that there was
no army in Europe that could be compared with the French. Clarendon's
Conservative successor, Lord Stanley, took a very relaxed attitude towards
the possibility of a war between France and Germany. Such a conflict would
be disagreeable but it would not be dangerous. Disraeli, now his prime minister, had famously remarked, as Austria was being defeated, that Britain
now 'almost systematically' declined to interfere in the affairs of the
European continent. It was not averse to intervention as such. It did so in
other parts of the world, but that was because it was 'really more an Asiatic
Power than a European'. It is scarcely surprising that there was no change

when Clarendon came back as Liberal foreign secretary in 1868. His successor from June 1870, Lord Granville, had a shot at mediation but his approaches have been dismissed as more appropriate to solving a dispute over fishing rights than one between major European powers.[67]

The most reflective, though scarcely dynamic, commentary on 'Germany, France and England' came in an anonymous article in the October 1870 issue of the *Edinburgh Review*. It happened to be written by the prime minister in a secrecy that was supposed to be absolute, but that soon became known. It argued that a new law of nations was taking hold of civilized mankind. The enthronement of the idea of public right 'as the governing idea of European policy' would be a triumph loftier than electricity and steam. The aggression of France was censured as was any greed that Germany might display. It fell to Britain 'to found a moral empire upon the confidence of the several peoples'.[68] Such doctrine, accompanied by certain practical steps, perhaps preserved the independence of Belgium, but did little else. Between Gladstone and Bismarck there was no meeting of minds.

The subsequent course of European history has sometimes led to the belief that failure to prevent the rise of Prussia, and the accomplishment of a kind of German unification, pointed to a particularly anaemic period in the conduct of British foreign policy. Despite the observations that have been cited, it is inferred that Palmerston would have intervened effectively to prevent both. If that means militarily – naval power was of little value in the circumstances – it is difficult to believe that it could have been done successfully. Such speculation, while one can see what prompts it, has little value. At the time there seemed no good reason to suppose that a united Germany constituted a particular danger either to Britain specifically or to the prospects for European stability in general. According to Congreve, Germany was only the central state of Europe if you looked at a map and allowed Russia and the eastern elements to be part of political Europe. It ceased to be if, as he wanted, you excluded them. In that case Germany would be at the margin of a western Europe whose geographical and political centre would happily be France.[69] Whether that applied culturally, however, might be another matter.

By the 1860s most leading critics – R.H. Hutton, Matthew Arnold, Walter Pater and Leslie Stephen, for example – learned German as a matter of course. What came from Germany was no longer automatically associated with bad taste, immorality and mysticism.[70] Baron Bunsen, Prussian minister in London, had become 'an ingratiating and controversial figure in English religious and intellectual life', liberally dispensing wisdom from Carlton Terrace.[71] His thoughts on the constitution of the church of the future had aroused the interest of Anglican broad churchmen. There was less reaction to his thoughts on Egypt's place in universal history. No more agreeable intermediary could be envisaged, married as he was to a wealthy Englishwoman he had met in Rome. Her sister initiated him a little into

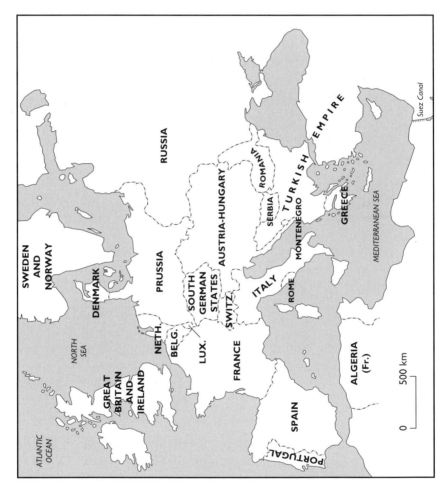

4. Europe in 1870, before the Franco–Prussian War

matters Welsh. At another level, the heir to the Prussian throne – and now emperor-to-be – had married the eldest daughter of Queen Victoria. It was not '*every day* that one married the eldest daughter of the Queen of England', Her Majesty had remarked at the time.[72] Bismarck saw trouble if his future queen remained the least bit English. She might be a blessing only if she became a Prussian.[73] In fact, of course, the death of her husband Frederick was to nullify both hopes and fears for the significance of this royal wedding. This sad event joins the unknowns – what would have happened if someone other than Bismarck had been in charge of Prussian policy or if France had intervened in the Austro-Prussian war of 1866 – that could have altered the course of German history, and the course of British–German relations.[74]

Overall, the balance of 'informed opinion', with historians in the van, favoured Prussia rather than France.[75] Goldwin Smith, erstwhile professor of modern history at Oxford, admittedly now safely ensconced in Canada, wrote to Friedrich Max Müller, the German philologist installed as a professor in Oxford, to say that 'Germany is the hope at present of European civilisation'. More than any other country, she was 'under the dominion of the knowledge and the ideas on which the edifice of the future is to be built'.[76] The Cambridge historian, J.R. Seeley, was taking the view that in the organization of research the example to be followed was that of Germany. William Stubbs, Smith's successor at Oxford, had no doubt that the English were 'a people of German descent in the main constituents of blood, character, and language [and] in the possession of the elements of primitive German civilisation and the common germs of German institutions'.[77] Yet, while England might, substantially and satisfactorily, be Teutonic, Matthew Arnold believed that there was 'a Celtic element in the English nature, as well as a Germanic element'. Saxons, he proceeded to elaborate, got things done. They busied themselves with doors that opened, and with windows that shut. The Celtic temperament was mercurial, permeated by a passionate and penetrating melancholy and, presumably, indifferent to draughts.[78] And if there was a Celtic element in the English nature, there was indubitably a Celtic element in the United Kingdom that could be caricatured if not characterized.[79] Englishmen and a few Germans were at one in exploring the foreign in Wales.[80] Whatever substance, if any, these stereotypes of 'races' possessed – and they seemed an inescapable pastime – the hybridity of the state became more apparent in post-1867 United Kingdom politics.[81] It remained 'hypocrisy' in relation to Ireland on which continental critics chiefly fastened but it seemed that Mr Gladstone's new administration was about to take that matter in hand.

Matthew Arnold sought to send English readers scurrying to appreciate the delightful tales in the Welsh *Mabinogion* (his own interest having been stimulated by the French scholar, Ernest Renan) but he also had a stark message. He believed that the fusion of all the inhabitants of these islands into one homogeneous, English-speaking whole, the breaking down of barriers between us, the swallowing up of separate provincial nationalities, is a consummation to which the natural course of things irresistibly tends.[82]

But what was a 'provincial nationality'? Was it even possible that 'nationalities' would be swallowed up in Europe and themselves become 'provincial'? Although he did not put this question, Arnold had immersed himself in schools and universities on the continent, saw that they were different in practice and ethos, and hoped that desire for *Wissenschaft* might seep into England.[83] A 'European mind' might then emerge.

It seemed unlikely, however, to put it mildly, that, whatever happened in the United Kingdom, Europe after 1870 would become 'one homogeneous, English-speaking whole' and therefore, presumably, its barriers would not be broken down and its inhabitants would not fuse. Indeed, the plurality of its languages within its states, even within its new supposedly 'unified' states, was becoming more, not less, apparent. Even so, although 'unity' therefore by no means seemed the consummation to which the natural course of things irresistibly tended, whenever it hit the 'world beyond' there was a 'European civilization'. In 1870, Britain stood out in the extent of its extra-European territoriality, but in the decades that were to follow the aspiration to extend or entrench outside Europe became a paradoxical hallmark of Europe. Disraeli's 1866 hyperbole might apply to others too. It was axiomatic, almost by the very fact of expansion, that it was a superior civilization, a view underpinned by ethnographical theories, purporting, subsequently and inaccurately, to derive from Darwin's *Origin of Species* (1859), which ranked the peoples of the world on a scale.

To what 'natural course' did the United States tend? If one sought 'English-speaking wholes', consummation with the great state across the Atlantic might be more 'natural'. Yet the American Civil War (1861–65) showed that unity of language, at least at a certain level, could not prevent the most catastrophic conflict – in casualties exceeding any of Europe's wars. Gladstone, in a speech in Newcastle in October 1862 went so far as to state that the leaders of the south had made a 'nation'. Relations between 'the English-speaking peoples' had by no means been harmonious. It was still thought in London that Canada might not be safe from American designs. In relation to the war itself, some believed that a North America divided into a multiplicity of states ('like Europe') was not undesirable. The abolition of slavery, however, produced contrary enthusiasms. However, although what happened in the United States was of particular importance to Britain – and somehow or other a diplomatic path was found – it was increasingly a country taking its immigrants from Europe as well as from Britain. Whether its emerging civilization was consequentially a kind of 'second Europe' (though paradoxically one whose founding fathers had thrown off Britain and whose new citizens had frequently escaped 'oppressive Europe') rather than another pole in the 'English-speaking whole' left many issues unresolved for the future.

'These are not the days for small states,' wrote J.A. Froude in 1870. Natural barriers that once divided kingdom from kingdom were being broken down. The interests of nations were becoming so intertwined that every one felt the benefit of belonging to a first-rate power. The empire still ensured that 'England' would remain such a power. There was no cause to quarrel with America but 'From the day that it is confessed that we are no longer equal to a conflict with her, if cause of rupture should unhappily arise, our sun has set'.[84] Benjamin Jowett, in the same year, wanted Britain 'to tie herself as closely as she can to America, removing causes of quarrel at any cost'. That was because he was worried about the equilibrium in Europe. 'It would be a serious loss to Europe', he wrote to Florence Nightingale, 'if either the German or French element were seriously weakened'. If French pride were humbled that would only lead to a war in the next generation. As things stood, German nationality was a very delusive idea, meaning really the ascendancy of a military aristocracy. It was the military spirit that was becoming rampant in Europe and in the end Europe would blow up like a powder magazine. England would be slow to join in but would at last fight, not in any good cause, like Poland or Italy, but to show that she was not afraid.[85] It remained to be seen whether, and if so where, she would do so.

|7|

Imperially detached,
c.1870–c.1900

New Germany and old Europe

There was a general recognition in London that German unity under Prussian aegis had profoundly changed the structure of continental politics.[1] Even so, though guardedly and ambivalently, the new German state was broadly welcomed. 'The North Germans are socially a hateful race', wrote Lord Kimberley, the colonial secretary, in his private journal in September 1870, 'but their supremacy would be less dangerous than that of France'.[2] The Franco-Prussian war itself, he thought, would throw Europe back 20 years. The future looked even more uncertain than usual. Prussia was seen by other writers as a disconcerting mixture of German, Slav and Huguenot blood – a lethal combination. Benjamin Jowett, master of Balliol and a breeder of politicians, expressed a common ambivalence in admiring the Protestantism of Prussia but disliking what he called aristocratic, vulgar and military Prussia. Speaking in the Commons in February 1871, Benjamin Disraeli talked about 'the German revolution', which he described as a greater event than the eighteenth-century French Revolution. It would bring about a new order in Europe, and Britain would feel the consequences most sharply because the balance of power had been destroyed. If there was ambivalence about the new Germany, however, there was also relief that the *grande nation*, which had once again been hankering to dominate Europe, had been defeated. French pride had come before a fall. The subsequent extraordinary events in Paris – the uprising of the Commune – provided observers with further proof that the French could not govern themselves sensibly. Fratricidal tendencies were once again rampant in the land of fraternity. France, endemically oscillating wildly between anarchy and despotism, could not be relied upon.

Great Powers

In 1876, Bismarck, the German chancellor, scribbled in the margin of a note he had received from Alexander Gorchakov. The Russian statesman claimed that a particular issue under discussion was neither a German nor a Russian problem but rather a European one. Bismarck wrote that anyone who talked about Europe in this way was simply wrong-headed. Europe was simply a geographical notion. Talking about the needs of Europe was simply a device by foreign statesmen who wished to obtain something from a foreign power that they would not risk requesting for themselves.[3] His bluntness was realistic as well as being characteristic. The events of 1870–71 had certainly not suggested that the statesmen of Europe were itching to become 'Europeans' and eager to find a 'European' framework. On the contrary, national stereotypes had been strengthened and state objectives reinforced.

It appeared to be the case that Berlin, as the capital of the German Empire, was on the way to becoming 'the capital of Europe', though it did not always inspire. To a young British diplomat joining the embassy there as late as 1884, the city still seemed rather modest and lacking in individuality.[4] Even so, it had now joined London, Paris, Vienna and St Petersburg as a centre where European policy was made. This was a Europe of Great Powers – Britain, France, Germany, Austria-Hungary and Russia. The mid-nineteenth-century dream of a voluntary federation of European nations faded away. The new Italy was also anxious to be thought 'among the Great Powers' and did not want to be kept waiting. The gap between these Great Powers and the 11 lesser powers of Europe – Spain, Sweden-Norway, Denmark, the Netherlands, Switzerland, Belgium, Greece, Serbia and Montenegro, and not forgetting Turkey – was enormous. Serbia and Montenegro, although now autonomous, were still legally part of the Ottoman Empire. The independence of Greece was limited by the requirement that it should follow the advice of its 'protecting' Powers – Russia, Britain and France. Belgium was required to be neutral. Switzerland and the Netherlands chose to be. Portugal found it advisable to listen to Britain.

Some observers in the 1870s thought that, with the 'German' and 'Italian' questions apparently settled, this patchwork called Europe could settle down to a period of peace. Whatever Disraeli thought, the balance of power had not in fact been destroyed. Their assumption was correct in that, with the exception of the Balkans, the state boundaries of 1900 were those of 1871. The 'management' of Europe by the Great Powers, through the system of alliances and alignments, could be held to be successful. It had not been accompanied by any fresh attempt to 'manufacture' a Europe that transcended the interests of states. Other commentators, however, were sceptical about this 'management' by the Great Powers. There seemed good grounds for supposing that the alliances of the period created rather than contained conflict and suspicion. One day Europe could explode.

European maps and minds

Even as the geographical expression that Bismarck preferred, this Europe remained a sum of diverse parts. What was 'western', 'central' or 'eastern' remained loose and imprecise. 'Frontiers', 'boundaries' and 'borders' – all words with rather different connotations – existed in minds, whatever maps might say, or could be manufactured to say. Physical Europe might be one thing, political Europe another.

When talking about Europe, western Europeans found it quite natural to begin with western Europe. However, in the light of 1870/71, the 'western Europe' envisaged by Congreve and his friends in the 1860s now looked a phantom. Bismarck's annexation of Alsace-Lorraine created a running sore. No French government could appear to have abandoned the provinces for ever but no German government could give them up. Whether their fate would ever merit war was another matter. In addition, France was now, once again, a republic. Monarchical Germany would not look to Paris to 'lead' a 'western Europe' towards which Berlin felt little emotional attachment. As for Spain, its politics still seemed self-contained and not 'western European'. It clung on to its colonial possessions with increasing difficulty. Its defeat by the United States in the war of 1898 substantially ended its overseas empire but 're-entry' into European politics was still problematic as its politicians wrestled with nation-building.[5] Rome, now the capital of new Italy, was disinclined to defer to a French leadership of 'western Europe'. Planners and architects had set to work immediately to transform the papal city into an appropriately grand expression of the new state and establish its claim to inherit classical Roman moral and political virtues.[6] Indeed, irritated by the French occupation of Tunis in 1881, Italy drew closer to Germany and Austria-Hungary. It looked as though 'western Europe' would amount to a Britain and France acting in unison – an unlikely contingency.

The events of 1870/71 could be said to have made central Europe, *Mitteleuropa*, easier to conceive. It consisted, on one formulation, simply of two empires, the German and the Austro-Hungarian. The Russian Empire, on this analysis, constituted 'eastern Europe'. It remained the case, however, that some observers wanted to exclude Russia from Europe. If that was done, of course, where central Europe began and ended and where eastern Europe began and ended remained problematic. In any case, to allocate states was one thing and to allocate peoples was another. All three empires, in varying degrees, were multi-ethnic and 'faced' in different directions. Not without internal controversy in doing so, they all endowed themselves with European missions, missions that British observers, whether from afar or at hand, found difficult to comprehend.

What did the German Empire conceive itself to be? In 1875, after nearly 40 years in construction, the *Hermannsdenkmal* was unveiled near Detmold in Westphalia. It commemorated a victory in AD9 of the German chieftain

Hermann (Arminius) over invading Roman legions. Whatever might be going on in new Rome, one might conclude, the Germans had successfully resisted old Rome. Quite what past now moulded Germany's present was contentious. Some prominent Lutheran voices linked 1871 to 1517 (the 'year of the Reformation') when Germany had 'broken free' from the ecclesiastical tyranny of Rome and had formed, as it were, an alternative and competing spiritual universe in Europe. It could not be straightforwardly of 'the West'. Yet the new German Empire was equally not straightforwardly a 'nation-state'. Bavaria, for example, retained its own constitution, army and postage stamps. 'Catholic' Munich and 'Protestant' Hamburg had very different pasts.

It became customary to talk about 'German unity', but there was no German uniformity. The 'integration' of Germany, even supposing it to be desirable, was still some way off. Whether the 'nationalization' of Germany was part and parcel of its 'modernization' was disputed. However, to some observers, the drift towards centralism in Germany seemed inexorable. Cities like Munich, Leipzig, Dresden and Frankfurt had their particular functions and importance, but Berlin was increasingly dominant. Its population in 1900 approached two million – Hamburg, the next biggest German city, held some 700,000 people. Traditional centres of government were being challenged by the new patterns of wealth and power emerging from industrialization. The contrast between Germany west and east of the Elbe became more marked. The *Kulturkampf* of the 1870s, which resulted in the consolidation rather than the undermining of German Catholicism, revealed another division. British observers conceded that this new empire was an elaborately constitutional state – political parties, parliaments and universal male suffrage – but it did not have 'parliamentary government' in the British sense. While that was no doubt regrettable, it was not in itself alarming. What was more worrying was how this Germany might use its power in Europe. 'Great Germany', it seems, was not on Bismarck's agenda but the suspicion that it might be did not disappear.[7] In fact, in 1879 he pressurized the kaiser to agree to a (secret) treaty with Austria-Hungary under which both states promised each other support in the event of a Russian attack, and benevolent neutrality in the event of an attack by a fourth power. This dual alliance was supplemented by a triple alliance in 1882, with Italy as an additional participant.

The Austro-Hungarian empire thus buttressed – though Bismarck sought, nevertheless, to keep 'on side' with Russia – was increasingly not a 'German' power in central Europe. Its multi-ethnic and multi-lingual complexity became steadily more apparent – though mapping the distribution of peoples frequently embodied political messages. Those who could be defined as Germans constituted in 1900 only 36 per cent of the population in 'Austria' and a mere 11 per cent in 'Hungary'. The Magyars fell short of being a majority in Hungary itself. Austro-Germans, however, remained in disproportionate ascendancy at court and in the army and business. Jews, in different parts of the empire, were awkwardly placed at the crossroads of identity and tilted differently in different locations. They were not alone, however, in not being quite certain where they 'belonged'. Vienna was, at one level, a 'German city' but its population was increasingly diverse. Prague was on its way to becoming a Czech rather than a German city. Politics in the empire, particularly after the advent of universal male suffrage in 1896, seemed to entail deals between different national groups. As in Germany, however, executive government was not parliamentary government. The role of the emperor, Franz Josef, who had succeeded in 1848, remained crucial. In short, Austria-Hungary could be regarded as a 'mini-Europe' in itself. Keeping its nationalities in a condition of 'even and well-modulated discontent', as Count Taaffe famously described his task between 1879 and 1893, was arguably what was also required to keep the peace in Europe as a whole. The monarchy would continue to survive, as Europe itself survived, by concession and accommodation. Diplomats, British among them, asked themselves what might replace the Habsburg monarchy and generally concluded that it was a question better not put. It looked increasingly realistic to suppose that in the European scheme of things Vienna punched below its weight.

The most north-easterly part of the German Empire (East Prussia), was further east than the western part of the Russian Empire (Russian Poland). In itself this indicated the limitation in regarding the German Empire as central European and the Russian Empire as eastern. Neither could the two empires be simply identified as 'Teuton' and 'Slav' respectively. The Finns and Estonians, of the Russian Empire's north-west were neither 'Teutons' nor 'Slavs', and with the Latvians and Lithuanians could be classified in a general sense as 'the Baltic people'. The word 'Slav' was as slippery in what it might embrace as was the term 'Teuton'. A major issue of the late nineteenth century was whether the Russian Empire would, in due time, become a Russian nation-state. Did the suppression or at least the restriction of non-Russian cultures reflect 'Russification' or did it stem from a desire to preserve the state from centrifugal pressures?[8] There were tensions, too, within the 'eastern Slav family'. Was there a separate Ukrainian nationality? If all 'East Slavs' could be categorized as Russians, Russians at the end of the century constituted some 75 per cent of the empire's population, but if only 'Great Russians' were 'really' Russians then they constituted less than half. Then again, the notion of some Czechs in Prague that Russia, although unfortunately ruled by a tsar, was their 'mother' was a further example of the awkward intersection of sentiment and geography.[9]

If, therefore, Bismarck was right to stress that Europe was a geographical concept it was an awkward one, and not only at its eastern edges. Both 'northern' and 'southern' Europe raised issues that to some extent ran counter to the predominant concern with east/west and the elusive middle. 'Scandinavia' remained a term of uncertain political significance. The future of the Swedish-Norwegian state looked increasingly uncertain. If the Finns were Scandinavians, their struggle against Russian political authority was paralleled by the desire to escape Swedish cultural hegemony. Likewise, while the European countries of the Mediterranean littoral largely lacked any means of common expression, they had a sense of distance from the great world of the European 'heartland'. In Athens, in 1890, Rodd reported that people still talked of 'going to Europe' if they travelled westwards from Greece.[10] It was a cast of mind not dissimilar to that of another European people accustomed to ships and seafaring.

Getting the picture

Relatively few Britons would have been comfortable conceptualizing such a Europe. However, the profusion of guide and travel books pointed to an accelerating desire to explore the continent. In sales terms, such books came second only to novels. The print run for a single-country handbook was between 500,000 and 700,000. Bradshaw's guide to continental trains had been available since mid-century. It had to cope, as decades passed, with a European rail network that became ever more extensive. So great was the propensity of 'the English' to travel that 'continentals' thought it a good joke to ask whether there were any left living at home. Currency transactions often proved a nightmare for British travellers, but in 1874 Mr Cook helpfully produced the precursor of the travellers' cheque. Travellers, it must be stressed, still tried to distinguish themselves from ordinary 'tourists' or 'sightseers'. The former, it seems, did a little *thoroughly*, while the latter did a lot *indiscriminately*. George Gissing, the depressed novelist, liked being a traveller in Calabria in southern Italy. Rome, he thought, was afflicted by swarms of the vulgar English who were determined not to let even a hen roost go undescribed for their benefit.[11]

There were some parts of Europe that eluded them, but the reputation of the British for inquisitiveness was not unmerited. Guide books themselves, by deciding how much space to allocate to particular countries, established a kind of travelling hierarchy. Anywhere east of Germany or Austria rarely received a mention in a general guide. If one went to Hungary – though Murray's guide noted that most English travellers did not venture beyond Pest – one should note that no Hungarian gentleman thought of travelling without his sheets, pillow, pillow case and leather sheets. One who did venture beyond Pest was the historian, politician and climber James Bryce. He journeyed across the Hungarian plain in 1866 until he found himself in Arad (now in Romania). The people seemed, he wrote, 'more like savages than one would expect to find in Europe'. In the market square, wearing strange dresses and possessing strange faces, he found Magyars, Wallachs or Romanians, Jews and Gypsies. The scene made him feel 'an enormous distance from home'. It is not clear whether he had taken his own pillow case with him.[12]

In comparison, Switzerland, Italy and the south of France was much more familiar territory.[13] Nice had its notable *Promenade des Anglais* where Queen Victoria could sometimes be seen. The Alps proved particularly congenial to outward-bound men. John Ball, one of the founders of the Alpine Club in 1857, had boldly concluded that being an Alpinist was better than being under-secretary for the colonies and consequently resigned his government position. Whether in Iceland, Turkey or the Carpathians, James Bryce could never resist a mountain. He became president of the Alpine Club, though in 1884 he feared that Swiss scenery was perishing at the hands of the crowds it attracted, 'or rather of those who build for their convenience cog-wheel railways and monster hotels'. Robert Louis Stevenson spent several gloomy winters in Davos for the good of his health. Queen Victoria established a notable presence.[14]

It was perhaps Italy that still held first place in British affections.[15] Florence and Rome were prime locations but, with the incentive offered by cheapness, Venice was rediscovered.[16] An extraordinary array of islanders came, saw and sometimes stayed. One scholar has concluded that insular travellers 'never became a truly cosmopolitan class, linguistically versatile and culturally receptive'.[17] It would perhaps have been better, he thinks, if they had stayed at home cultivating their gardens. The extent to which the English or the Scots lived in a ghetto in Rome or Nice, for example, can be overstated. If they built Anglican churches for themselves that was what all European Protestants living 'out of area' did.[18] British residents, however, naturally noted that Italy was 'nationalizing' itself and that Rome was losing its 'European aspect'. Rodd had been 'emancipated' by living in Rome as a boy in 1865–66. Arriving in the Rome embassy in 1891 he found the city 'had changed its aspect tragically, from the picturesque and sentimental point of view'.[19] The British ambassador at this juncture, Lord Dufferin, had been born in Florence. In order to avoid the boredom apparently engendered by the new Italy, his lordship returned to reading the Latin and Greek texts he had studied as an undergraduate.[20]

Regular travellers could not fail to be aware of the social and political changes taking place throughout Europe. Diplomats sometimes felt a certain nostalgia for the *couleur locale* that it seemed was being lost in newly unified or centralizing states. Earlier, when in Berlin, Rodd had accompanied his ambassador to the small ducal court of Dessau. He concluded that an 'old-world life' supposedly 'patriarchal, kindly and picturesque' was passing away in an increasingly homogenized continent.[21] It was perhaps this awareness of what 'unification' might entail that made Switzerland's constitution of particular interest. James Bryce thought that Switzerland offered a better example than any other continental country of how self-government could work in practice.[22] The idea of consulting the people by means of referendums on specific issues also excited interest in 'progressive' quarters. For J.A. Hobson, Switzerland proved 'that a people of different nationalities, different religions, different customs, different climates, different allegiance, and divided by barriers, can agree and disagree in political harmony'.[23] Why could not Europe become a kind of big Switzerland?

Mr Gladstone's Scandinavian thoughts

Sometimes, travel triggered home thoughts. Late in life, Mr Gladstone felt the pull of northern Europe. On 13 September 1883 he received the Freedom of Kirkwall on Orkney. The appearance of the people there, he noted, bore 'testimony to their Scandinavian character'. The following day his party set sail for Norway, a country then inaccessible to 'all but the more moneyed classes' – a limitation, incidentally, remedied a decade later by Quintin Hogg's 'really courageous' Polytechnic Tour.[24] The people of Christiania (Oslo) seemed to Gladstone 'most courteous & apparently happy'.[25] He was well aware of the fact that then Norway had its own constitution within its union with Sweden under the Swedish Crown. Gladstone proceeded to Copenhagen where he had the privilege, somewhat to Queen Victoria's consternation, of meeting no less than 25 'royalties'.

How could all the peoples of the British Isles be made as happy as the Norwegians seemed to be with their constitutional arrangements? Gladstone, a Liverpool Scot who lived in Wales (sometimes), had more understanding than many of his English contemporaries that a reconciliation between nationality and empire was perhaps the greatest challenge faced by European states (the United Kingdom included). Two years later, setting out on another cruise to Norway, this time in the fjords, he was again reflecting on Ireland, aware of that standing reproach which it constituted for Britain in Europe. Proving there was 'a due regard to the unity of the Empire' there could be considerable change in the relationship between Britain and Ireland. He scorned the idea, put forward by Parnell in a speech in Dublin, that Scotland had lost its nationality as a result of the Act of Union. Nationality and statehood, for Gladstone, were distinct. He embarked on what turned out to be a futile attempt to square the circle. In the 1886 general election, only seven months after that which had brought him to power, Gladstone lost. He had disastrously split his own Liberal Party. A majority of MPs in Ireland, Scotland and Wales favoured home rule, but England said 'no'. Twenty years later, after Gladstone's death, the happy Norwegians were even happier when they separated from Sweden.

In July 1886, Lord Selborne, Gladstone's lord chancellor, but an opponent of home rule for Ireland, met Sir James Lacaita in the inner library of the Athenaeum Club in London. Lacaita was a naturalized Italian, a fact that apparently did not prevent him from becoming an Italian senator. He had assisted Gladstone decades earlier in uncovering repression in Naples, and was in tears as he expressed his hostility to Gladstone's Irish ambitions. Could not Gladstone understand that the principle he was employing would 'lead to an agitation for the dismemberment of the kingdom of Italy, in

Sicily first, and afterwards (not improbably) in all the provinces which were formerly independent States'?[26] He was only too aware of the fragility of Italian unity. It would be disastrous to reverse what he regarded as a process of beneficial integration. Lord Salisbury's incoming administration took the same view. In an article on *Disintegration* published in 1883, Salisbury had deplored how, with the encouragement of the Liberal Party, the English race was being denigrated. As a result, the national impulses of Englishmen were beginning to disappear.[27] He was firmly of the view that there was no halfway house. Ireland was either with Britain or against it. Ministers in Berlin, Vienna and St Petersburg did not much like halfway houses either.

Trying democracy

Hippolyte Taine, the French *savant*, reflecting on his time in England in the 1860s, admired the way in which Britain, unlike France, had retained a free constitution thanks to, rather than in spite of, the survival of social hierarchy. British foreign policy in the final decades of the nineteenth century remained, almost without exception, in the hands of politicians securely located within the social hierarchy. The same point largely holds for diplomats and Foreign Office officials. Their social homogeneity, the similarities in the education they received at school and university, and their personal relationships across party-political boundaries all perpetuated deeply entrenched convictions about Britain's relationship with 'Europe'. They had to work, however, within a framework of more popular government. The 1872 Ballot Act had made voting secret and an 1883 Act had targeted corrupt practices. Although the franchise had been further extended and seats redistributed in 1884/85, only just over 60 per cent of the male electorate was eligible to vote in 1891. The 'right to vote' was not 'fundamental'.

The approach of democracy might require a reconsideration of 'foreign policy'. Governments heretofore had been able to conduct policy, make treaties, even go to war, if parliament approved, with scant regard for what 'the democracy' felt. Would that continue? The answer, as far as the remainder of the nineteenth century was concerned, appeared to be that the policy-making elite would not be unduly hindered. All foreign secretaries in these years sat in the House of Lords. They therefore did not have to deal with irritating constituents or worry about their own re-election. They had under-secretaries who could speak for them in the Commons. This arrangement reflected the sense in which the foreign secretary dealt with a 'national interest' in a sphere beyond party politics. It could still be assumed that interest in 'foreign affairs' on the part of the electorate was a minority taste. It was an area best left to specialists. Recruitment into both the Foreign Office and the diplomatic service (still separate) remained aristocratic and 'upper middle class' – as was normal also in continental Europe. In practice, of course, this lofty separation of 'foreign policy' from domestic issues could not invariably be maintained. Even though they might not relish doing so, elite politicians had to 'carry the country'. The prejudices and preconceptions of 'the people' had to blend with their own.

Ministers and 'the foreign'

Ministers made no pretence that they had 'Europe' at their fingertips. Their pattern of knowledge and experience was largely fortuitous, but it was not as scanty as is sometimes suggested. Whether, and in what sense, they considered themselves to be 'men of Europe' was something addressed only rarely. Generations overlapped in cabinets as different ministers carried in their heads images of Europe formed at different times and in different circumstances.

Lord Granville, who served as Gladstone's foreign secretary after the death of Lord Clarendon, was familiar with the great world of European diplomacy from birth. He was born in the year of Waterloo. After Eton and Oxford, he entered the Commons at the age of 21 in 1836. His father was ambassador in Paris and, according to his biographer, he had early entered the *vie intime* of the entire diplomatic circle of Europe.[28] He succeeded to his father's peerage a decade later. He had been foreign secretary briefly in 1851. In 1856, with his young stepson, the budding historian John Acton, he had represented Queen Victoria at the coronation of Tsar Alexander II. He had been struck by the 'disparate' character of St Petersburg, where beauty and wretchedness mingled. He formed the view that Russia had immense resources, if properly developed – but they would not be properly developed.[29] It would be difficult to argue, however, Granville's European experiences flowed directly into his policy-making. Granville again served Gladstone from 1880 to 1885 but his tenure of the Foreign Office has not excited modern interest. It did not excite his stepson either. Granville had 'very little knowledge of foreign countries', Acton complained in 1871 – but the requirements of this particular historian must be judged to be rather exacting.[30] Gladstone himself complained, at least retrospectively, that he was conducting British foreign policy 'almost single-handed'.

As for Gladstone himself, his earlier European views have been referred to previously, but the continent had now changed. It would be only a slight exaggeration to say that he hated Bismarck. He talked about 'the violent laceration and transfer of Alsace-Lorraine', predicting that it would be 'the beginning of a new series of European complications'.[31] Bismarck, in turn, scornfully referred to Gladstone as 'Professor', a devastating indictment indeed. Gladstone's handling of the Franco-Prussian crisis, as has been noted earlier, was bizarre and his ruminations on the public law of Europe, while undoubtedly profound, did not always seem immediately pertinent to the issues on hand. The personal duel between Bismarck and Gladstone, which lasted nearly a quarter of a century, with interruption, was capable of being presented as embodying national approaches to the practice of state-craft. It was a contest Bismarck won – at a European price.

The arrival of an unambiguously Conservative government in 1874 was a novelty. So was Disraeli. 'My mind is a continental mind', he had rashly and privately written in 1833. No other British prime minister had or has emulated this dangerous achievement. His grandfather, an Italian Jew, had settled in London in 1748. His father had permitted Benjamin to be baptized in the Church of England. The 'continental mind' had been prudently achieved, as it could only be achieved, by avoiding public school and university in England. He had instead made copious notes on Mme de Staël's *Germany* and read German literature (in translation). He had travelled in the Rhineland, and Lord Byron's boatman, no less, had rowed him at night on Lake Geneva.

The continental mind then expanded to embrace the Near East. He toured the eastern Mediterranean in 1830–31 and was 'thunderstruck' by Jerusalem. His 'Jewishness', for good or ill, was something he thereafter neither could avoid, nor wished to. On the plains of Troy, 'standing upon Asia, and gazing upon Europe', he conceived a poetic epic in which he would present the two continents as 'the Rival Principles of Government that at present contend for the mastery of the world'. Disraeli had an engaging conversation in Cairo with Mehemet Ali, in which the Egyptian ruler revealed that his interest in the idea of a parliament was so great that he had drawn up a list of the people he intended to make members.

Few of Disraeli's foreign interlocutors would have suspected that this unconventional and 'unconnected' young man would end up as prime minister of the greatest country on earth. Despite his 'continental mind', *England*, as he put it in 1832, summed up his politics. Even so, it has been persuasively argued that his inspiration came from outside England's atmosphere and his 'leaps of mind occurred in travel beyond its shores'.[32] He was 70 when he reached the political summit and began fresh mental leaps.

Disraeli had Lord Derby as his foreign secretary, which office he had previously held in 1866–68. Derby had also been a traveller in his youth, to South America and the West Indies. He had later put up with visits to France, which were made necessary by his wife's health. When in office, the management of his estates apparently took as much time as managing the foreign policy of the British Empire. Derby, however, was an efficient man who had taken a first in Classics at Cambridge. Disraeli was disconcerted by Derby's initial inclination to think that foreign policy was a matter for cabinet discussion. Around the foreign secretary's final years in office there lies mystery – concerning his health, his effectiveness and his propensity (or perhaps his wife's) to pass on cabinet secrets to the Russians. He resigned in April 1878.[33]

His successor was Lord Salisbury who again became foreign secretary in his own first government in 1885. In his second administration, Lord Iddesleigh was initially foreign secretary but Salisbury took the two posts from 1887 to 1892, as he did in his 1895 government, though he resigned as foreign secretary in 1900.

Salisbury was the first British prime minister to be born after Waterloo (about which battle his godfather, the Duke of Wellington, supplied pertinent information). His father had served in Lord Derby's father's cabinet in 1852. This had marked the reappearance on the national scene of a family that had found fame and fortune under Elizabeth I. Like Lord Derby, however, it was not on a European Grand Tour that Salisbury had embarked as a young man.[34] After distinctly mixed experiences at Eton and Oxford, he had set off in 1851 on a journey to the Cape, 'Australia' and New Zealand. It transpired that the manners of the British race he encountered in these parts were not quite what he had been used to as a Tractarian undergraduate at Christ Church. Back home, two years later, he entered the House of Commons at the age of 23. Easily depressed, he found satisfaction in rebutting the notion that the natural savagery of mankind could be tamed by civilization.[35] He detested the Crimean War.

Largely for financial reasons – his marriage had alienated his father – Salisbury turned to journalism. He reviewed, by no means uncritically, works of contemporary European historians and political philosophers. He was fully acquainted with the language, literature and history of France, an acquaintance capped by residence. The ample Châlet Cecil was built near Dieppe in 1870 for family use, followed by a less ugly building in the south of France decades later. It would have been out of character, however, had he believed that location broadened the mind. He opined that 'the more the facilities of travelling bring the two nations into contact the less goodwill is likely to be generated'.[36] He reviewed a dozen books of German history, philosophy and literature, usually once a month, between 1859 and 1864.[37] He had no doubt that national affairs could not be conducted on principles prescribed for individuals. In sum, an aristocratic MP who reviewed both the theology of Schleiermacher and the political economy of Karl Marx cannot be accused of indifference to currents of European thought. His stance was determinedly against the spirit of the age. He disliked Napoleon III's 'democratic Caesarism', found it odd that Germans should wish to venerate Hermann, dismissed Abraham Lincoln as a 'personal nullity' and described Greek independence as 'artificial and premature'. It seemed that the democratizing world held few attractions.

His political career began in 1866 when he briefly became secretary of state for India (an office he held again from 1874 to 1878). He hated the Second Reform Act, even more because his own party had passed it. Perhaps it was his Indian responsibilities that reinforced his conviction that splitting up mankind 'into a multitude of infinitesimal governments' simply on the basis of language or race was a great mistake. Civilization, in his view, was 'constantly tending' to the 'agglomeration and not the comminution of states'.[38] That was a perspective he brought to the consideration of Europe. He hated German nationalism. It was false to believe that language should form the basis of a state. He also hated (the repetition of this verb is inescapable) the Communards and deplored any attempt to 'ape' the French. He had hinted in an 1862 essay at an underlying incompatibility of temperament between Englishmen and Frenchmen. All of this commended him to the University of Oxford, which made him its chancellor in 1870.

Salisbury had earlier detested 'oriental cunning' in Disraeli, but gladly accepted office as foreign secretary in 1878. Now 48, the disposition of his mind was set. He was not averse to displaying cunning himself. In 1864, reflecting on the recent vacuous European interventions of Lord John Russell, he had expressed the view that the influence of England in the councils of Europe had passed away. Englishmen, he suggested, might not have been liked but their 'bull-dog characteristics' had formerly been respected. No longer. It was time to realize that peace without honour was not only a disgrace, it was a chimera.[39] England had obligations to 'the European Commonwealth of which she is a citizen', but needed to be strong to carry them out effectively. Any journalist, however, could *write* such things. What Salisbury could do as foreign secretary might be another matter. He would be his own man because it was not for a statesman to consult the wishes of the people – the people had no enduring and settled interests.

Lord Rosebery (b. 1847) became Gladstone's foreign secretary in 1886, though he then professed 'no knowledge of diplomatic practice or forms, and little of diplomatic men', and served again in his last government (1892–94). He succeeded Gladstone as prime minister for 15 miserable months before resigning in 1895. Another Scot, he had succeeded to the courtesy title Lord Dalmeny as a small boy, when his father, author of a pamphlet commending gymnastic exercises, died from a sudden heart attack. He then set about reading Macaulay and studying Thiers on the *History of the Consulate and Empire*. At Oxford, as at Eton, he was known to be brilliant, but too devoted to horses – at home and abroad. He adored Naples. His pleasure in visiting Florence in 1868, however, was diminished by finding it 'swamped with Cook's Tourists'.[40] Two years later, he spent three months in Italy. In the early 1870s he paid three extensive visits to the United States – it fell to him to persuade Queen Victoria, 20 years later, that the United States merited an embassy rather than a mere legation. After spending several weeks in Paris in 1873 he concluded that 'so bastard and ridiculous a Republic was never seen'.[41] In the years that followed he developed further European contacts. He was on friendly terms with Herbert Bismarck and talked with his father 'as one gentleman to another' in 1885.

It was, however, the idea of 'empire' not 'Europe' that excited his imagination.[42] He set off for Australia in 1883 and in a speech in Adelaide recognized an Australian nation 'in performance and fact'. There was, however, no need for any nation to leave the Empire because it was in reality 'a

Commonwealth of Nations'. The British Empire was the greatest secular agency for good that the world had ever seen and he was proud to declare himself a 'Liberal Imperialist'. Both as foreign secretary and prime minister, Rosebery 'tilted' in a German direction since it was with France that Britain most frequently clashed in Africa. It so happened that William Henry Waddington, the French ambassador in London, somewhat unusually, had rowed for Cambridge against Oxford in the Boat Race but this feat did not significantly remove Rosebery's suspicions of France.

This brilliant prelude, however, ended in nothing. The 'man of the future', as Gladstone had once described Rosebery, faded away to a villa in Naples where it became his habit to spend several months every year. There he indulged a passion for Napoleon unequalled among former British prime ministers. He had acquired Napoleon's travelling library and studied his last days at length. He contemplated the cushion (which he possessed) on which Napoleon's head had rested after his death.

Lord Kimberley (b. 1826) was briefly Rosebery's foreign secretary. Like his young master, he was an Etonian who had proceeded to Christ Church, Oxford. He graduated with a first in Classics in 1847 and then wintered in Italy, keenly observing events there. He sat in the Lords, having inherited his father's title as a child. Somewhat to his surprise, having never expressed an opinion in public on foreign affairs, he was made foreign under-secretary under Lord John Russell and Lord Clarendon in 1852. In the aftermath of the Crimean War, he had the delicate task of becoming minister in St Petersburg (1856–58). He was not impressed by Russian society. Russian gentlemen might have facility in languages – speaking Russian to their serfs, German to their upper servants and French in polite society (and learning English from their nurses) – but they apparently had an extraordinary want of sound knowledge. Wodehouse, as he was then known, believed that the Crimean War had answered its purpose. The nightmare that had weighed upon Germany, and in some degree upon all Europe, had been removed. He supposed that the Russians were realizing that before they could take up a great position in European affairs they had to become civilized. Such a Russia, he conceded, might be a more formidable factor in Europe than the existing semi-barbarous one – but it would be years before Russia became civilized.[43] Wodehouse met Bismarck in December 1863, having been despatched to Berlin and Copenhagen to mediate (unsuccessfully) in the Schleswig-Holstein crisis of that year. Bismarck gave him the impression of being a cunning and unscrupulous man. His career thereafter took him away from Europe. He served for two spells as colonial secretary and Indian secretary between 1870 and 1894 before his brief tenure at the Foreign Office. Even in that capacity, however, imperial rather than European issues engaged his attention. However, in conversation, he did agree with the Empress Frederick of Germany that the expenditure of the European powers on armaments was ruinous. It might well be that Europe was heading for a 'cataclysm'.

Isolation and intervention

It is evident from these sketches of the leading formulators of British policy in these decades that they had some personal knowledge of 'the continent' but it was patchy and incidental rather than comprehensive or systematic. They were in a general sense Europeans but had experienced the world beyond Europe as much as the continent itself. Their responsibility was to blend these twin perceptions in the formulation of British policy. They almost all came into office lamenting either that their immediate predecessors had been too 'isolationist' or too 'interventionist'. If there had been 'isolation', it was either 'splendid' because it demonstrated that Britain did not need allies, or 'dangerous' because enemies threatened and allies were necessary. 'Splendid isolation', ironically, was a phrase coined in a debate in the Canadian parliament. Incoming prime ministers frequently saw advantage in 'intervention', particularly in the case of a Disraeli who might have little time in which to make his mark, but in practice 'intervention' could mean different things (as could 'isolation'). All terminology in this area is slippery. It is not difficult to demonstrate that Britain was never completely 'isolated' (where Europe was concerned) if that is taken to mean the absence of any continental commitment whatsoever.[44] Nevertheless, in comparison with other powers, British partiality for a 'free hand' was marked. Britain might want to 'lean' on occasion to the Triple Alliance of Germany, Austria-Hungary and Italy, but it would not belong to it. It might, at another juncture, wish to 'lean' to the Franco-Russian alliance (which had emerged in the early 1890s), but would likewise not join it. There was, of course, a rich irony in the fact that Salisbury was apt to invoke 'the people' as a reason why British governments could not be committed. Alliances, he considered, entailed 'burdensome conditions' that Britain's 'insular position' enabled it to avoid. Even so, in 1887 Britain had concluded a series of 'Mediterranean agreements' with Italy and Austria-Hungary, designed to uphold the status quo in the Mediterranean and the independence of the Ottoman Empire – fear of Russian designs on the Straits remained. This was perhaps as close to a continental alliance as Britain came. A decade later, however, perceptions changed. Britain's pre-eminence in Egypt had come to make the question of the Straits negotiable and the agreement with Austria lost its significance. The government was confident that it could deal with France without needing the support that the link to the Triple Alliance had provided.[45]

Insular security, however, required the maintenance of naval supremacy. 'The fleet of England is her all-in-all', wrote Lord Tennyson in his poem *The Fleet* (1886). Sir Henry Campbell-Bannerman pleasantly explained in 1889 that British naval supremacy was 'a traditional possession'. It was maintained with 'the consent of, and without any injury or grievance to, neighbouring countries'.[46] There is, however, no record of any such consent being given. From the mid-1880s onwards, there were regular naval scares in the British press. It was observed that if the French and Russian navies were combined the Royal Navy's traditional dominance of the Mediterranean would become untenable. The preservation of supremacy over the next two largest navies proved increasingly difficult for the Royal Navy to maintain as warships became ever more sophisticated and expensive.[47] And no amount of warships could prevent the landward expansion eastwards of the Russian empire.

'Anxious detachment' therefore perhaps comes closest to characterizing the sentiments of British political circles overall. It is misleading, however, to think of this being a detachment from 'Europe' as if, in these decades, there was a 'Europe' from which one could be detached. Although there were still examples of a European congress – that of Berlin in 1878 will be considered shortly – and a conference in 1884/85 on Central Africa attended by 15 states, there was no standing 'system' that was established to settle European problems. In addition, it was becoming evident that 'Europe' now spread beyond its home continent. Germany joined Britain and France in seeking power and status outside Europe.[48] Italy aspired to do the same, though it suffered a humiliating defeat in Ethiopia in 1896, something that was not supposed to happen to real European powers. Belgian royal enterprise led to the establishment of the Congo Free State.[49] The scale of extra-European activity was becoming a sign of status within Europe. 'It is not to be wondered at', Sir Harry Hinsley remarked, 'that an older and purely European habit and system of collaboration proved increasingly impossible to uphold'.[50]

The problems posed for Europe by 'Europe-in-Africa' were new. The 'Eastern Question' was old, but it seemed to be coming to a head. In May 1876, Bulgarian nationalists attempted an insurrection in eastern Rumelia. It was ruthlessly crushed – that is, some 15,000 men, women and children were crushed. It was not an unprecedented Ottoman response to rebellion. In Britain, the 'Bulgarian atrocities' sparked renewed condemnation of Ottoman rule in which, eventually, Gladstone joined. His pamphlet on the *Bulgarian Horrors* sold over 200,000 copies. According to the Anglo-Catholic *Church Review*, Turkish excesses were an 'insult to European Christendom'. The scale of the agitation in Britain, in the eyes of *The Spectator* demonstrated the country's 'moral healthiness'. It was not an agitation, however, that had any counterpart in its scale and righteous fury in any other European country.[51] 'European Christendom' might indeed have been insulted, but the term had little political significance. It was, of course, conceivable that 'European Christendom' might be reconstructed. In Bonn in 1874/75 there had been a 'Reunion Conference', the inspiration of Dr Döllinger, the 'Old Catholic' dissenter from the decision of the 1870 Vatican Council. The idea was to consider restoring communion between eastern Christendom and some parts of western Christendom. Henry Parry Liddon, Canon of St Paul's, was impressed by the 'Orientals' – Russians, Romanians, Constantinopolitans and Athenians – he met there. He noted that these eastern Europeans could only understand each other through the medium of German.[52] It was evident from these discussions that the restoration of 'European Christendom' would not be swiftly accomplished.

Agreeing that the Turks should be expelled from 'Europe' was one thing, agreeing on the subsequent structure of south-eastern Europe was another. A conference with the Porte in Constantinople, which Salisbury attended, ended in failure in January 1877. It was followed by an Austro-Russian agreement and then, after further exchanges with the Porte, by Russian military intervention. The peace of San Stefano, concluded by Russia and the Ottoman Empire in March 1878, established 'Big Bulgaria', a Slav state extending from the Black Sea to the Aegean. Whether Britain should or should not intervene in this development was debated fiercely both in the cabinet and in the country. Disraeli took the position that the San Stefano treaty had turned the Black Sea into a Russian lake. He argued that any changes to the treaties of 1856 could only be made by the powers collectively. Preceded by much diplomacy, a congress assembled in Berlin in June/July 1878, presided over by Bismarck, notable as an 'honest broker'. It was attended by Britain, France, Russia, Austria-Hungary, Italy and the Ottoman Empire. The outcome was a small autonomous principality of Bulgaria and an 'eastern Rumelia' equipped with a Christian governor but still under Ottoman jurisdiction. The independence of Serbia, Montenegro and Romania was acknowledged, accompanied by certain territorial adjustments. Austria-Hungary was allowed to occupy Bosnia-Hercegovina and the Sanjak of Novi Bazar. It was a settlement that lasted, after a fashion, into the next century. The Ottoman Empire was still in Europe but had been forced to retreat. Not for the first time, undertakings were given that there would be 'reform' in the territory it still directly controlled.

This Balkan arrangement agreed by the Great Powers could not be said, however, to have attempted anything as grandiloquent as 'reincorporating' the Balkan peoples into Europe. What had prompted the vigorous British reaction was fear that 'Big Bulgaria' betokened a permanent Russian predominance in the Balkans. Who knew where that might lead? Whether Russian overlordship might be a good thing for the Bulgarians was not a relevant consideration. It was rather tiresome that they seemed to regard the Russians as liberators. The small Balkan nations were not negotiating their own fate. They were only on hand in Berlin to hear what the Great Powers had decided. The Austrian occupation (not annexation) of Bosnia-Hercegovina was another piece of Great Power balancing.

Britain had no mind to grapple with this part of Europe which was 're-emerging'. Phil-Hellenism had lost much of its fervour and the 'experiment on a puerile nation' had turned into a rather 'messy' family business.[53] *The Times* did have a correspondent in the Balkans by the early 1890s. He drew attention to plans for 'a Confederation of the Christian Peoples of the Balkans', which the nations concerned, he thought, would obligingly put into execution 'when the favourable moment arrives'.[54] Over the years, the correspondent, J.D. Bourchier, came to be idolized in Bulgaria, being described by a Bulgarian prime minister as 'a martyr to the Bulgarian cause', but at the same time 'a martyr to what is noblest in the English soul'.[55] In fact, Bourchier was an Irish Protestant. So far, he remains the only man born in County Cork to have his visage reproduced on a Bulgarian postage stamp. The efforts of one *Times* correspondent, however, could not substantially alter a generally pervasive ignorance in Britain concerning Balkan developments. The situation was not helped by the fact that British outsiders tended to 'adopt' one or other Balkan nation and be blind to the virtues of others.

Britain had agreed to guarantee Asiatic Turkey against Russian attack in a convention signed in June 1878. In return Britain was permitted to station troops on Cyprus. The island was perceived as a *place d'armes* with an eye on Russia. The long-term consequences of another British encounter with Orthodoxy and Islam received little attention – although it was not to be until the First World War that Britain annexed Cyprus. Crete, with its recurrent insurrections, was another island which demonstrated that British 'patience' with pan-Hellenism had largely disappeared. London had been critical of the renewed but disastrous Greek war against Turkey in 1897. When told that a possible new governor of Crete, under the then latest proposals for the administration of the island, knew no Greek, Salisbury was not upset. 'So much the better', he retorted to the Foreign Office, for he would 'hear fewer lies'. 'The Protecting Powers', said the British representative in Crete, 'hardly realized what a hedgehog they had laid hold of when they made themselves responsible for its administration'.[56]

The aspirations of Balkan states had clearly taken second place behind the requirements of European balance as perceived by the Great Powers. Even so, conflict in south-east Europe brought back onto the agenda deep historical issues about the nature of Europe. Henry Parry Liddon felt that the Christian races in the region were now the predestined heirs of the future. He set off to inspect them at first hand. It was the Roman Catholic Bishop Strossmayer of Diakovar in Croatia who most impressed him. He was even more influential, Liddon supposed, as a politician than as an ecclesiastic. They talked vivaciously in French. Liddon was a little surprised to find himself waited on by servants who wore livery, which was not something that normally happened to him. It was gratifying to be able to conclude that St Sophia in Constantinople would once more be in Christian hands.[57]

European culture and civilization

According to the Russian historian Sergey Mikhaylovich Solov'ev in 1877, the 'Eastern Question' surfaced in history from the moment when 'European man' saw the differences between Europe and Asia, 'between the European and Asian spirit'.[58] It was, however, not the only matter that brought the question of culture and civilization to the fore. What did 'European man' stand for? It was a question, of course, that men addressed. The Franco-Prussian war had involved the two nations who saw themselves in the vanguard of European progress. At a personal level it ignited a celebrated controversy between David Strauss, from a German Protestant background and Ernest Renan, from a French Catholic. They had both written *Lives of Jesus* that demolished the 'Jesus of the Church' to their satisfaction and thought they were setting European civilization and culture on a progressive path. However, at this juncture, they disagreed bitterly. Renan was furious that Strauss saw Prussian victories as a just punishment for French arrogance, and proof that Prussian culture was vital whereas French was decadent. Their personal relationship came to an end.[59] This particular quarrel was symbolic of what was happening across the continent. Who 'owned' European civilization? Where was it heading?

The two words 'culture' and 'civilization' were recognizable in many European languages but whether there was common understanding of them was another matter. It was sometimes held on the continent that Victorian England had such a commercial and 'practical' ethos that it had no contribution to make to such discussion. Even 'proud England', Strauss thought, had been compelled to acknowledge the achievements of Prussian culture. Certainly Mr Gladstone read Strauss's *The Old Faith and the New*, though without admiration. He did acknowledge that 'in the ulterior prosecution of almost any branch of inquiry' it was to Germany and to the works of Germans that the British student had to look for assistance. The Germans, he suspected, unlike his own countrymen, had not yet learned to undervalue or despise 'simplicity of life'. Britain, he feared, as a wealthy country, was being afflicted by the corroding pest of idleness.[60] Even so, some Britons joined Frenchmen and Germans in Venice – a place not without a suspicion of idleness – to brood over the future of European civilization.[61] There were clearly some, like Mr Gladstone himself, who could not be accused of idleness and joined in a Europe-wide debate. The writing of Renan and Strauss had spread to Moscow where one of the city's suffragan bishops was anxious to learn from Henry Parry Liddon about their reception in England.[62] Even so, whether due to idleness or wealth, British agony on the subject of culture and civilization did not quite have the intensity to be found in countries better endowed with universities.

There were more questions than answers. Was 'culture' the Jewish-Christian-Greek-Roman inheritance of Europe and 'civilization' its modern expression through the exercise of reason and the advance of science? Was 'Kultur' a 'typically' German concern and 'civilization' a 'typically' French concern? Was 'civilization' replacing 'culture' – or did they both still vibrantly co-exist? Was there really a 'Jewish-Christian-Greek-Roman' inheritance or did it make more sense to distinguish between the 'Jewish-Christian' and the 'Greek-Roman'? Could one speak of a 'Jewish-Christian' inheritance at a time when Jewish and Christian communities were sharply distinguished? Was it 'culture' that would preserve society from 'anarchy'? Even more pressing was whether 'Europe' had any inheritance at all given the emphasis, evident in so many quarters across the continent, upon national pasts that were 'unique' and 'authentic'. 'National revival' insisted upon difference not upon commonality.[63]

The 'European' character of European civilization, not surprisingly, appeared more apparent to non-Europeans than it did to disputatious Europeans themselves. Likewise, in Africa or Asia, British politicians or administrators, who might fight shy of thinking of themselves as 'Europeans' at home were prepared to assume that mantle abroad. Lord Salisbury, for example, in supporting the foundation of Gordon College in Khartoum in 1898 wrote that the only way in which the wall of prejudice that separated 'the thoughts of the European' from 'the thought of the Egyptian and Sudanese races' could be thrown down was by giving the conquered 'access to the literature and knowledge of Europe'.[64] The lords of human kind were not reticent about the merits of European civilization.[65]

It was the scale of the British Empire that placed it in pole position in the dealings of Europe with the wider world. Queen Victoria became empress of India in 1876. For a long time, in the subcontinent, the British continued to represent 'Europe' – even to those Indians whose understanding of 'the West' was quite sophisticated. Although, with greater familiarity, that equation changed, the words 'British' and 'European' were frequently taken to be synonymous.[66] The experiences of British statesmen, civil servants, merchants, soldiers, missionaries and even some historians ranged across the world. It followed that for many Britons Europe was seen through a global haze. We have noted the Lords Derby, Granville, Kimberley and Salisbury had all served as colonial or Indian secretary before becoming foreign secretary subsequently. With his familiarity with the Caribbean, Lord Derby did not need to be told where Jamaica was when a black rising had taken place on the island in 1865. Salisbury had met Kaffirs in South Africa and concluded that their language bore traces of a very high former civilization – the word 'former' was important. Governor Eyre's suppression of the 1865 rebellion triggered a substantial mid-Victorian debate on 'race', 'gender', 'civilization' and 'self-government'.[67] The debate about 'rights' and 'representation' had a particular immediacy in the Birmingham of John Bright, but it reverberated throughout the British Empire.[68] Lord Ripon, convinced as Viceroy of India in 1883 that British rule should be 'for the benefit of the Indian peoples or all races, classes and creeds' rather than 'in the sole interest of a small body of Europeans' asked the legal member of his council, young Courtenay Ilbert, to draft a bill whose purpose was to enable Indian judges to conduct trials of white defendants. In the event, the bill had to be watered down.[69]

Talk of the 'unity of the British Empire' was becoming rather like talk of 'the unity of Europe'. Both were clubs of a kind. Club members felt themselves to be most 'British' or 'European' when non-members were present. On members-only nights, differences became apparent. 'Colonials' were no longer unequivocally British, but they were not unequivocally anything else either. Touring 'Greater Britain' in 1866–67, Charles Dilke recognized that divergencies of lifestyle were inevitable and that 'mixture with other peoples had modified the blood' but he still believed, and remained faithful to the view that, the British race would be always one.[70] Being in Sydney or Toronto would be just like being in Kent or Cornwall. The Anglo-Saxon of the future, spread across the globe, would not be everywhere the same but would still be 'essentially' one. In such a context, Dilke suspected, the future of the world would belong to the Anglo-Saxon, the Russian and the Chinese races.[71] Given this kind of language, it is perhaps not surprising that Disraeli, the great British 'imperialist', distanced himself from 'you English' when in conversation with Dilke.

It is noteworthy that few contemporaries, when they gazed into their crystal balls, identified 'Europe' (including Britain) as one of the blocs that would make up this world future. Russia was singled out by Dilke, for example, not because in any sense it represented Europe but simply because of the land mass that it now embraced. France and Germany, on this analysis, looked likely, when viewed globally, to become second-class powers. The same thing would happen to the Anglo-Saxons if they thought of themselves as European and nothing else. There was, however, a difficulty. Real Anglo-Saxons were hard to come by at the end of the nineteenth century. It might be, of course, that it was not only within the British Empire that they now roamed. They could be transmuted into 'the English-speaking peoples' and one common 'transatlantic civilization'.

In his *American Commonwealth* (1888), James Bryce gave a not unattractive picture of a complex and dynamic country. There had been, and were to continue to be, disputes between London and Washington – from the aftermath of the American Civil War to the Venezuelan/British Guyana boundary question – and the 'balance of power' in North America was still a matter of British concern. However, as A.J. Balfour, Salisbury's nephew, put it in a speech in 1896, a war with the United States would carry with it 'some of the unnatural horror of a civil war'. Journalists and letter-writers on one side or the other of the Atlantic did not necessarily agree, however, about the strength of 'sentiments of kinship'.[72] Talk of 'the two great Anglo-Saxon states', as Balfour recognized, somewhat overlooked populations that would not have considered themselves 'Anglo-Saxons' at all. It was, however, to the United States rather than to Europe that some members of the British political elite now looked when seeking brides, and not only for financial reasons. Joseph Chamberlain, Salisbury's colonial secretary was one of the latest to do so. It scarcely needs to be said, though, that Salisbury himself loathed the United States. His willingness to conclude arbitration treaties with Washington did not reflect devotion to the Anglo-Saxon bond.[73]

Creating historical perspectives: transcending nationality?

Pursuit of Anglo-Saxons, both real and latter-day, continued to engage a burgeoning British historical profession that viewed its contribution to national self-consciousness with increasing seriousness. At Oxford and Cambridge, in the early 1870s, 'history' was turned into an academic discipline in its own right. Tutors, not all devoted to research, taught young men enrolled in the 'school for statesmen'. It was professors who became conscious of the necessity of creating a scientific school – as epitomized in contributions to the *English Historical Review* (1885). Writing history, it seemed, was very different from writing novels, though some professors could not altogether suppress a desire to write for a wider audience.[74] It was proper to focus on British (i.e. English) history, but some strayed across the Channel. William Stubbs gave lectures in Oxford on German medieval history and discerned English institutional origins emerging from Teutonic soil.

It fell to the young Richard Lodge, however, to supply something new to assist the student in understanding foreign mysteries. His *Student's Modern Europe*, covering the period 1453–1878, established 'Europe' in the minds of English and Scottish students over several decades in its many impressions. Deciding that singing choruses with German students in Heidelberg in his long vacation constituted an insufficient grasp of the continent, Lodge had travelled over a period of years through Germany, Austria, Hungary, Italy, the Low Countries and France. His immediate academic reward was an invitation to assist in translating the Swiss, Johannes Bluntschli's, *Lehre vom modernen Staat*. He also wrote an *Encyclopaedia* entry on Spain. His later reward was the opportunity to introduce European history to the west of Scotland as professor of history at Glasgow University.[75]

Other historians ventured abroad in this period. C.G. Coulton found himself in Heidelberg and was surprised to be told by a German-Jewish friend that Germany and Britain could not go on indefinitely without a serious quarrel. What would happen to the British, he was asked, who had not one soldier to ten Germans? Coulton did not then know the answer.[76] Sucked from Saxon obscurity in Somerset to succeed Stubbs in Oxford, Edward Freeman's primary concern was with England down to the fourteenth century – though he also wrote a *History of Sicily*. Armed with copious railway timetables, he had scampered about Europe drawing notable buildings in France, Germany, Italy and Dalmatia.[77] Where the modern history of Europe was concerned, however, he was said to be 'coming to that', though this delay did not prevent a detestation of the presence of the modern Turk in Europe. York Powell, who became regius professor at Oxford in 1894 was a somewhat eccentric choice as a historian, but his linguistic knowledge reached parts of Europe – including Icelandic, Welsh and

Portuguese – not normally at the fingertips of English historians. He had the advantage that his build and beard made him a passable imitation of Lord Salisbury, but he owed his appointment to Lord Rosebery, who had been his pupil. One might conclude, but not very persuasively, that Rosebery was acknowledging how much his European perspective was indebted to Powell's linguistic attainments.

Indeed, it would be unwise to make any clear correlation between the history created by these Oxford historians and the perspectives of the British political leaders that emerged from the university over these decades. However, patchy and idiosyncratic though their attention to Europe was, they did acknowledge that the English past could not be detached from it – whatever that context might imply in the present, and it might not imply very much. Despite this 'imperial moment', J.A. Froude, Freeman's successor, was the only regius professor to risk seeing the Empire for himself. He came back enthusiastically from Australia to write *Oceana, or England and her Colonies* (1886).[78] It was not to Cape Town or Toronto, but to Paris and Göttingen, that York Powell sent young H.A.L. Fisher in 1889 – the most influential British *History of Europe* of the mid-twentieth century was already in gestation.

At Cambridge, where he succeeded Charles Kingsley, John Seeley wrote a full study of the Prussian minister Stein (1757–1831), reformer of the Prussian state, but it was not his work in modern European history that brought him fame. That was achieved through *The Expansion of England* (1883), a bestseller that demonstrated what a regius professor could do if he caught a public mood. Politicians read him, none more avidly than Joseph Chamberlain, the Radical-Imperialist who was to become Salisbury's colonial secretary in his last government. Seeley reiterated Dilke's point that only by ceasing to be absent-minded about empire could Britain survive as a Great Power. Seeley himself, however, never left Europe and the lectures that became the book were conceived in Switzerland.[79] 'Anglo-Saxons' do not appear in his text and its tone was different from Froude's. Central to Seeley's thinking, and pursued in subsequent books, was the idea that only where the national interest was deliberately pursued externally did a nation become fully conscious of itself as a nation among nations. Such an emphasis, it is argued, was common enough in Germany but almost peculiar to Seeley in Britain.[80] It was one that Lord Rosebery thought fit to reward with a knighthood for the author.

The background and approach of Seeley's successor, Lord Acton, could hardly be more different. For him, history was not politics, though Acton once told Gladstone that his vast library had been bought with a view to understanding the public life of the time and the world in which he lived. It was a measure of changing attitudes that a man who had been turned down by three Cambridge colleges when young because he was a Catholic (which led to him studying in Munich instead) now occupied the regius chair. No more European Englishman than Acton could be imagined at this juncture.

He was born in Naples in 1834 – though in a villa with an English land-scaped garden – and died at Tegernsee, Bavaria. The Actons were a Shropshire family but John's grandfather had been educated in France, had commanded the ships of the grand duke of Tuscany and had ended up as prime minister of Naples. John's father married a Dalberg, one of the lead-ing families of the Holy Roman Empire, with large estates in the Rhineland. Acton himself married a Bavarian countess. His connections in Europe – family, ecclesiastical, political and historical – were wide and diverse, and not at all 'typical'. He was, however, an Englishman, indeed from 1869 a peer of the realm, but could not be easily pigeonholed. It is hardly surpris-ing to hear him arguing that the historian had to rise above nationalism. 'The process of civilisation depends on transcending Nationality,' he wrote, 'for patriotism cannot absolve a man from his duty to mankind'. The his-tory that had to be written should be neither British, nor European but uni-versal. Acton knew very well that 'national missions' were being trumpeted in many quarters but he thought that the historian should be detached. It was a solitary business and might make one sad. By the time of his death in 1902, Acton was sad. He had, however, a long after-life as successive gen-erations of Cambridge historians succumbed to the study of his papers and tried to establish how an Englishman might write history.

The dilemmas with which Acton had wrestled as a historian were echoed in other areas of academic reflection. Even Acton had a nationality. There was a place for patriotism but it needed to be restrained by an awareness of the duty to mankind. How, though, could nationality be both recognized and yet transcended? If it was not, Europe would destroy itself.

In France, it was Ernest Renan who returned to these issues in the wake of the Franco-Prussian war. He took the view that Europe was 'a confeder-ation of States united by the idea of civilization that they share'. Each state had an individuality derived from race, language, history and religion. He had no doubt that there were superior races and inferior races. The regener-ation of the latter by the former was part of the providential order of things. But that could not be the end of the matter. A nation also stemmed from 'the agreement and desire of its various provinces to live together'. His analysis in *What is a Nation?* (1882), and repeated in other writing, was that states and nations were transient phenomena.[81] They had their place, purpose and time but they could give way, possibly, to a European confederation. After 1871, however, it looked to him as though France and Germany were divided by a chasm that would take centuries to fill – but only when there had been a bridging of this political, cultural and spiritual chasm could Europe become a 'willed community'. 'Before French, German, or Italian culture,' he concluded, 'there is human culture'. Like many others at this time, as we have seen, he was attracted by Switzerland as an example of a confederation in which race, language and religion were transcended. Renan had stated that his aim in life had been 'the intellectual, moral and political union of Germany and France'. He did not think it appropriate to include 'England' in such a project. He admired the way in which the English were dealing with issues of religious toleration, but somehow they were not on his wavelength. It was the continent that needed to be reconciled. The sole conclusion that he drew from his visit to Oxford in 1880 was that fellows of its colleges did not work. Such a conclusion did not suggest that England would be to offer much by way of a *via media* in European intellectual life. It fell to a Scotsman, Sir Mountstuart Grant Duff, a keen though ineffective observer of European politics, to champion Renan in Britain. Duff perhaps found solace for his dismal political career in his election to the presidency of the Royal Historical Society.

Internationals: palaces, popes and the proletariat

The nation-state was not the sole occupant of the space that was Europe. The 'Royal International', after a fashion, still operated. Personal visits by the crowned heads of the five major European powers to their 'cousins' took place some four times a year.[82] Her longevity had ensured that Queen Victoria had a superior status. Even as early as 1869 she was describing herself to her daughter as 'the *doyenne* of Sovereigns' in Europe. The award of honours and dignities to foreign royalties was a matter of considerable seriousness. In 1877 Victoria agonized between the Order of the Bath and the Order of the Garter as a suitable accolade for the emperor of Germany. Stock selection in the European royal marriage market also much exercised the queen. In Victorian Britain there was always an undercurrent of complaint, and not only in radical circles, against the 'German-plated' British monarchy. German additions to Victoria's family were represented as expensive drains on the pocket of 'John Bull'.[83]

European monarchs, of course, did not all have the same capacity to exercise political power. Although with less power than a German, Russian or Austrian emperor, Queen Victoria had not turned into a cipher and had real though circumscribed influence.[84] Nevertheless, although trans-European royal contact continued, both official and unofficial, the 'royal international' could not be effectively mobilized to thwart the interests of states as perceived and presented by ministers. There were some 'grey areas' where, on occasion, the 'royal network' was valuable but it was not an alternative decision-making mechanism. The royal relationship between Queen Victoria and her grandson Wilhelm, both before and after his accession as kaiser, was important.[85] The death of his father, married to her daughter, the Princess Victoria, came as a severe blow to the queen. Wilhelm II did not get on well with his mother. However, despite occasional lapses, Queen Victoria did prove able to separate her personal feelings and political needs, though initially Wilhelm had complained that she was treating him 'more as a Kaiser than a grandson'.[86] The time had passed, however, when in Britain the visit of a foreign monarch could be treated as simply a 'family visit'.

Such occasions, duly accompanied by pomp and circumstance, had inescapable political aspects. The queen well understood this point but declined to be used for such a purpose in relation to Ireland. She discouraged visits and residence there by members of the royal family in 1872, 1885, 1893 and 1897.[87]

Whatever they may have felt about each other, European royalties were certainly superior to any other kind of royalty. The shah of Persia came to London in 1889. Lord Kimberley, having been required to 'kow-tow' to the visitor at Buckingham Palace, was scathing: 'what a ridiculous fuss is made about this semi-barbarian'.[88] The prime minister later entertained the shah at Hatfield House, but was not overawed by him, at least not physically.

'Transcendence' of a rather different kind was to be found in the formation of the Second (Socialist) International in Paris in 1889. Its congresses were held in Brussels (1891), Zürich (1893) and London (1896). Here was the latest manifestation of the view that workers of the world, or at least of Europe, should unite. Class loyalty could transcend national loyalty. It proved difficult, however, to agree on either ideology or organization. Although it was the British Trades Union Congress that could be said indirectly to have launched the International, the British were scarcely in the van of its subsequent evolution. There was no mass party in Britain, both the Independent Labour Party and the Social Democratic Federation were small and competing against each other for members. It was the German Social Democratic Party that largely constituted the 'model' for European socialist growth. Most of the British trades union officials, it seems, had come to regard the International as a forum for theoretical debates between continental Marxists and their British socialist colleagues.[89] There were only a couple of occasions (London being one) when the British delegation was larger than the French or German. It is suggested, however, that British delegations were of a size that demonstrated that Britain was a 'top nation', and one that normally voted against 'continental extremism'. There were few translations of Marx or the post-Marx generation that were available in English. It was conspicuous that it was between the strongest national constituents that the strongest tensions arose: between the French and the Germans, and also between the British and both the French and the German delegations. It was a triangularity repeated in other spheres.

'Transcendence' might also be located in the Vatican. The Protestantism of Europe, Lutheranism, Calvinism and Anglicanism was almost by definition national in structure and organization. There was no Protestant 'locus' to challenge the nation-state. Pope Pius IX, however, was in a challenging phase. In December 1864 he had issued a *Syllabus of Errors* of formidable comprehensiveness that concluded by condemning the belief that the Roman pontiff could or should reconcile himself with progress, liberalism and civilization as lately introduced.[90] It was an announcement that was greeted with derision by liberal opinion throughout Europe. Indeed, it seemed to confront all that modern Europe believed itself to be achieving.

The calling of the first Vatican Council in 1870 looked to some like a further step to assert the 'temporal power' of the papacy. The question of the pope, Gladstone could not help feeling, was a question for all of Europe. Both his foreign secretary and the British envoy counselled him against intervening in the matter. It could be argued that a declaration of papal infallibility would weaken rather than strengthen the Roman church.[91] For his part, however, Cardinal Manning welcomed the prospect of an infallibility decree. He suspected that Newman was lukewarm on the matter and had earlier seen 'much danger of an English Catholicism, of which Newman is the highest type'.[92] It was a contradiction in terms, thought Manning, to think that one could have a Catholicism that was English. But a Catholicism that was English was just what Gladstone wanted. Acton, hostile to infallibility, was on site in the Vatican and kept him informed.[93] The dogmatic constitution, which affirmed infallibility, was passed.

Two days later, the Franco-Prussian war broke out and Italian troops occupied Rome. The Vatican Council dispersed. Four years later, having resigned office, Gladstone burst into print with an expostulation, as he called it, on the Vatican decrees 'in their bearing on civil allegiance'. He was convinced, he wrote to Granville, that there was a conspiracy afoot to manipulate the war in Europe in such a fashion that it would lead to the re-establishment by force of the temporal power of the papacy.[94] Controversy raged. Bismarck took the opportunity to send Gladstone a private letter declaring his pleasure at seeing 'the two nations which in Europe are the champions of liberty of conscience, encountering the same foes'. It took a common dislike of the papacy to produce such an exchange. In the event, of course, the temporal power was not restored. Whatever influence the Vatican might be able to bring to bear on the future of Europe could only be exercised by other means.

A perverse interpretation of geography?

In one of his last orations, in the Guildhall, Disraeli declared that so long as the power and advice of England was felt in the councils of Europe peace would be maintained, and for a long period. If one of the most extensive and wealthiest empires in the world turned 'an indifferent ear' to the feelings and fortunes of continental Europe because of what he called 'a perverse inter-pretation of its insular geographical position', it ran the risk of becoming an object of general plunder.[95] It has been evident from this chapter that the British ear had been extended, at many levels and by many people. It had not been 'indifferent', but neither had it been fully attentive or receptive to the rather discordant sounds of an increasingly cacophonous continent. European peace of a kind had been largely maintained after 1870/71, though whether in any sense this could be due to 'insular advice and power' was another matter. Yet, as the century drew to a close, there was apprehension rather than satisfaction.

In October 1899 Britain went to war against the Boers in South Africa. It looked like another 'little imperial war' but might turn out not to be. In European capital after European capital British action was strongly condemned. Might this be the moment when Britain and the British Empire might be the object of that 'general plunder' which Disraeli had feared?

8

Civilization and cataclysm, c.1900–c.1919

Britain's South African war: Europe's opportunity?

The conflict in South Africa might have proved the occasion when 'the continent' united in opposition to British arrogance. Here was an opportunity, perhaps, to transcend the two blocs – Germany, Austria-Hungary and Italy on the one hand, and France and Russia on the other – in a common explosion of beneficial indignation. Only by identifying Britain as 'the Other', might some kind of 'European' solidarity be discovered. Certainly there was no lack of abuse directed at individual British people who happened to find themselves abroad. In Germany, the young Robert Vansittart, later permanent under-secretary at the Foreign Office, had to endure gibes in the house, press, theatre and street, and narrowly avoided a duel.[1] In the Netherlands, the cause of the Boers could unite the Catholic south and Protestant north in criticism of British action. In the spring of 1900, Queen Victoria expressed her displeasure at French criticism by cancelling her normal visit to the south of France. She went instead to Italy, where the atmosphere was less hostile.

Newspapers across Europe heaped praise upon the noble army of farmers. Feelings were perhaps strongest in France. French press hostility was so vitriolic that the German occupiers saw benefit in reproducing it in 1940. It seemed that decades of pent-up resentment of Britain was now being given free rein across the continent. President Kruger was greeted by enthusiastic crowds when he landed at Marseilles. The vision of a vast French African Empire had excited certain sections of French opinion. British control of Egypt continued to rankle. Then the two countries confronted each other at Fashoda (hitherto not a place of note) in the Sudan in 1898.[2] The British government demanded, and eventually obtained, the withdrawal of the small French expeditionary force that had arrived there. This French 'humiliation', though it was followed by a convention between the two countries that more or less established French predominance in West Africa and British in East Africa, was nevertheless bitterly resented in Paris. The German ambassador reported to Berlin that Frenchmen had even forgotten Alsace. The French president told a Russian diplomat that Britain, not Germany, was France's real enemy. Nevertheless, while French diplomacy thought there was some possible leverage – over Egypt, for example – neutrality was the official position of the government. The foreign minister, Théophile Delcassé, publicly dissociated himself from the press attacks on Britain. The extent to which he was already going further and envisaging an understanding with Britain, remains contentious.[3]

German support for the Transvaal had been manifested in various ways over the immediately preceding years. The kaiser had sent a telegram of congratulations in 1896 to the president of the Transvaal, Paul Kruger – a raid led by Dr Starr Jameson from Rhodesia into the Transvaal had failed. This gesture brought upon Wilhelm the wrath of much of the British press. A year later, however, the journalist and MP, Justin McCarthy, thought that English people had pulled themselves together and had agreed that it was 'only one more of the odd performances of the young German Emperor'.[4] In 1899, however, Germany would not become involved. The kaiser, 'a man whose remarkable personal qualities', *The Times* now observed, 'are hardly less fully appreciated in England than in Germany itself', visited his dear English grandmama in November. The *Daily Mail* printed his photograph with the caption 'A Friend in Need is a Friend Indeed'. Two years later, though with a number of further 'odd performances' in between, not least concerning the 'Hunnish' qualities expected of German troops in China, the kaiser was again in England. In Victoria's funeral procession, the press agreed that he appeared every inch an emperor. In a departing speech, Wilhelm declared that Britain and Germany ought to form an alliance: 'with such an alliance not a mouse could stir in Europe without our permission'. On his previous visit to England, it was reported that 178 pheasants and 328 rabbits had stirred in the kaiser's presence, though they did so for the last time.[5]

In other European capitals, a disposition to find the British hypocritical was not absent. There was some hope that the powers would obtain 'compensation' somewhere in return for non-intervention. That did not happen. Gestures, like the invitation to a Boer representative to attend the marriage of the tsar's younger sister, upset the British ambassador, but had little material consequence.[6] As far as Italy was concerned, though there were some sources of friction – the British downgrading of the Italian language in Malta, for example – relations between the two countries were good. The French ambassador in Rome (who had been brought up in London, where his father was living in exile after the coup of 1851) reported in 1899 that it was British predominance in the Mediterranean that reassured the Italians, though, by the end of the war there was some improvement in Franco–Italian relations. Italy appeared to indicate that in any war involving France, it would remain neutral and received, in return, a signal that certain Italian aspirations in North Africa would not be opposed. The way was opening up for Italy's conquest of Libya in 1911.[7] For his part, basking in his seventieth birthday, following so closely on the golden jubilee of his reign, the emperor of Austria expressed himself as 'completely English' where the war was concerned. In sum, such reactions indicate why Britain was able to 'escape' a 'continental league'.

Mightier yet?

'Europe' could not challenge an empire that ruled approximately a quarter of the globe and consisted of some 400 million people, only approximately one-tenth of whom lived in the United Kingdom. It fell quite naturally to Foreign Office men, for example, writing of Russia, to state that its frontiers were 'coterminous with ours or nearly so over a large portion of Asia'.[8] The Himalayas, on this reading, were as much a 'British' frontier as was the English Channel. The 'golden link of the race', as the *Daily Telegraph* described Victoria, had however apparently united more than just the 'Anglo-Saxons' at home and abroad. Vast crowds had gathered in Calcutta on the day of Queen Victoria's funeral and sat in mourning throughout the day. Muslims in London had offered prayers for 'the Sovereign of the greatest number of The True Believers in the world'.[9]

The South African war, which had dragged on until the Peace of Vereeniging in May 1902, nevertheless showed the empire's weakness. British forces had indeed proved victorious but it had taken some 300,000 men to achieve the defeat of 'farmers with rifles'. Continental powers drew conclusions about British military incapacity – as indeed were drawn at home. Throughout, there had been a minority of 'pro-Boers' who were appalled by the way in which Milner, as high commissioner in the Cape, and Chamberlain, as colonial secretary, had, in their different ways, engineered the conflict in the first place. The outcome, too, had not settled the 'isolation' question. Victory could be cited as evidence that Britain still did not suffer 'practically' from its absence from the alliance systems of the continent. During the war's course, however, the opinion had been expressed in various quarters, notably from India, that Britain was no longer strong enough to sustain its global position on its own. Salisbury, however, at the very end of his career, could see no advantage in 'novel and most onerous obligations' (he was thinking of assisting Germany and Austria-Hungary against Russia) in order to guard against a danger in whose existence there was no historical reason for believing. On the other hand, there remained those who feared a vulnerability to 'a combination of Great Powers'. What was to happen to China or, on a different scale, to the Samoan islands? The possibility of a German 'alliance' was pursued up hill and down dale. It has subsequently been interpreted variously as a 'mirage' or a 'lost opportunity'.[10] The German assertion that Britain 'needed' an alliance was found particularly galling in London. A detailed further examination of this episode is not attempted here. The fact that an alliance was canvassed, however, notably by Joseph Chamberlain, indicates that the 'continental question' had entered a new phase. Chamberlain, momentarily at least, talked the language of Teutonism and saw it as providing the necessary substructure of a lasting British-German relationship.

The problem was to decide what kind of state the United Kingdom/British Empire was. Perceived from one angle, it was a 'world-state', with a structure and scale quite unlike that of any other European state. Russian and French expansion was feeble in comparison. German colonial enthusiasts knew that it was the real thing. Carl Peters, one such, had come to England in the 1880s to discover its secret at first hand. Max Beer, the London correspondent of the official organ of the German Social Democratic Party believed that the empire embodied a great dream – the political and economic unification of the world.[11] 'World politics' was what the British did and they might even be regarded as the emissary of Europe. A party of German students, visiting England in 1910, expressed their gratitude that it was 'English people who extended the sounds of the Continental masters [composers] all over the world'.[12]

No one felt 'globalization' more strongly than George Nathaniel Curzon. In the 1880s and 1890s, he travelled twice round the world. Although he had also sat through three Wagner operas at Bayreuth, and had gone on short jaunts to Spain, Paris and Italy, he preferred the khanates of central Asia. Both his wives were American. Destiny had marked him out as a future president of the Royal Geographical Society. 'No Englishman', he had noted, could 'land in Hong Kong without feeling a thrill of pride for his nationality. Here is the further-most Eastern link in that chain of fortresses which from Spain to China girdles half the globe'.[13] In 1907, having served as viceroy of India, he reminded a Birmingham audience that 'England' could not be separated from 'empire'. 'If the empire fell,' he declared, 'so would England, and your ports, coaling stations, dockyards would disappear, and England would become the inglorious playground of the world, with her antiquities, castles, parks and the like remaining to attract tourists, a crowd of meandering pilgrims'.[14] Had the term 'theme park' existed, Curzon would have used it. The thought that Britain might be nothing more than 'a glorified Belgium' was too dreadful to contemplate.

At one level, therefore, the participation of colonial troops alongside British troops in South Africa had indeed testified that the British Empire was a going concern. It was evidence that it was not simply 'Britain' that was at war. The eventual formation of the Union of South Africa in 1910 as a kind of federation was to be later used as a demonstration that English- and Afrikaans-speaking South Africa could be reconciled within the imperial framework (black South Africans could be left until a later day). Yet it was also clear that the countries of settlement, which had sent contingents to fight alongside the motherland, could not have been coerced into doing so. The corollary of this help, however, was the need for consultation with 'imperial public opinion'. The existence of 'colonial nationalism' could scarcely be denied.[15] 'It is difficult to believe henceforth', wrote a contributor to the *Nineteenth Century* in March 1902, that 'any man can be Prime Minister of Britain-within-seas who had not gained in equal measure the confidence and support of Britain-beyond-seas'.[16] At the least, that would entail mechanisms of consultation. However, the Colonial Conference of 1907 rejected plans for an imperial council with a permanent secretariat. The assembled colonial premiers seemed, well, rather 'colonial'. Foreign observers, particularly Germans, were apt to suppose that some philosophy must underpin the vast British imperial project, but the more one looked at its structure, the more incoherent and ramshackle it appeared.[17] That it all somehow worked, had to be put down to a British genius for government.

In claiming that old ideas of trade and competition had changed, Chamberlain struck a chord. It was obvious that Britain no longer possessed the kind of commercial dominance that had existed in mid-century. It was equally clear that 'pure' free trade had not been universally adopted, nor would it be.[18] It was time to draw more closely the ties of sentiment, sympathy and interest within the empire. It would be possible to envisage the economic unity of the empire – 'British trade in British hands' – in such a way that it would matter little whether its 'centre' was in London, Sydney or Ottawa. Such a view corresponded with Curzon's indifference as to whether the king held court in London, Quebec or Calcutta. In 1903 Chamberlain launched his Tariff Reform Campaign. It was indeed the case that Britain traded and invested globally, overwhelmingly outside Europe (but not overwhelmingly within the empire). He split the Conservative government in doing so.[19] Balfour's administration petered out in December 1905, and Chamberlain himself suffered a debilitating stroke in the following year and sat speechless in the House of Commons until his death in 1914. 'Defence of free trade' played a significant part in the Liberal electoral victory of January 1906. Yet, while in the short term the 'tariff reform' campaign failed, the underlying issues of alignment and identity of which it was in part an expression, did not disappear. Proponents of imperial federation remained ardent lobbyists. The pressure group the Round Table, founded in 1910, continued to seek ways of integrating the states of the empire.[20] Such activity was, of course, the work of enthusiasts, though not all of them displayed in their persons the 'clear, healthy, though dry-looking tan' acquired, at least in fiction, by sons of MPs who forsook the decadent lifestyle of Europe for Australian ranches.[21] It was, however, very gratifying that such tanned specimens returned to fight in the European war of 1914.

'Citizens of Europe'?

Yet this quasi-world-state, this 'Land of Hope and Glory', as Edward VII's coronation ode, written by a son of an archbishop of Canterbury, described it in 1902, could not avoid its European location. (The author's father had also been the first headmaster of Wellington College in Berkshire, set up for the sons of officers in memory of Wellington.) Edward Elgar, composer of the sumptuous tune to which the words were now sung, 'modern in a peculiarly English way', was an artistic embodiment of this national split personality.[22] Europe was where music was. It had been to Leipzig that he had gone as a teenager. Later, he had made several trips in the 1890s to Bayreuth. A large engraved portrait of Wagner was hung at Elgar's house in Malvern Link. Richard Strauss was his contemporary musical hero. Birmingham, home to Joseph Chamberlain, was set to become 'an English Leipzig'.[23] Music was European and Elgar's 'eastern' pieces (*In Smyrna*, *Serenade Mauresque* and *Crown of India*) have rightly been seen as little more than 'nods' within a style that remained uncompromisingly western.[24] After 1914, the severance of his ties with the German conductor, Hans Richter, who had done so much to promote his music, profoundly saddened him. Richter rejected the English honours that had been accorded him. The widow of August Jaeger, 'Nimrod', the naturalized German who had been Elgar's musical publisher, changed her name to Hunter. An Anglo-German civilization, in which Elgar had partly lived, was coming to an end.

Such a sundering of a particular network of relationships by war can be paralleled in many other fields and many other instances. It was perhaps very agreeable to be described as a 'citizen of Europe', as was Maurice Baring, diplomat, journalist and novelist, but in reality no one could measure up to this awesome title. In circumstances of conflict, individuals had to choose between the cultures and civilizations: the whole European package was not available. Britons did not all feel 'at home' in the same places. A man like Baring belonged to what G.K. Chesterton called 'a microscopically small minority' of men of good English culture who, quite unaffectedly and warmly, were 'devoted to some particular foreign culture'.[25] Insular inhabitants were thought to be more 'linguistically challenged' than continentals. A Foreign Office official explained to the German state secretary, 'Englishmen are bad at learning languages, whereas Germans are not.'[26] This, he thought, gave German commercial travellers an advantage, but this linguistic incompetence, supposing it to be as true as it was often assumed to be, had deeper implications for the way in which 'Europe' could be experienced. The stereotypes and images of Europe formed by the British, conveyed by correspondence and conversation, could scarcely ever be described as genuinely comparative. Diplomats, moving from mission to mission, form something of an exception to this generalization, but naturally even they could not have posts in every European capital. In addition, the fact that ambassadors were frequently chosen because their personal attributes were held to match those required by particular countries reinforced stereotypes.[27] Whether the diplomacy and ambitions of Germany were more devious than those of Russia, or vice versa, could therefore be construed very differently in the light of individual experience.

A considerable number of Englishmen fell to wondering about their identity in circumstances in which it appeared that they might have to decide whether, as it were, they were 'Teutons' or 'Slavs'.[28] Two opposing examples may be given. Stephen Graham, interpreter of eastern Christianity, passing through Germany on his way to Kiev in January 1914, was impressed by German efficiency. The English, he thought, were not inefficient but 'thanks to the ancient Briton in us, we are more like the Russians than the Germans ... naturally the Russians can't stand the Germans'.[29] John Clapham, the economic historian, was quite clear, however, that he was a Teuton not a Slav.[30] It did indeed seem to many that Europe would be likely to be dominated by one or other of these imposing aggregates, presented either as 'racial' or 'cultural'. Lord Cromer, the authority on the government of 'subject races', wanted to see Germany defeated but not crushed, for then 'the only result would be an extreme predominance on the part of the Slav, which would be only one degree better than Pan-Germanism'.[31]

Such crude but politically significant perceptions of the 'pan-' phenomenon obliquely expressed what individuals thought 'our race' to be. The United Kingdom, in the second half of the nineteenth century had 'led' Europe in the export of population, with some 10 million out of a total of nearly 23 million.[32] The 1901 census revealed that more than a million people then living in Britain had been born elsewhere. Although half of that total had been born in the United Kingdom's other island, the other half had come mainly from the mainland of Europe. The largest single category among such immigrants was Jews (a population that had reached some 300,000 by 1914). The influx had prompted the passage of the Aliens Act (1905), although its restrictions applied only to foreign 'undesirables' – the destitute or those with a criminal record. By 1911, Jews constituted 2 per cent of the population in London, 5.8 per cent in Leeds and 5.5 per cent in Manchester. They now constituted the largest (and initially the incomers were largely Russian-speaking) identifiable community from Europe in Britain.[33]

The Irish presence in Britain could not be 'alien' but it was 'different' – Englishmen in Ireland were not 'aliens' either, but they knew themselves to be 'different' too.[34] Whether such difference would remain, vanish or strengthen would depend on inclination (the immigrants themselves) and reception (the reaction of 'natives'). The 'Irish question' in England, Scotland and Wales, would play differently, as it had done throughout the nineteenth century, from place to place and had an inherent ambivalence. Ambivalence, indeed, characterized the entire relationship between Britain and Ireland at this juncture. The empire of settlement, in the composition of its population, was not English, not British, but 'British Isles'.[35] Looked at globally, what was developing was a 'British/English imperial race'. Within the United Kingdom itself, the separate nationalities of Welsh, Scots and English could seem merely local divisions.[36] With the return of a Liberal government in January 1906, however, the question of home rule for Ireland was back on the political agenda. It proved as bitterly divisive at the level of Westminster politics as it did in Ireland itself. Liberal ministers had little difficulty in recognizing that in a certain sense the United Kingdom was a multi-national state. Indeed, the very membership of the Liberal cabinets testified to this fact. Sir Edward Grey, the foreign secretary, argued in a speech in May 1912 that nothing but harm would come from attempting to make out that there were no separate units in the United Kingdom and no differences of national opinion.[37]

Was political devolution a helpful and beneficial corollary of such recognition, both for the United Kingdom as a whole and for its territorial components? Alternatively, was it likely to lead to the break-up of the kingdom and the emergence, in an acrimonious atmosphere, of competing new states whose acceptability and definition might in turn be subject to enduring challenge, both internally and externally? Where was the 'middle way' to be found? In relation to Ireland, it had by now come to be an old issue, though even more pressing, but it also had some point in relation to Wales, Scotland and a possibly regionalized England as well. In such circumstances, though fleetingly and unsuccessfully, the comprehensive federalization of the structures of the United Kingdom was mooted. What had happened in Canada and was just happening in Australia, could scarcely be thought un-British. And, indeed, it might be thought an essential ingredient in the functioning of a world-state, with multiple levels of competence and decision-making pertaining throughout.[38] Yet Ireland's complexity resisted such easy accommodation. Home rule, as a solution, was at once too much and too little for different elements both in Ireland and in Britain. In 1914, at long last, a home rule measure was on the statute book after a protracted parliamentary struggle between the two houses, but whether, when implemented, it could work, was another matter.[39]

In such circumstances, it was not a straightforward matter to present the identity of the United Kingdom in the European arena.[40] The divisions within the United Kingdom, and how such divisions were to be compared with, and related to, the divisions of Europe were coming to seem increasingly problematic. Even so, it was still the gulf between all 'Europeans' and the 'East' that received most emphasis.[41] Curzon may have thought that Britain's subject peoples in the East displayed a 'satisfied and grateful acquiescence in our domination', whereas French rule was 'irksome' to them, but *au fond* the imperialisms of Europe all rested on a basis of the continent's superiority.[42] Benevolence, though not absent, was not a defining characteristic of the British version, differentiating it from all others. Since, according to Curzon, the day of 'great nations' had apparently dawned, it was surely unreasonable for Britain to complain if Germany embarked on *Weltpolitik*, whatever that meant, or if Russia continued to push east.

By 1917, having listened to three years of war-time propaganda, which had either lauded or vilified the qualities of 'the great nations', A.C. Benson was perhaps regretting his extravagant ode of 1902. 'The world at large', he now wrote,

> outside of the people I actually touch & know, seems to me a great dim abstraction. I am not the least interested in the human race, nor can I back our race against all races. I believe in our race, but I don't disbelieve in theirs.[43]

Old diplomacy's last fling: Balfour and Lansdowne

It fell to new men in office (though most of them were chips off old blocks) at the top of Edwardian and Georgian politics to address these contradictions, or at least paradoxes, seemingly inherent in the United Kingdom's position. Politicians and diplomats inevitably felt in their bones many of the assumptions, prejudices and sentiments that have been alluded to. Their experiences, and the orbits in which they had moved, fashioned their perspectives. Even so, the pursuit of the 'national interest', however defined, could run counter to such likes or dislikes. On 28 July 1914 the historian G.M. Trevelyan wrote that 'our whole British civilisation' would be made or marred by the decision whether or not to go to war.

The fifth Marquess of Lansdowne (1845–1927) became foreign secretary in November 1900.[44] Educated at Eton and Balliol, Oxford, he had succeeded his father in 1866. His grandfather had served in every Whig/Liberal cabinet in the period 1830–63. The Lansdownes held large estates in Ireland (and in England) and it was opposition to Gladstone's Irish policy that led him to forsake its Whig traditions. He was fluent in French, his mother being the daughter of an aide-de-camp to Napoleon who had later, on making his peace with the Bourbons, served as French ambassador in London. Before becoming foreign secretary, Lansdowne had served far away from Europe – in Canada as governor-general (1883–88) and in India as viceroy (1888–94). On his return, he became war secretary in 1895. As foreign secretary, he favoured a good working relationship with Germany but felt that an alliance would 'oblige us to adopt in all our foreign relations a policy which would no longer be British but Anglo-German'.[45] That was not a prospect to be contemplated. An Anglo-Japanese alliance, however, would provide a reliable ally in the event of an attack on the British Empire by two powers, such as Russia and France, combined. It was concluded in January 1902, though it did not, in itself, preclude an understanding with Germany. The Russo-Japanese war followed in 1904–05.[46] The British press recognized that a global shift was evident in the alliance and in the Japanese victory, but was uneasy. While the 'Europeanization' of Japan (the substitution of western ideas and modes of life for those of the Chinese) was welcomed, the signature of a treaty with an Asiatic power had great significance. 'Great Britain', declared *The Economist*, 'has quit decidedly ... that unwritten alliance of all white Powers against all coloured races and through which alone the supremacy of Europe over Asia and Africa can be finally be established'.[47] Was it wise, in other words, for the British in this way to 'break European ranks'? Nevertheless, the alliance was subsequently renewed. In 1910 a Japan-British exhibition further celebrated the links between the two 'island empires'. In the same year, *The Times* noted that since Britain kept the ex-king of Upper Burma prisoner in India it could scarcely object to the Japanese annexation of Korea.

In Europe, it was Lansdowne who concluded, on 8 April 1904, the set of arrangements, public and secret, that came collectively to be referred to as the *entente cordiale*. The preceding negotiations had considered colonial questions – Newfoundland fisheries, West Africa, Morocco, Egypt, Siam and the New Hebrides. Centrally, France accepted the British position in Egypt, while Britain accepted that Morocco 'appertained' to France. The previous year, King Edward VII had paid a state visit to Paris, a visit returned a few months later by the French president. The diplomatic atmosphere had certainly improved but more public relations exercises were needed to turn a hard-argued colonial deal into a cordial relationship between the two peoples. Indeed, the arrangement still ran against the prevailing stereotype of Britain in France.[48] The agreement was generally welcomed in the press and across the political parties in Britain – the only significant opponent was Lord Rosebery. It was, however, not an alliance of a comprehensive kind and, on the British side at least, was not seen as the prelude to one. Nor would it necessarily lead to an Anglo-Russian agreement. Yet there was always a possibility that international developments might bring about one or other, or both, such extensions. The kaiser's landing in Tangier nearly a year later served to solidify rather than to disrupt a still fluid understanding.[49] Lansdowne's European legacy remains ambiguous, capable of being interpreted, in its restraint, as Salisburian 'continuity' but also, in its break with severe detachment, as a first step towards greater commitment. After leaving the Foreign Office at the end of 1905, Lansdowne's energy was chiefly displayed, as leader of the House of Lords, in obstructing any step that could lead to Ireland becoming 'foreign'. In 1917, however, having lost a son and fearful that the prolongation of the war would spell 'ruin of the civilized world', Lansdowne emerged in public as an advocate of a negotiated peace. It was a letter, said H.G. Wells, of a peer who feared revolution more than national dishonour.[50]

Balfour, who succeeded his uncle as prime minister in 1902, did not clear away uncertainty.[51] He had been round the world in 1875, travelling through the United States and thence to New Zealand and Australia, and then back from Singapore. In 1878 he had attended the Congress of Berlin with his uncle. Balfour's only notable contribution there, it seems, was to disabuse Bismarck of the notion that he was descended from the Balfour of Burleigh who featured in Scott's *Old Mortality*. In general, however, he preferred English country houses and golf in Scotland to continental haunts and jaunts – though he was persuaded to go to Bayreuth to listen to Wagner in 1895. It was not an experience that gave him much pleasure. 'Travelling is worse than drinking', he wrote to George Curzon. Nevertheless, he pondered more than most on where he really 'belonged'. Prompted later by the home rule controversy, he admitted in 1912 to a general regard for mankind, but was also moved by a patriotic feeling

> for a group of nations who are the authors and guardians of western civilization, for the subgroup which speaks the English language, and whose laws and institutions are rooted in British history, for the communities which compose the British Empire, for the United Kingdom of which I am a citizen, and for Scotland, where I was born, where I live, and where my fathers lived before me.

Such patriotisms, he believed, were not only consistent but might mutually reinforce each other – if they were not 'forced into conflict'.[52] What would happen if they were? It was to fall to him, as foreign secretary from December 1916 and, as a 70 year old, to plan the future of Europe in 1919 after just such a contingency.

Old diplomacy's last fling: last year in Marienbad (or was it Biarritz?)

The Liberal governments after 1906 contained prominent members with varied European experiences. The new 70-year-old prime minister's Glaswegian father had been keen to send his son to Europe and learn languages – 'C-B' was held to speak French like a Frenchman, to be fluent in Italian and competent in German. After his marriage in 1860 he had normally spent at least six weeks each year on the European mainland. From 1872 until the death of his wife there in 1906 (in August), he took the waters, and read French novels, at Marienbad in Bohemia (now the Czech Republic). Various kings (including Edward VII), princes and politicians provided congenial conversation at this healthy hub of Europe. The return to England was leisurely. It normally entailed a week in Vienna and a week in Paris. There was ample evidence that he liked nothing better than to roam about Europe – additionally Paris at Whitsuntide and Italy in the winter. In addition, he loved French bull terriers.[53] Two years later, however, but only just before 'Europe', as epitomized by Marienbad, came to an end, Sir Henry died.

His successor as prime minister kissed hands in another of Sir Henry's favourite places, Biarritz, where the king was ensconced and was evidently disinclined to leave. It had been with some difficulty that the royal suggestion that, afterwards, the new cabinet should go over to Paris en masse and receive their seals of office in the Hôtel Crillon, had been resisted. As a young barrister, Asquith (b. 1852), a brilliant Balliol man, had travelled a little to Germany, Switzerland, the Riviera and Italy, though on a more modest scale than Sir Henry. As prime minister, the availability of the admiralty yacht *Enchantress* made cruising to Cannes, the Dalmatian coast, Greece and Malta particularly congenial, as it did to Winston Churchill. These were not occasions, it is evident, when the intrepid sailors sought to test the political temperature in the capitals of Europe. Asquith, however, although known as an imperialist, did not venture to see the British Empire for himself.[54] He could not compete with his younger colleague's imperial adventures in India and Africa. The prime minister's friend, R.B. Haldane, the war secretary, likewise failed the imperial test. Haldane's father, fearing that Oxford would be a rather unwholesome experience, had sent the young Scotsman to Göttingen to study. As a result, no other cabinet colleague could match Haldane's knowledge of German philosophy or his understanding of what *Kultur* meant. The extraordinary outsider who moved up to become chancellor of the exchequer had also publicly lamented the linguistic deficiencies of British commercial travellers, though he restricted himself to English and Welsh. David Lloyd George was neither English, nor Anglican nor Oxbridge-educated. The advent of the motor car enabled him – at a rate of only two punctures per diem – to undertake appropriately individual, though not exotic, trips to Genoa, Lisbon and Biarritz. Sometimes, he had purposes other than pleasure in mind. A trip to Austria and Germany in August 1908, specifically to investigate social insurance, culminated in dinner with Bethmann Hollweg and discussions with Edouard Bernstein, leader of the Social Democrat 'revisionists'. France, however, was his particular love – his mistress, oddly, thought him more French than Welsh – and he found himself able to reassure a Welsh audience that the Welsh religious revival of 1904/05 was much talked about across the Channel, and even in Italy. French Algeria seemed a good place to go in January 1914 and Lloyd George disappeared into the Sahara for five days.[55] It is not certain that this eremitic experience was specifically undertaken to prepare himself for the battles that shortly lay ahead. His unorthodox behaviour was perhaps to be expected from 'a Celt from the lower regions', as the diplomat Sir Cecil Spring-Rice undiplomatically but privately called Lloyd George. When this Anglo-Irish Protestant vowed his country to God, above all earthly things, he would no doubt like to have excluded its lower regions.[56]

Sir Edward Grey (b. 1862), foreign secretary, gallantly stood out among his oddly and relatively cosmopolitan colleagues in not straying into Europe.[57] His first encounter was delayed until 1914, when he visited Paris. He had, however, toured India and inspected the West Indian sugar industry at first hand. Product of Winchester and Balliol, grandson of a home secretary, he also stood out as unambiguously English. He was regarded, at home and abroad, as a gentleman, though one tinged with radicalism, and perhaps not without subterfuge. His benevolence towards the government over the South African War had confirmed the impression that he was a

Liberal imperialist.[58] He had already identified Germany as the main threat to Britain. He scarcely wavered in this conviction through all the twists and turns of European diplomacy until 1914. It was a rigidity that upset many backbenchers in his own party and some subsequent historians.[59]

Extended entente?

The preservation of the entente was something to which Grey was absolutely committed and from which he would not waver. What precisely it entailed, however, constituted an enduring ambiguity. Franco-British military conversations in 1906 were not disclosed to the whole cabinet, but they were supposedly for information only. The British stance seemed enigmatic in France, as it did in Germany. Grey seemed largely content that it should remain so. There were moments of crisis when its significance was tested. The Agadir crisis of 1911 was one such. Germany sent a gunboat off the Moroccan coast as an indication that the establishment of a French protectorate would require some 'compensation' to be offered – as indeed it subsequently was. However, the German action seemed unduly belligerent. It was Lloyd George who caused a stir by proclaiming that in this matter Britain would not be treated as of no account in the 'Cabinet of Nations'. It was a public speech generally taken to be directed at Germany. The fact that it has subsequently sometimes also been thought a warning also to France is a further illustration of the ambiguity surrounding British intentions and policy in these years. Ambiguity might have been removed had the entente been formally transformed into an alliance. The possibility was mooted in 1911/12 but there was insufficient support in cabinet. Instead, Grey wrote to the French ambassador in terms that did not greatly clarify what precisely would happen in the event of an unprovoked attack by a third power.[60] It is not surprising that obligations, including 'obligations of honour', were disputed in the summer of 1914 when the crisis came.

The Franco-British entente had been complemented by a British convention with Russia in 1907. The deal involved Tibet and Persia. The former became a buffer state and the latter was divided into spheres of interest. The Russians held the north, the centre was neutral and the south-east went to Britain. The liberties of Persia, such as they were, were extinguished. Grey's argument was that a frequent source of friction and possible cause of war had been removed. Curzon denounced the agreement as an abdication of all that Britain had been fighting for. The foreign secretary's subsequent acquiescence in Russian infringements of the agreement, when Russia had later recovered strength, proved to some critics that it offered no real check on Russian ambitions. It was in reality a capitulation before an anti-Semitic and illiberal power.[61] Its only justification, on this analysis, could be that Russia constituted a vital counterpoise to Germany on land. In the spring of 1914, however, it could look as though Russia was relentlessly pursuing her ambi-

tions to a point at which Britain's very existence as an empire would be at
stake. And, according to some, the endowment of Germany with Napoleonic
ambitions, a conviction that had settled itself in important British military
and diplomatic circles, was fantasy. All of this leads to the conviction, now
popular, that 'standing aside' in 1914 would have been preferable to British
intervention. While Germany forced the continental war upon an unwilling
France, it was the British government that made it into a world war, with far
greater casualties than would have occurred had it acquiesced in what is presented as Germany's first 'bid for European Union'. It is sometimes conceded
that it could have made sense to intervene if there had been a bigger British
army to put immediately into the field. The corollary of 'covert commitment'
should have been such expansion – but it was not possible either politically
or financially. Yet exclusive reliance on 'blue water' had also been abandoned. Policy-makers, with Grey at the helm, had created the worst of all
possible worlds. 'German objectives', it has been contended,

> had Britain remained out, would not in fact have posed a direct threat
> to the Empire; the reduction of Russian power in Eastern Europe, the
> creation of a Central European Customs Union and acquisition of
> French colonies – these were all goals which were complementary to
> British interests.[62]

Even if these three 'objectives' are accepted as accurate – and there is a
deceptive simplicity in their presentation – their complementary character
depends on the assumption that 'isolation' was not dangerous and that a
German hegemony or domination over mainland Europe could be (and
should have been) regarded with indifference. If that had happened, we are
asked to believe, in a matter of weeks, Europe would have been transformed
'into something not wholly unlike the European Union we know today'.[63]
'Not wholly unlike', we observe, but perhaps also not 'very like' either.

All counterfactual speculations, however seductive, remain speculations.
What German objectives in fact were, and what foreign perceptions of those
objectives were, has continued to be a subject of ongoing debate on a massive scale.[64] It remains necessary, too, to ponder over the relationship
between 'immediate' and 'long-term' causes and between 'intention' and
'structure' in trying to assess what happened. Then there is the fact that the
war that was waiting to happen was made possible, as it were, by the assassination of Archduke Franz Ferdinand of Austria-Hungary in a particular
place by a particular person at a particular time. Europe's precipitating
catastrophe came from Europe's periphery.

Boundary pressure

Put another way, 1914 was a demonstration of Europe's inability, with certain exceptions, to accommodate ethnic and linguistic diversity within

acceptable structures by peaceful means. Few states in Europe in 1914 were 'comfortable'. It looked, for a time, as though civil war was going to break out in Ireland, something that might in turn cause turmoil in Great Britain. There had been unsettlement even in Scandinavia. After decades of increasing tension, the Norwegians forced the issue of separation from Sweden in 1905. Edward VII was a figure of importance in these rearrangements. He had facilitated the process whereby a Danish prince became king of Norway and his wife, Edward's own daughter, Maud, became queen. Edward's excessive conversation during a command performance of Grieg's music, however, caused the composer to stop the orchestra and decline to compose the 'Coronation Cantata' that was expected of him. In 1903 Iceland was given home rule within the framework of the Danish kingdom, but an independence party pressed for more freedom. The Finnish position was more complicated because the struggle against Russification, which met with only spasmodic results, was also accompanied by a desire not to return to the Swedish sphere.[65] The Scandinavian countries, however, stayed out of 'Europe's war'.[66]

It was in both parts of Austria-Hungary and in the Balkans generally, however, that this issue of nationality and statehood remained central. It was certainly no part of British policy actively to try to dismember the Habsburg monarchy, but Vienna's annexation of Bosnia in 1908 had caused a crisis. For some years thereafter, relations between London and Vienna cooled and perhaps, indeed, they never fully recovered before 1914. A young British diplomat, admittedly writing retrospectively, smelt decline and decay in the running of the empire, notwithstanding the fact that the aged emperor allegedly began work at 4.30 in the morning each day. The diplomat interpreted matters thus: 'the Asiatic was already apparent: the lack of will power and purpose, the need to be moulded from above and without; the static mind generally'.[67] In various parts of the empire Britain was presented as the friend of the subordinate nationalities. A former Irish MP suggested to Vienna that, in return, it might care to stir up trouble in Ireland or India – but it did not.[68] A Czech crowd paraded around Prague waving the Union Jack. There were indeed individual British visitors who interested themselves in the nationality question. H. Wickham Steed, *The Times* correspondent, was a mine of information. So was the remarkable Robert Seton-Watson.[69] In August 1914 his first thought was that a 'Great Serbian State' would be inevitable, to include Dalmatia, Bosnia, Croatia and Istria. That, he must be presumed to have supposed, would settle another of Europe's boundaries.

The Foreign Office needed no reminder of the complexity of the area or of the fact that it was in south-eastern Europe that Vienna and St Petersburg stood on the brink of conflict as they sought to extend their spheres of influence or direct control. G.P. Gooch, a historian/politician, who had a German wife, argued that, if a choice had to be made between Austrian or Russian domination of the Balkans, 'most of us would prefer the more tolerant and cultured German influence'.[70] Others felt just the opposite. Although individual Britons, many of them members of a 'Balkan Committee' pressure group, interested themselves in Albania, Macedonia or Bulgaria, to give three examples, and sought to exert political influence on their behalf – pressure sometimes partial for one cause or another – direct British interests were not great.[71] Paris or Vienna proved the main source of Balkan finance. The British Treasury was so uninterested in Balkan finance that it told the Foreign Office in the first decade of the century that it no longer wished to receive reports on the subject.[72] In 1908 the 'Young Turk' revolution took place in Constantinople and promised equality for all communities within the Ottoman Empire. The British ambassador was a little surprised by the enthusiasm for Britain displayed in popular demonstrations. However, another 'new beginning' faltered.[73] In any case, the new national states saw their opportunity to remove the Ottomans from Europe. In October 1912 Serbia, Montenegro, Greece and Bulgaria launched a successful attack, followed by an armistice, followed by negotiations, and then followed by resumed hostilities. It was in London that a settlement was signed. Although Grey rarely found Balkan disputes other than 'very tiresome', his role as a conciliator and promoter of non-intervention on the part of the Great Powers received considerable praise at home and abroad.[74] In 1913 a second Balkan war began in which Bulgaria was attacked from all sides, and, in the ensuing Treaty of Bucharest, lost Macedonia to Serbia and Greece. 'It is only a mockery to abolish Turkish rule in the Balkans if it is to be succeeded by what is a worse tyranny in many ways', wrote Bourchier from Sofia in March 1914 as refugees poured into Bulgaria from Greek Macedonia.[75] The Ottomans took advantage of this renewed conflict to regain a small amount of territory, but even so they had lost what had been the richest and most developed provinces of the empire for 500 years.[76] Muslim refugees flooded into Constantinople as the new frontier of Europe was finally established, or so it was said.[77]

Finding the right perspective

The war that broke out in the summer of 1914 was first known as 'the European War'. Its subsequent scale and its global ramifications led then to it being described as 'Great' and 'World'. It was, however, a conflict that was essentially both in Europe and about Europe. Historians, one might suppose, could put it all in perspective. By 1900, 'history' had become a subject of central importance in British universities. At Oxford, in the decade to 1909, it had become the most popular subject, having been taken by almost a quarter of undergraduates. State and nation remained the central focus of writing and teaching. There were individual historians who initially supposed that war 'in the interest of Serbia and Russia' would be a 'sin against civilization', but most focused on the sins of Germany. In Oxford, some historians set out swiftly to explain *Why We Are At War*.[78] Eight years earlier the Historical Association had been founded with the aim of uniting university teachers, schoolteachers and the general public in an awareness of the importance of history. For some this meant that teachers of history should 'interpret the national character, the national ideals, and educate their pupils in the ethos of their own race'. For others, however, European history should also be given attention and 'need not undermine patriotism at all'.[79] A.F. Pollard, editor of the Association's new journal, *History*, wanted pupils to grasp how English history (he was a Tudor specialist) had unfolded into British imperial history. The defeat of Russia by Japan in 1905 had alarmed him. In *The History of England: A Study in Political Evolution, 55 BC–AD 1911* (1912) he thought that the 'slumbering East' had awakened. Would 'the yellow hordes of Asia' now turn against the West?[80] Before they had chance to do so, however, the white hordes were turning on themselves.

The graduates in the British cabinet in July–August 1914 had evaded the study of history, however, and were not able to glean what it might be able to tell them. The following month, Oxford University Press obligingly sent three advance copies of *Why We Are At War* in order to explain to the foreign secretary what historians thought the answer was. The choice that faced the British cabinet in July–August 1914 could not have been more momentous. The ambivalences of identity and interest, evident in previous chapters, could not be avoided. If this was indeed the climax, or at least a climax, to that struggle for mastery in Europe that was apparently inescapable, could the United Kingdom stand aside and let the outcome be what it would? The 'decision' was, at one level, a matter for the particular collection of men who made up the British cabinet at that juncture. The scrutiny of their assumptions, spoken and unspoken, has continued ever since. The meticulous analysis of the decision-making process is a necessary enterprise. We now know how, within the constraints imposed by previous understandings, obfuscations, 'obligations of honour' and formal commitments, individual members of the cabinet wavered and vacillated. Men were forced to face the incompatibility of various 'principles' to which they had given optimistic assent. Opinion was finely balanced and it is not implausible to envisage different outcomes. Mr Lloyd George contemplated retirement to Cricieth, his home in north-west Wales, but then contemplated again.

The cataclysm, so widely if vaguely predicted, was about to engulf the much-vaunted 'civilization of Europe'. H.G. Wells admitted that he could rarely resist invitations to prophesy (or indeed, one might add, any invitations whatsoever). In a New Year message in 1909, having just tasted the 'go' in things American, he speculated on the possible collapse of civilization. Looking back on the nineteenth century, men had perhaps become over-confident and forgetful of the ruins of great cities and confident prides of the past that littered the world. He instanced in particular the extent to which, in his view, everything crawled forward but the science of war; that rushed on: 'Every modern European state is more or less like a cranky, ill-built steamboat in which some idiot has mounted and loaded a monstrous gun with no apparatus to damp its recoil.' The twentieth century, instead of going inexorably onward, was going to have a set-back.[81] The guns of Europe had indeed become monstrous and offered a wry commentary on its civilization. The scale of armies and navies across the continent frightened very disparate observers, from Tsar Nicholas II downwards. Peace conferences held at The Hague in 1899 and 1907 had established a body of apparently agreed restraints on the conduct of land and naval warfare. The participating states, however, had no intention of circumscribing the prior right of initiating hostilities. As for arbitration, despite the attention devoted to its possibilities, it was clear that states were only prepared to agree to treaties that contained crippling reservations on its use.[82] Pacifists (the word was new) of various hues struggled against the view of the international scene perpetrated by 'scaremongers'.[83] The French-educated Norman Angell's book, *The Great Illusion* (1910), could be reduced to the simple but compelling contention that 'war could not pay'. Territorial gains, he thought, – supposing that was what war was about – would be offset by the losses caused by financial dislocation. It had an enormous, though ultimately unavailing, impact.[84]

The first version of Angell's thinking had been *Europe's Optical Illusion* (1909) and it pointed out to Europe 'the complex financial interdependence of the capitals of the world'. He argued that New York was dependent on London, London on Paris and Paris on Berlin.[85] A corollary, as already apparent to some, was that if there were ever to be a European Union it would have to operate in a world setting. It was noticeable that whereas only five out of the 26 states at the first Hague conference in 1899 came from beyond Europe, 24 out of 44 were non-European at that of 1907.[86]

The United States could not be ignored and Britain, in particular, had not ignored it. James Bryce, appointed as ambassador to Washington in 1907 – he served until 1913 – proved an exemplary emissary. Sir Charles Hardinge, who had declined the post, thought Bryce had the quality of liking to make long and rather dull speeches on commonplace subjects. The American masses liked that kind of thing.[87] Bryce did not disappoint, in this and other respects, though whether the universities, bar associations, and chambers of commerce he addressed saw themselves as 'the masses' may be doubted.[88] Such an effort further contributed to the portrayal of 'kinship across the Atlantic'. It had been American assertiveness that had pushed Britain into finally dropping the idea of the United States as a potential enemy. British naval and military forces were withdrawn from North America and the West Indies in the decade after 1895.[89] Yet, the language of kith and kin could not and did not completely eliminate subdued resentments. 'The Englishman', or at least Lord Cromer, did not expect the United States to have joined the war but when President Wilson adjured his fellow-countrymen to construe neutrality into a denial of sympathy with a just cause, his surprise 'deepened into a feeling very akin to shame and contempt'.[90]

When it came to the point, nothing availed to stop the war in Europe or British involvement in it. In 1911 Ramsay MacDonald had written that the international socialist parties had some way to go in perfecting their organization before they had 'established finally the conditions of the world's peace'. That was rather an understatement. He feared that, before it was done, the chancelleries of Europe might have precipitated war. An 'anti-war strike', which would place the working classes of Europe in opposition to those chancelleries, was a fine rhetorical flourish but, in actuality, no more than that. It was only late in July, in Britain as elsewhere, that socialist leaders came to think that a war was actually going to happen. The large crowd assembled in Trafalgar Square on Sunday 2 August 1914 seems to have felt powerless in the face of the drift of events. Even so, Keir Hardie stridently complained that the people had had no voice in the treaties that were now leading to war.[91] 'Democracy' had become a watchword but it had not 'controlled' foreign policy.[92]

The great states of Europe, Britain among them, all believed that a decision for war had a defensible political rationale. The advice of treasuries, interior ministries and general staffs was that it would be fierce and short but would not destabilize the domestic economic and political order. A Great Power could not abandon its willingness to threaten to use force without ceasing to be a Great Power. Sir Eyre Crowe (who, like a number of other senior British diplomats, had a German mother, and had received a German education) even minuted on 31 July 1914 that if 'England' could not engage in 'a big war' it was abdicating as an independent state.[93] And, initially, with the exception of Serbia and Belgium, the war for 'Europe' was something the Great Powers of Britain, France, Germany and Russia kept to themselves.[94]

Clashing philosophically

A.J. Balfour, lately released from the cares of prime ministerial office, had turned his philosophical attention to 'decadence' in a lecture given at Cambridge in 1908. He was not thinking of lawn tennis, to which he was addicted, or of literary or artistic descents into dream-worlds, drunkenness and morbidity, a phenomenon detectable in *fin-de-siècle* Europe, and not without insular examples. He wrestled, rather, with the internal causes by which, in any given community, progress was encouraged, hindered or reversed. He remained sanguine that whatever perils lay ahead there were no symptoms either of pause or of regression in the onward movement of western civilization.[95]

The lecture had been delivered as a tribute to his brother-in-law, Henry Sidgwick, the Cambridge political philosopher. In a posthumous book, *The*

Development of European Polity (1903), Sidgwick had assumed that 'the growth of civilization' would lead continually to larger societies. It was 'not beyond the limits of a sober forecast' – a guarded observation even for a philosopher – that some further integration would take place in the west European states and would take the form of an extension of federalism.[96] There was indeed around this time a revived interest in Britain in the idea of a United States of Europe. The lawyer, Sir Max Waechter, took up the idea in 1909 and founded a European Unity League in 1913. Of course, anyone can found such a league, and its political significance was negligible, but it does say something about the way some opinion was moving. But was there a consensus on 'civilization' that could make it work? 'The best thing for Europe', wrote the author of a treatise on Kant's *Perpetual Peace* in 1903, 'might be that Russia ... should be regarded as a serious danger to all the civilized Powers of the West. *That* would bring us nearer to the United States of Europe'.[97] France, however, one of those 'civilized Powers', clearly saw the serious danger to its civilization coming from elsewhere. In and after 1914 an explosion of publications trembled before the notion that it would be German *Kultur* that would put its stamp on Europe. The vice-chancellor of Leeds University, lecturing in 1915, claimed that 'intelligent Frenchmen, Russians and English, when they get below the surface of things, find that their thoughts are sensitive to the same problems'.[98] That was the mental basis of the alliance. Here, now, was a great chance for the islanders. 'At this crisis in the history of European civilization,' he wrote, 'Great Britain (and especially England) stands for a synthesis which attempts to combine what is good in two, sometimes polarised, views of national duty and personal obligation.'

A decade before Balfour's lecture, however, his uncle, Lord Salisbury, had famously divided the nations of the world into the 'living' and the 'dying'. The living would gradually encroach on the territory of the dying, and the seeds and causes of conflict among civilized nations would readily appear.[99] The previous year Salisbury had referred to the competition in armaments. Unless the powers could be brought together and act in a friendly spirit on all questions of difference that might arise the competition might well end in a terrible effort of mutual destruction that would be fatal to Christian civilization.[100] The Council of the Baptist Union described the German invasion of Belgium as an attempt 'to destroy the very fabric of Christian civilization'.[101] It was a far cry – two years – from Bishop Boyd Carpenter's view that the kaiser was 'a lover of peace, earnestly desirous of promoting the welfare of mankind' and who was known 'to have a simple trust in Divine guidance'. The British Council of Associated Churches for Fostering Friendly Relations between the British and German peoples proved as anaemic as the Socialist International when confronted by the power of states.[102] Pope Pius X was reported to be 'depressed' when he heard of the murder of Franz Ferdinand and his wife at Sarajevo. He died the following month as 'Christian Europe' went to war.

Women arise!

The decision-makers and the inhabitants of the power structures who had brought Europe to this pass, and whose activities have filled the narrative of this and all preceding chapters had one thing in common. They were men. Many women, active in maternalist politics in various international organizations, largely European (with an American admixture) as they were, had concluded that there was a connection between male dominance and the world at war. Whether biologically or socially grounded, women were different from men and, in time, modern women would undermine the institution of war and the obsession with power that had led to it. Sir Edward Grey's late wife dissented from the political norms of the world in which she had reluctantly lived. 'We are not a really Christian nation', she had written in 1900, 'Our Church of England is not a Christian Church. If anyone had talked to Christ about *Empire* he would have laughed, I think.'[103]

|9|

European civil war?
c.1919–c.1939

The 'Twenty Years Crisis'

The 'Twenty Years Crisis' can be looked at from various perspectives. Sometimes, the term 'European Civil War' is used, though it is capable of being given different interpretations. It can refer to the rivalry, and then resumed warfare, between the states in Europe. It was essentially 'European' because in 1939/40 the United States was not a participant. In such a perspective, the United Kingdom was a European state of the front rank, participating once more in 'the struggle for mastery'. It can also refer, however, to an ideological war, common to all the states of Europe, one within as much as between them. Some supposed that the struggle was between Nazism/Fascism, on the one hand, and Communism on the other. Alternatively, it was a struggle between 'liberal democracy' and both Nazism/Fascism and Communism. Sometimes, the latter could be lumped together, despite their proclaimed hostility, as 'totalitarian'. Ever since, of course, historians have explored these ideological issues in detail.[1] There is no necessity, however, to concentrate exclusively on 'inter-state' aspects or on 'inter-ideological' aspects. Few European states, by the 1930s, had escaped a mingling of the two. Students of international relations at the time could change their minds as the scene unfolded. E.H. Carr, for example, writing at the end of 1936, argued that 'The current habit of classifying countries by the type of political theory professed by their government is misleading' but in the 1939 edition of his book he did talk about a 'European civil war' in Spain, given the support to the respective combatants from 'Fascist' states and the Soviet Union.[2]

To speak too glibly about a 'European civil war' however, makes too simple an analogy with the 'civil wars' that did take place in Ireland or Spain.[3] To refer to a European civil war presupposes that 'Europe' was pervasively 'owned', yet such 'ownership' was frail at best. As will appear, some enthusiastic exponents of 'Europe' specifically excluded Britain from their purported definitions, an exclusion that caused little dismay in some insular quarters. Lumping, say, the north-west and the south-east of Europe together at this time, as if their experiences were 'common', is unpersuasively artificial. 'Placing' the Soviet Union as state successor to the Russian Empire, and as non-state harbinger of revolution, also remained problematic. This chapter, however, naturally concentrates upon Britain 'inside' its Europe with all the tensions, aspirations and contradictions its stance entailed in a continent supposedly 'settled' in 1919.

The Battle of Europe: 1940

The mood in Paris on 3 September 1939 was sombre and resigned when Britain and France declared war on Germany. The two countries did not do so at precisely the same hour – out of step to the end, even if marching together. In anticipation of crisis, American and other tourists had been leaving the city over the previous few weeks.[4] The contrast with proud Paris in 1919 could not be greater. France as victor had then hosted the Peace Conference and saw itself as the leading power in Europe, albeit with assistance from its partners. The Great War had been 'the war to end war'. The German army was successfully invading Poland, a state recreated as part of the peace settlement. On 23 August news had come of the extraordinary Nazi-Soviet Pact under which both countries pledged neutrality if the other was engaged in hostilities. Secret clauses gave Germany a free hand in Lithuania and western Poland, and gave the Soviet Union a free hand in Latvia, Estonia, Finland, Bessarabia and eastern Poland. The largest state in eastern Europe was thus partitioned a fifth time. Such a pact with the ideological enemy, supposedly in the interests of the Soviet state, naturally caused dismay and confusion among Communists elsewhere. There was then a 'phoney war' before German forces occupied Denmark and Norway in April 1940 and then, the following month, conquered Belgium and the Netherlands and swept into France. After a six-week campaign, France was forced to sign a humiliating armistice. Paris was under German occupation. The country was split in two: half, including Paris, was under direct German control, the remainder under a puppet government led by Marshal Pétain, hero of the first war, established at Vichy. Sweden remained neutral but, in the circumstances, might be compliant. Spain was non-belligerent but was expected to be compliant. Switzerland would be Switzerland. The Irish Free State declared its neutrality. Italy, initially non-belligerent, joined the war so as not to be neglected. Compliance would be required from the states of south-eastern Europe, Albania being already under Italian occupation. In the summer of 1940 there seemed little to prevent the consolidation of a lasting 'new order' in Europe. A book by the exiled Hungarian writer Paul Tabori, entitled *Epitaph for Europe*, seemed entirely appropriate.

The only immediate obstacle was the continued willingness of Britain to fight – though there was obviously speculation about Hitler's intentions with regard to the Soviet Union. The march of events produced dramatic political change in London. Winston Churchill, who had been out of office during the 'low dishonest decade' returned as prime minister, determined to fight on. The 'Epitaph for Britain' might be imminent. The pressing needs of the moment squeezed out protracted reflection on the past or preparation for the future, but the questions would not go away. There were so many oddities in what had happened. As in 1914, so in 1939, Britain was once again performing ambivalently. It was both a 'European Great Power' and a 'Great Power' once again reluctantly fighting in Europe. There was some doubt about the wisdom of going to war at all – though, when it came to the point, less than there had been in 1914. Back in 1931, the French Protestant commentator, André Siegfried, published a book on *La crise britannique* in the twentieth century. It was translated (incorrectly but revealingly) as 'England's Crisis'. Its general tone was gloomy, appropriate for a year of financial and political crisis. The moment for decision, he thought, had come. Was her future to be with the youthful trans-oceanic 'Anglo-Saxon societies' or would she return to the old world from which her culture sprang? As things were, he suggested,

> England has in a sense fallen between two stools, the European conti-
> nent to which she does not belong, and the non-European world for
> which she has neither the youth nor the temperament. She is beginning
> to realise slowly and rather regretfully that her splendid isolation has
> come to an end.[5]

In 1940, the split personality was still very evident. The peace settlement of 1919 had failed to establish a harmonious Europe. Britain had not found, perhaps had not wanted to find, a 'home' within the continent. For some commentators in 1940, those two sentences explained why things were as they were, but there was no consensus, as there had not been for 20 years.

Relighting the lamps

Once wars have begun their outcome can rarely be accurately predicted. All the belligerents in 1914 harboured illusions about what lay ahead.[6] In the House of Commons on 2 August, for example, Sir Edward Grey stated that the country was going to suffer terribly in the war 'whether we are in it or whether we stand aside'. The 'short war' illusion, the idea that the conflict, one way or other, would be settled in months rather than in years, was widespread across Europe. Instead, a protracted conflict in which some nine million men died throughout the world, around half coming from Britain, France and Germany, shattered 'old Europe'. The scale of the upheaval and the ensuing psychological, political and social consequences are even now difficult to grasp. Country after country experienced a vast war of words

5. Europe in 1919, after the First World War

explaining what was at stake. Defeat, it was claimed by each belligerent, would entail disaster because its values were sometimes presented as being best for Europe. Claims (and counter-claims) for the most part, however, rested on the superiority (or inferiority) of national civilizations *tout court*. It was unfortunate that allies sometimes had to make do with partners who might not fully come up to scratch. The dialogue, if such a term can be used, was basically between the civilizations of the Great Powers. The clash between Britain and Germany, which was perhaps the fiercest of all, was sometimes thought to have the intensity of a 'family quarrel'. It was inconceivable that, in the moment of their success, the victors would contemplate any diminution in national sovereignty. The mobilization of all available resources had strengthened the power of the state in each belligerent country.[7] In fighting 'Prussianism', British critics of the war never tired of pointing out, Britain had 'Prussianized' itself. 'New Europe' would remain a 'Europe of states', though within a rather vague penumbra of 'internationalism'.

Peacemaking in 1919 has been scrutinized by historians for decades. A century earlier, the Vienna Congress had attempted to draw lessons and provide fresh mechanisms for resolving disputes. The Versailles Conference (use of 'conference' rather than 'congress' was put down to the nefarious influence of journalists) was under a similar compunction. The bloodiest conflict, thus far, in human history seemed to make a 'fresh start' imperative.[8] The year 1918 had started with far-reaching proposals, or at least rhetoric, from both Lloyd George and Woodrow Wilson. The latter's 'Fourteen Points' did make specific commitments – for example, to erect an independent Polish state and, more opaquely, to give to the peoples of Austria-Hungary 'the first opportunity of autonomous development'. Before the United States came into the war the Allies had made certain agreements among themselves and the reconciliation of these commitments with the new principles would not be easy.

The interplay between principals and principles has exerted a lasting fascination.[9] In Britain, it became commonplace, surprisingly quickly, to regard the Treaty of Versailles as a disaster. It turned out to be only a 20-year truce, as Marshal Foch had presciently predicted. No detailed examination of 'Versailles' is repeated here, but certain contextual points need emphasis.[10] Germany was defeated but neither destroyed nor occupied. It was easy for Germans to come to believe that the army had been 'stabbed in the back'. The Allies did not abandon their belief that Germany had caused the war. The central problem was simply how best to prevent another attempt in the future. Solutions, however, were not simple since, inevitably, the leaders of the victorious states had their individual agendas. As far as Britain was concerned, the outcome would be likely to establish its relationship with Europe for a generation. David Lloyd George, prime minister since December 1916, came to Paris buttressed by a general election, held in December 1918, the first since 1910, which had given the coalition he headed an overwhelming majority. During the campaign, the tone of government candidates in relation to the impending settlement became stronger. The electorate had been barely eight million before the war but in 1918 it expanded to 21 million (of whom 8.4 million were 'mature' women (i.e. over 30). It was in the tranquillity of academic Cambridge that Sir Eric Geddes had demanded that the German lemon be squeezed until the pips squeaked. It was clear that politicians, in the new peacemaking, could not ignore the emotions of the electorate. Such a fact shocked the young J.M. Keynes, who was trying, or so he thought, to bring economic rationality to the conference proceedings. Virginia Woolf reported him depressed 'by the dismal and degrading spectacle of the Peace Conference, where men played shamelessly, not for Europe, or even for England, but for their own return to Parliament at the next election'.[11]

At Vienna, aristocratic diplomacy had not required France to accept a 'war-guilt' clause. Democratic diplomacy did now require one of Germany (even though its purpose was rather more limited than it was subsequently presented in Germany as being). The allied leaders did not have the degree of latitude and detachment from public pressures possessed by their predecessors in 1815. France, Italy, the United Kingdom and the United States were all democracies of a kind. The direct personal involvement of an American president was a novelty. The other leaders were to a degree subject to cabinet constraint. Wilson, by contrast, was a 'monarch' and also, to many hopeful Europeans, a messiah. His presence was a reminder that without American help the Allies would not have won the war and might even have lost it.[12] In quadrilateral discussion, would Wilson and Lloyd George produce *la paix des Anglo-Saxonnes* that they would impose on the 'Europeans' (France and Italy) or would the 'Europeans' (Britain, France and Italy) successfully resist the American shaping of Europe? In the event, the overall outcome contained elements of both. It was Britain, predictably enough, that struggled to keep its options open.[13] Smuts, Afrikaner general turned imperial visionary, was arguing in December 1918 that the British Empire should regard the United States rather than France as its main ally. 'We must remember', Sir Eyre Crowe retorted, 'that our friend America lives a long way off; France sits at our door'.[14] That was the problem.

Recovering

The reality was that governments, to an extent, were prisoners of wartime propaganda that they had themselves instigated. The British government dismantled its machinery for this purpose, but its legacy remained.[15] 'Secret diplomacy' as conducted before 1914 had been widely criticized during the war. President Wilson aspired to 'open covenants, openly arrived at' – a doctrine that, in the event, proved capable of refinement. In this changed climate, Lloyd George had his own men. Sir Charles Hardinge, the permanent under-secretary at the Foreign Office, was marginalized. He, in turn, was scandalized by negotiations conducted in what he considered 'a thoughtless and light-hearted manner'.[16] The precise extent to which the influence of the Foreign Office was 'eroded' remains a subject of debate. The biographers of Sir Eyre Crowe, Hardinge's successor, assert that the Foreign Office proposals for the territorial settlement were very far from being wasted.[17] Official insights, however, were more subject than ever before to politicians who were themselves susceptible to gusts of democratic opinion. The wartime Union of Democratic Control had wanted democracy to assert itself.[18] 'The people', wrote Arthur Ponsonby, later to be under-secretary at the Foreign Office under Labour, were not inspired by any racial animosity and their combative instincts were normally in abeyance. It was a comforting belief.

The transition to 'peace' could not be easy anywhere.[19] A small amount of bombing apart, Britain had suffered little direct damage during the war. This very fact caused enormous difficulty when it came to trying to assess the overall costs of the war for the belligerents. The issue of who should 'pay' for the war became a major element in the international relations and domestic politics of the next decade.[20] The amount to be paid in 'reparations' was not fixed until 1921 and the issue in effect came to an end in 1931. Its feasibility was bitterly disputed at the time, and sharply different views remain on the consequences for the newly established Weimar Republic. At many meetings and in the production of various 'Plans', the governments concerned sought to protect their interests, while at the same time proclaiming the need for an overall settlement. British ministers, in successive governments, looked in vain for a change in United States policy on debt. They were reluctant, however, to make common cause with European allies in confronting the major creditor. One authority also concludes that governments were also doing their best to evade the domestic financial consequences of the war.[21] While common opposition to reparations in Germany may in one sense have stabilized Weimar democracy, inflation helped to undermine confidence in its capacity. 'Recovery', of course, had been very much in Britain's interests commercially. It was a task, however, that was believed to be too great for private enterprise alone. The general perception remained in Europe that Britain was still a rich country. In London, there was an uncomfortable awareness of the extent to which British investments in the United States had been realized to pay for the war. Invisible earnings no longer covered an adverse trade balance. New York was now on a par with London as a world financial centre.[22] It was the United States that provided the largest single source of loans to Europe in the 1920s, though of the share which went to central and eastern Europe, under the auspices of the League of Nations, almost half was subscribed in London. The overall pattern of British overseas long-term investment remained overwhelmingly outside Europe.

'Recovery', however, touched on deeper issues. Cultural historians continue to explore, with differing conclusions, the extent to which the war, in its totality, constituted a fundamental break in European culture. Some of them stress the elements of continuity in which old frameworks of explanation and consolation endured. Others emphasize the iconoclasm of a modernism set loose in country after country from old moorings. That debate continues. While 'memory' found some different expression, the belligerent countries of Europe had one common fundamental experience. After 1919, as Jay Winter puts it, 'almost all towns and villages in the major European combatant countries were ... communities of the bereaved'. Huge cemeteries in northern France presented enduring witness to the fact that part of

'Britain' was left in France. Winter discounts a sharp differentiation between the outlooks of the 'victorious' and of the 'defeated'. Collective slaughter was the 'special path' that all the major combatants had taken.[23]

A 'community of bereavement' did not translate into any other kind of 'community', certainly not a 'European' one. There was, however, some growth of pacifism in post-war Europe, though there was no uniformity in the understanding of the term.[24] A conviction of the absolute inadmissibility of violence remained restricted to small groups, usually Protestant, whose political impact was modest. There were other organizations that sprang up with a more general 'pacificist' orientation – that is to say bodies that sought to promote peace but did not rule out the use of force in all circumstances. Differences of conviction among pacifist bodies often made collaboration difficult within countries and to speak of a 'European peace movement' in the 1920s would exaggerate the degree of contact and cooperation across national boundaries. Broadly speaking, both pacifist and pacificist bodies emerged in countries with Protestant rather than Catholic or Orthodox cultural/religious backgrounds.[25] Only in Britain during the war had the government recognized the right of conscientious objection to military service. The British 'peace movement' in the 1930s was the strongest in Europe and was able to capitalize on a wider public reluctance to contemplate another war.[26] Its almost 'official' character gave it a standing and political significance not to be found elsewhere. The extent to which its strength actually inhibited rearmament in the middle 1930s is difficult to gauge accurately. For a time, however, no British government could construct its European policy without taking account of a broad swathe of organized 'peace' opinion. It is probably true to say that no other European government felt the same degree of constraint.

Not an 'insignificant island'

For Britain to 'put things right', as Sir Edward Grey had expressed it in 1914, was no small task, and not one in which he would be engaged. The 'old régime' may have persisted into the twentieth century but its day had now surely come.[27] Despite Siegfried's assertion, however, Britain's 'temperament' for dealing with the non-European world did not seem unduly impaired. After all, the 'Britain' that had fought in Europe had involved troops from the self-governing dominions and from India. It had been an imperial war effort. Such mobilization had not been without strain, but it appeared to demonstrate that the empire was a going concern. The dominions pressed for greater clarity concerning their constitutional status. The agreement on 'parity of status' was codified in the 1931 Statute of Westminster. Despite increased internal opposition, there was no disposition to end British rule in India. It would be possible to head off emerging nationalism.[28] The detailed evolution of the British Empire/Commonwealth in this period has been amply covered elsewhere.[29] What must be emphasized here, however, is that this complex and unwieldy structure – difficult for foreigners to understand – remained of central significance in British thinking, whether in relation to commerce or defence. The Germans, for example, found it difficult to understand the relationship between the Irish Free State and the British Commonwealth of Nations, and did not know quite how to deal with the Irish minister plenipotentiary when he arrived in Berlin in 1929. Nor did the British ambassador.[30] 'Empire-mindedness' characterized the military and naval establishments. Of course, in an ideal world, it might have been possible, financially and industrially, to maintain all three services at a high level of readiness for either European or global involvement, but the world was not ideal. There is general agreement among historians that the 'continental commitment' remained the lesser priority for most of the period.[31] 'It is our Imperial position which gives this country its great voice in the world,' declared Chatfield, the first sea lord, 'Unless we are willing to maintain that Imperial position,' he continued, 'we shall become once more nothing but an insignificant island in the North Sea ... and should carry as much weight in the councils of the world as Italy or Spain.'[32] That was not a congenial prospect. What might suit a 'significant island', therefore, might not suit Europe, and vice versa.

Heartbeats

It has not infrequently been argued that when Britain became 'directly involved' with Europe after 1918 its political classes were unable to understand or deal with a changing continent.[33] Both the making and then the unravelling of the Versailles settlement have been thought to provide a perfect illustration of British incomprehension. The claim has some substance but is overstated. 'For one who spent in Paris the greater part of the six months which succeeded the Armistice,' wrote J.M. Keynes in 1919, 'an occasional visit to London was a strange experience. England still stands outside Europe. Europe's voiceless tremors do not reach her. Europe is apart and England is not of her flesh and body.' He claimed that his membership of the Supreme Economic Council of the Allied Powers had made him 'a European in his cares and outlook', something that was a 'new experience' for him.[34]

By now, it needs scarcely to be said that 'understanding and dealing with Europe', however imperfectly, was not a novel challenge for the political elite or for other sections of British society in 1918/19. Even Keynes pre-war had a German governess, as had many other British families of his social background.[35] In 1912 he had visited a Hungarian Cambridge friend who lived, implausibly some believed, at Rum in Hungary. In 1919 Keynes further took the view that Europe was 'solid with herself'. France, Germany, Italy, Austria, Holland, Russia, Romania and Poland, to name the countries he singled out, all apparently 'throbbed' together. Their structure and civilization, he stated, were 'essentially one'. Whether such an implausible conclusion – Keynes was no historian – was reached only by the deliberate exclusion of Balkan countries other than Romania, and of Scandinavia and the Iberian countries, is not clear.

The notion that Europe was 'solid with itself' was advanced, it now appears, at just the point when radically different 'essences' were appearing across the continent. Over the next 20 years, the countries of Europe, in their political, social, constitutional and economic development certainly 'throbbed', but not together. To an extent, Europe as a whole was beginning to manifest the characteristics of a 'consumer' culture, and was perhaps in evident transition to a 'mass consumer society', but, if so, it was at vastly different speeds both between and within European countries. It has been pointed out that the triumph of 'modern', nationally integrated markets over 'traditional' subsistence systems was far from complete. In Italy, for example, less than one-third of all farms produced for the market as late as the 1930s.[36] The British consumer's heart was in good shape and was beating soundly, even if Keynes' stethoscope could not pick it up.

Family likenesses and imperfect imitations

The 'essences' of Europe after 1919 were supposed to embody democracy, national self-determination, parliamentary government and the rule of law. The British believed that they were adequately, indeed emblematically, equipped in these areas. The only phrase that caused difficulty was 'national self-determination'.[37] Application of this 'principle' would simply cause the British Empire to dissolve, though it might take time for some of its component parts to decide on their nationality. There was, however, no serious prospect of the application of the principle outside Europe. There was difficulty, however, in relation to Ireland. The suppression of the 1916 Easter Rising in Dublin had the effect, over subsequent years, of strengthening the determination of Irish republicans to break the British connection completely. A constitutional convention broke down. The pre-1914 'solutions' ceased to be available. Was Ulster to be 'thrown over'? Could one 'give in' to Sinn Fein? The British government attempted coercion. Years of bloodshed and violence finally led to a settlement at the end of 1921, which established an 'Irish Free State' on the model of a dominion within the British Empire but also maintained 'Northern Ireland' in the United Kingdom. Its narrow acceptance in Dublin in turn led to civil war in the south. A new constitution in 1937 further emphasized the Free State's determination to emphasize its independence, a step further symbolized by its neutrality in 1939. These events, and the new status of Northern Ireland, with self-government within the United Kingdom, disabused any who thought that in

1919 the United Kingdom was a nationally integrated state able to prognosticate on the application of national self-determination in Europe from a position of political and moral comfort.

It did not take very long, after 1919, for the other 'essences' of the 1919 settlement to crumble. By 1929, Agnes Headlam-Morley, whose father, Sir James, had been the effective head of the wartime Political Intelligence Department of the Foreign Office, acknowledged that democracy was 'no longer lauded as the only intelligent, the only possible way by which a civilized people can be governed'.[38] The American Foreign Policy Association followed European developments closely. In 1934, with the Nazis now in power in Germany, its president, Raymond Leslie Buell, believed that 'the majority of the people in Russia, Italy and Germany support their present leaders', believing them to show 'more disinterested devotion to the national good' than was demonstrated by political leaders in supposedly democratic countries.[39] Mussolini's regime had produced equivocal responses in Britain ever since its consolidation in 1922. It might be 'good' for Italy and it might also be 'good' to have Mussolini 'on side' after Hitler came to power in Germany in 1933.[40] Headlam-Morley saw many dangers ahead. The failure on the continent of 'an imperfect imitation of our constitution' might make it vulnerable at home. Constitutions, she thought, were products of 'character'. There was now a danger that some British politicians might try to create institutions in Britain 'which are probably as unsuited to our country as ours are to theirs'. For his part, Buell noted what he called the virtual abandonment of the party system in Britain in August 1931. He expressed concern at the emergence of Sir Oswald Mosley and Sir Stafford Cripps, both products of the same public school, Winchester, who might, in their opposite ways, justify Headlam-Morley's fears.[41]

The British constitution was indeed under stress but Britain did not succumb in the 1930s to what was sometimes perceived as a continental virus. Its 'first-past-the-post' electoral system, initially scorned as undemocratic in the 'new democracies', helped to marginalize both Communism and Fascism in Britain.[42] Representative democracy was not under serious threat. Class was an element in British politics but, with considerable success, Conservatives projected themselves as the party that stood for the unity of the nation.[43] There were major social and economic problems, but Britain's poor did not become destitute, its lower-middle-class did not become 'obsolete', and there was no breakdown in law and order.[44] Contemporaries were apt to explain this behaviour in terms of 'national character'.[45] Even if this explanation no longer satisfies, the contemporary construction of Englishness/Britishness in the skilful hands of Baldwin, in particular, is relevant.[46] In sum, there was no simple correlation between British political behaviour and that manifested in different countries of the 'European Civil War'. The Spanish Civil War, which broke out in 1936 and lasted until 1939, illustrates rather than nullifies this contention. Certainly, both sides in Spain had their British supporters, some of whom went out to fight, but even so there was no precise correlation between the forces in conflict in Spain and the categories of British politics.[47]

Master classes

'Misunderstanding' of Europe on the part of the British 'political classes' was therefore paradoxically an aspect of their 'understanding' of Britain. The political and official elite, all late-Victorian men, interpreted Europe on the basis of pre-1914 images mingled with more recent direct experience.[48] There seemed little reason to want to be more 'like' any part of the continent. They were past the age, as the following sketch shows, when men radically change their perspectives. Lloyd George (b. 1863) did not hold office again after the collapse of his coalition in 1922. Bonar Law (b. 1858) died in 1923 after a premiership of less than a year. His successors, Baldwin (b. 1867), Ramsay MacDonald (b. 1866) and Neville Chamberlain (b. 1869), were 70, 69 and 70 when they resigned. Among foreign secretaries, Balfour resigned in 1919 though was still active thereafter. He devised the 'formula' for inter-imperial relations in 1926 when he was 78. Curzon (b. 1859) was 59 in 1919 but six years later he was dead. Austen Chamberlain (b. 1863) took office in 1924 and Arthur Henderson (b. 1863) in 1929. Six years later, Henderson was dead.[49] Reading, 70 in 1931, was a stop-gap minister. Simon (b. 1873), Hoare (b. 1880) and Halifax (b. 1881) lowered the age profile somewhat. Only Eden (b. 1897), who followed Hoare until February 1938, belonged to the new and war-serving generation. He had gained the Military Cross and still liked to be referred to initially as Captain Eden. Mussolini (b. 1883) and Hitler (b. 1889), of course, did belong to this new generation.

There was also – in comparison with Mussolini or Hitler and their entourages – strong institutional/educational continuity among the British elite. Public school and Oxbridge predominated. Lloyd George, Bonar Law, MacDonald and Henderson were the exceptions. If 'understanding Europe' is assisted by the possession of a history degree, as historians urged, the boom in the discipline was now having results. His father had sent Austen Chamberlain to read history at Cambridge (though the syllabus stopped at the Peace of Amiens). Afterwards, his command of French and German enabled him to listen to Albert Sorel in Paris and Heinrich von Treitschke in Berlin. Baldwin took a first in Part I of the Cambridge History Tripos, a feat he did not sustain. Hoare and Halifax gained firsts in history at Oxford. Neville Chamberlain's degree in metallurgy was enhanced by occasional (though unsolicited) historical advice from Professor Harold Temperley of Cambridge. While it would be unwise to endow this academic formation with too much significance, it should not be discounted. Linguistic competence and travel was greater than might be supposed, though no one set out to verify Europe's essential unity. Ramsay

MacDonald's visit to Georgia in 1920 might have established its outer limit. Austen Chamberlain paid regular visits to Switzerland and the Italian lakes, by now almost home ground for comfortably-off Englishmen. He conversed with Mussolini in French in five private meetings, though in 1927 he felt obliged to take his holidays in Spain to avoid 'undesirable political speculation'. Chamberlain regarded such meetings as promoting the Locarno spirit of friendship and mutual trust.[50] Before 1914, Baldwin had regularly spent a month in western Europe (and a month's winter sport in Switzerland). Post-war, he largely settled for annual residence in Aix-les-Bains. His French was good, his German passable and he could apparently read Russian without difficulty (the first British prime minister to do so). Reading, who was Jewish, had been sent by his father to learn German in Hamburg. In the years before 1914, he and his wife joined the European notables at Marienbad. Simon, apparently, could speak French, Spanish, Portuguese and Italian. He could also read German and had some knowledge of Russian. His knowledge of Hindustani is a reminder that these men also travelled beyond Europe – to North America, the Antipodes and India. Hoare spoke French, Italian and Russian (he had spent time in pre-revolutionary Russia). Eden spoke French and German but had studied Persian and Arabic, with distinction, at Oxford. Since these men usually still travelled by train or car, they had some understanding of how one European landscape merged into another. It was Hoare who was the enthusiast for flying (as befitted a former air secretary). His efforts, however, had largely been devoted to developing key imperial routes to India and South Africa. Hoare's wife became the first woman to fly from Britain to India. That seemed more interesting than flying to Paris.

This pattern of education and travel among prime ministers and foreign secretaries reflected personal choice and did not constitute a deliberate programme to 'understand' Europe, but it also reflected genuine interest. Examination of the travel undertaken by other politicians and other elites might show a different pattern, but there was no lack of curiosity about 'abroad'. How much they 'understood' of what they saw and heard in Europe is more problematic, as is its bearing on policy-making, but there is sufficient here to puncture the picture of invincible insular ignorance. There was always the danger that travel brought only 'misunderstanding'. British 'eye-witnesses', observing life in the Third Reich, very often found evidence that confirmed the impressions with which they had started.[51] So did visitors to the Soviet Union. Eden, when he was a junior minister in the Foreign Office, liked travelling, and visited Berlin and Moscow. Talking to Hitler in Berlin in 1934, he thought the new chancellor had 'charm' and was 'more sincere' than he had expected. This made him disposed to condone a particular rearmament proposal Hitler wished to put forward. Vansittart got Simon to send his junior a stiff rebuke. Here was the rub. Unless politicians 'familiarized' themselves at first hand with their European peers and saw for themselves the context in which they worked, how could they understand what was going on? Baldwin reacted strongly against the 'conference diplomacy' that had taken Lloyd George to various European cities in the immediate post-war period. Neville Chamberlain did not undertake any official foreign travel between 1932 and 1937. His flight to confer with Hitler in September 1938 was his first. Asked in 1933 whether it would have made any difference if he had met Bethmann-Hollweg, the German chancellor in 1914, Edward Grey replied, 'Not a bit.'[52]

Grey's response would have gratified Britain's professional diplomats. They still believed that they could give cool and disinterested advice. The men on the spot would not be bamboozled by the natives as visiting politicians were liable to be. They could represent the British nation. The interlude of Lloyd George could be portrayed as an aberration. There were few Welshmen in the Foreign Office to challenge Keynes's presentation of him as the epitome of 'final purposelessness, inner irresponsibility, existence outside or away from our Saxon good and evil'.[53] After 1922, foreign policy could return to 'normalcy' in good Saxon hands. Until the premiership of Neville Chamberlain in 1937, the Foreign Office, particularly in the person of Sir Robert Vansittart, poet, playwright and novelist, and Etonian contemporary of Lord Halifax, appointed permanent under-secretary in 1930, regained authority in the policy-making process.[54]

Becoming 'continentals'?

There was, however, a growing belief that diplomacy, in a democracy, was too serious a business to be left to diplomats, or at least to the elite from which they continued to be drawn. There needed to be a deeper and wider public engagement with international relations. C.R. Buxton, for example, a convert to Labour from Liberalism, sought to banish 'the too commonly accepted idea that the sister nations of Europe can never be more than a name to the English democracy'. The people would be able to 'break through the age-long conventions of diplomatic intercourse'.[55] His brother Noel had been attempting to do that in the Balkans, a task that made him 'an amiable nincompoop' in official eyes.[56] A 1930 Fabian Tract, having analysed the 'upper class' composition of the Foreign Office and the Diplomatic Service, concluded that such men had been secluded from the common people. What was now needed was men who could mix easily with all classes and standpoints – a capacity apparently precluded by an 'upper-class' upbringing. The Foreign Service ought to be able to present abroad 'the mental attitude of the nation it stands for' and conversely to convey to government at home the mind of foreigners. Only a democratic diplomacy would be capable of exploiting the 'moral forces' that were then, allegedly, rallying behind the cause of world peace.[57]

A constituency of academics and commentators had a similar perspective. The post-war world required the cultivation of 'the international mind'. States, including Britain, had been too concerned with 'national interests' and such a focus had led to disaster. 'Now we stand at the parting of the ways. It is for British citizens', wrote Arthur Greenwood, subsequently a Labour MP, 'to choose whether they will fly in the face of international tendencies and relapse into an illusory insularity, or whether they will assume the responsibilities of that wider citizenship without which international life is chaotic.'⁵⁸ The volume in which he wrote was sponsored by the newly formed Council for the Study of International Relations.

The study of international history received fresh impetus from historians – A.J. Grant, L.B. Namier, H.W.V. Temperley, J.R.M. Butler, E.H. Carr, C.K. Webster, E.L. Woodward and Lillian Penson – many of whom had been temporary 'insiders' in the Foreign Office, writing handbooks ahead of the Peace Conference.⁵⁹ 'Nationality', A.J. Pollard believed, 'has come to stay', but there needed to be a League to provide means for its expression in any form but war.⁶⁰ No boy, thought Eileen Power, should leave school without understanding 'the place of his country within the larger whole of mankind, swept by great movements common at least to Europe'. The only way to cure the evils that had arisen out of a concentration on purely national history was to promote a strong sense of the solidarity of mankind.⁶¹ Two historians of the ancient world, Alfred Zimmern and Arnold Toynbee, turned their attention to their own times with similar intent.⁶² Chairs of International Politics were established in Aberystwyth, London and Oxford. Arnold Toynbee took on the task, for the newly formed British Institute of International Affairs – to become the Royal Institute (Chatham House) in 1926 – of completing a Survey of International Affairs on an annual basis.⁶³ 'What all the nations now need', Lord Bryce declared in his final lectures on international relations, delivered in the United States in 1921, 'is a public opinion which shall in every nation give more constant thought and keener attention to international policy, and lift it to a higher plane'.⁶⁴ 'Well-connected' individuals, such as John Wheeler-Bennett, made it their purpose in life to find out what was going on in Europe.⁶⁵

It was the relationship between Britain and Europe that was considered to need most urgent attention. G.M. Trevelyan, historian of Garibaldi, who had commanded the British Red Cross Unit in Italy from 1915 to 1918, came back to England convinced, as he lectured to the British Academy in 1919, that 'we are, whether we like it or not, part of the Continent'. No doubt excepting himself, he feared that the British had no training in how to mix with their neighbours. It should become a national priority to study modern languages and modern history.⁶⁶ Alfred Zimmern, son of a German Jew who had come to England in 1848, addressed the problems of Europe 'in convalescence'. Britain, he thought, should become a good European, and that meant seeing Europe as more than a market or a field for investments or consortiums. 'Is it not time,' he asked, in this age in which men fly the Channel in ten minutes, that we become Continentals, that we should break down our island inhibitions and seek to relate ourselves to the deeper problems and issues which are engaging the minds of men throughout the wider world?[67]

He devoted his own subsequent career in Aberystwyth, Geneva, Paris and Oxford to this end. Surprisingly, perhaps, F.S. Oliver (b. 1864), 'amateur' historian and enthusiast for federalism in the United Kingdom and British Empire, now concluded that Europe was a 'vital and organic unity'. People whose home was Britain could not escape from their own particular environment. They were forced, he believed, not merely by material but also by spiritual causes 'to be European first and Anglo-Saxons afterwards'.[68]

Europe, the world and the League of Nations

In the cultivation of 'internationalism' there was a tension between the global and the continental. The formation of a League of Nations, the 'great experiment' as one of its most ardent advocates, Lord Robert Cecil, son of the former prime minister, described it, emerged from ideas put forward by various groups during the war, largely in Britain and the United States. A league, as Lord Grey expressed it in May 1918, would impose some limitation upon the national action of each member state. If any nation broke such a limitation then, in theory, all the other nations would have to use their combined force against it.[69] Schemes that had been put forward showed considerable variation in detail – some advocates thought that no force should be used, only 'sanctions', whereas others wanted to see the League given an international enforcement role.[70] It was recognized that the participation of the United States would be vital if the League was to be a truly effective world organization. It then became clear that President Wilson could not deliver that participation. That being the case, some official and political opinion believed that Britain too should not participate. However, the strong current of public opinion could not be resisted. At the first meeting of the League Council in Paris in January 1920, the foreign secretary pledged Britain's commitment to 'an association of sovereign states' whose purpose was to reconcile divergent interests and promote international cooperation. Such a guarded endorsement disappointed those who thought that the League ought to have been, and could still evolve into, a 'superstate'.

The League of Nations, as an international body meeting at regular intervals, with its own permanent secretariat and headquarters at Geneva was a new phenomenon.[71] The League's International Committee on Intellectual Co-operation, created in 1922, drew together luminaries, largely from across Europe, with the objective of fostering intellectual relations, envisaged as a necessary prelude to fiscal and military disarmament. Optimistic minds were fascinated by the dawn of the 'electric-machine-power-age'. The physical dimensions of the planet were being virtually reduced by the evolution of three machines – the aeroplane, radio and television.[72] It was time to throw off the shackles of the past.

British participants were prominent in various other new agencies that appeared under League auspices. One such body was the International Labour Office. 'What on earth is an international official?', asked the then chancellor of the exchequer in 1921, 'Is he both British and non-British? Is he a - - - hermaphrodite?'[73] Vansittart, considering that the ILO never did anything of importance, expressed the view that 'it is really of no particular interest of ours who is Director'.[74] Sir Harold Butler, who got the job, took a different view. Hermaphroditism did of course pose some difficulties. Some men who had worked with Americans during the war found their approach positive and refreshing. Continentals could be trying. Butler, however, had found the American outlook 'far more remote from our own than that of the continentals'. It took him time to perceive that American and British ways 'were rooted in the same subsoil of ideas and ideals'.[75]

A wide swathe of Liberal, Labour and some Conservative opinion in Britain invested its hopes in the League, though some wanted to see it 'modified' or 'improved' before it could receive unconditional support. Some thought there was significance in the fact that it was the League of Nations, though in reality it was the League of States. It frequently turned out, however, that one person's 'improvement' was another person's 'retrograde step'. The League of Nations Union became the most influential pressure group and educational agency on international issues in inter-war Britain.[76] Historians of the League have frequently felt obliged to consider a long list of 'if onlys' when considering its performance. This or that aspect of its structure or remit might indeed have been ordered differently, but the 'lesson' to be drawn from its inadequacy in dealing with the serious political disputes that arose is not that it could have been more effective if it had been given more authority but that it was a condition of its creation that it could not have that authority.[77]

The purported universality of the League precluded it from being a direct instrument for the fashioning of 'Europe' and, initially, the defeated powers were excluded. Austria and Bulgaria joined in 1920, Hungary in 1923, and Germany in 1926. In Germany, in particular, as far as Europe was concerned, the League appeared little more than a 'front' for the wartime victors. Thus, in the eyes of Lord Robert Cecil, the September 1926 League Assembly marked 'the real end of the war' since 'Europe was no longer divided into two groups'. In his mind, it was 'Geneva' that 'had effaced the evil memories of Versailles'. The Soviet Union, which did not apply until 1934, was accepted in that year. 'Geneva' was initially somewhat overshadowed as a forum by the inter-allied conferences that took place at Genoa and Cannes, and by the Conference of Ambassadors and the Inter-Allied Commission of Control, but by the middle 1920s it had established itself as the place where foreign ministers, including the British, met. Politicians from new European states, Dr Benes of Czechoslovakia in particular, relished the European platform it provided. When Germany, Italy and Japan left the League, however, Geneva as a meeting place declined in importance.

For Britain, the League of Nations added complexity rather than clarity to the question of its relationship with 'Europe'. The League's pretensions were global, not European, however incomplete its membership. In practice, however, it was Eurocentric. 'The League is much too much of a purely European affair already', wrote A.L. Kennedy, *The Times* correspondent who covered its affairs in 1926.[78] The impressive new *Palais des Nations* was naturally erected in Geneva. It was a Briton, Sir Eric Drummond (later earl of Perth), who became its first secretary-general, a post he occupied until 1932. According to one observer, Drummond was 'a typical Scot' – though an aristocratic one – who 'concealed beneath the surface a vision and a fire which his great office had inspired in him'.[79] To others, however, his cautious and unemotional demeanour was concealing nothing at all. His successor, a Frenchman, emerged after a flurry of exchanges between London, Paris, Rome and Berlin. British scholars seemed justified in concluding in 1933 that 'The destiny of the League lies mainly in the hands of the Great Powers of Europe.' France and Britain had given what they called 'reiterated pledges of their loyalty' to it – provided the system accepted their point of view. They had even shown signs of beginning to understand each other's point of view.[80] 'Pledges of loyalty', however, did not suffice. The 'failure' of the League in the Far Eastern Crisis of 1931–33 could be explained by its remoteness, but no greater success was achieved in the Abyssinian/Ethiopian crisis of 1935.[81] Supporters of the League criticized what they regarded as the feeble response of the British government, but it became obvious that 'national interests', as the government perceived them, took priority. Thereafter, the League dwindled into irrelevance. Old-style inter-state relations had not gone away.

The problem of France

In February 1940, Sir Orme Sargent, a Foreign Office official, wrote about the need to create 'a permanent system of Anglo-French amity'.[82] In a broadcast on 30 March, Churchill spoke about the need to establish 'indissoluble union'. In the event, the proposed Anglo-French Union never got off the ground. Lord Hankey who, as cabinet secretary, had been at the heart of British decision-making for decades, was certain in June that 'the French were more responsible for our present troubles than anyone else'. He could not believe that the British people would stand for 'a policy which merges our nationhood'. Lord Halifax hastened to reply that the proposal had been considered only as a wartime exigency. In the circumstances, he added, the idea was now quite dead. The British 'island story' received a fresh lease of life amid dire danger. King George VI was not alone in seeing merit in not having to bother with tiresome allies. Other contemporaries thought that the trouble with France was that, in spite of its intellectual and artistic brilliance, it was a country still fractured from top to bottom on the great social and political issues of the age. France, it was argued, had neither wholly embraced nor wholly rejected democracy.[83] 'The history we have written together since the 1918 Armistice,' wrote the French writer Georges Bernanos in exile in Brazil in 1941, 'with the blood of five million men, is not of a kind for children to read'.[84] The Franco-British relationship was indeed the key element in creating, or failing to create, a stable Europe.

In 1919 Britain and France were the two dominant European powers, with Italy a poor third. Together, they had 'won the war' but they had not 'won the peace'. Despite the rhetoric of the *entente cordiale*, deep mutual understanding had proved elusive. During the war, at various levels, there were difficult moments in the relations between the two allies – as was perhaps only to be expected with some two million British troops on French soil. One English chaplain reported that the French peasantry were the meanest people he had ever met. 'They will not give a glass of water to a British soldier ... unless they are paid for it. Our men's common talk is that they hope our next war will be with these peoples.' French soldiers, on the other hand, were 'all right with our men'.[85] Robert Graves, possibly unreliably, recorded in his autobiography that anti-French feeling among ex-soldiers 'amounted almost to an obsession'.[86] 'Tommy' and 'Jock' in north-eastern France displayed customary British indifference to the French language. The 'occupation' of Calais seemed to its inhabitants to be making it almost an English town (again!). When the Scottish entertainer Harry Lauder landed in Boulogne it seemed to him 'like a bit of Britain picked up, carried across the Channel and transplanted successfully to a new resting place'.[87]

The armies of the two countries had stood alongside each other in mutual support, but they did not fuse. French and British politicians and soldiers were sometimes at loggerheads as to how the war should be run. That was hardly surprising, as Marshal Foch, the supreme allied commander, subsequently wrote, given that the armies were 'strange' to each other and differed significantly in their structures. 'The French mean to take us over body and soul', complained the British chief of the imperial general staff in May 1918, 'They are proposing to pool oats, and to have a Frenchman to say how many horses each country is to have ...'. And Sir Henry Wilson, the French-speaking writer of this letter, was sometimes supposed to be 'the only British General of his day who got on with the French'.[88] Lord Milner, the war minister, wrote to Lloyd George in the same month stating that while Britain had indeed gladly agreed to strategic unity of control 'we never contemplated the administrative unification of the French & British Armies, & ... it is quite impossible for us to agree to it'.[89] Nevertheless, despite points of friction, the two countries had 'come through' together.

Clemenceau, the 'tiger' of France, was not a stranger to the 'Anglo-Saxon world'. He was an admirer of J.S. Mill, whose work he had translated into French half a century earlier. In 1911 he had taken the distinctly unusual step (as a foreign politician) of joining Lord Roberts' National Service League. He had attended races at Ascot and apparently shook hands like an Englishman. He spoke excellent idiomatic American English and, during his years in the United States, had acquired an American wife.[90] In 1919, however, he exclaimed '*L'Angleterre est la désillusion de ma vie*'.[91]

The two countries had agreed in September 1914 (as had the Russians) not to make a separate peace, but that did not mean that they planned for peace together.[92] At the conclusion of the war, therefore, there was plenty of scope for disagreement and the casting of doubt on the contribution each had made to victory.[93] It was the treatment of Germany, the central issue, on which Britain and France diverged. A country that had been partially occupied (again) had its own future security uppermost in its mind. A country that had not been occupied could not share that anxiety to the same degree. Britain wanted Germany somehow to pay for its misdeeds and to be 'rescued' for its own sake and that of Europe as a whole. Some believed, though Balfour did not, that Germany had undergone a conversion and was now absolutely a different nation.[94] The continuance of the Allied blockade at the end of the war caused more upset in Britain than in France. Paris, frightened by the possibility of a third invasion, and sceptical of a regenerate Germany, looked to ways in which it could hem Germany in by territorial adjustment (and France would naturally simply take back Alsace and Lorraine). Conscious that it paid reparations after the Franco-Prussian war, France could not understand the tender hearts of the British.[95]

The argument, fundamentally, was between those who thought that the security of Europe would best be served by prudent reconciliation and those who thought it best served by punitive exclusion. In the end, as has been observed, Britain and France were more or less able to thwart each other's ideal policies towards Germany, but in the outcome neither could agree to uphold the treaty nor agree on a means of alleviating it.[96] The British Empire may have 'unquestionably left the negotiating table as the most satisfied, if not satiated state' but in doing so it left 'Europe' unbalanced.[97] The British willingness to guarantee France, agreed conditionally on the United States joining, lapsed when it refused to do so. There was at this time a fresh review of the Channel Tunnel question, but financial, strategic and emotional arguments were successfully deployed against it.[98] Relations with France, concluded Sir Charles Hardinge, would never be sufficiently stable and friendly to justify construction. The idea of a guarantee to France still had its British supporters post-war but opponents successfully argued that France wanted something for nothing. Lord Derby, lately ambassador in Paris, wrote to Lloyd George in June 1921 that he wanted Germany re-established as a commercial nation, but he did understand French feelings that a revived Germany might be tempted to launch a war of revenge. He wanted these things to be reconciled – but could not think how.[99] He was not the only man in this condition.

In January 1923, France, supported by Belgium and Italy, moved into the Ruhr, using, as grounds, a German failure to make a specific reparation payment. The British declined to take part but did not formally condemn.[100] Allied division encouraged German 'passive resistance', though by September it was called off. It had been made clear to the new German chancellor, Gustav Stresemann, that he could not look for direct British support.[101] The French action, even though it appeared to have been vindicated, had aroused much criticism in Britain, drawing on old memories of French military dominance. However, French financial weakness enabled the British and the Americans, the latter particularly, to impose a new plan, the Dawes Plan, to deal with reparations. France evacuated the Ruhr in the summer of 1925.

The Treaty of Locarno, initialled in October 1925 and signed in December, appeared to represent a new beginning, or perhaps pre-war 'stability' had been regained.[102] The Franco-German and Belgian-German frontiers, as established at Versailles, were accepted by the three powers concerned and guaranteed by Britain and Italy, as was the demilitarized Rhineland. This was an agreement, not a *Diktat*, and appeared to open up a new era. Was not a British guarantee significant? Its practical importance was minimal, however, and has indeed been described as 'valueless'.[103] Both France and Germany had to be 'guaranteed' against each other – a requirement that nullified any possibility of effective military action in support of either. It was the British hope that Germany and France were achieving a *modus vivendi* that would eliminate or minimize any need for future British military action on the continent. As has been argued, it was not the prelude to constant intervention.[104] Emphasis on the limitations of the pact is appropriate, but Chamberlain had to endure considerable criticism that the direction of British policy had been placed in French hands.[105] His personal engagement with his European counterparts was exceptional. In the year after leaving office, 1930, he gave an address to the Royal Institute of International Affairs, on 'Great Britain as a European Power', which left no doubt of his basic conviction on this point.[106]

That could not mean, however, that Britain had ceased to be a non-European power, and neither had France. There was little to lead to the conclusion that Britain should forget its far-flung empire and think only about Europe. That empire, after all, post-1919, had expanded to what was to prove its largest territorial extent. The German colonial empire in Africa was ended and Britain (and South Africa) took control.[107] From the former Ottoman Empire, Britain took control of Iraq and Palestine. It was in the Middle East that Franco-British tension was most acute as both countries sought to get maximum benefit from their wartime Sykes–Picot agreement, which set out their respective spheres of influence (France had Syria and Lebanon). It is true that these allocations were 'mandates' rather than annexations, though the practical difference did not amount to much. British influence in Iraq, which became independent in 1932, was paramount as indeed it was in Egypt, which had become independent a decade earlier. The 1917 Balfour Declaration, which envisaged a 'national home' for Jews in Palestine brought a fresh complication, the practical consequences of which increasingly taxed the British administration. In sum, the ambitions and rivalries of Britain and France, particularly but not exclusively in the Middle East, made fundamental accord in Europe more difficult.

The hopes of the 'Locarno era' soon withered. The 'Great Crash' of 1929, and its repercussions, the death of Stresemann, Nazi election success in 1930 and the financial crisis of the summer of 1931, all produced a different climate. Comments in his diary by the prime minister in these months are striking. France had become 'the peace problem of Europe'. French behaviour was 'inconceivably atrocious'. The pursuit of world disarmament in 1932–33 failed.[108] 'Can we keep trying to work with these impossible people?', MacDonald asked himself in December 1932.[109] French obduracy, or at least that of the French government, was frequently blamed for the failure of disarmament talks. Writing in November 1931, for example, the journalist Robert Dell, indicted the rulers of France (by which he meant the big banks, the *Comité des Forges* – the powerful association of steelmakers – and the general staff of the army), who knew that French armaments far exceeded what was needed for national defence. They were needed rather as an instrument of political domination. When they spoke of security, they meant French hegemony.[110] A couple of months later, Vansittart likewise wrote that France had obtained hegemony, if not dictatorship, political and financial – the very thing that Britain had sought to avoid in Europe.[111] The Foreign Office did recognize that there would be no 'give' from Paris unless security fears were dealt with. 'We do not minimise the risks of involving Great Britain yet further in the fate of Europe', a lengthy memorandum of December 1931 argued, '... but we believe that we are already committed by our geographical position and by the extent of our economic relations.'[112] The cabinet reiterated, however, that it was not prepared to enter into any guarantee over and above Locarno under which British forces might be engaged in a war on the continent of Europe.[113] Years later, the advent of the Popular Front government under Blum in June 1936 added another factor: it was seen as a front for the Communists.[114]

Dell's charge became standard. We have noted the animus that existed in 1940. British politicians in private, and sometimes in public, criticized France sharply, and vice versa. In Britain, the litany focused on the number of 'missed opportunities' to achieve an understanding with Germany for which France could be blamed. In France, it focused on British unwillingness to contemplate a real continental commitment. Despite the fact that *au fond* both countries recognized the need for partnership, in all the crises of the 1930s it proved virtually impossible to reach a common understanding, either on strategy or tactics. It remained an orthodoxy in Britain, on the analogy of 1914, that alliances led to war. France, on the other hand, signed a treaty with the Soviet Union in 1935. French opinion could not understand why British opinion had objected so strongly to the Italian invasion of Abyssinia. The hypocrisy of Britain, it was suggested, caused the alienation of an Italy that should have been kept 'on side'. In the Rhineland crisis of 1936, when German troops reoccupied the demilitarized zone, and in the Austrian and Czechoslovak crises of 1938/39, London and Paris proved more adept at blaming each other for their own inactivity than in formulating common policies.[115] The Franco-British partnership had become dysfunctional.[116]

The gripe about French 'hegemony' of course reflected the deep-seated British preoccupation with 'the overlordship of Europe'. 'It has nothing to do with rulers or nations', Churchill had stated at a private party meeting in March 1936, 'it is concerned solely with whoever is the strongest or the potentially dominating tyrant'. This 'wonderful unconscious tradition' had lasted for 400 years and still applied. It was a 'law of public policy' that was being followed, not a matter of likes and dislikes, of being fundamentally pro-French or anti-German, or vice versa. It happened now to be 'a Germanized Europe under Nazi control' that threatened, and therefore Britain's national salvation required her to gather up 'all the forces of Europe' to contain and if necessary frustrate it.[117] In doing so, of course, she would again be the guardian of 'the liberties of Europe'.

The problem of Germany

Such a classical exposition can explain why, with relatively few exceptions, the British political establishment had moaned about French 'hegemony' before it turned to lamenting French demoralization as its own apprehensions about German 'hegemony' deepened in the late 1930s. It had not been the business of the 'wonderful unconscious tradition' to assess whether there was a Franco-British 'solidarity of values', albeit differently embodied, that should be deepened and strengthened. The tradition implied that Britain should rather concentrate on undermining French hegemony in a mechanical way. 'Bringing Germany back' was the only way that could be achieved. Of course, initially after 1919, Britain looked to support a 'Germany-in-Europe' that would see the stupidity, as much as the wickedness, of what had been attempted in 1914. J.L. Garvin, editor of the *Observer*, was only one of those who quickly saw the folly of trying to keep the German race as 'international serfs' for decades to come. The 'incorporation' of Germany in Europe was vital because, in 20 years, it might possibly be again 'the strongest on this side of the world' and might seek to 'gain back what it had forfeited'.[118] Such convictions can be identified in many other quarters. As foreign secretary, Curzon in 1921 commented that any idea of obliterating

Germany from the comity of nations or treating her as an outcast was not only ridiculous but insane.[119] The presence of British troops in Cologne, as part of the post-war Allied occupation, arguably successfully blocked French attempts to create a separate Rhineland.[120] It continued to be a standard refrain for the next decade, although what 'bringing Germany back' precisely entailed was not always clear. In May 1932, Alexander Cadogan of the Foreign Office was still looking to bring the 'post-war period' to an end and to allow Germany to be a Great Power on an equal footing.

There was, however, some irritation that important political elements in post-war Germany appeared not to be attracted by the prospect of such 'incorporation'. The Soviet-German Treaty, signed at Rapallo in April 1922, whereby the two states normalized their relations, seemed to show how quickly Germany might emerge from its containment by the western powers.[121] There was much talk in Germany of the 'revolutionary self-disarming' to which it had allegedly been subjected. British observers asked themselves how firmly and acceptably based was the Weimar Republic. German intellectuals asked themselves whether democracy in Germany would have some specifically German essence. The functioning of a democracy rested upon certain cultural preconceptions. Was there a cultural continuum – Germany, western Europe, Anglo-America – or did the cultures remain, in certain important features, at loggerheads. What was specific about 'German freedom'? It seemed not infrequently that British liberalism was inappropriate for Germany. 'Anglicization' was to be feared.[122] One who wrestled with these problems was the theologian-historian Ernst Troeltsch. He had never been to England but received an invitation to lecture there in March 1923. He died, almost symbolically, however, before he could make the journey.[123]

The president of the British Academy expressed the hope that British scholars 'might assist the process of conversion by which alone Germany could win readmission to the fellowship of civilized nations' but that would evidently take time – and presupposed an understanding of 'civilization' that was not yet settled.[124] British observers found the apparent preoccupation with 'a new birth of the German soul' rather trying when it might have been better to concentrate on the material betterment of society.[125] At various levels, renewed contacts did go some way towards blotting out the legacy of war, but suspicion remained not far below the surface.[126] Mr Christopher Isherwood (in the years 1929–33) was not the only Englishman to be drawn to a certain lifestyle in Bohemian Berlin.

> And in cold Europe, in the middle of Autumn destruction,
> Christopher stood, his face grown lined with wincing
> In front of ignorance – 'Tell the English,' he shivered,
> 'Man is a spirit.'[127]

The advent of Hitler to power in 1933 reawakened such suspicions. It was frequently suggested that Nazism was the inevitable reaction of the

German people to the Versailles settlement. Even if this was so, however, what followed? Some suggested that the rhetoric of the regime should not be taken too seriously but others believed that a kind of official madness had overtaken Germany. Could one do business with Hitler? What was the real nature of 'National Socialism'? How 'popular' was it? These and other questions were frequently aired but less frequently settled.[128] *The Times* recognized 'the absolute right' of Germans to have the kind of constitution they preferred. The distinction it tried to draw was between the internal affairs of Germany, which were her own concern, and such national activities that might threaten the peace and security of other countries or strike at the worldwide freedom of religious belief.[129] But was this traditional distinction tenable? Anti-Semitism and the ecclesiastical policy of the regime received increasing British attention, though there was no unanimity in interpreting what lay behind it and the goal to which it was leading.[130] There was a minority that was enthusiastic about Nazi Germany.[131] Individual Britons in Germany and Germans in Britain awkwardly straddled an increasing divide. Was it possible to 'resist' the regime and yet remain a German patriot? Where did a 'double life' end and 'duplicity' begin? The career of the German Rhodes Scholar at Oxford, Adam von Trott zu Soltz illustrated this ambiguity.[132] After 1933, refugees, largely German Jewish, came to Britain but by the end of 1937 Great Britain harboured only about 5500 of a total of 154,000 refugees who had left Nazi Germany. At the beginning of the war there was a total of 74,000 Germans and Austrians in Great Britain.[133]

It was against this background that Neville Chamberlain, prime minister since June 1937 considered Europe. Whatever else may be said about Chamberlain, and much has been said, he thought war futile, whether or not Britain was 'ready' for it. He would get Hitler, or at least Germans, to see that there could be some 'peaceful change' so long as the security or independence of the United Kingdom was not jeopardized. He was prepared to accept some reordering of central Europe to this end. If he had succeeded, the 'Europe' that would then have emerged was one in which it was an enlarged Germany, rather than France, that exercised 'hegemony'. That some degree of subordination or subservience might then have been required of France was regrettable but probably inescapable. It would have been a Germany in the grip of an ideology with which, in a world of states, one would have to live, as one had to live with the Soviet Union, also in the grip of an unpalatable dictator and ideology. It would have been for Germany to determine how much latitude to extend to Italy as an ideological 'partner'. Such a Europe would not have been congenial but it would have been tolerable – provided that its premise, that Britain would not then become vulnerable but could exist, imperially, at arm's length from such a continent, was accepted. There were increasing numbers who thought the scenario implausible. It was imperative, rather, to collect 'all the forces of Europe' so as to provide effective deterrence. It was by no means clear, however, that 'Europe', even if the Soviet Union is included in that description, was available for collection in this way. Whether Chamberlain's policy was 'the only way which offered any hope of avoiding war' or whether he 'stifled serious chances of preventing the Second World War' will continue to be argued over indefinitely.[134] The irony is that whether or not Britain went to war came to hinge, in 1938/39, on developments in that awkward space known as 'central Europe', occupied by the products of 1919 'national self-determination'.

'Central Europe' and the Balkans

Vienna in 1919 was a city lost.[135] It seemed a far cry from the congress of a century earlier. An application of 'national self-determination', which incorporated 'Austria' within Germany, probably what most Austrians favoured, was not acceptable to France. The Foreign Office would have allowed it. The city became a disproportionately large capital of a small state uncertain of its *raison d'être*. 'What a funny shape Austria must be,' Lord Robert Cecil had noted at Versailles. It was certainly not the heart of Europe, nor was it even the heart of 'central Europe' since the neighbouring new states of Poland, Czechoslovakia and Hungary, in their independent existence, distanced themselves, in their different ways, from the Habsburg legacy. It contained about an eighth of the territory of the former Habsburg Empire and about a sixth of its population.[136] It was a state that soon achieved bankruptcy but that was rescued financially under the auspices of the League of Nations. Sir Arthur Salter, the British official who arrived in this connection, thought that starvation and desperation would soon lead to chaos and disorder.[137] The country survived but excited no admiration. The idea of a Customs Union with Germany in 1931 was quashed because of French rather than British objections. Austria's politics were made acrimonious by the gulf between Vienna, with a large Left presence, and Catholic conservative country areas. Clerical 'authoritarianism' did not appeal in Britain. Young Michael Stewart, later foreign secretary, thought there could scarcely be two more different cities in Europe at this juncture than London and Vienna.[138] Fighting broke out in Vienna in 1934. Naomi Mitchison left Oxford to express her support for the workers. She had to confess to Viennese she met, however, that 'Austria is no longer news in England'. Her conclusion was that 'Dear little Dollfuss, whom everyone in England feels all motherly about, appears to be extremely well hated'.[139] Dollfuss, the Austrian chancellor, was under five feet tall. Wheeler-Bennett, who met him, saw him as 'the tragic and almost predestined victim of a political dilemma virtually impossible of solution'.[140] The comments of British diplomats in Vienna suggest that they found the factions in Viennese politics virtually impossible of comprehension.[141] Sir Walford Selby, the minister, greatly enjoyed stalking roaring stags in the early dawn of an October morning in the Austrian mountains. He was sent off to Portugal to deal there with another clerical-authoritarian regime, that of Dr Salazar. Dollfuss was assassinated later in 1934 but a Nazi coup attempt failed. Austria 'slipped downhill' as the British correspondent G.E.R. Gedye chronicled its fate.[142] In 1938, having completed his stalking of the Austrian scene, Hitler brought his native Austria 'home' to the Reich. 'A World-War on the subject', wrote J.L. Garvin in the *Observer* on 13 March 1938, 'would be an insanity and a crime, and there can be no question of it in any responsible quarter in this country'. Nor was there. In 1815, Vienna had been the centre of Europe when Europe was the centre of the world. By 1919 the Habsburg Empire had ceased to exist. By 1938, Vienna was no longer the centre of anything. The first alteration in the map of central Europe had been unilaterally made. It would not be the last.

The most famous observation Austen Chamberlain ever made was that the Polish corridor (which gave Poland its access to the sea and separated West and East Prussia) was something 'for which no British Government ever will or ever can risk the bones of a British grenadier'. It was the Franco-German border that Britain would 'guarantee' at Locarno, but Britain could not contemplate a guarantee of the German-Polish border. The Polish minister in London was reassured in 1925 that Poland and Germany would find common interest in coming to terms. No sensible man in Germany wished for a new partition. Before he died, in 1937, he discovered that not all men in Germany were sensible.[143] Despite emollient words, there was an obvious implication that Poland could not expect support. In 1918/19, enthusiasm for the new Poland in high places had been limited. Lloyd George thought Poles greedy and grasping, and Lord Robert Cecil thought them 'unsatisfactory'. Lewis Namier, whose knowledge of Poland and eastern Europe in general, the House of Commons was told in 1919, was 'remarkable' tried, not very successfully, to use it. A British subject since 1913, he had been born in Russian Poland, the son of polonized Jews. He loathed what he regarded as Poland's territorial greed. He was later to make his name as a historian of British eighteenth-century politics. Headlam-Morley concurred that Polish imperialism was a 'disease by now well known to all'.[144]

In the immediate post-war years, complicated territorial struggles ensued involving Poles, Lithuanians, Byelorussians and the Bolsheviks.[145] The Treaty of Riga in March 1921 brought the Polish-Soviet War of 1919–20 to an end. Polish forces achieved the vital victory in August 1920. The Poland that resulted contained large minorities. The Labour movement, under the slogan 'Hands off Soviet Russia' sided with the Bolshevik version of events and threatened a general strike to prevent British aid to the Polish government.[146] Poland generally received a bad British press. Lloyd George in 1925 spoke scathingly of Poland as 'that possessor of five Alsace-Lorraines' and in 1930 the local correspondent of the *Manchester Guardian* in 1930 denounced the 'Polish terror in the Ukraine' as 'worse than anything else that is happening anywhere else in Europe'. Poland's denunciation of the Minorities Treaties in 1934, its anti-Semitism and its annexation of Teschen

– which had been within Czechoslovakia – in 1938 continued to make the country unpopular in liberal circles.[147] The British guarantee to Poland in March 1939 did not reflect any particular regard for the country. It was to indicate to Hitler, after the invasion of Prague, that he could go no further without a likelihood of war. In such a war Britain would not be able to offer Poland meaningful assistance.

In September 1938, Neville Chamberlain also made a famous observation. It was 'horrible, fantastic, incredible', he declared, that the British people were digging trenches and trying on gas masks 'because of a quarrel in a far-away country between people of whom we know nothing'.[148] During his years at the Prague Legation in the early 1920s, Bruce-Lockhart received letters, even from government departments in London, addressed Prague, Czechoslavia; Pragu, Yugoslovakia; Prague, Czechoslovenia; Prague, Vienna; and even The Prague, Poland. Writing in 1934, he thought such mistakes understandable since apparently 'Englishmen take less interest in foreign affairs than any other nation in the world.'[149]

It was, of course, not absolutely true that the British people knew nothing about central Europe, but they did not know much. Individuals adopted the causes of particular countries. Hungary provides one such example. The loss of Slovakia and Transylvania had been bitterly resented. There was a Communist government in Budapest for five months in 1919.[150] It was overthrown by the Romanian army. White Terror replaced Red Terror. Miklos Horthy, a former Habsburg admiral, established his own kind of dictatorship, which lasted until 1944. Lord Rothermere, vocal proprietor of the *Daily Mail*, took up the cause of the lost Hungarian territories in the mid-1920s. It was thought possible that he might make a bid for the Hungarian throne – Horthy was only 'regent' – an idea first proposed by Hungarian supporters in 1928.[151] According to Collin Brooks, one of Rothermere's editors, all of this had more than a touch of *The Prisoner of Zenda* (a popular novel by Anthony Hope).[152] Emil Nagy, a former Hungarian minister, counted among 'the most momentous hours' of his life his talks in England on the shortcomings of the Trianon settlement. He never met a single Englishman who was not shocked at what he had to say.[153] Rothermere rejoiced when, following the 'Vienna Award' of November 1938, a million Hungarians were released from 'the impositions, humiliations and cruelties which were heaped upon them by Czecho-Slovakia'. It was a tragedy that it was to the totalitarian states and not to the 'democracies' that Hungary was grateful.[154] Hungary, even without King Rothermere, was embedded in Europe. 'This stalwart Asiatic people', as H.A.L. Fisher described the Hungarians, had not since the days of King Stephen 'been regarded as aliens in Europe'. They had played such a valiant part in the defence of Europe against the Muslim peril.[155]

Further south, where 'the Muslim peril' was a more recent memory, a kingdom of Serbs, Croats and Slovenes had been created (subsequently turning itself into Yugoslavia). Britain had declined to join France in

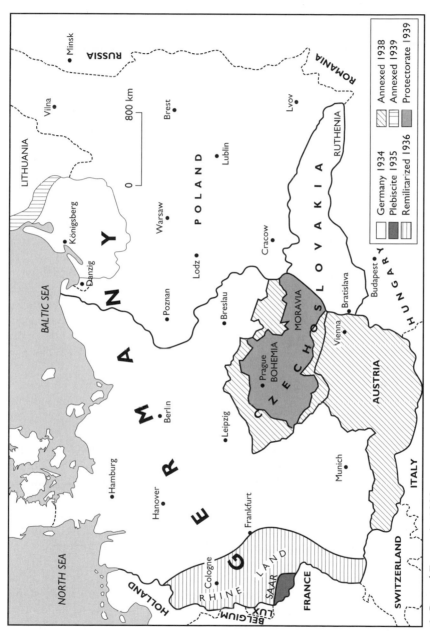

6. Central Europe in 1939

Legend

Germany 1934	Annexed 1938
Plebiscite 1935	Annexed 1939
Remilitarized 1936	Protectorate 1939

0 ————— 800 km

NORTH SEA

BALTIC SEA

HOLLAND
BELGIUM
LUX.
FRANCE
SWITZERLAND
ITALY

G E R M A N Y

•Hamburg
•Hanover
•Berlin
•Leipzig
•Cologne
•Frankfurt
R H I N E L A N D
SAAR
•Munich

LITHUANIA
•Vilna
•Königsberg
•Danzig

P O L A N D
•Poznan
•Warsaw
•Lodz
•Breslau
•Cracow
•Lublin
•Brest

RUSSIA
•Minsk

C Z E C H O S L O V A K I A
•Prague BOHEMIA
MORAVIA
RUTHENIA

AUSTRIA
•Vienna

HUNGARY
•Bratislava
•Budapest

ROMANIA
•Lvov

offering treaties of guarantee or in seeking a 'little entente', but kept a close watch on developments in the Danube region.[156] This was the 'new Europe' without empires. In varying proportions, however, these states all had ethnic minorities whose position was supposedly to be guaranteed through the League of Nations.[157] Their creation had received both official and unofficial British support at the close of the war, though all those involved, as they examined the options, knew very well that awkward choices had to be made. States that would be ethnically or linguistically homogeneous, supposing that to be 'ideal', could not be created except by what would be later described as 'ethnic cleansing', which would be unacceptable. Jews, existing in large numbers, could not have a state of their own in Europe but would have to receive 'minority' protection in whichever state they found themselves – or pursue the Zionist vision and emigrate to British-administered Palestine.

In relation to the frontiers of 'Czechoslovakia', for example, Robert Seton-Watson could see why the 'pan-Germans' would insist on union with Germany, but to permit the partition of Bohemia would deprive the new republic of security and economic independence. He supposed that the Czechs would have every interest in conciliating their German fellow-citizens.[158] From the start, however, in this instance and in others, British writers recognized that 'National minorities in a state may become, even unwillingly, the tools and cats' paws of the state's enemies; they may be used as a mean of political blackmail'.[159] It was an assessment that proved accurate in relation to the linguistic and ethnic struggles within the Czechoslovak state, particularly, but not exclusively, between Czechs and Germans.[160]

British historians, noting the number of new states in Europe, had speculated that in future the Great Powers would not 'so overwhelmingly dominate the Councils of Europe as they did in the nineteenth century'.[161] New states arrived in the Baltic as well as in central Europe. The British took time before giving full *de jure* recognition to Estonia, Latvia and Lithuania (1921/22). Initially, no one in the Foreign Office claimed to know much about their native inhabitants and leading men. Sir Harry Brittain, politician and publicist, visited all three countries on a pioneering official British delegation in 1923. In each one he came across evidence of 'a real virile race'. His encounter was a 'revelation'. Another revelation was that Lithuania offered very good wild boar hunting.[162] It did not take long, however, before Britain began a more vigorous commercial drive in the region. The states, a Foreign Office official claimed in 1925, would welcome 'the quiet assurance that England at any rate considers that these countries are sufficiently stable for her own economic expansion in them'. The region was to be another area of British-German commercial rivalry.[163] E.D. Simon wrote enthusiastically about Scandinavian states.[164] British diplomats, however, were rarely carried away, although one future permanent under-secretary was, in Belgrade in 1919, when he expressed himself eloquently on behalf of south

Slavs. It was wrong, he thought, to expect an immediate miracle of a country that had hardly learnt to walk.[165] Rebecca West's record of a journey through Yugoslavia in 1937, brilliant in its observations, confirmed that no miraculous integration of its diverse elements had yet taken place.[166] In Bulgaria, listening to curses directed at Serbs because of a fourteenth-century battle, Arthur Salter sadly concluded that a thousand years were as a day. Such observations can be replicated from many sources. The British Legation in Sofia in 1928 referred to the 'semi-civilized races inhabiting the Balkan peninsula' and the Office tended to concur that 'everything in these benighted countries is mediaeval'.[167] A 'Balkan Locarno' was a will-o'-the-wisp.

South-eastern Europe had also witnessed one further major upheaval in the post-war settlement. Out of the wreckage of the Ottoman Empire came a new Turkey under the leadership of Kemal Atatürk, hero of Gallipoli. Constantinople, city of decay and decadence, designated at this point as a neutral zone, would be replaced by a new capital, in Anatolia, Ankara. Smyrna (now Izmir) then had a Greek population larger than that of Athens, though who was a Greek remained part of the problem in a collapsing political situation.[168] Lloyd George supported the Greek push into Anatolia, partly because it might be advantageous to British interests in Asia Minor, but also because of a certain Grecophilia. The operation proved a disaster for the Greeks – and, politically, for Lloyd George himself. Arnold Toynbee was on hand to witness the disaster the Greeks experienced. The details of the war of 1921–22 cannot be recounted here, but the upshot, the Treaty of Lausanne of 1923, resulted in a massive 'exchange of populations'. Approximately 375,000 Muslims/Turks and 1.25 million Greeks/Christians were transplanted. Lord Curzon, Britain's negotiator, thought he had 'the art of getting on with Orientals'. The 'unmitigated evil' of the Turkish presence in Europe had finally come to an end. There was, however, little reason to gloat over the conclusion, which left Greece with a major problem of 'accommodation' of a population whose distinctiveness has not altogether disappeared even today. The final paradox was a Turkish republic, under Atatürk's guidance, bent on becoming, in central aspects, a 'secular' and 'European' state.

Diplomats, however, were representatives of a Great Power. They could be distinctly superior in their observations on the new systems of government – Bruce Lockhart, who thought of the Czechs as lowland Scots in disposition, and 'provincial', came to see that he must have appeared patronizing. They noted, in some instances, the ease with which peoples who had escaped oppression began to oppress. They wondered whether it was sensible to have small fractious states at what had been the heart of old Europe. The states had been created when Germany and the Soviet state had no say. If one had to choose between German influence and Soviet influence, the former was preferable. There was recurrent talk, both in the region and outside it, of federations. 'There is no complete peace for Europe until we have a great Balkan State, a great Central European State', wrote a British Conservative in 1938, 'and then the other countries around it such as France, Italy and Scandinavia'.[169] In 1919, the geographer and politician Halford Mackinder had argued that 'securely independent the Polish and Bohemian nations cannot be unless as the apex of a broad wedge of independence, extending from the Adriatic and Black Seas to the Baltic'.[170]

By 1939, however, the 'broad wedge' had no unity. If Britain should ever be in a position to determine the future of central Europe, which might be doubted, there was scarcely a British politician who thought that a simple restoration of the status quo, as established after Versailles, was the answer. *Mitteleuropa* could not exist in itself as a European entity. It had to be anchored to western Europe – or perhaps absorbed in eastern Europe, that is to say an expanded Soviet Union. No one could tell, however, whether Britain's role in eastern Europe should be that of 'a disinterested *amicus curiae* [friend at court]', as Austen Chamberlain fondly characterized it in 1925, or whether it should be a 'partner', as he characterized Britain's role in western Europe.[171]

Russia/the Soviet Union

The absence of 'Russia' in the conclusion of the peace treaties with Austria, Bulgaria, Germany and Hungary was perhaps the greatest surprise of the overall settlement. As has previously been noted, it had been frequently supposed (and feared) from 1914 onwards that the defeat of Germany and Austria would inevitably have one consequence – the dominance of a still autocratic Russia over an undefined 'eastern Europe' (not to mention elsewhere). If that had happened, the 'central Europe' that has just been discussed would not have taken the form it did. The triumph of the Bolshevik revolution in 1917 meant the end of the 'Russia' of 1914. The Bolshevik government, after months of negotiations, made a separate peace with the central powers at Brest-Litovsk in March 1918.[172] It entailed the loss of almost half of its 'European' possessions. Ukraine, Finland, Poland, Estonia, Latvia and Lithuania became nominally independent states – though within the sphere of influence of the central powers. It was an agreement that gave Germany its chance of victory in the West, a chance nearly taken. The Bolsheviks dissociated themselves from previous agreements made by the tsarist government with its allies, one of which was that which had promised Russia Constantinople and the Straits. Lloyd George would have been willing to see a Bolshevik delegation in Paris, at least to discuss economic issues, but Clemenceau objected. The French premier's alternative location, an island in the Sea of Marmora, used by the Turks as a canine refuge, proved unattractive to the potential participants.

Until its demise in 1917, the Anglo-Russian alliance had inevitably been difficult to manage. Close cooperation had never materialized. Direct high-level consultation was impossible and, in many respects, the two countries have been characterized as rivals rather than allies.[173] Revolution, therefore, did not bring an abrupt change from intimacy to enmity. However, British troops were in Archangel in northern Russia as part of an intervention designed to keep Russia in the war and safeguard allied supplies. In the changing circumstances it was easy to portray their presence as an attempt to destroy the new regime.[174]

The new regime claimed to be more than 'Russia' under new management. The new Soviet Union was to be different from the Great Power stance of its predecessor. Workers worldwide would regard it as their 'home', whatever state (temporarily) they happened to live in. 'No force on earth', declared Lenin in March 1919, could 'hold back the progress of the world communist revolution towards the world Soviet republic'.[175] Whatever a 'world Soviet republic' might be, it would clearly have little resemblance to the Europe of states. The aspiration seemed so outrageous to Winston Churchill that he suggested instant strangulation. A great pan-European army (including Germans) could liberate Russia and then establish a durable 'eastern Europe'. His call for such a crusade went unheeded. Nevertheless it seemed to many observers at the time that a new kind of rivalry was being born which, as it were, bypassed old issues in Europe. 'Europe was superseded', wrote A.J.P. Taylor in 1954, 'and in January 1918 there began a competition between communism and liberal democracy which has lasted to the present days'.[176]

Was the post-1922 'Soviet Union' simply the successor state to the Russian Empire? As has been noted, few British historians have regarded its reconquest of Ukraine or the Caucasus as anything other than an internal 'Russian' event and have taken little interest in it.[177] In 1924 the Estonian Consul in London objected to the *Manchester Guardian*'s practice of lumping the trade of the 'successor states' under 'Russia'. He plaintively pointed out that the British public should be made aware of the fact that the successor states were independent and 'the rest of the former Russian Empire is now known as the Union of Soviet Socialist Republics'.[178] A struggle to differentiate was never wholly won. It reflected the fact that 'old Russia' was still perceived in the attributes and aspirations of the Soviet state, despite its ideological transformation. Its characteristics, to some minds, strengthened the notion that the Soviet Union was not 'European'. Stalin (who was not even Russian) was truly a barbarian. From the beginning, Catholics in Britain shared the perception of Catholics in Europe that the Bolshevik regime was bent on the destruction of the Christian church. The prospect that it would be desirable, from the middle 1930s, to succour small nations by making terms with a godless and anti-democratic state 'such as Russia' was anathema to most of the Catholic press.[179]

The reaction of the British Left was necessarily more nuanced. Although 'international socialism' had failed in 1914, there had been various attempts during the war to re-establish the solidarity of workers in the belligerent countries. Communism in the Soviet Union brought the 'labour question' to the forefront in the early 1920s across Europe. In its critical reflections on peacemaking, the Labour Party stated that it did not approve the methods of the Russian Socialistic Republic, but the attempt to graft industrial self-government on to democracy was 'an experiment which mankind direly needs'.[180] A Labour and TUC delegation visited the Soviet Union in 1920. Reactions varied, but hostility to Marxism was accompanied by a 'hands off' stance, the belief that the Soviet people should determine their own destiny.[181] Of course, the relationship between 'Communists' and 'Socialists', and their respective 'Internationals' was the subject of much rancour, in Britain as elsewhere in Europe. The Communist Party of Great Britain was founded in 1920. No less than other continental Communist parties, its domestic strategy had to be aligned with the requirements of Moscow, though this was no straightforward business. The Comintern kept a watchful eye.[182]

It was one thing, therefore, to assert that the international labour movement 'must be reckoned as one of the most important factors in international politics' but another to identify what that meant in practice.[183] Certainly, Labour saw itself as 'internationalist' but a 'Labour foreign policy' was problematic. Initially, the party had comparatively few foreign policy 'experts' and drew heavily on ex-Liberals such as Arthur Ponsonby and C.R. Buxton.[184] MacDonald's first Labour government in 1924 extended *de jure* recognition to the Soviet Union and negotiated two treaties, but the 'Zinoviev Letter' played a part in his electoral defeat in that year. Neither MacDonald nor Henderson wished to be thought indifferent to patriotism. Their personal relations were difficult and they differed somewhat on the question of the League of Nations, but the 'European Labour Movement', in its non-Communist manifestation, meant something to them in their attitudes towards European affairs.[185] Quite what, depended on how the Labour Party 'fitted' in a movement where its 'counterparts' across Europe had normally to operate (or be closed down) in contexts very different from that in which it operated. Some accounts have stressed Labour's insularity and ideological distinctiveness. Others have placed the party within a European 'mainstream', and more specifically within a 'north-west European type of labour movement'.[186] In any case, with the party split in 1931 and out of office for the remainder of the decade, the British were in no position to 'give a lead'. It was that very powerlessness that made the idea of a 'popular front' appealing and the Soviet Union itself increasingly attractive. Literary intellectuals lauded proletarian virtues. In their seventies, Sidney and Beatrice Webb set off for the Soviet Union in 1932 and published *Soviet Communism. A New Civilization?* three years later. The question mark in the title was removed in the second English edition in 1937.[187] Walter Citrine, general secretary of the TUC, who paid a second visit in 1935, was less enamoured.[188] In the years immediately before 1939 a centre-left grouping pressed for an alliance with 'Russia' as the only way to deter Germany. A sceptical prime minister declined to follow this course, or at least only to explore it tardily. The Nazi-Soviet Pact ruled it out. News of its conclusion brought 'deep peace' to Evelyn Waugh's 'Guy Crouchback', but this heroic figure was perhaps not a typical Englishman.

Civilization in danger?

If the Red Army had not been defeated at the Battle of Warsaw, the British ambassador to Germany had written in 1920, the very existence of western civilization would have been imperilled. A peril had clearly returned in 1940, but what was the civilization that was in danger? Lord d'Abernon had also prognosticated a 'dangerous reverse' for Christianity.[189] Others, who had been exploring its ails for years, thought that it was 'European civilization' that was on the brink of obliteration. Perhaps it was 'democratic civilization' that would become extinct. Many writers, from Salamanca to Stockholm, pondered these matters, very well aware of the difficulties of definition they presented once one moved beyond their function as political slogans. For some, there were important distinctions to be drawn between 'western' and 'European' and 'Christian' and 'democratic' civilizations. For others, these words were virtually synonymous. Perhaps the most problematic was Europe itself. In September 1914, the English journalist W.T. Stead had published an article entitled 'The United States of Europe: The Only Way Out' but a quarter of a century later it was obvious that the way had not been taken, though the 'European idea' had indeed had its proponents.[190] After informally consulting other European leaders in 1929, the French prime minister and foreign secretary, Aristide Briand, announced his intention to propose a federation of Europe. It would tie France and Germany at its heart. A further significant impulse came from a widespread feeling that the continent ought to organize itself economically to meet 'the American challenge'. Culturally, too, in some quarters, Europe needed to protect itself against black men playing jazz. The initiative, obscure in particular as it was, failed. 'Pan-European clap-trap at Geneva' was dismissed by E.H. Carr, then in the Foreign Office. Nevertheless, for a time, serious consideration had to be given to the possibility that something might emerge.[191] British consideration took place in the context of a desire to promote imperial economic cooperation. There were, of course, deeper cultural considerations. Some fear of 'Americanization' existed in cultural discourse in Britain, but the reality was that America provided the bulk of the films that were being shown in cinemas. It was the source of fashion and glamour for the masses, whereas, for the elite, 'Europe' had been the cultural arbiter.[192] To be 'part of Europe', however, with the United States of America as the 'Other', was not an attractive or even conceivable goal, notwithstanding considerable wariness about Washington, not least on the part of Neville Chamberlain.

Perhaps the most active movement in favour of European integration was that inspired by Count Richard Coudenhove-Kalergi, son of an Austrian diplomat and a Japanese woman. His *Paneuropa* was first published in 1923. Neither his pedigree nor his theme suggested a large British following, but perhaps that did not matter because, in the count's opinion, Britain had grown out of Europe and had become a political continent on its own. The Soviet Union was likewise excluded, being a federal empire in itself. 'Pan-Europe' included all the rest of Europe. It went without saying that both the British and the European 'power fields' extended far beyond Britain/Europe.[193] Shunting Britain into an insular-globalism, however, seemed to tilt Britain's balancing act too far. In *We Europeans*, Julian Huxley and A.C. Haddon argued that in Europe both ethnic inter-crossing and culture contacts had proceeded so far that 'racial purity', like complete isolationism or self-sufficiency, was impossible.[194] The British were Europeans. And it was left to a historian to sum it all up. European civilization, thought H.A.L. Fisher in 1936, could be distinguished from that of the Semites, the Indus or the Chinese, but then it dissolved into a thousand different colours. Europe had refused to be unified by the egalitarian plan of the French Revolution, as he put it, just as it now declined to accept the 'iron programme' of Russian Communism. Yet the dream of unity had persisted and haunted the imagination of statesmen and peoples. There was no more pertinent question 'to the future welfare of the world' than how the nations of Europe, whose differences were so many and so inveterate, might even so be combined into some 'stable organization'.[195] It was to be the war that would provide some sort of answer.

10

War, reconciliation and restoration, c.1940–1975

1975: joining a community?

The United Kingdom of Great Britain and Northern Ireland, together with the Irish Republic and Denmark, joined what then became the nine-member European Economic Community on 1 January 1973. It was a momentous occasion with global ramifications. In New Zealand, which Anthony Eden had visited in 1949 and where he had talked glowingly of the 'British family of nations' with its common inheritance, loyalties, ideals and sense of kinship, there was a sense of betrayal.[1] It was a New Zealand historian who first propounded a case for a 'New British History'. It seemed obvious to Professor Pocock that British entry into the EEC would entail redefinition of 'Britain' and its history, either as European and nothing else, or as 'European' in a sense that would be privileged above all others. Such a step, he thought, whatever it might do for the British, would require the inhabitants of the 'neo-Britains' settled across the world in the nineteenth century to establish that they were British without being European.[2] Reformulating 'Britain' out of the British pasts therefore moved in tandem with the rebadging of Europe.[3]

The accession negotiations had been conducted under the Conservative government of Edward Heath (b. 1916).[4] Heath stressed on a number of occasions how much his wartime experience as a soldier in Germany had influenced his view of Europe's future.[5] The Labour opposition, under Harold Wilson (b. 1916), who had not been a soldier in Europe, had stated in the Commons in 1971 that a Labour government would seek to renegotiate the terms of entry. Both men belonged to a new British political generation. In its manifesto for the February 1974 general election, Labour had further stated that renegotiated terms would be put to the people, either through a general election or consultative referendum. Now in office, James Callaghan (b. 1912), the Labour foreign secretary, began negotiations in April 1974, a process completed – with a further general election in October intervening – at the Dublin summit of the Council of Ministers in March 1975. There were considerable internal Labour Party divisions on the issue. In cabinet, Wilson won a 16 to 7 majority in favour of a government 'yes' recommendation, but in the Commons in April more Labour MPs voted against membership (145) than in favour (137). It was Conservative and Liberal votes that gave him a Commons majority on the issue.[6]

A referendum was set for 5 June 1975. Clearly, not everyone shared the view of the philosopher Michael Oakeshott, who declared that he did not find it necessary to hold opinions on such matters. The campaign in the country for a positive vote was orchestrated by 'Britain in Europe' under the direction of Sir Con O'Neill, a former diplomat, who had led, at official level, the negotiating team for Britain's entry in 1969–72. Nearly two-thirds of the electorate voted, with 67.2 per cent in favour of remaining in and 32.8 per cent against. The EEC consisted, at that juncture, of three substantial states (France, Federal Germany and Italy) and three small ones (Belgium, Luxembourg and the Netherlands). The 'Common Market', as it was normally referred to at the time in Britain, came into being, together with the European Atomic Energy Community, on 1 January 1958, following the signature of the Treaty of Rome by the six states concerned in March 1957.[7] So, in 1975, 30 years after the end of the war, Britain, it was said, had at last joined 'Europe', though there remained those like the Labour MP and 'No' campaigner, Douglas Jay, who not only firmly rejected any idea that Britain was 'merely' a European power but also expressed scepticism as to whether 'Europe' was anything more than a stretch of land from the Urals to the Atlantic.[8] The Trades Union Congress had urged trades unionists to vote against. Claiming that 'democracy' in Britain had been based for centuries on the supreme power of an elected parliament, it believed that the British people would cease to have the final say on the way in which their country was run.[9] The rocky road to British membership has by now been explored in many detailed studies.[10] This chapter draws on them but does not attempt a complete narrative. Its purpose, rather, is to continue to explore how both 'Britain' and 'Europe' shifted in meaning over 30 years of national, continental and global post-war change.[11] It is written, too, in the knowledge, as demonstrated in the final chapter, that 1975 did not in fact 'end' the matter. In the twenty-first century, neither 'Britain' nor 'Europe' is what they were then taken to be, and meanings will no doubt shift again.[12]

The decades immediately after the Second World War seem in retrospect to constitute the apogee of a certain kind of Britishness.[13] It was only in the 1960s that questions about the structure and nature of the United Kingdom came to the fore. It seemed to some that such questioning was the inevitable corollary of the rapid end of the British Empire, beginning with India and Pakistan in 1947, and continuing thereafter across the globe. In fact, that empire had been substantially disposed of without precipitating, in the process, the kind of 'metropolitan meltdown' that had occurred in France and was to occur in Portugal. Secure, or supposedly so, in the possession of its own nuclear deterrent, Britain no longer needed colonial symbols of eminence. Even so, some writers continue to assert that there was a direct correlation between imperial 'decline' and 'territorial' questions in Great Britain and Northern Ireland.[14] The United Kingdom, some said, was little more than the 'grubby wreck of old glories'.[15] The end of the British Empire would be followed by the end of Britain.[16] The first Plaid Cymru MP was elected at a by-election in 1966.[17] The Scottish National Party won a by-election in the following year. These were only two manifestations of far wider questionings about identity and governance. A commission set up by the Labour government to investigate the constitution reported in 1973 in favour of legislative assemblies, and corresponding executives, in Scotland and Wales. In Northern Ireland, by the autumn of 1974 1100 people had been killed. The Stormont Parliament had been prorogued in 1972 and replaced by 'direct rule' from Westminster. There appeared to be no solution in sight that could satisfy the conflicting aspirations of the province's two 'communities', as they were frequently called. It was inconceivable, some supposed, that such disturbance on the 'periphery' would not, in turn, see a more determined assertion of 'Englishness'. Any author forecasting the 'break-up' of Britain seemed to many to be correctly interpreting the signs of the times.[18]

There was, therefore, an irony in the United Kingdom's adherence to a 'community', even if one only described as 'economic', at the very moment when the discordance of its own 'communities' had become more pronounced. A cluster of issues were coming together both within the United Kingdom and within the 'Europe' it was now joining – how did regions, nations, states and supranational entities relate to each other?[19] If a sense of 'community' was the prerequisite for a viable political order, at what level did it need to exist? Moreover, whatever political elites might envisage as a desirable outcome, at some stage or other, as had just happened in the United Kingdom, electorates would dispose of what governments proposed. Was there, therefore, a continuum of identities – English/British/European (and equivalents within the other members of the EEC) – that could be reconciled? Puzzlingly, both 'integration' and 'disintegration' seemed to be taking place simultaneously.

'White cliffs' and 'finest hours': war and its legacy

Such issues had surfaced by the 1970s, but they would have seemed unlikely 30 years earlier. No understanding of the mentality of Britain in the immediate post-war decades is possible without an appreciation of its wartime circumstances and their enduring legacy, though it is rightly argued that the 'price-of-victory' formula should not be advanced as a complete explanation of British post-war European policy in these years.[20]

In 1940, Britain had fought on, though in May the war cabinet had aired the possibility of a compromise peace.[21] The new prime minister, Churchill, had been able to persuade colleagues that there should be no talk of peace until Britain had proved that it could not be invaded and conquered. It can only be a matter of speculation what such a future negotiated peace might have looked like. Certainly, a 'new order' was being created in Europe.[22] In Berlin, the economics minister, Walther Funk, sketched out its basis. European currencies would be fixed in relation to each other. The whole continent, under German hegemony, would be 'planned', with benefits for all Europeans. English was among the languages into which the outline was translated. The British, however, showed little sign of sense. In July 1940, fearful that the French fleet would fall into German hands, the war cabinet authorized drastic action. The attack on French warships at Mers-el-Kébir constituted the most conspicuous example of the fractured relationship between erstwhile allies.[23]

In retrospect, it can be seen that at this stage it was the continuing resistance of Britain that prevented Hitler consolidating his kind of Europe. Defeating him, however, was another matter. 'England's only hope is Russia and America', Hitler told his generals at Berchtesgaden in late July 1940. Many British policy-makers would have agreed, though there still remained a belief that the German economy (and morale) could be undermined by bombing, blockade and subversion. In September, however, the chiefs of staff modestly discounted the possibility of creating a British army for the continent that would comparable in size to that of the Germans. In such circumstances the special operations executive came into being. It would be a revolutionary organization that would 'set Europe ablaze'. In the years that followed, much ingenuity, energy and enthusiasm was devoted to British 'cloak and dagger' operations in Europe, sometimes with complicated results. Such an 'irregular' strategy placed great faith in the existence of a smouldering opposition in Europe for which, initially at least, there was little evidence. German success seemed so complete that 'resistance', whatever that word encompassed, could seem futile. From the very start, any kind of organized subversive activity raised divisive questions about future structures. 'Resistance' rarely existed in straightforward antithesis to 'collaboration' (and raised particular issues in Germany and Italy). In each occupied country its strength, unity and effectiveness varied. When British officers came to support 'resistance' in the Balkans they became very well aware of the fact that a struggle was being waged not just against Germans or Italians but for the future political order when peace returned. They encountered immediate problems on the ground but there were strategic political issues to be considered in London.[24]

In invading the Soviet Union in June 1941, Hitler supposed that he would be removing one of the remaining 'hopes' that he had thought, a year earlier, Britain might still possess. An attack on 'Bolshevism', in defence of 'European civilization', had a wide appeal beyond Nazi ranks. Having failed in the 1940 'Battle of Britain', Hitler was determined to raise the stakes.

Germany and Japan, he believed, should concert their actions against their common enemies, the United States and the Soviet Union. The Japanese attack on Pearl Harbor took place in December 1941 and Hitler declared war on the United States in the same month. These developments fundamentally changed the nature of the war. Britain seemed likely to be able to 'win' only as part of a coalition operating globally. Moscow and Washington would not leave the future of 'Europe' to the Europeans (or the British).[25]

'Home' to exiled 'Europe'

There was a sense during the war, momentary no doubt, that Britain, by default, was 'home' to such peoples and political forces of defeated 'Europe' as could reach her shores.. This 'friendly invasion' was sometimes seen, however, as a 'mixed blessing'.[26] Fears of a 'fifth column' could at times place all aliens under suspicion and lead to the internment of some.[27] There were some nationalities – like the Belgians – whose presence brought back memories (and memories of problems) of 1914–18. The fact that the 'foreigners' were all hostile to Germany did not obliterate the differences between exiled 'communities' that had themselves, on their home ground, sometimes been rivals (for example, Poles and Czechoslovaks). These differences could also exist within such 'communities' (for example, between Walloons and Flemings, or between Czechs and Slovaks). Ideological differences were also pronounced. Some exiles had arrived by deliberate choice but others just happened to be in Britain at a particular moment.[28] Individuals found roles in broadcasting to their countries of origin or scientific capacities and there was a direct combat role for Czechoslovaks and Poles.[29] Quite apart from the direct contribution made, it suited Britain to be seen to be 'fighting for Europe'.[30]

There were, of course governments-in-exile, with varying status, access and prospects. They hatched various ideas for 'cooperation' with neighbouring countries – for example, a new arrangement between Belgium, the Netherlands and Luxembourg – but they did not wish to see themselves put out of business.[31] The British government let it be understood that it was not invariably beholden to their wishes or aspirations. It was a relationship in which friction, to some degree, was inevitably present. The situation was further complicated by the anxieties of the exiled 'Londoners' that their authority was being undermined in their home countries. There was a real sense, therefore, given the variety of uniforms on show, that Europe – in reality only a small part of it – was on parade in London. A stream of publications appeared that told British readers about the recent experiences of communities now represented in Britain.[32] Britons in turn published their experiences of operating in strange places.[33] Even so, when London was urged to 'Carry on!' it was the quintessential qualities of the British people, galvanized by a new sense of purpose, that were identified and lauded. London could take it, and so could Glasgow and Swansea.[34] Quite who the British people actually were, however, was a question made meaningful by the presence of foreigners.[35]

By the time 'Victory in Europe' had been gained, Britain appeared to have 'carried on' to achieve a unique status. Through the early months of 1945 the BBC Home Service offered weekly talks on *Europe and Ourselves*. Asa Briggs, the historian of the BBC, has noted how many broadcasters at that date were what would now be described as 'pro-European'.[36] Listeners were told that what European peoples feared most was 'our losing interest in the continent'. They looked to Britain 'as a bulwark against tyranny and poverty'. 'Pierre Maillaud', a Frenchman in England, noted in 1945 that alone of the main western powers of Europe, 'England' was still on her feet, ethically as well as physically. 'Her first task is to decide whether she will follow the European path, and follow it decidedly.' The literary critic, Raymond Mortimer, in commending Maillaud's book, felt that unless England and France could 'join hands' and then gain the sympathy of Scandinavia and the Low Countries, each would 'dwindle into a satellite upon one of the more multitudinous powers'. The traditions of 'our gallant Allies, the USA and the USSR' were 'so different from our own'.[37] It rested with the British electorate 'to see that the coming opportunity is not thrown away'.[38] The electorate did indeed sweep Churchill out of office, but where that electorate stood in relation to the 'European futures' that were being suggested by these writers was another matter.

How to start again?

There was to be no overall grand peace settlement, like Vienna or Versailles, at the close of the Second World War. The next Europe emerged rather in dribs and drabs. It was to have a 'provisional' character for many years. It was easy for commentators in Britain and on the continent to agree in 1945 that the 'Europe' of 1919–39 had been a failure. That did not necessarily mean, however, that the nation-state itself was obsolete, although a plethora of publications suggested that it was. G.D.H. Cole, a socialist intellectual, looked to a 'western Europe' with predominantly socialist institutions. There would be two, or perhaps more, continental groups with which Britain would have to 'come to an accommodation'.[39] However, other writers had no patience with the idea of a regional or continental bloc. It was a heresy, wrote E.H. Carr, to suppose that Great Britain could ever become 'a predominantly European Power'. The British role was to serve as 'a bridge between the "Western civilization" of Europe and the same "Western civilization" in its new homes in other continents'.

'Broadly speaking,' E.H. Carr wrote in 1942, 'the problem of Europe is the problem of Germany'. The only way to make young Germans into good

Europeans, he thought, would be to give them a role in the reorganization of Germany and Europe.[40] German 'national character', however, had continued to be a topic of controversy in Britain.[41] It was an argument in which exiles joined, not always predictably. Victor Gollancz, who had denounced 'Vansittartism', was accused by some German exiles of operating on the erroneous idea that Germans were, after all, much like Englishmen. They were not.[42] The historian A.J.P. Taylor, having studied the course of German history, came to the conclusion that it had no more been a mistake for the German people to end up with Hitler than it was an accident when a river flowed into the sea.[43] A Chatham House Study Group reported in 1943 that, even after defeat, Germany might again 'unloose a cataract of evil upon the world'. There was an 'all-embracing will to mastery' in Germany, which lay at the heart of the matter.[44]

Some resistance groups in wartime Europe put forward 'federal' solutions of one kind or another.[45] There had also been such stirrings in Britain. 'Europe must federate or perish', wrote the man who was to become British prime minister in 1945 in *Labour's Peace Aims* (1939). G.D.H. Cole was firm that the pre-war state-system in Europe could not be put back. 'We Europeans', he wrote 'can no longer live under national governments, each asserting its own independent sovereignty'. The inclusion of Poland, the Balkans and Hungary as Soviet Republics within a vastly enlarged state based on the USSR would be a better solution than the restoration of capitalism in that area. It was 'very doubtful' whether 'the backward countries of Eastern and Southern Europe are suitable for parliamentary government'. Dislike Stalin's methods as one might, the USSR remained 'fundamentally Socialist'.[46] 'Federal Union', a new 'think-tank', continued to suggest the advantages of a federal structure, though without unanimity as to whether to focus on Europe, on 'western Europe' or on the world.[47] The primary purpose of a federation, the constitutional lawyer Ivor Jennings declared, was the perpetuation of European peace. A federation that included Germany, France and the United Kingdom would bring together the important participants in the three major wars of the previous 60 years. Such a 'western Europe' would not only bring peace to that area, it would prevent aggression elsewhere in Europe. In eastern Europe, Britain would give preponderant weight to Russian views and interests.

E.H. Carr was sceptical of neatly defined geographical divisions. He looked to Great Britain and the United States accepting permanent military and economic responsibilities beyond their borders in a 'revolutionary' way.[48] Whether they would in fact be prepared to do so, however, was another matter. Clarence K. Streit, a journalist, had been proposing to his fellow Americans that they invite the United Kingdom and six other English-speaking democracies to start a Union of the Free, in turn a prelude to a Future United States of Man.[49] Lord Davies of Llandinam, Welsh millionaire, a man much given to writing on international security and federation, echoed such a prospect from the British side.[50] These and other suggestions in the political literature of the time pointed to a changing mood, in some quarters – but perhaps little more.

Europe: savagery and civilization

Federal systems, as many of their advocates recognized, did presuppose a considerable sharing of political and cultural values if they were to be effective. It was, to say the least, questionable whether the 'Europe' of 1945 had any such basis. A continent that had portrayed itself as in the van of civilization and progress had been scarred by savagery – and brutality continued into 'peace'. In August 1944 there were some 2.8 million Russians, 1.7 million Poles, 1.3 million French and 600,000 Italians working under compulsion in the German war economy.[51] Returning 'home', for those who survived, was traumatic, supposing 'home' still existed. Altogether, it has been suggested that some 30 million people had to be 'repatriated'. That included some 6,500,000 *Volksdeutsche* (ethnic Germans), who were driven out of eastern European countries in which they had been substantial minorities. The same fate befell *Reichsdeutsche*. The Sudeten Germans were expelled from Czechoslovakia.[52] Some 100,000 Italians left Istria when it became part of Yugoslavia. Several million Poles moved around what was the new Poland as its borders shifted westwards. The catastrophe that had befallen the Jews of Europe through the Holocaust – some six million dead – radically changed the ethnic balance of many European countries, most conspicuously in the case of Poland.[53] Expulsion, destruction and expropriation seemed ubiquitous in a world where people had literally lost their bearings in their landscape. From a British perspective, both actually and metaphorically, the continent was full of 'displaced persons' (some of whom had found or were finding a home in Britain).[54] When British observers 'lifted the lid', and saw what was inside, they feared a spread of one-party dictatorships and the constant danger of concentration camps in this ravaged, vicious and unstable continent.[55] 'We have seen the greatest degradation of the human race of all time and every one of us has become defiled' was the reaction of one British officer in May 1945.[56] Visiting Belsen concentration camp in April 1945, Patrick Gordon Walker, briefly to be foreign secretary in 1966, was adamant that the German soul had to be 'purged' for the 'crime against the West' represented by Belsen and Buchenwald.[57] The British general, Sir Brian, later Lord Robertson, who was successively deputy governor, military governor and then high commissioner of the British zone of occupation, had no European background, spoke no German and had never visited Germany. Perhaps that was just as well.[58]

The British historian A.G. Dickens had held up 'the western tradition' as the hope for the continent.[59] The German philosopher Karl Jaspers, however, claimed to have identified the characteristics of the 'European spirit'.[60] Germans in exile had repeatedly stressed that 'a thoroughly democratized

Germany' would not be a danger to European peace. A 'Europeanized Germany' would be a guarantee of a united Europe.[61] It seemed that if Germans were to become suitable Europeans they had to be 're-educated' – though there were some writers, like H.N. Brailsford, who believed that 'one nation cannot educate another'.[62] Germany was divided into zones of occupation – Soviet, American, British and French.[63] Specifically in the field of education, Robert Birley, headmaster of Charterhouse, went out in 1947, to see what could be done. He brought idiosyncratic authority (his 'equivalent rank' was that of major-general) to his relationships with Germans. His ideas did not always find favour. It was, for example, at that time a 'British way' for universities to be governed 'locally' rather than being under the direct control of a Ministry of Education. That was too revolutionary a step to be introduced in Germany.[64] This issue was but one example of the difficulties of 'cultural transfer'.[65] It should not be forgotten, too, that there was once again a German community in Britain itself, and it was not entirely made up of footballers.[66]

The restoration of democracy in Germany under the auspices of an occupying power was necessarily fraught with difficulty.[67] How surviving supporters of the defeated regime (not to speak of 'fellow-travellers') should be punished/integrated remained contentious. It was not even as though the 'western' occupiers shared, in detail, an understanding of what democracy entailed. The new French fourth republic was itself a shaky creation. 'Re-education' also sat uneasily alongside the transfer of 'industrial capital equipment' supposedly to be done without trenching on the requirements of a peaceful Germany.[68] Needless to say, the British occupation was not without its sour moments, but there were British-German relationships and networks established that were to endure after the British occupation ended.[69] Dickens, stationed in north Germany, asked himself whether Germany would ever become 'an integral part of the West, or merely use its intellectual techniques to create a new barbarism'. The Allies had displaced the Nazis – even if 'de-Nazification' somewhat ran into the sands – but it was up to German intellectuals who truly understood 'the western tradition' to wage the fight for it within the German mind.[70] It was not clear that 'Westminster' should constitute a model for the new *Bundestag* of the Federal Republic.[71] Over time, both at the level of high politics and in cultural and other exchanges, 'normalization' between Britain and Germany was to be achieved by 1975, though not without occasional flashes of animosity that reawakened old anxieties.[72]

It was not only Germany that needed 'restoration', all of Europe needed it too. One writer thought that a promising start might be made by removing 'the fungus growth of suburbia'.[73] There was a realization that 'Europe' was at a crossroads, but there was no unanimity as to which direction it should take. For some, 'Europe' was already a museum, and a ruined one at that. It would never regain its place in the world. For others, it was not 'restoration' but 'revolution' that was needed in order to create a better social order and a higher standard of living. It might take a very long time. Freedom might indeed only be realized in community, but where was the balance to be struck? The paradox of the 'European idea' might be, as Jaspers put it, that Europe had developed the counter-position for every problem. Europe was Europe 'perhaps only because it is capable of becoming everything'[74] Sir Ernest Barker who, with 'European' colleagues, had been seeking to identify the European inheritance, included 'parliamentary democracy' but did not mention 'autocracy' in its various forms, from the Greek tyrants to Hitler and Stalin, as another inheritance.[75] Despite his age, Barker – whose teaching had much impressed the undergraduate Attlee at Oxford – briefly took up an academic post in Germany to assist in 'renewal'.

The arguments about freedom and order, justice and equality, cooperation and competition, communism and capitalism raged across the continent, as states recreated themselves, devised new constitutions or renovated old ones. Political parties re-established themselves or new ones were formed. 'Christian democracy' emerged as a major factor in France, Federal Germany and Italy.[76] This process of 'revaluation' did not pass Britain by, but neither its ingredients nor its intensity were precisely replicated.[77] Although T.S. Eliot obligingly offered further thoughts towards the definition of culture to the good people of North-Rhine Westphalia, the British tended to be witnesses of European *Angst* rather than sharing fully in it.[78] In introducing the essay by Jaspers for a British readership the Scottish theologian Ronald Gregor Smith knew that he had to try to explain what 'existentialism' was. He had to admit that 'in this country there is as yet no strong awareness of the urgency of such matters'. Britain, under Labour, was simply getting on with 'its vast social experiment'.[79] It was, of course, not alone in doing so.

The nature of the 'vast social experiment' required in Europe dominated the continent's post-war politics but its form divided rather than united. In Bulgaria in 1943, Frank Thompson, an Englishman fighting with Bulgarian partisans, dreamed of a United States of Europe for which he could feel a patriotism transcending his love of England. He wanted to be able to think of Krakow, Munich, Rome, Arles and Madrid as his own cities.[80] He was dead before he discovered that the dream too was dead. Whether by oversight or conscious decision he had not included Kiev or Moscow as 'his own cities'.

He might well have included them, however, for the prestige and status of the Soviet Union had greatly increased in Britain after 1941. Booklet after booklet endeavoured, with more or less guarded enthusiasm, to explain 'this dark crystal', as H.G. Wells had referred to it in 1920. Margaret Cole particularly praised the way in which, allegedly, 'the Soviet Union has succeeded in bridling and harnessing the modern devil of "nationalism"'.[81] Authors were casual as to whether they spoke of the 'USSR' or 'Russia'. A Chatham House guide to Britain's new ally noted in 1942 'the seemingly successful efforts of the Soviet leaders to encourage the traditional culture of each national group'. It admitted to be groping in the dark as to what the effects of wartime association might be.[82] The dean of Canterbury in his *The Socialist Sixth of the World* (1939), a book that by 1942 had been translated into 13 languages and that had an English-language circulation of two and a half million, had admitted to 'shadows as well as lights', but moved on to ever more enthusiastic accounts.[83] Small and sovereign states had to go. Europe would see a set of federations – Slav, Teutonic and Latin – while 'our own country would find its appropriate environment in the extension and equality of all its Colonies'.[84] Writing in the United States in 1944, and drawing on his deep knowledge of Russia, Sir Bernard Pares concluded that the 'life of common purpose' had made both sides more aware of each other. The similarities would be greater and the understanding stronger.[85] Walter Elliot, Conservative MP, visiting Russia in March 1945, saw 'great and fundamental resemblances to ourselves' and thought that in this light 'we must read all of the baffling characteristics which separate us'.[86] It was a commonplace on the Left that the Russians had much to learn from Britain about authentic political democracy, but Britain had to learn from Russia 'the basic elements of scientific economic planning'.[87]

Jennie Lee's notion that the 'older democracies' had 'half the answer' but that Russia also had 'half the answer', and that it was in 'Europe' that the new synthesis would be found, had echoes in many parts of the continent. 'Nobody in Europe', claimed the historian A.J.P. Taylor in a radio broadcast in 1945, 'believes in the American way of life, that is, in private enterprise'.[88] The reality, as it turned out, was that each 'half answer' came to be identified with 'half' of the continent. 'New Europe' was not to be a new synthesis but a continent in which 'half answers' blossomed into full but different ones in its different parts. The pursuit of a 'third force' or a 'bridge' by some writers and politicians on the Left, both in Britain and on the continent, proved fruitless. The synthesis they purported to offer was, in any case, seen in other quarters as shallow and implausible.[89] One had to choose, if one could, between the freedom embodied in 'the West', however flawed, and the 'totalitarianism', with whatever mitigating features it might possess, embodied in the 'East'. There was an 'iron curtain', according to Winston Churchill, now leader of the British opposition, which had 'descended across the Continent from Stettin in the Baltic to Trieste in the Adriatic'.[90]

Ally into enemy

Iron curtains became global in the enveloping confrontation that goes under the name of the Cold War.[91] The literature on its origins is now formidable. Scholars will continue to debate what part ideology, geopolitics, psychology and technology played in its development.[92] That debate cannot be followed in detail here. The important point, for our purposes, is that the Cold War soon came to overshadow, and perhaps render obsolete, many of the assumptions about the future of the continent made both by government and in the public discussion that has just been referred to. The relationships between the states within an inter-war Europe that had still seen itself as the political centre of the world were no longer possible. It was no accident that the successor to the League of Nations, the United Nations, was to have its location in New York. That body, its supporters hoped, would learn lessons from its predecessor but, whether or not that would turn out to be the case, it would clearly be a 'world' body rather than the European club that the League had latterly become.[93]

'Europe', it has frequently been stated, was now 'between the super-powers'. The United States and the Soviet Union were going to determine the parameters of the possible.[94] Arguably, however, there was no 'Europe' *between* the superpowers. It became apparent that each superpower, through its partners, clients, subordinates and satellites (and each of these words has an appropriate context) sought to offer a new Europe whose structures and values bore the strong imprint of its own. The United States and the Soviet Union, as it were, 'repatriated' their own versions of what might be called a European inheritance.[95] To point to some similarity in this process, however, is not to say that both 'hegemons' exercised their new supremacy within their spheres in same way. Within bi-polarity, there remained significant capacity for independent action. There was another substantial difference. The Americans in Europe were indubitably 'out of area'. Circumstances might arise in which they would 'go home'. The Soviet Union, on the other hand, it could be assumed, would always be there, constituting, as 'Russia' had done in the nineteenth century, a perpetual if puzzling 'European' presence. This ambiguity surrounding the Soviet Union/Russia in relation to the continent was something the British, in par-ticular, were conscious of since now, as then, it continued to match their own – notwithstanding that global circumstances were different.[96]

Old and new guards

In such a context, 'dwindling into a satellite' was as abhorrent to the politi-cal 'old guard', whose minds had been formed and careers forged before the 'post-war world' began, as it had been to Mortimer the critic. For prime minister Clement Attlee (b. 1883) or foreign secretary Ernest Bevin (b. 1881), such a status should be delayed as long as possible.[97] Attlee had stud-ied the Italian renaissance when an undergraduate at Oxford. He had visited Spain during the civil war. His European perspective did not go much fur-ther. Perhaps Attlee was only half-joking when he remarked that one could not trust Europeans because they could not play cricket.[98] Bevin's pre-war trades union work had taken him to France, Germany and central Europe on a number of occasions – not to mention trips to Australia and America.[99]

Herbert Morrison, foreign secretary in 1951, tended to the view that continentals 'ganged up'.[100] Attlee's successor, Churchill, was 76 when he became prime minister again in 1951. Anthony Eden and Harold Macmillan, who then came to the fore as foreign secretaries and prime ministers had both been born in the nineteenth century, and both had directly experienced the fighting of the First World War and the high politics of the Second. Macmillan, like Churchill, was the son of an Anglo-American marriage. He spoke French fluently and dabbled with 'the European idea'. He was the last prime minister to be familiar with the Classical Europe of Greece and Rome. Selwyn Lloyd (b. 1904), his first foreign secretary, had seen parts of Europe as a soldier. The last dead German he saw happened to be Heinrich Himmler. Lloyd noted that the Foreign Office had to learn 'the importance of renascent Europe'.[101] Lord Home (b. 1903), his second, had travelled in South America as a young man – but not widely in Europe.

It was only with the prime ministerships of Wilson in 1964 and Heath in 1970, however, that men reached the top who had not been active in high politics before or during the Second World War.[102] Their foreign secretaries, with the exception of George Brown (b. 1914), had all been born before the First World War. Brown had been a trades union official through the second war and had not been abroad. By the time he became foreign secretary, he claimed to know the Middle East and the continent of Europe 'fairly well'. He believed that 'our destinies' pointed in the direction of Europe.[103] Michael Stewart (b. 1906) was exceptional in his first-hand knowledge of pre-war Europe. After leaving Oxford, he had learnt German in Dresden and spent a period at the School of International Studies run by Zimmern in Geneva.[104]

Initially, after 1945, it seemed clear that the United Kingdom was the most powerful state in Europe (if the Soviet Union were excluded from Europe). It had been neither defeated nor occupied. It was a proud country, if an exhausted one, dependent, it seemed, on loans from the United States and Canada. Recovery would come – as indeed it did, after protracted austerity.[105] Austerity was followed by the burgeoning consumer society and the 'swinging sixties'. This 'cultural revolution', however, it need hardly be said, was not a peculiarly British phenomenon, though in its specifics it played differently from country to country. A kind of inchoate youthful internationalism temporarily seemed to threaten the post-war 'establishments' and the 'contaminated' social order of reconstructed western Europe.[106] There were political ripples in Britain but it seemed again that the threat of terror and political violence for revolutionary objectives was a continental proclivity. The political atmosphere then shifted again. There had long been concern about the performance of the British economy. It now turned into a period of protracted gloom and despondency – and industrial confrontation. It became common to talk about 'the English disease' or 'the British sickness' – all in contrast, or at least so it appeared, to the 'modernization' of the economies of the leading countries of western Europe. After

30 years, the sense that Britain was the most powerful state in Europe had evaporated. It was widely supposed that if Britain was to regain confidence and again become successful it could do so only by moving itself closer to the 'norm' now represented by the institutions and conventions embodied in the 'Europe' that 'the Six' had established over nearly a quarter of a century.

On the other hand, the Second World War had made Britain more 'mixed up together' with the United States than ever before. Between 1942 and 1945, some three million young Americans had passed through the United Kingdom, ultimately on their way to 'Europe'. 'Brits' and 'Yanks' found that they did have many things in common, but equally realized that there were important differences in the way they looked at things.[107] The disparity in power between Washington and London had become steadily more evident in the last two years of the war. Roosevelt had not entered the war to save Britain. He had done so to preserve and extend the financial, political and strategic interests of the United States. So, while talk of the 'big three' continued, Britain was taking a place as 'junior partner in an orbit of power predominantly under American aegis', as one British official in the Washington Embassy put it in August 1945.[108] In such a relationship there could be, and were, substantial differences of approach and opinion, but partnership was both inescapable and necessary. Whether in Palestine, India or in other parts of the world, the British still believed that they could handle the unwinding of their empire themselves, so far as that was going to be necessary. They needed no advice on how, and how quickly, it should be done. There was resentment in Britain over failure to share nuclear information. Such important matters of controversy apart, however, it was the general view in London that it was important to keep the United States interested in the fate of Europe. On the other hand, by maintaining the imperial preference system, the British resisted American wishes that Britain should participate in a European economic bloc. The relationship overall, therefore, was pervasive and fuzzy but fundamental.[109] The link with the United States would not be jeopardized, but only in France did it seem to be one simply between 'Anglo-Saxons'. The US ambassador in London in 1950 was to describe the 'special relationship' as 'inescapable'.[110] He thought there was no country on earth whose interests were so wrapped around the world as the UK. Even so, looked at from America, Britain was equally inescapably European. When the celebrated American reporter John Gunther had gone *Inside Europe* in 1936 he had not excluded 'England', described as 'that dominant island', from his scrutiny (nor did he exclude the Soviet Union). In the post-1945 world, even if the island was no longer dominant, it was still a critical bridge between the United States and whatever 'Europe', at any given moment, was turning into. The fiasco of the 1956 Suez expedition, mounted by Britain and France but 'sabotaged' by the hostility of the United States, made clear how limited was the European capacity for action that Washington opposed. It has also been noted, however, that during that crisis, British and American codebreakers decrypted the messages of all the Middle Eastern powers except Israel and shared them with each other – but, despite planning the invasion of Egypt with France, the British did not pass this information to Paris.[111] France, particularly after de Gaulle's return to power in 1958, emphasized its nuclear capacity, and became obsessed with the nuclear relationship between Britain and the United States.[112] It was a divergence that went deep.

A European coat of many colours: NATO, the Council of Europe, Economic Community – Six and Nine

The behaviour of Britain towards 'Europe' between 1945 and 1975 must be seen against such a background. A 'united Europe', it soon became apparent, was capable of being given many meanings, but it could not mean a European polity that stretched from, say, the Urals to Iceland. Rather, old geographical categories were reconfigured and fresh alignments invented. There were different kinds of integration. There were two contrasting developments in 1949 and then there was the EEC.

Europe of the North Atlantic

The 'North Atlantic Treaty' was signed in Washington in April 1949. The location was significant – the United States and Canada were indeed signatories, but the other members were all European – Belgium, Denmark, France, Iceland, Italy, the Netherlands, Norway, Portugal and the United Kingdom. The treaty provided for mutual assistance should any one member be attacked. Here was a conspicuous example of a 'western European/American' defence community. Greece, in whose internal affairs Britain had played a significant part during and after the war, joined in 1952.[113] So did Turkey. The latter's inclusion, of considerable defence significance, did however raise the question, in other contexts, of that country's status alongside its 'European' partners. The Federal Republic of Germany joined in 1955. Over the previous few years there had been an attempt to form a European Defence Community but, despite the fact that it had been seen by its sponsor, the then French prime minister, as a means of reconciling French opinion to West German rearmament, the French National Assembly rejected it. It was a stillborn project. The inclusion of the Federal Republic, which had become sovereign in 1949, indicated its acceptance within the Euro-American world of the 'Atlantic community' and, at the same time, testified to a growing sense – public statements to the contrary notwithstanding – that the division of Germany was 'permanent' and, with it, the division of 'Europe'.[114] Subsequently, the erection of the 'Berlin

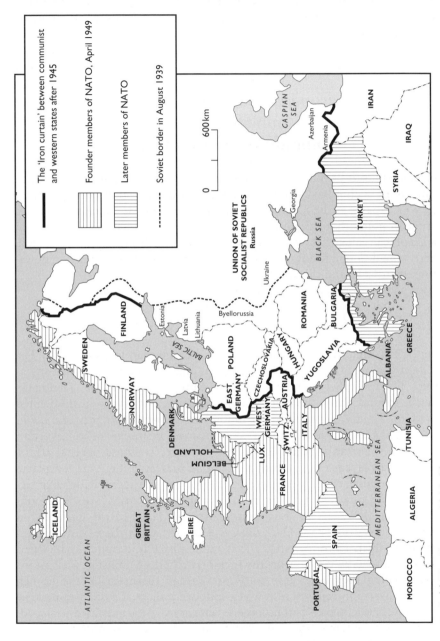

The 'Iron curtain' between communist and western states after 1945

Founder members of NATO, April 1949

Later members of NATO

Soviet border in August 1939

600km

0

ATLANTIC OCEAN

ICELAND

GREAT BRITAIN

EIRE

NORWAY

SWEDEN

FINLAND

DENMARK

HOLLAND

BELGIUM

LUX.

FRANCE

SWITZ.

PORTUGAL

SPAIN

ITALY

MEDITERRANEAN SEA

MOROCCO

ALGERIA

TUNISIA

BALTIC SEA

Estonia

Latvia

Lithuania

EAST GERMANY

WEST GERMANY

AUSTRIA

POLAND

CZECHOSLOVAKIA

HUNGARY

YUGOSLAVIA

ALBANIA

GREECE

ROMANIA

BULGARIA

Byellorussia

Ukraine

UNION OF SOVIET SOCIALIST REPUBLICS

Russia

BLACK SEA

Georgia

Armenia

Azerbaijan

CASPIAN SEA

TURKEY

SYRIA

IRAQ

IRAN

7. Cold War Europe, 1945–89

Wall' in 1961 brought the point home. Britain did not share, or at least to nothing like the same degree, French resentment of American hegemony within the alliance, a resentment that grew ever stronger and led to its partial disengagement. Paris grumbled at the apparent willingness of other European states to accept American leadership – a complaint that might have disappeared had France rather than Britain been America's 'second'.[115] Such alignments could lead to the conclusion that 'European history', conceived as a self-contained entity, was at an end. It was now a case of jockeying for position within 'Euro-America'.

The Council of Europe

The Council of Europe, set up in May 1949, represented a different starting point. The 10 states initially in membership – Belgium, Denmark, France, Ireland, Italy, Luxembourg, the Netherlands, Norway, Sweden and the United Kingdom – included states that had been on opposite sides in the late war as well as neutrals. It was scarcely 'Europe', however, though the strong presence of Scandinavian states represented an enhanced 'European' consciousness on their part. It made the Council more than a gathering of 'western Europe'. Not that it was a potent body. It functioned through an executive committee of ministers, and their deputies, together with a non-legislative consultative assembly. British participation was lukewarm and had been conditional on such a limited basis.[116] It was a stance that frustrated some members. At the December 1951 assembly meeting, its then president, the Belgian Paul-Henri Spaak, spoke of the simple choice he felt confronted 'Europeans'. In his view, 'We' had either to 'line up' with Great Britain, which meant renouncing the attempt to create a 'united Europe', or 'we' had to create Europe without Great Britain. If it did come to such a choice, he favoured the latter. Spaak (b. 1899) had become his country's first socialist prime minister in 1938/39. In 1940, after the invasion of Belgium, he had come to London as foreign minister in the government-in-exile and remained there for the duration of the war. It was no doubt his experience of British attitudes that led him to suppose that Europeans 'lining up' with Britain could say farewell to 'a united Europe'.

Precisely what creating a 'united Europe' would mean, however, remained obscure. In Britain, a 'United Europe Movement' had been launched in May 1947 in a Royal Albert Hall 'crowded to capacity'. Europe, Churchill declared, had become a breeding ground for pestilence and hate. It was time to proclaim that the spiritual conception of Europe should not die. United Europe should form one major regional entity – alongside the United States, the Soviet Union and the British Empire and Commonwealth – within the structure of the new United Nations Organization. He had no doubt that if Europe united was to be a living force, Britain had 'to play her full part as a member of the European family'.

He denied any notion that such an ambition constituted a sinister plot against the Soviet Union. He largely reiterated the approach he had adopted famously in a speech at Zürich in 1946 and was to repeat publicly on a number of occasions over the coming years. Fêted at a 'United Europe' gathering in The Hague in 1948, it could not be doubted that this great Englishman was the great European of his time. There was an expectation, when he again became prime minister in 1951, that he would throw himself into a 'United Europe'. That was to misread his stance. He had no doubt that European civilization existed and that Britain shared in it, but he still believed 'in the august circle of the British Crown', by which he meant the British self-governing dominions. Such is the exuberance of Churchill's rhetoric that it is difficult to judge just what all his fine phrases entailed; perhaps he did not know himself.[117]

European Economic Community

When Spaak spoke of 'creating Europe' in 1951 – by implication without Britain – he well knew that it would not, could not, include most of the peoples and states of Europe as it had existed in 1939. What was in prospect was a limited western European grouping. 'The Six' can be said to have first come together as such in June 1950 when the French foreign minister, Robert Schuman, successfully proposed the creation of a supranational organization that would oversee the coal and steel production of participating countries. Its council, according to the Federal German chancellor, Konrad Adenauer, stood at the crossroads of two kinds of sovereignty, national and supranational. The national interests of member states had to be 'safeguarded' but its paramount task was to promote the interests of the 'community'.[118] Acceptance of such a high authority was made a precondition of participation in the negotiations. The ECSC, and its attendant institutions, came into effect in August 1952. Technically, until 1967, there were therefore three 'communities' but in that year they were merged and all of these entities were subsumed under the EEC. Ever since, 'safeguarding' and 'promoting' have existed in uneasy dialectic. The tension has in turn been reflected in historiography as historians have variously estimated the balance between these two elements and tried to distinguish between economic priorities and strategic political objectives in the evolution of these institutions.[119] It may be questioned whether a clear distinction between these two motive forces is ever possible. The EEC itself came into being when Belgium, France, the German Federal Republic, Italy, Luxembourg and the Netherlands signed two treaties in Rome in March 1957 – treaties that were the outcome of a conference held in Messina in Sicily in 1955.[120]

Britain did not join the ECSC and did not sign the Treaties of Rome. These 'failures' have now been much debated. They have frequently been seen as *the* critical moments when Britain 'missed the bus' or 'abdicated leadership in Europe'. Edmund Dell, Labour politician and historian, wrote that the origins of 'Britain's European problems' lay in the 'myopic reaction of the Attlee and Churchill governments to the Schuman Plan'.[121] The former US secretary of state, Dean Acheson, recognized that it was not Britain's last clear chance to 'enter Europe', as he put it, but it was the first wrong choice.[122] At the time, Attlee had told the House of Commons that Britain could not hand over the most vital economic forces to an authority that was 'utterly undemocratic and responsible to nobody'. The Messina conference had been viewed from outside by the Conservative government with a comparable mixture of suspicion, scepticism and hostility.

When 'Britain had walked out of Europe in 1955', as it has been put, it was, rather, a refusal to join in the unfolding process.[123] Not that 'Europe', as such, was 'on offer'. The enterprise was that of a group of six western European states. Notwithstanding this fact, however, articles, lectures and books regularly appeared in Britain, at the time and subsequently, which, in addressing 'Britain and the unity of Europe' or 'Britain and European integration', related almost exclusively to Britain's relationship with the EEC as it then existed.

One British reaction to 'the Six' was to try to set up its own 'Europe'. Under an agreement signed in Stockholm in January 1960, Austria, Denmark, Portugal, Sweden, Switzerland and the United Kingdom agreed to set up the European Free Trade Association (EFTA), whose members undertook to establish a free trade area among themselves within a decade.[124] As a kind of Europe this grouping had no geographical coherence but, Portugal apart, it could be portrayed as 'social democratic' in contrast to the predominantly Catholic and conservative 'Six'.

The following year, however, Macmillan announced the United Kingdom's wish to become a member of the Community, provided that Britain's interests, those of the Commonwealth, and those of EFTA could all be safeguarded.[125] Edward Heath, who led the British delegation, claimed that, faced with the threats that all could see, Europe had to unite or perish. The United Kingdom, being part of Europe, could not stand aside. The British people were anxious to become full, wholehearted and active members. The Labour Opposition, however, could scarcely be included in this description. The party's National Executive Committee took a different view. Britain's history had certainly overlapped with that of the existing Community members but it had also significantly diverged. It reiterated that Britain's connections and interests lay as much outside as inside Europe. Hugh Gaitskell (b. 1906), the party's leader, thought that membership would mean the end of Britain as an independent nation-state.[126] That might be a good or a bad thing but independence was what was at stake. Gladstone, son of an Indian civil servant, and married to the daughter of Russian Jews who had settled in London, spoke fluent German and had spent a year studying in troubled Vienna in 1933–34. The thought, however, that Britain might become 'just a province of Europe' was intolerable.

In the event, though after months of negotiation, President de Gaulle declared that the British people were not sufficiently 'European' to merit admission. As has been noted, there was a certain irony in the fact that the British, who had made clear their inability to become part of a 'federal Europe', found in de Gaulle, as he was to demonstrate in his later behaviour within the EEC, a believer, like themselves, in a *Europe des Patries*, even if he did not want the British *patrie* inside.[127] There is, of course, no denying de Gaulle's personal stature – and his long memory when it came to dealing with 'Anglo-Saxons'.[128] It has been reasonably pointed out, however, that he was in reality only able to thwart the enlargement process because his partners, who were broadly favourable to admission, hesitated and because the principal applicant remained rigid and ambivalent.[129] 'The Five is not an entity,' Gordon Walker observed, 'it does not exist as such'.[130] Five years later, the Wilson government tried again, but with no greater success. It seemed in London and to visitors to London, such as the Dutch foreign minister, that only if Britain dismantled its ties with the United States would the general change his mind. It did not and nor did he.

Stripping out the personal factors, it was fundamentally the shape of 'Europe' that was at stake, an argument as always complicated by imprecision among those who argued. A Fabian publication in 1962, for example, whose combative author made 'the political case for staying out' in the context of the first British application to join the EEC was entitled *Not with Europe*.[131] Historians, subsequently, found themselves using such titles in their own studies of this period.[132] The 'Background to the Negotiations' produced in 1962 by the Information Division of the Treasury and the Central Office of Information, was given the title 'Britain and the European Communities', but its contents described the idea of 'Europe', as a political economic or defensive unity, as 'particularly strong' since 1945. Among the reasons given for 'this resurgence of the European idea' was the fact that the two world wars had started in Europe and shattered the European economy. That should not happen again. Britain, it was stated, though having close relationships with the Commonwealth and the USA, had 'taken a major part in efforts to express the European idea'. Such a publication, perhaps understandably, did not dwell on what, in detail, that 'idea' might be.[133] European unity remained a slippery concept – as was whether such unity as existed, or should be sought, best found expression in a confederation, a federation or a 'union of states'.[134] Recognition of the inter-dependence of western Europe might be one thing, its full integration another.[135]

The end of Europe?

Some observers considered that 'European history', as it had been thought about in the first half of the twentieth century, had ceased to exist.[136] By the same token, it was meaningless to talk about 'Britain and Europe' within old categories. What was the point in talking about 'Europe', some argued, if it was simply where soldiers from the Urals and soldiers from Texas met? There did not appear much prospect that 'all Europe' would re-emerge. What it meant to be 'European' had therefore to be constantly revisited. The new nine-member Community of 1975 was unlikely to constitute a final 'Europe', but it might come to constitute an integrated 'western Europe' – though what was meant by integration was rarely spelt out. In that same year General Franco died and a transition to democratic pluralism began in Spain.[137] Portugal was in turmoil in the same year but it, too, might successfully develop democratically. 'Iberia' could be expected to reappear as a factor in Europe. It looked, though, as if 'central Europe/*Mitteleuropa*' had disappeared for ever. The terms of the Austrian State Treaty of 1955 saw the withdrawal of occupying troops and the country's neutrality within its 1937 borders.

Austria, however, had an exceptional status. The Warsaw Pact, signed a couple of months later, brought Albania, Bulgaria, Czechoslovakia, the German Democratic Republic, Hungary, Poland, Romania and the Soviet Union together in the 'Eastern European Mutual Assistance Treaty'. A united military command was created with its headquarters in Moscow. Signatories were bound to assist each other in the event of an armed attack on any one of their fellow-signatories in Europe.

'Western Europe' and 'Eastern Europe', newly defined, therefore directly confronted each other – both sides employing, in due course, propaganda strategies to harden the unpalatable image of the other.[138] It was not just defeated Germany (and Berlin itself) that was divided, but Europe itself. In such a situation, the duality that had to be wrestled with was not 'Britain and Europe' but 'Britain and western Europe'. What did it mean to be a 'west European'? British writers at the time, like others, found terminology problematic. Britain, France, Federal Germany and Italy were held by one author, for example, to constitute the 'core' of western Europe.[139] For another, western Europe was 'the Six', to which should be added the United Kingdom and the Scandinavian countries.[140] Both authors agreed that Spain and Portugal did not form part of this western Europe, but that was only because their political systems at that time ruled them out.[141] Perhaps whether this 'western Europe' had meaning fundamentally related to the possibility of a quite new relationship between France and 'Germany'. Among British observers, it was not only Harold Macmillan's private secretary that expressed the view that the French and the Germans would never sufficiently bury the hatchet to make the 'Common Market' work.[142] They were wrong. Federal Germany, under Adenauer's direction, firmly took 'the path to the West'.[143] History, therefore, was dictating that western Europeans were placing new meanings on the European space they occupied.[144] It involved the major states in an agonizing appraisal – sometimes insufficiently agonizing – of their immediate pasts in the search for a plausible and coherent 'community'.[145]

'Eastern Europe' had no place in the consultations of the 'Council of Europe' when Spaak purported to address 'Europeans'. The formation of the

Warsaw Pact was but one further step in the consolidation of the 'Soviet bloc'. Its membership now seemed to give 'eastern Europe' a coherence, under Soviet auspices, that, in its new form, it had not previously possessed. Communism was now superimposed on earlier images of 'backwardness' as an additional defining feature of a strange region. Further, 'the Balkans' in a sense disappeared in an alliance that purported to link Bulgaria and Albania with Poland – with Greece, a NATO member, anchored in 'the West' after its civil war.[146] In practice, within the Warsaw alliance, Albania and Romania proved 'uncooperative'. Yugoslavia, under Tito, had never joined and sought a non-aligned stance that enabled his historically fractious country to hover uneasily between East and West and maintain its own precarious unity. As time passed, however, the sense that Eastern Europe was a 'different world' deepened in western European perceptions. Events in East Berlin, in Poland and, most dramatically in Hungary in 1956, confirmed that the regimes were unpopular but also that 'the West' would not be able or willing to intervene to change the situation. The suppression of the Hungarian Uprising led to a crisis in British Communism. Some prominent historians left the party on this issue.[147] The Warsaw Pact (excluding the Czechoslovaks and Romanians) engaged in only one joint action – to intervene to oust the reformer Alexander Dubček in 1968.[148] Soviet troops remained stationed in Czechoslovakia, as they had not been before.

So far as could be judged, therefore, it looked as though the division of Europe was going to be permanent. The continent's future remained bound up with the global struggle between 'East' and 'West'. The division of Germany would solidify with the passage of time (though there was no lack of plans that could possibly have both united and neutralized Germany). 'Western Europe' and 'Eastern Europe' would drift further and further apart in their social systems, political values and perhaps in their economic performance. Communists in the West and non-Communists in the East might hanker for the Other, but with little likelihood that their hopes would be realized. Yet, notwithstanding this apparently frozen scene, there was in the early 1970s some diplomatic movement, some relaxation and tentative reconciliation. The *Ostpolitik* pursued by the Brandt government in Federal Germany resulted in separate treaties with the Soviet Union, Poland and the German Democratic Republic (1970–72) in which, respectively, both sides renounced the use of force, recognized the western frontier of Poland and declared that the sovereignty of each was confined to its own state territory. Broadly speaking, Britain supported this approach.[149] Alec Douglas-Home, as foreign secretary, wrote to Brandt expressing British appreciation of all he had done to improve East/West relations – though below the surface there had been a lingering British anxiety that the Soviet Union would achieve a loosening of German links with the West. In November 1972 preliminary talks started in Helsinki on the calling of a 'Conference on Security and Cooperation' in Europe. Perhaps 'all-Europe' was not defunct after all.

|11|

Home and dry? 1975–2005

Let the people decide

In 2005/06 the inhabitants of 25 member states of the European Union were to decide, by a referendum or other process, whether they will accept the European Constitution agreed, at the second time of asking, by their governments and signed (symbolically) in Rome in October 2004. The United Kingdom government decided, having initially resisted the call, that a referendum would be held – later fixed for May 2006 – so that the UK electorate could give its verdict. The consensus among UK commentators in 2004, however, was that it would vote against the proposed Constitution. If no other EU electorate or parliament did the same, it would be an outcome that would confirm that the UK was the 'awkward partner'. Such a result might, in turn, produce pressure within the United Kingdom to withdraw from the European Union or at least seek fundamentally to alter its position within it. It would also, of course, even if there was assent everywhere else, make it impossible for the EU to proceed with the Constitution, at least not in its existing form. If, however, the Constitution were also to be rejected elsewhere within the EU, possibly before the United Kingdom voted, the EU would be thrown into another crisis, particularly if rejection occurred in a major member state. Its structure, identity and purpose would again come under serious scrutiny. If, on the other hand, the Constitution were to be upheld in all member states it would undoubtedly be a major landmark in the crystallization of a certain idea of Europe in the twenty-first century. It would mean, too, that the British people, after all the twists and turns that have been the subject of this book, had come to accept their 'common home'. The stakes were indeed high, both for Britain and Europe.

Referendum

The 1975 referendum had raised questions about decision-making within the United Kingdom, particularly in relation to 'Europe'. At key points in the previous chapter, the evolution of British policy had been a matter for governments. Decisions had been reached through the 'customary processes', as official advice blended with political pressures. There remained, however, and there was to continue, a lasting uncertainty about decision-making. What should the relationship be between 'the Foreign Office' – accepting that the advice of its London staff and that received from ambassadors abroad was never likely to be absolutely uniform – government, and 'the people'. Incoming foreign secretaries, particularly Labour ones, still harboured suspicions that the Foreign Office, despite further reforms aimed at broadening its recruiting base, was still socially exclusive. Ernest Bevin, on hearing that the young Gladwyn Jebb had allegedly been given a job because, when interviewed, he had the good fortune to know the French for 'seaweed', claimed at last to have discovered how one got into the Foreign Office.[1] Lord Gladwyn later had a distinguished career.[2] George Brown, having come to the conclusion that the British Embassy in Paris was completely out of touch with what was going on, or so he believed, arranged for the appointment of Churchill's son-in-law Christopher Soames as ambassador.[3] Margaret Thatcher stood in this line. From her perspective, the Foreign Office had too great a willingness to 'see the other side'. It was for politicians, elected by the people, to decide policy, not dislocated officials. It might, of course, be the case that 'the professionals' had a better assessment of their country's interests than either politicians or people. Just occasionally, as in the case of Sir Nicholas Henderson's 'farewell despatch' on retiring from the Paris Embassy in 1979, diplomats let slip what they really felt about what was happening to their country and the policies they had a duty to implement.[4] This issue continued to run in the twenty-first century. Sir Stephen Wall, a retiring head of the European secretariat at the cabinet office, was reported as criticizing the prime minister and the chancellor for failing to promote a case for 'positive engagement' in the Union. 'Too much democracy – a mandarin's lament' was the verdict of the *Daily Telegraph*.[5] Academics and journalists turned again to discussing diplomats and the foreign policy process in the era of mass communication.[6]

Parliamentary debate and public commentary in the press, on radio and, perhaps now most formatively, on television formed the backdrop. 'Democratic control' of European policy, in any direct sense, had remained both elusive and illusory. The parties who formed governments had their broad policies on 'Europe' but how far, in the general elections of 1959, 1964, 1966, 1970 and 1974 (two) voters had voted for their parties primarily or even significantly because of their stance on 'Europe' may be doubted. At best, 'Europe' was an element in the mysterious portfolio of factors that determine voting behaviour. In any case, it was difficult to know consistently where the Conservative and Labour parties stood on 'Europe' since it was obvious that internal divisions were strong. The perception was that the Conservatives 'tilted' towards EEC membership and Labour against, but voters could not have predicted with any confidence what course Macmillan or Wilson would actually have followed or been at all certain about their negotiating positions on significant matters. People changed their minds. Macmillan, noting that two trusted friends, who had been strong 'Europeans' had become violent opponents of entry, observed in 1962 that the controversy was 'beginning to crack the old Party alignments'.[7] In 1970 and 1974 few could have doubted that Edward Heath was more energetically and explicitly committed to membership of and enthusiastic participation in the EEC than any other post-1945 British political leader, but such were the political circumstances of those general elections that people can be presumed to have voted him in or out for other reasons.

The referendum campaign in 1975 demonstrated the degree to which the issue of 'Europe' transcended party. There was no question, Roy Jenkins wrote retrospectively, of trying to persuade the electorate that Europe 'was an affair of packages and nothing else'.[8] It was a matter of the political future of Europe. The referendum, still formally 'consultative', asked for a verdict on what had been negotiated. Voters had not been previously asked whether they wished to 'mandate' the government to enter into negotiations, neither had they been requested to express their opinion on matters that were central to the negotiation. They were simply being asked to approve or reject what government had accepted. The result was in a sense unequivocal – if one discounts the electorates of the Western Isles and of Orkney and Shetland – but it also seems to have been unenthusiastic. The verdict gave little real indication of the depth of support, or lack of it, for the EEC conceived as an evolving entity. 'Endorsement' having been obtained, the initiative returned to governments who knew, whether they liked it or not, that membership entailed participation in a process, probably a roller-coaster process, whose end was to be 'European unity', a unity whose form was to be unprecedented, unpredictable and inescapably contentious. It is likely, however, that a substantial portion of 'Yes' voters thought in terms of an 'event' rather than a 'process'. Opponents argued at the time that the purpose of the Community was to merge Britain with France, Germany, Italy and other countries into a single nation. Britain would become 'a mere province'. That theme continued to resound over subsequent decades.

Europe (of Nine)

France and Federal Germany, their bilateral relationship strengthened in the 12 years since the signature of the Elysée Treaty (1963), had formed the core of the Community since its formation. Initiatives had proliferated with the intention of promoting mutual understanding. French and

German historians and geographers, for example, set about establishing, for school purposes, parallel texts that examined contemporary issues in both countries. The two governments almost invariably worked closely together. It is shorthand, but not a distortion, to say that Federal Germany had financial and economic muscle but France gave political direction. It was France, under de Gaulle, that precipitated grave debate in the mid-1960s on the powers of the Commission, a controversy that for a time threatened the functioning of the Community before the 'Luxembourg Compromise' was reached in 1966. At the time of British accession there was a good working relationship between Heath and de Gaulle's successor, George Pompidou which some saw as the renewal of a Franco-British axis. It was with Bonn and Paris that London equated itself, or which it sought even to lead – for there were assumptions, sometimes spoken, that when Britain joined it would 'lead'. It remained the 'great powers' of the Community – with Rome anxious not to be left out – which believed that they could shape its future direction in ways that suited them. The 'common' policies already in place, notably the Common Agricultural Policy – were scarcely ones that Britain would have formulated.

It is generally admitted that the initial tone adopted by British ministers was querulous, even hectoring, in their early encounters with their counterparts. A certain way of working had grown up among the original members and where it differed from British practice the British supposed that it was inferior and inefficient in comparison with their own. The British, it was said in response, did not understand what it was to be *communitaire*. Much of this was a matter of tone and style, but British standing was damaged. It did not lead Belgium, the Netherlands and Luxembourg, for example, to feel that the United Kingdom was as much of an asset as, for historical reasons, they had supposed it would be. The progress of 'Benelux' integration seemed to its members a pattern to be followed on a larger scale, but the British did not wish to take note. They saw no call to take lessons on integration from a 'Belgium' that seemed on the point of complete disintegration as its two language communities, French and Flemish, moved further and further apart.

This 'Europe of Nine' did not readily map onto any past. The simultaneous accession of Denmark and Ireland, however, did have some interesting geopolitical aspects. Danish membership, taken in conjunction with the fact that the Norwegians, in a bitterly contested campaign, had declined to join, signified something of a rupture in 'Scandinavia'. Copenhagen, as it were, came into the 'mainstream' and now looked south and west. Finland, still anxious not to offend the Soviet Union unnecessarily, had to stand outside. Stockholm still talked about 'neutrality' but it was not clear whether as reason or pretext. The Irish Republic, too, had a policy of 'neutrality' and stood outside NATO but (helped by the fact of its still largely agricultural economy) joined the EEC with relish. Although its application was largely a consequence of the UK's, it seized its opportunities with skill, eager to demonstrate that an island to the west of Britain could be 'thoroughly European'. There were obvious historical reasons, compounded by the crisis in Northern Ireland, that stood in the way of a common British/Irish standpoint. Dublin was anxious to stand distinct, but in practice could not altogether disguise the fact that it was another English-speaking state in the Community.

Europe (10 to 12)

The 'Europe of Nine' lasted until January 1981 when Greece was admitted. Its application had been lodged in mid-1975, though it was a controversial step for the country to take. It had just emerged from the regime of the colonels who had been in power since 1967. Cyprus was in a condition of near-anarchy following a coup by Greek-born officers in the Cyprus National Guard. Turkish forces had landed in the north of the island and established a 'Turkish Federated State' there. The fact that Greece and Turkey were both members of NATO did not seem to rule out the possibility of a clash in the Aegean between the two countries. The argument was that Greek admission would strengthen the fragile Greek democracy. Equally, however, it could not be denied that Greek membership would draw the EEC into a troubled area and a poor country, with implications for its own cohesion. Hence the rather protracted discussions before Greece was admitted. Despite all the talk about admitting 'the birthplace of European civilization', in terms of its social, political and economic development Greece did not yet correspond to the European 'norm' that the nine members believed themselves broadly to constitute. As far as Britain specifically was concerned, relations with Greece had been strained during successive phases of the Cyprus question (on which island Britain still retained a 'sovereign base' under the terms of its 1960 independence). The advent of Athens into the Community was greeted with considerable caution in London.

Once the 'strengthening of democracy' argument had been given considerable weight in the Greek case it was difficult to reject it when Spain and Portugal applied in July and March 1977 respectively. There was, however, considerable resistance, particularly from France and Italy, where agricultural lobbies were very active. An attempted coup in Spain in 1981 was also used as a reason to delay. Belgium and the Netherlands were not keen. Greece campaigned for more financial support before agreeing. In comparison with these obstructions, the United Kingdom was broadly supportive. As far as Spain was concerned, the question of Gibraltar was always likely to be a source of friction but in other respects the country might be a welcome ally. In relation to Portugal it was always possible for Britain to bring its long historical connection into play. Portugal also presented itself as a self-consciously 'Atlantic' country in what was now the 'Atlantic rim' of the

EEC. Both Spain and Portugal eventually joined at the beginning of 1986. Although their cases had been considered in parallel, there were considerable differences in their situations, notably the fact that Portugal was undergoing a post-colonial adjustment comparable to that which Spain had gone through after the Spanish-American war at the beginning of the century.

The arrival of 'Iberia' naturally gave the EEC a further 'southern' dimension, both culturally and economically. Its institutional bases, however, remained firmly located in the narrow northern triangle, which had suited the original Six (Italy apart). The Commission remained in Brussels, the Court in Luxembourg (as were banking institutions and the secretariat of the Parliament), the Parliament in Strasbourg. Even so, there was increased talk of the 'Mediterranean dimension' the EEC now possessed – and, judged in terms of gross national products this dimension was poorer. Denis Healey took a sardonic British view that the 'olive line' was as real a frontier as any in Europe. South of the line where olives grow people had little respect for government and used their discretion when it came to paying taxes.[9] 'Mediterranean solidarity', however, as the admission negotiations had shown, was a frail plant. The negotiations had also revealed the extent of strains between the outlooks and interests of north and south within France and Italy.[10] Indeed, across the Community as a whole, it became steadily more apparent that statistics of 'national' performance, used for comparative purposes between its members, disguised very considerable disparities between regions within states. This became additionally very apparent in the case of Spain, where the economic success of Catalonia was particularly marked. Such disparities scarcely constituted a new discovery, but they received additional political prominence through the processes of membership expansion. Perhaps they could only be mitigated, if not eliminated, outside the framework provided by the nation-state itself.

Purpose, structure and function

The 12-state Europe of 1986 was thought likely to settle down at this size for some time to come. Its composition, in relation to past inter-state and international relationships, formed a novel partnership. This particular dozen had never before all come together in close association. How much direct interaction had taken place in the past varied very considerably. The historian would be hard put to it, for example, to write volumes on the interaction between Denmark and Greece. In some cases, however, there were substantial bilateral histories, sometimes long and sometimes poisoned, which could still have ramifications in the present (Britain and Ireland being a case in point). The United Kingdom, it could reasonably be claimed, had as many, if not more, long-established and not insignificant bilateral relationships within this grouping as any other of its members. All of the members, with the exception of Greece, Ireland and Luxembourg, had been colonial powers beyond Europe (and some still had residual colonial possessions). Greece and Ireland, however, like Italy, had significant and continuing global diasporas – in Australia and South and North America. This 12-state (five monarchies, a grand duchy and six republics) Europe overlapped substantially but not exclusively with the European membership of NATO (which Spain joined in 1982 and to which Greece returned in 1980). Only Ireland, of the members, was outside NATO. Norway and Iceland, NATO members, were not in the EEC and did not wish to be. Such a close correlation between EEC and NATO membership enhanced the solidarity of the 12 in one sense but also in another it entailed their 'defence' remained fundamentally linked to the United States. France, however, remained hostile to American 'hegemony' and maintained its semi-detached status within NATO.

The Community, thus enlarged, was in itself a kind of 'European unity', if in a weak sense. To function at all, it needed 'orchestrating' beyond the customary levels of diplomatic representation. It needed its own institutions and mechanisms. Their basic form, of course, had been established before the United Kingdom and other members joined. The newcomers had little alternative but to accept its tripartite structure: Commission, Council of Ministers and Parliament. They knew well, however, that this structure had been a compromise between the views of its original members. There had been, throughout the Community's existence, a tension between the elements of supra-statism and inter-governmentalism. That tension had not always been creative, but was inescapable. Pressure to move in one or other of these directions had been frequently associated with particular countries, but, as the example of France had demonstrated, state approaches could oscillate significantly as a consequence of political developments within member states. Both approaches could be plausibly represented as 'what Europe needed', given where individual member states were coming from. Both approaches, however, moved the participating states in new directions.

The Commission consisted of a body of civil servants in Brussels drawn from the member countries under the guidance of nationally selected commissioners, one of whom was president. The UK joined France, Federal Germany and Italy (and Spain on its accession) in being able to nominate two such commissioners, who were appointed for four-year renewable terms – the other countries could nominate one. The first, and thus far the only British president of the Commission was Roy Jenkins (1977–81), whose enthusiasm for the Community had been evident in Labour politics for many years. He himself noted, however, that while his conviction was complete, his experience of the business of the Community was negligible. He also confessed, subsequently, that he had been initially too starry-eyed, both about the economic and social achievements of the other Community countries and about the position and power of the president of the Commission. France, Italy and Germany he knew fairly well, but had visited Brussels on only four occasions between 1945 and the date of his

appointment.[11] Commissioners are required to jettison their national allegiances on taking up their respective portfolios (an allocation requiring
much juggling, with Jenkins having a more significant role in this process
than his predecessors had done), but a British appointee at this juncture
was significant.[12] He had ideas to bring fresh life to a bogged-down
Community – the most significant of which was to revive the proclaimed
objective of 'economic and monetary union'. The British decided not to
participate in the ensuing exchange rate mechanism (ERM) of the
European monetary system (EMS), though they indicated an intention to
join eventually. The national habit, as Jenkins subsequently put it, 'of
never joining any European enterprise until it is too late to influence its
shape' had been upheld.[13] His experience of the negotiations, however,
showed him just how difficult reaching a 'European' consensus on such an
issue was.[14] The Commission might propose, but the heavyweights
decided, that is to say France and Federal Germany.

The 'European Council' (which was not written into the original treaties)
evolved out of the informal meetings of the heads of state and government
after 1973. Such 'summits' were initially held three times a year at varied
locations (e.g. Copenhagen, Paris, Dublin, Brussels, Bremen, Fontainebleau,
Milan, Luxembourg and London (December 1986) with attendant media
attention. The composition of the Council of Ministers, which stands below
the European Council in the decision-making hierarchy, fluctuates, in terms
of ministers attending, according to business under discussion. It is chaired
by a minister from the state that holds the rotating six-monthly presidency
of the Community. The actual balance of power and influence between the
Commission and the Council, however, has never been static. Elections in
member-states threw up new governments, personalities and domestic policies – as, for example, those attempted by the French socialists under
François Mitterrand after 1981 – which resulted, each time, in significant
shifts of direction. Whether the Commission has been 'declining' or 'reviving' in relation to the broad sweep of policy has depended upon a multiplicity of factors. The momentum regained by Jacques Delors in the mid-1980s,
for example, was only possible because his vision had the clear support of
the French government. The pendulum would swing again.

The constitutional thinking that informed these structures drew, very
naturally, on the traditions from which the founding members came.
Periodic new 'Plans' emerged, which advocated or produced some changes
of procedure or structure to cope with a constantly evolving process. The
United Kingdom itself mysteriously and uniquely continued to function
without a written constitution or basic law. All member states had parliaments but only the United Kingdom had a doctrine of parliamentary sovereignty – that is to say the supremacy of Acts of Parliament over any other
source of law. A Community could not function effectively, however, unless
its law (arising out of its founding Treaties) took precedence over national
law in any case of conflict. The European Court of Justice, drawn from each

member state, plus one, and sitting in Luxembourg, consistently upheld this principle, and ingenious legal devices were required to reconcile it with the United Kingdom notion of parliamentary sovereignty. Such devices could not altogether disguise the fact that there was a 'clash of principles'.

The question of a 'parliament', in relation both to British 'parliamentary sovereignty' and 'accountability' within the European institutions also brought a 'clash of principles'. During the 1975 referendum campaign, even Michael Foot, a Labour orator normally drunk with words, could not at that time find sufficient superlatives to describe the merits of Britain's parliament. No comparable institution, he wrote, had shaped so continuously the life and society of any western European state. It was being made farcical and unworkable by the semi-secret law-making process of the Council of Ministers.[15] It was a plea made to no avail. Steps were then taken, however, to turn the European Assembly (which had originally been made up of delegated members from the parliaments of member states) into a directly elected European Parliament.[16] The Labour government dragged its heels in implementing this change and it was not until 1979 that the first directly elections to the Parliament took place in member states. Seen by Edward Heath as 'one of Europe's crowning achievements after centuries of warfare', direct elections did not enthuse the UK electorate.[17] The UK turnout of 32 per cent was the lowest figure in the Community and the UK electorate thereafter consistently failed to recognize the significance of this 'crowning achievement' by voting in 'European elections'. It was a commonplace observation that few could actually name their MEP or had any real notion of what they actually did, apart from draw what were perceived to be generous expenses. There was a paradox, here. It was frequently suggested that the way the Community operated was 'undemocratic' but at the same time there was resistance to giving the European Parliament the enhanced powers for which many of its members periodically asked because that would give it 'legitimacy'. A lot of parliamentarians still thought that only the Westminster Parliament was a real parliament and wanted to keep it that way.

A European Parliament, it has often been commented, would only become 'real' when it developed pan-European parties derived from a voting base that was itself European.[18] There were indeed ideological groupings, ranging from far left to far right but the biggest were the Socialists, the Christian Democrats and the Liberals but it would be a mistake to see them as tight-knit, in organizational terms, or to believe that national perspectives, on particular matters, had been eliminated. The extent to which MEPs followed closely the line of their 'home' parties could vary significantly, as could the regard, as individuals, in which they were held by their home parties. The variables are such that generalization in this area is hazardous. British Labour fitted relatively comfortably into the socialist group. British Conservatives found it more difficult to establish a place for themselves in this European spectrum. Soon after becoming leader of the party, Margaret Thatcher paid a visit to Federal Germany and, in discussions with the leadership of the Christian Democratic Union, came away feeling that the two parties had much in common. Discussions with Italian Christian Democrats, however, she found very depressing. They had nothing to contribute on what she considered the great question of the post-Cold War world – the long-term relationship between nation states and supra-national institutions. She found it disconcerting that under a 'Christian Democrat' banner one could find anything from 'full-blooded free enterprise' to corporatism. She was present at the launch of the European Democratic Union in Salzburg in 1978 but learnt enough about her 'partners' to know that British conservatism, as she understood it, was somewhat anomalous among the continental company it kept (sometimes).[19] The seating of the House of Commons, of course, ensured that government benches directly confronted opposition benches. Neither in the European parliament nor in the national parliaments of other member states was this the pattern. The symbolism of such seating arrangements continued to reflect different traditions of government and the prevalence, as it still appeared in this period, of a 'two-party system' in contrast to the coalition-juggling politics that often occurred elsewhere in the Community – itself in substantial measure a reflection of different electoral systems. In party terms, however, 'fitting in' was not simply a peculiarly British problem. There were other major parties, in France or Ireland, for example, whose colouring derived from particular national circumstances. It was possible, therefore, to see in the British participation both distinctive and common political aspects – a situation that, of course, obtained throughout the Community.

Clubbing?

The way 'Europe' worked, as expressed through the institutions that have been sketched, therefore remained rather an arcane mystery in this first period of UK membership. It did not seem that there was any public eagerness to enhance understanding of the Community and bring its development into the public 'mainstream' of the UK. Attention to its affairs in the media was spasmodic and unsystematic. Correspondents were certainly established in Brussels, and reports were published or broadcast at moments of major decision-making, but there was little sense that it was 'Britain in the Community' which now required constant and informed coverage. It was, for example, virtually impossible for the UK voter to gain any information on a regular basis concerning the proceedings of the European Parliament – a factor that no doubt contributed to the lack of UK interest in voting at elections. In the press, such marginalization stemmed, at least in part, from continuing 'scepticism', to use a word which came into public vocabulary. Such 'scepticism', however, was virtually indistinguishable from 'hostility'. Back in 1962, Lord Beaverbrook had written to Harold Macmillan that his newspapers would support him in everything but that blasted Common Market, which is an American device to put us alongside Germany. As our power was broken and lost by two German wars, it is very hard on us now to be asked to align ourselves with those villains.[20]

Over the ensuing couple of decades, different pens and different proprietors, (some not British) showed comparable dislike for the 'blasted Common Market' (and some, at least, of the peoples who lived within it).

The lack of press attention to 'Britain in the Community', however, should not be exclusively seen as political bias on the part of proprietors. It was an aspect of a more pervasive 'depoliticization' of the popular press in favour of sex and sport.[21] The readership of the *Daily Star* (launched in 1978), for example, relished its focus on 'bums, tits and bingo', and did not wish to be disturbed by discussion of the ERM. The 'quality' press, too, felt unable to resist human interest and celebrity stories. Sketch writers gave readers amusing glimpses of the 'show' that was Parliament but it was no longer possible to read verbatim parliamentary reports. *The Times*, then owned by Lord Thomson and edited by William Rees-Mogg, an enthusiastic European at that time, launched *Europa* a supplement in conjunction with *Le Monde*, *La Stampa* and *Die Welt* in the early 1970s but it did not last. Owned by Rupert Murdoch after 1981, it had no disposition to become 'European' in orientation. Television and radio services proliferated in a communications revolution that played havoc with 'public service' paternalism. It was not a cultural climate that encouraged or even made room for 'the European project' as a significant national enterprise. A newspaper, the *European*, launched by Robert Maxwell, did attempt to provide coverage but could not attract sufficient readers or advertising. Of course, the technological developments that made possible the transformation of the British media scene were not an insular peculiarity. The density of its tabloid constellation, however, in comparative terms, was conspicuous. The inability of the UK television watcher even to receive the output of other Community channels contrasted with the facility with which, if viewers were so inclined and linguistically competent, cross-national viewing could occur elsewhere in the Community.

Necessarily, however, membership of the Community did entail some meshing of British bureaucracy with its procedures and institutions. There was, however, no 'Department of European Affairs' within the machinery of government. Individual British nationals, usually from Whitehall, joined the relatively small bureaucracy of the Community as 'Eurocrats'. A European secretariat within the cabinet office in Whitehall was given a central coordinating role in relation to Community matters. Naturally, some UK departments (Agriculture, Trade and Industry, the Environment, the Treasury) were drawn more deeply into 'Brussels' than others, but there was scarcely any area of UK government unaffected by Community developments. In Brussels itself, the office of the UK's Permanent Representative to the European Communities (UKRep) was represented on the body of all such representatives of member states. Stated succinctly, its function was to provide expertise for the benefit of Whitehall negotiators and keep constant contact with the Commission and other bodies. UK lobby organizations also needed its advice and assistance. The cumulative impact of these changes, coming as they did at a time of more general enquiry into the structure of Whitehall, necessarily produced some blurring of boundaries between existing UK departments and also between 'London' and 'Brussels'. It also made the process of administration more complex in so far as it involved additional 'players' who now had to be taken into account.[22] There were, too, continuing differences of administrative culture. 'European' civil servants did not invariably display that deference to their political masters which British civil servants were at least groomed to display. British civil servants, in turn, had their own private opinions, by no means invariably enthusiastic, about the Community.

'Oui', now and then – and 'no, no, no'

Such administrative adjustment was not of a character to hit the headlines. There were sufficient domestic political developments for this purpose. Wilson resigned as prime minister in 1976 and was succeeded by an older man – James Callaghan (b. 1912). Callaghan, had been Labour's foreign affairs spokesman after 1972 and had served as foreign secretary when Labour came into office. Although he had struggled with the problems of Cyprus and Rhodesia, it had been 'Europe' that had dominated his time at the Foreign Office. Intelligent, but not intellectual, he prided himself on common sense. He was not inclined to put forward visions of European unity. To the French president, Giscard, he seemed a typical politician of the fourth republic, an observation not regarded as complimentary. Helmut Schmidt, the West German chancellor, found him more congenial, but the twosome did not become a threesome. 'Non, merci beaucoup' – a remark that largely exhausted his command of French – had been Callaghan's stance towards a further deepening of the EC and his demeanour during the renegotiation might best be described as dogged. The overall position of the country seemed parlous. The government still wrestled with economic crisis. After much debate, the cabinet agreed to the cuts that were required as a condition of the loan obtained in 1976 from the International Monetary Fund (IMF). Britain was not in a position to 'lead' anywhere. In addition, the structure of the United Kingdom itself seemed problematic – though in the event, proposals for devolution to Wales and Scotland were defeated and failed to carry a sufficient majority when put to the vote in those countries in 1979.

David Owen (b. 1938) (originally trained as a medical doctor) became a youthful foreign secretary in 1977 on the death of Anthony Crosland. He had been one of the organizers of the vote by 69 Labour MPs – in defiance of the party whips – to join the Common Market, but in office, preoccupied with Rhodesia, there was little scope, given the mood of the party, for divergence from a rather frigid stance. Leading Labour figures – Tony Benn, Peter Shore and Michael Foot – continued to be hostile to membership of the Community. It has already been noted that Callaghan would not join the EMS. In November 1978, speaking at the annual lord mayor's banquet in London, he gave notice that the UK could not become the largest contributor to the Community budget – the Common Agricultural Policy, in particular, consumed a far greater proportion than had been envisaged during the accession negotiations – when it was seventh in the Community's economic league table. The 'Bloody British Question' – what 'rebate' Britain might receive – moved up the agenda, to the embarrassment of the British president of the Commission. However, it was not Callaghan who went into battle. Following the 'Winter of Discontent' of 1978/79, the Callaghan government lost a vote of confidence in the Commons in March 1979 and lost the ensuing general election in May 1979. It brought into office the first woman prime minister of the United Kingdom. It was her avowed intention, among other things, to 'get our money back'.

Margaret Thatcher (b. 1925) was the first Oxford science graduate – she studied there in 1943–47 – to become prime minister. Her family background was modest and Methodist. She had been in the Commons since 1959. In her attitude to foreign affairs, it has been argued, 'she remained the Grantham schoolgirl of the early wartime years'. The same author notes that she spoke no foreign language and allegedly gave no evidence of having read anything about Europe beyond the *Reader's Digest*.[23] Of course, even if she had the resources to do so, she could not have used her vacations, as Heath had done in the pre-war years, to travel in Europe. This assessment, however, may have too mandarin a tinge. In her own account of her schoolgirl reading there is in fact no mention of the *Reader's Digest*. There were, apparently, books in Grantham.[24] In the immediate post-war decades, her circumstances were such that familiarizing herself with 'Europe' by travel and networking would not have been feasible, even had it appealed to her. Family holidays took place on the Sussex coast or the Isle of Wight. Skiing in Switzerland began in 1960. Her view of 'Europe' was one shared by the 'middle Britain' of her generation on whose behalf she spoke with increasing authority. It was a universe with which Giscard d'Estaing (b. 1926) was not familiar.[25] Nor was his successor in 1981, François Mitterrand, who apparently commented that she was 'a little bourgeois ideologist' – the damning element in this indictment presumably being that she was 'bourgeois'.[26]

Her foreign secretary, Lord Carrington (b. 1919), who had been defence secretary in the Heath government, was not bourgeois. He brought urbanity (as did other Etonian members of the cabinet who might, *sotto voce*, have been inclined to echo Mitterrand) to a cabinet presided over by a grocer's daughter. It fell to him to make noises of greater British commitment, as Jenkins put it, while the prime minister limbered up for the fight on the budget. Carrington had seen wartime service in Europe and shared with another prominent figure in the cabinet, William Whitelaw (b. 1918), who had commanded a tank squadron in the invasion of Normandy, a determination that Europe would never again be at war with itself. In addition, Carrington had come away from his service as High Commissioner in Australia (1956–59) with the belief that Britain's destiny lay in Europe.[27] It was another matter, however, to translate such youthful 'lessons' from the war and afterwards into detailed policies for Europe decades later. In addition, Carrington's tenure proved short. He resigned in 1982, accepting responsibility in relation to the Falklands crisis of that year.

The successful recapture of the islands after their invasion by Argentina boosted the prime minister's fortunes and was a considerable factor in her re-election in the following year. It was an episode that showed how British opinion could still be galvanized by an issue very distant from Europe. By contrast, the German contingent attending the annual Anglo-German exchange of views – the Königswinter conference – had to be shown where the Falkland Islands were on the world map. The British success had in substantial measure depended on the cooperation of the United States. It was a particular expression of that intimacy with the United States that Thatcher had cultivated from the outset. She prided herself on her association with President Reagan and infinitely preferred to deal with the Americans than with 'the Europeans'. With only a few exceptions, this remained a central stance throughout her premiership. Britain would accept the stationing of Cruise missiles on its territory. She was wary of any moves, particularly from Paris, that might undermine the structure and remit of NATO.

'Our money' and the Single European Act

Immediately, within the Community, it was Britain's budget dispute that occupied the headlines. A temporary agreement had been reached in May 1980, but it was not until the Fontainebleau Summit in 1984 that the rebate question was settled. The Common Agricultural Policy, which gave preference to Community farmers and subsidized their exports, had long been something the British wished to see 'reformed'. Thatcher had been prepared in 1982 to try to hold up agreement on agricultural prices for 1982/83 as a tactic in the budget dispute. Mitterrand in turn publicly suggested that Britain should cease to be a full member of the Community and negotiate a 'special status', a suggestion the prime minister dismissed.[28] Her stance played well with that section of British opinion which thought that 'Europe' understood only tough talking. Others thought that she upset her European 'partners' unnecessarily. Only when the budget dispute was settled could the acrimony dissipate and discussion begin again on the future direction of the Community.

Thatcher had stressed that she attached great importance to the Community as an economic bond with other western European countries. She had been sceptical, however, of the assumption frequently made in the early 1970s that merely joining the Community would somehow galvanize Britain. There were confrontations to be had at home too if Britain was to be pulled out of its malaise, and she would not duck them.[29] The programme her government embarked on – trades union reform and 'privatization' – was a deeply contentious 'neo-liberal' assault on hallowed social and economic doctrines. The Labour Party, committed under the leadership of Michael Foot to withdrawal from the Community, lost the 1983 general election conclusively.[30] The German SPD also lost in the German election in the same year. As the bitter industrial disputes of the years after 1983 demonstrated, Thatcher was prepared to fight it out. Helmut Kohl, however, the new Christian Democrat chancellor, would not risk fundamental challenge to the 'consensual' structures of German society. The 'British way', although sometimes portrayed as a conservative revolution rippling out through the Community, was in fact special. For her part, the prime minister made no pretence that she thought other than in terms of British interests and sought British solutions. Other member states, she believed, did the same in relation to their interests – the Common Agricultural Policy being the classic instance – but cloaked their self-interest in European terminology. They were also hiding their heads in the sand. She believed that the passion for Europe displayed by her predecessor had now become an obsession. She accused Heath of thinking of Europe first. The clash of personality was also a clash of dogma – within the party and within the country. For the moment, the tide domestically was with the prime minister.

Towards the European Union

'Europe – The Future' was the title of an ambitious document submitted by the British government to the Fontainebleau summit. Its stress was upon what it saw as the need for practical solutions, that is to say British ones, but in doing so was able to draw upon a more widespread European anxiety about the technological gap with the United States and Japan. The British emphasis was upon the creation of a real internal market for the Community. There was also reference to developing a common approach to external affairs. The document showed little interest in institutional reform and reiterated the importance of the national veto. The new foreign secretary was Geoffrey Howe (b. 1926). As a Cambridge undergraduate in 1950 he had been taking the view that British leadership in some form of European union was politically 'essential'.[31] He had been on family boyhood holidays in Belgium and France before the war. Two decades later, now as solicitor-general, he had played a major part in drafting the European Communities Bill. In 1984, claiming that Britain had played a 'full part' since joining the Community, he wanted to see real achievements, not proclamations masquerading as achievements.

Community debate now centred, following a French initiative in February 1985, on institutional reform, despite British reservations. The Fontainebleau Council had agreed to set up a working group, under an Irish chairman, and it reported in March 1985. It seemed that some modification of the veto was inevitable. Much manoeuvring then took place over the summer. In June a Franco-German paper entitled 'Draft Treaty on European Union' was presented at the Milan summit. It was agreed after a vote on which the Italian presidency had insisted that there should be an inter-governmental conference to consider the way forward. In the same month, Lord Cockfield, a member of the Commission presented detailed proposals with an accompanying timetable to create a unified market. Eventually, at the Luxembourg summit in December 1985 a compromise was reached. From Thatcher's perspective, the creation of a single market by 1992, with rules that would ensure that there would be equal opportunities for all states operating within it, was a great prize, even if that entailed some extension of EC competencies to achieve it. The stated objective of economic and monetary union, however, was another matter. The British could also claim certain other general 'success'. There was to be no major increase in the powers of the European Parliament. On the other hand, as the next few years demonstrated, the emphasis which the Commission wished to place on ensuring 'social safeguards' in relation to the internal market, was not congenial. When the Social Charter (on the Fundamental Social Rights of Workers) was adopted at the Strasbourg Council in December 1989, the British government insisted on an 'opt-out'.

The Single European Act, however, was a major milestone. The British remained suspicious about continental willingness to incorporate the necessary legislative instruments into their national legislation. 'Continentals', in turn, well understood that Britain was sceptical about 'ever-closer union'. The prime minister made known her preference for a Europe of nation states in a celebrated address delivered at the College of Europe in Bruges in 1988. It deeply depressed her foreign secretary who in turn could be accused of possessing a romantic longing for Britain to become part of some European consensus.[32] This underlying difference found expression in the difference of opinion about whether Britain should join the ERM, which all member states were expected to join as a prelude to establishing what was later to be the euro. Howe was sacked as foreign secretary (Nigel Lawson, chancellor of the exchequer, had earlier resigned). His replacement, John Major, announced in October 1990 that Britain would join the ERM. It turned out to be a step taken at the wrong time and the wrong rate. It was also made clear that Britain was not thereby committed to monetary union in Europe. At the Rome summit in that same month, however, all the other states reiterated their commitment to that objective. The following month, however, after a devastating resignation speech from Howe (deputy leader), which had focused on the prime minister's handling of Europe, Michael Heseltine (b. 1933) mounted a leadership challenge. He had been involved in a spectacular quarrel with the prime minister as to whether the Westland helicopter company, which was in financial difficulties, should be taken over by an American rival or by a European consortium. This was one example among many, particularly in the defence field, where the political dimensions of a particular case could scarcely be excluded from financial or technical appraisals. Heseltine resigned. He was another example of that Conservative generation that was by instinct 'pro-European'; he even had a dachshund called Rudi. His leadership challenge, however, also proved personally unsuccessful but the prime minister eventually calculated that she could not carry on. In the eyes of her critics, her 'rejection of the European idea', the product of ignorance and nationalism, had greatly reduced Britain's influence in Europe and, inevitably, the world. The United States, it was said, was looking to Germany and France as the key players in a uniting Europe.[33] To her supporters, still a not insubstantial section of the Conservative Party, she had robustly defended democracy against the machinations of the Commission.

Meanings of Maastricht

What 'the end of the Thatcher era' signified for 'Britain and Europe' was problematic. She had articulated the sentiments of a large section of the governing party and it was possibly her stridency rather than the substance of her contentions that had latterly been her undoing. It could be argued, however, that she 'spoke for Britain', although, under Neil Kinnock after 1983, the Labour Party moved away from its commitment to withdrawal and shifted towards acceptance. Support for membership had been a major factor in the defection of erstwhile leading Labour figures (Roy Jenkins, David Owen, Bill Rodgers, Shirley Williams) to form the SDP. In the 1983 general election the SDP/Liberal 'alliance' had polled only a few percentage points fewer than Labour, though it obtained only 10 per cent of Labour's seats. The Conservatives, although possessing a massive parliamentary majority, had obtained less than half of the popular vote. During the mid-1980s, as part of its search for electability, Labour edged towards being identified as 'pro-European', but the 1987 election result still left the Conservatives with a very strong majority. Jacques Delors, the president of the Commission, a French socialist by background, helped the process along later by speaking to the Trades Union Congress in September 1988 and presenting an image of a 'social Europe' that was more attractive to his audience. It was denounced by the government as an inappropriate intervention in British domestic politics. John Smith, the shadow chancellor, found himself advocating British membership of the ERM ahead of the government.

The observer would therefore have found it difficult to say how 'Europe' aligned itself in the British party structure and what was signified by it. It became conventional to talk in a general way about opinion within and without political parties being divided between 'Europhiles' and 'Eurosceptics', but such a division was not very illuminating beyond the 'orientation' it disclosed. In so far as they immersed themselves in the nuts and bolts of the Community, Europhiles could differ considerably at any given point in the process of its evolution. 'Euroscepticism' could be, and frequently was, no more than a euphemism for 'Eurohostility' or 'Europhobia', and could only have been satisfied by complete withdrawal from the Community, but it could also include a genuine scepticism about whether the Community could in fact 'deliver' what it professed to aspire to.[34] Sooner or later, even some well-wishers suspected that it would collapse under the weight of its ambition.

It was undeniable, however, that a loose kind of 'western European' identity had even penetrated to the United Kingdom. At all sorts of political, economic and social levels a certain mingling was taking place – with unpredictable consequences. Historians, to take only one humble category, wrote with distinction on the histories of countries other than their own – German writing on British history and British writing on German history being one example.[35] Refugee historians had made a name for themselves in post-war Britain and made a substantial contribution to raising the study of European history 'to a very respectable level'.[36] There was a German Historical Institute in London. Writers had largely ceased to be preoccupied with the construction of grand national narratives to serve public purposes, though there was a lively debate about history teaching and nationhood.[37] Whether 'British history' was also 'European history', however, remained obscure.[38] A British historian who wrote on British and European history was not to be taken, by that very fact, as expressing a personal commitment to the European Union.[39]

Mass tourism continued to grow from decade to decade, though in the case of Britain and France, the flow from the former to the latter was greater than vice versa by a ratio of about three to one in the decade after 1984.[40] Sometimes, as in the Dordogne and elsewhere, the British came to stay. Spain proved more than willing to provide a place in the sun for British holidaymakers on a scale never before achieved. Business travel within western Europe became a normal fact of life at a certain executive level. Direct trunk dialling facilitated telephone contact. The supreme symbolic expression of this 'unity' was the decision of both the British and French governments to support, though not to finance, the building of a Channel Tunnel. A project long speculated upon but often feared, and cancelled by Britain in 1975, was at long last to happen. The continent was no longer to be 'cut off'. Thatcher and Mitterrand announced the decision in Lille in January 1986, and the Tunnel became a reality in 1994. It was argued in some quarters that in itself the Tunnel would not bring revolutionary change – and in any case being 'on the edge of Europe' did not much matter in commercial terms.[41] British university students and staff were encouraged to spend periods in other universities in the Community as part of their normal academic experience.[42] The 'twinning' movement between towns and cities across the Community continued to expand. Europe, for English and Scottish football fans, consisted of a set of city-based clubs that regularly played each other in various cup competitions.[43] It was still the case, however, though the situation was to change dramatically, that English clubs normally fielded players from the British Isles. It could be argued that such proliferating contacts at different levels carried no political implications with them. It was indeed difficult to relate them to the processes of decision-making at the highest political levels. Tourism might be taking on the appearance of an annual British mass-migration southwards but bronzed Britons gained a reputation for remaining extravagantly British in their packaged and packed destinations.

It was this puzzling combination of involvement and detachment within western Europe that confronted John Major (b. 1943) when he took office in 1991. He was the first prime minister to have no personal memory of the Second World War. Apart from a honeymoon in Ibiza, he knew more about Nigeria, where he had worked for a while, than about Europe. His enthusiasm for cricket linked this avowedly classless man to Alec Douglas-Home among his predecessors, but it had no resonance with his European peers. The 'unfinished business' with which he had immediately to deal was the negotiation of the Maastricht Treaty (or Treaty on European Union) in December. Its genesis, essentially, was to provide the context within which European Monetary Union (EMU) would take place. It was agreed that EMU would be introduced in 1999 – it successfully took physical form in 2002. A stability pact was supposed to ensure that member states would limit their public sector deficits to 3 per cent of GDP and public-sector debts to 60 per cent of GDP. The British succeeded in getting an 'opt-out' in their own case (as did the Danes). They also opted out of the Social Chapter. Such exemptions could be represented as a notable success. Even more important, however, at least potentially, was the fact that 'subsidiarity' as a principle was written into the treaty, though in a form that left its precise meaning opaque.

By November 1993, provided the treaty was ratified by member states, a European Union would have come into existence. It had three elements. The Community continued as before but a fresh impetus was given, inter-governmentally, to working out a Common Foreign and Security Policy and to cooperation in the fields of Justice and Home Affairs. Citizens of individual EC countries would become citizens of the European Union. The foreign secretary, Douglas Hurd, saw that the European Union was a huge historical achievement compared with anything Europe had achieved in the past.

Unlike the prime minister, he knew about the past, having studied history at Cambridge. Not only was he the first foreign secretary to have been a diplomat in his early career, he was also the first to write that he felt 'at home' sitting in the sun in the Piazza San Michele in Lucca in Italy, sipping an espresso and reading the *Corriere della Sera*.[44]

Major won the 1992 election but 'Europe' continued to prove bitterly divisive within his own party. It was to lead him in 1995 to resign and successfully seek re-election. Even so, as he tacked back and forth seeking a middle course on Europe, his authority suffered. In September 1992 he had withdrawn sterling from the ERM, an enforced move which cast doubt on even the principle of EMU as far as Britain was concerned. Doubts about Maastricht were not confined to the United Kingdom, but other developments added to British disenchantment. No one could have forecast the outbreak of BSE (or 'mad cow disease') or the acrimony that accompanied the ban imposed by the Commission on the export of British beef. Getting the European Community (Amendment) Bill through the Commons in the early part of 1993 proved an exhausting business. On the third reading in May the measure was passed, but 46 Conservatives voted against it. Four years later, Tony Blair took office as the first Labour prime minister since 1974.

At the heart of Europe

Shortly after taking office, Major made a speech in which he claimed that his aims for Britain in the Community could be simply stated. He wanted his country to be where it belonged, at the heart of Europe. The problem was that in 1991 no one knew where to find the heart. In one sense, the heart of western Europe had come to be Brussels since it would obviously have been inappropriate for the burgeoning Community to have had its headquarters in the capital of one of its major states. The steps that have been traced, culminating in Maastricht, had been taken by a group of states which, despite their rivalries, had exhibited a sufficient capacity for symbiosis. They all appeared to be 'settled'. In Northern Ireland, the Basque country and Corsica there were indeed serious problems for the states concerned, but they were not likely to lead to inter-state conflict.

This relative cosiness concerning the 'integration of Europe' was shattered by the events in eastern/central Europe and the Soviet Union from 1989 onwards and which were still unfolding as Major spoke.[45] The real Europe had come back on the agenda. Its return had begun in Poland with the emergence of the Solidarity movement in the 1980s (though it appeared to have been crushed by the imposition of martial law). In 1985 Mikhail Gorbachev became general secretary of the CPSU, stating that one of the party's basic tasks was 'the further perfecting and development of democracy'. Faced with more unrest, and in a context where it was attempting economic reform, the Polish government allowed Solidarity to contest a limited number of seats in parliamentary elections in 1989. It won them all. The basis of Communist rule evaporated. In Hungary, too, some economic liberalization, which had been attempted for a decade, led to multi-party elections in 1990 and the appointment of a non-Communist prime minister. The pace of change accelerated across all the countries of the 'Soviet bloc' – Czechoslovakia, Bulgaria, Romania. Gorbachev's Soviet Union neither could nor would stop it. It was initially often assumed, however, that the Soviet Union itself would remain intact. All that was happening, it might seem, was that 'eastern Europe' was extracting itself from Russian overlordship.

Even before this rapid collapse of Communism, intellectuals in France and Germany, sometimes exiles from eastern Europe, had been addressing the question of 'Europe' with renewed vigour, though without agreement.[46] The events of 1989–90 took the debate further as the old issues resurfaced concerning 'central' or 'eastern Europe'?[47] Where did it 'fit'? Democracy had come again, but what kind of democracy?[48] The paradox was that just at the moment when its virtues were being celebrated, the democracies of western Europe had a tarnished appearance as glimpses began to be had of the scale of corruption or 'sleaze' at the highest level of politics in Italy, France, Germany, Spain and Britain, and in the European Commission itself. Old landmarks disappeared – in the collapse, for example, of the once dominant Christian Democrat party in Italy. In country after country, as old class alignments declined, the parties they had embodied lost their coherence or their distinctiveness. The 'brave new world' of the East, with a renewed zest for multi-party politics, met an old world of the West, whose electors seemed increasingly unwilling to exercise the vote in the multiplicity of elections and referendums they were being offered.

The crisis in the Soviet Union itself, which saw not only Estonia, Latvia and Lithuania regaining the independence – the former two with large Russian minorities – that had briefly been theirs between the world wars, but also the independence of Ukraine, Belarus, Georgia, Moldavia, Azerbaijan, Kyrgyzstan, Uzbekistan, Tadzhikistan and Armenia, brought a huge new dimension to the questions. In December 1991 the flag of the Russian Federation, not the Soviet hammer and sickle, flew over the Kremlin. The federation still embraced a large land mass with diverse and probably restless ethnic groups, but it was now more 'European' than it had been for many decades. It also remained to be seen how complete this independence was to be. A large state like Ukraine might want to tilt to 'Europe' rather than to Russia, although either option would divide rather than unite the country, largely on an east/west basis. The era of Gorbachev was over but he had made great play with the notion of 'a common European house'. Russia could be 'at home' in Europe other than with tanks and troops. Yet it was equally clear that its former satellites did not wish to see Russia playing a large part in their new Europe.

The events of 1989–91, which have been merely sketched here, were eagerly followed in the British media.[49] Thatcher had famously remarked that she had found in Gorbachev a Russian with whom it was possible to 'do business'.[50] Her support for the dismantling of Communism in eastern Europe was unambiguous and on her visits she found herself receiving a warmer welcome than she was then receiving at home. Believing that freedom flourished only in a free market, she had none of that hankering after 'reconstructed Socialism' still to be found among elements of the western European Left.

Major had spoken, in Bonn, of Britain being at the heart of Europe in a Germany unified and a Europe transformed (the heart of Germany was shortly to move to Berlin).[51] It had predictably been the crisis in the German Democratic Republic and the question of 'German unity' that had caused most concern in London. For more than 40 years reunification had been a distant vision. Two German states had in many quarters come to be seen as not inappropriate and a relationship of a kind had developed with the German Democratic Republic.[52] The situation that made German unity possible was not the direct result of the policies either of the Federal Republic or of the West as a whole. In October 1989 an *Economist* poll suggested that 70 per cent of Britons favoured German unity but that figure had dropped to 45 per cent by the following January. Nicholas Ridley had to be dismissed from the cabinet by the prime minister because of an article he wrote that spoke of a 'German racket designed to take over the whole of Europe'. This was a more extreme expression of an underlying anxiety felt not least by Thatcher herself. A German historian working in London concluded that, while unification was in the end accepted, there was 'no sense of relief'. Britain had still not accepted that its future no longer lay in keeping a distance from Europe but in existing 'in close proximity to it'.[53] Historical memories were not far below the surface. The Federal Republic had been the economic powerhouse of 'western Europe' but had been politically somewhat reticent. It would still not have a permanent seat on the United Nations Security Council or possess nuclear weapons (unlike Britain and France), but might it not now flex its political muscles as its most powerful state to shape the new Europe according to its wishes? The fall of the Berlin Wall and the ensuing German unification was the most striking sign that the post-1945 era had ended, but few grasped at the time how difficult unification was to prove.[54] Putting it crudely, one state could not easily eliminate two states of mind. Integration did not lead to overweening German ambition but rather to much self-doubt and despondency. It was an example that could even serve as a warning in relation to European integration as a whole.

There were fears, too, that release from Communism would also unleash pent-up ethnic quarrels. It had been among Romania's Magyar minority that the events that led to the overthrow of Ceauşescu had begun. Czechoslovakia separated into two states – the Czech Republic and

Slovakia. This latter step was achieved without violence but that it occurred at all testified to the strength of feeling and the rejection of that 'Czechoslovak' amalgam that had been invented in 1919. It was, however, in Yugoslavia – which had kept itself outside the Soviet bloc – that the explosion occurred.[55] In one sense, the country in its post-war form died with the death of its creator, Tito, in 1980. Its 'special' status within the Cold War lost its significance as the Cold War came to an end. It was an avowedly federal state with six autonomous republics (one of them, Serbia, also had autonomous republics). In December 1990 Slovene voters, by a large majority, wanted independence. A year later, Germany recognized both Slovenia and Croatia, as did the EU in January 1992. Britain had gone along reluctantly with this step. Conflict was engulfing the region and the most congenial, because least demanding, explanation was that 'ancient hatreds' had reignited. By 1995 some 200,000 people had been killed in the Yugoslav wars. It was in August of that year that NATO air sorties were launched against Serbian forces in Bosnia. The United States brought the leaders of Serbia, Bosnia and Croatia to reach a settlement in November 1995, which created two 'entities' in the Bosnian republic. Order would be kept by NATO, with US forces to remain for one year. Bosnia was followed as the storm centre by Kosovo (the province of Serbia which had an Albanian majority but had great significance in Serb national history). The position of Albanians within the Former Yugoslav Republic of Macedonia, as it at first called itself in deference to Greek objections to the appropriation of 'Macedonia', constituted a further flashpoint.

The salient fact about these bitter and bloody conflicts was that they were in Europe but that 'Europe', it appeared, had neither the will nor the means to intervene effectively either to stop the fighting or to produce a 'solution'. The intervention, when it came, had been by NATO (with British involvement). It was the United States that in November 1995 brought the leaders of Croatia, Bosnia and Serbia together and brokered a deal. A first stage of the Yugoslav wars had been settled at the US Air Force Base in Dayton, Ohio. It was a salutary reminder of the gap between 'European vision' and Europe's capacity to act – but, in contrast to 1912–14, there was no danger that the major European powers would go to war with each other because of events in the Balkans.[56] There was, however, something bizarre in the foreign minister of Luxembourg telling Slovenia that it was too small to be independent. Each of the major European states still had its own individual agenda arising out of both past relationships and more recent contacts with Yugoslavia. Where was the British 'national interest' in such a complicated dispute? Would it not be better for 'Europe' to distance itself, thereby sustaining the impression that the Balkans were still not 'part of Europe'?

The outside intervention, such as it was, had another twist. Both in Bosnia and Kosovo it was Muslim populations that were being given some support. There were times when attempts were made to present the

Croatian/Serbian conflict as the latest expression of the gulf between Catholic Europe and Orthodox Europe (not a fault-line that had much resonance in Britain). It could not be said, however, that 'Christian Europe' was patrolling its boundary to keep out Islam.

Whether one could still speak of 'Christian Europe' as a defining aspect of the continent's late-twentieth-century character was one of its major problems. Christianity appeared to be most flourishing in those continents to which it had been exported from Europe. The withdrawal of large segments of the population of Europe from the churches seemed to be a general phenomenon, whether seen as a rapid decline in the late century or as the climax of a very long process of 'secularization'. The categorization of European states as Protestant, Catholic or Orthodox now had only limited validity. It appeared possible for Catholics to admire Pope John Paul II, whose role in the transformation of Europe should not be discounted, while ignoring aspects of Catholic teaching that he emphasized. Whether Europe in some sense still believed but no longer belonged was a question for the sociologists of religion.[57] Agnostics and atheists did their best to ease the churches out of the public sphere. Additional justification for doing so could be found in the presence across western Europe of substantial post-1945 migrant populations of Muslims drawn from different parts of the 'Muslim world' in different European states. The scale of this presence presented issues that had not before been grappled with in Europe's past.[58] It has added a new twist to the long-drawn-out question of the admission of Turkey to the Union, on which very different stances were being taken.

In short, Europe of the twenty-first century had become a very different continent from the one it had been a century earlier. Some believed that this new Europe could be defined only by paradoxically emptying itself of any definition other than an adherence to notions of human rights, notions that, however, are in principle universal. Whatever answer was given to these questions, it had become clear that the discourse about its civilization on which western Europe had been relaunched after 1945 now had an archaic sound.

So did the British debate – even of 1975 – about its place in Europe. It had then been fought with a stock of notions about what Britain was, and what Europe was, which became increasingly obsolete with the passage of time. The United Kingdom had been constitutionally transformed at the end of the century by the creation of a Scottish Parliament and a Welsh Assembly. Northern Ireland trembled on the brink of getting its own Assembly to work. Relations between London and Dublin could be described as virtually 'normal', even harmonious.[59] For some, however, these pragmatic adjustments signified the end of the United Kingdom as its constituent parts made their journey to becoming 'European regions', though if so it was a journey that English regions seem disinclined to make. These decades have seen a continuing debate on what it is to be British on a scale without previous parallel, but all the time the European goalposts have been moving.[60]

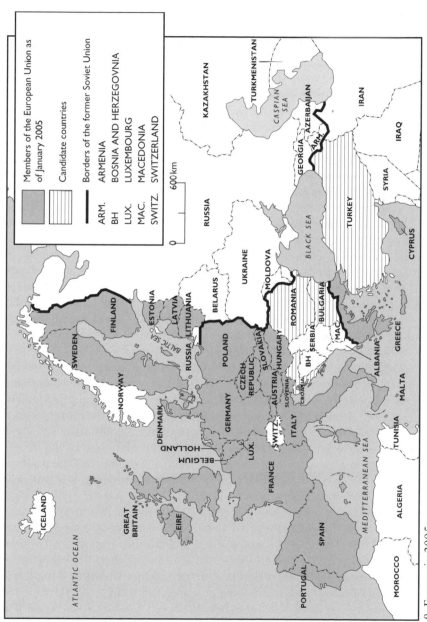

8. Europe in 2005

It is customary for incoming British prime ministers to make an initial 'pro-European' speech. New Labour, it was said after 1997, would make a 'fresh start'. The government did indeed sign up to the Social Chapter and Blair spoke to the French National Assembly in French.[61] It was a gesture to acute French sensitivities on the question of language. It was one that could be made, however, with the knowledge that in reality English had become the necessary common language for almost all members of the Union.[62] It was, no doubt, the ubiquity of the English language (albeit often with an American accent) that buttressed the substantial monolingualism of the British. At the beginning of the twenty-first century, as they had done at intervals over the preceding century, governments had preached the benefits of foreign language acquisition to a largely deaf audience. Where a European language was acquired, French was still the normal choice. Spanish was gaining and German losing ground. Languages from the Asian subcontinent had a greater presence in British society in the twenty-first century than those of north or east European members of the European Union.

The prime minister remarked in his Paris speech that as he watched his children grow up he wanted them to live in a Europe in which they felt as much 'at home' in Paris, Rome or Vienna as in London. He did not say in Warsaw, Riga or Budapest. Western European Britons still thought of capitals they knew at first hand themselves. Yet at the Copenhagen summit in 2002 it was agreed that Cyprus (hopefully reunited), the Czech Republic, Estonia, Latvia, Lithuania, Hungary, Malta, Poland, Slovakia and Slovenia would join the Union in 2004, followed by Bulgaria and Romania in 2007 – with Turkey's application still unresolved.

Such a Europe would indeed constitute a new creation.[63] It was an enterprise without exact parallel and eluded the categories of relationship offered by past diplomatic and constitutional history. The implications of its proposed Constitution remained capable of diverse interpretations.[64] The United Kingdom had declined to join the eurozone and its government had contrived to put off the promised referendum on adopting the euro.[65] The economic arguments for staying out might be cogent but the political impression it conveyed remained that of British ambivalence.[66] It was possible, however, that the awkwardness of the British stance would appear less anomalous in a Europe of 25 states than it had in one of 12. The British view of Europe might prove compatible with the approach of newcomers to the Union – it was noticeable that the new figures on the European scene from eastern Europe most frequently had English as their second language. This 'expansion of Europe' might well not be complete – as political upheaval in Ukraine demonstrated, bringing to power as it did a government that 'looked west'. These points had not escaped the British Foreign Office. 'Britain belongs in the English-speaking world' (not Europe) declared a *Daily Telegraph* editorial in 2004, but the editor seemed unaware of the extent to which Europe was becoming Anglophone as the only way of communicating with its complicated self, though what difference use of language made to a 'way of thinking' remained un-resolved.[67]

In any event, as the crisis over Iraq demonstrated, Europe's future would not be only a matter of the endless juggling of jurisdictions and competencies in trying to develop a workable system originally designed to handle second-order issues among a small group of states within a stable geopolitical context.[68] It would as much depend on what happened beyond its frontiers. Decades of talk about European political cooperation, although it had some results, could not prevent a deep schism between France and Germany on the one hand and Britain, Italy (and for a time) Spain on the other.[69] Poland sent troops to Iraq. France, on the other hand, criticized the United States and saw in Europe the means of creating what it described as a multipolar world. 'Europe', as a former president of Germany remarked in London in 2004, 'no longer seemed to exist'.[70] At an extreme it could be argued that just as western Europe had needed a Communist 'Other' to bind it together, so all-Europe now needed the United States (or even a diminished Russia) as its 'Other'. It was a view firmly rejected by Blair but not by Britain alone. There was renewed talk of Britain being a 'bridge' but it was not clear what that meant.[71]

Coda

The year 2004 witnessed two major commemorations that fortuitously illustrated the deep-seated ambiguities that remained at the beginning of the twenty-first century. Events to mark the centenary of the *'entente cordiale'* between Britain and France could not fail to note both that the two countries had developed an enduring, though peculiar, special relationship, but also that the celebration occurred at a moment of sharp political disagreement about Europe and the Atlantic relationship.[72] In the summer of 2004 Britain, France and the United States stood together in France, with others, to remember the fiftieth anniversary of the Normandy landings (and Germany was represented). In the second half of the twentieth century, with the exception of the Yugoslav wars, Europeans had stopped killing each other in large numbers. Even so, while the struggle for mastery over Europe appeared to have ended, the struggle to build a Europe in which all its peoples could feel 'at home' – while keeping certain rooms for family-only use – would be unlikely ever to end.

Epilogue

It would be rash to suppose that a study of some two and a quarter centuries in the relationship between 'Britain' and 'Europe' points inexorably towards a single conclusion about its 'essential' character. In any case, as has been repeatedly stressed in successive chapters of this book, neither 'Britain' nor 'Europe' has remained static. The history considered here has not been the unfolding, decade after decade, century after century, of the same set of enmities and amities. For more than half the period under review, in any case, 'Britain' was a United Kingdom of Great Britain and Ireland, a state that, ultimately, proved a failure and ended in violence. The relationship between the two parts of the island of Ireland and between both of them and 'Great Britain' remains an enduring conundrum in the twenty-first century. That failure may be readily admitted, but, even so, in the period under review 'Great Britain' can plausibly be presented as a 'successful' state, able, by accident or design, to combine diversity and unity. That balance has admittedly been more stable at certain junctures than others, and has tilted first one way and then the other. It has been a state that has maintained its territorial integrity and has not been conquered, annexed or partitioned. For most of the period under review it has also been an imperial state. Even if 'Greater Britain' proved a fantasy, 'Little Britains' were established across the world and still, in some sense, betray their origins. The language that had its origin in these islands has become the language of inter-continental communication in the twenty-first century. These features and facets of British history, whether welcomed, deplored or simply accepted as the dowry from the past, have combined to produce its particular and perhaps peculiar flavour. The 'grand narrative' that has undergirded the 'island story' has not, in this period, had to find a place for cataclysmic catastrophe, paralysing self-doubt or bitter civil war. That is not to claim, however, that the 'national past' as it has been represented by historians, politicians and 'the media', and referred to in this book, has in fact been uncontested. The central myths of British history have not been 'owned' equally by all sections of the community at all times. The 'success', too, has not been without periods of acute anxiety, whether in the Napoleonic Wars or in the two world wars of the twentieth century, not to mention periods in both the nineteenth and twentieth centuries when Britain seemed in congenital 'decline'. The predominant tone, however, as evidenced in this book, has been one of national self-satisfaction, sometimes of smugness.

It would be a mistake to suppose that such attributes and experiences have given Britain a 'special path' of such extraordinary individuality that it is thereby 'extra-European'. It is only by endowing the 'Europe' considered in this book with an internal coherence and common path of development that such a claim can even be made. It has been the underlying argument in these chapters, however, that there has been no such European 'template' but rather a set of paths that all have both 'special' and 'common' features. The travellers, at various times in their interacting journey have absorbed and copied, rejected and spurned. 'Europe' has been as protean an entity as 'Britain'. In the period under review, different nations and different states have sought to 'lead' if not to 'master' the destiny that should be Europe's. They have invariably come to it with their own individual senses of place. The pattern of interaction has largely been determined by geography. In these pages, it has been France and 'the French' or Germany and 'the Germans' that have at different times constituted 'the enemy' and that seemed likely, from a British perspective, to create a Europe in their own image. The British relationship with Russia/the Soviet Union and with the Ottoman Empire/Turkey has also, at particular points, loomed large. It has been a deliberate decision in this book, however, to present Britain's 'European encounters' as more than the story of the relationship between 'the Great Powers', while granting that it has been the Great Powers (and Britain as one of them) that have decided the fate of the continent at particular junctures. British encounters with less powerful 'Others', from Iberia to the Baltic and from Scandinavia to the Balkans, have also played their part in creating 'Britain's Europe'.

The 'European dialogue' encountered in this book, however, even when it has been a dialogue of the deaf, has operated within a context of memory and place that all those engaged in it could refer back to for support, encouragement or solidarity. Such remembrances still echo into the present, but both 'Britain' and 'Europe' now exist in a world in which the stock of their pasts cannot easily cope with the reality of the present. 'Identities' once firm now seem fluid and less clear-cut in the world of population transfer and instant communication across boundaries and borders. 'The sea' no longer has the place in British consciousness it still had in 1945, but the year 2005, the two-hundredth anniversary of the Battle of Trafalgar, is designated 'Year of the Sea'. Even as all such past intra-European encounters echo into the present, however, so they recall a Europe that is no more.

Notes

Chapter 1

1. Charles E. McClelland, *The German Historians and England: A Study in Nineteenth-Century Views* (Cambridge, 1971), p. 13.
2. Fania Oz-Salzberger, 'Adam Ferguson's Histories in Germany', in Benedikt Stuchtey and Peter Wende (eds), *British and German Historiography 1750–1950* (Oxford, 2000), p. 53.
3. N. Campbell and R.M.S. Smellie, *The Royal Society of Edinburgh (1783–1983)* (Edinburgh, 1983), p. 7.
4. The observation is cited in Paul Langford, *Englishmen Identified: Manners and Character 1650–1850* (Oxford, 2000), p. 76.
5. Prys Morgan writes that, 'In the eighteenth century London was without doubt the cultural capital of Wales, there alone was congregated a large moneyed and leisured middle class'. P.T.J. Morgan, *Iolo Morganwg* (Cardiff, 1975), p. 7. Morganwg himself never visited Europe.
6. Emrys Jones (ed.), *The Welsh in London, 1500–2000* (Cardiff, 2001), p. 77.
7. David Williams, *Cymru ac America/Wales and America* (Cardiff, 1946), p. 39. The date of this publication is significant. It was desirable to point up the significance of a Welsh-American community of perhaps a quarter of a million.
8. R.J.W. Evans, *Wales in European Context: Some Historical Reflections* (Aberystwyth, 2001), p. 9.
9. Norman Davies, *The Isles* (London, 1999); Richard S. Tompson, *The Atlantic Archipelago: A Political History of the British Isles* (Lewiston/Queenston, 1986).
10. S.J. Connolly, *Religion, Law and Power: The Making of Protestant Ireland 1660–1760* (Oxford, 1992), p. 314.
11. In discussing these years, R.F. Foster argues that it is 'the British connection that should be stressed'. R.F. Foster, *Modern Ireland 1600–1792* (London, 1989), pp. 251–2.
12. T. Barnard, 'Integration or Separation? Hospitality and Display in Protestant Ireland, 1660–1800', in Laurence Brockliss and David Eastwood (eds), *A Union of Multiple Identities: The British Isles c.1750–c.1850* (Manchester, 1997), pp. 127–46.
13. H. Schulze, *States, Nations and Nationalism: From the Middle Ages to the Present* (Oxford, 1996), pp. 124–5.
14. E. Evans, 'National Consciousness? The Ambivalence of English Identity in the Eighteenth Century', in C. Bjørn, A. Grant and K.J. Stringer (eds), *Nations, Nationalism and Patriotism in the European Past* (Copenhagen, 1994), p. 160.
15. Norman Davies, *Europe: A History* (Oxford, 1996), pp. viii–ix.
16. Geoffrey Treasure, *The Making of Modern Europe 1648–1780* (London, 1985), pp. xv–xvi.
17. William Doyle, *The Old European Order 1660–1800* (Oxford, 1978).

18. Thomas Munck, *The Enlightenment: A Comparative Social History 1721–1794* (London, 2000), pp. viii–ix.
19. Hagen Schulze, *Phoenix Europa: Die Moderne. Von 1740 bis Heute* (Berlin, 1998); see also his rich collection (with Ina Ulrike Paul) of texts on various themes from across Europe *Europäische Geschichte: Quellen und Materialen* (Munich, 1994). I was the British member of a small team of European historians whose task, in working with Jean-Baptiste Duroselle, was to endeavour to weed out Francocentrism (or any other -centrism) in the book that appeared in English as *Europe: A History of its Peoples* (London, 1990).
20. Davies, *Europe*, p. 35.
21. For further discussion, see Keith Robbins, 'National Identity and History: Past, Present and Future', reprinted in his *History, Religion and Identity in Modern Britain* (London, 1993), pp. 27–44.
22. D.B. Horn, *The British Diplomatic Service, 1689–1789* (Oxford, 1961) remains the standard account of its development.
23. Derek McKay and Hamish Scott, *The Rise of the Great Powers 1648–1815* (London, 1983), p. 202.
24. Roy Porter, *Enlightenment: Britain and the Creation of the Modern World* (London, 2000) sets out to rebut a Francocentric view of 'Enlightenment'.
25. W.R. Ward, *The Protestant Evangelical Awakening* (Cambridge, 1992).
26. Robin Eagles, 'Beguiled by France? The English Aristocracy, 1748–1848', in Brockliss and Eastwood (eds), *A Union of Multiple Identities*, pp. 60–1.
27. McClelland, *German Historians*, p. 12.
28. Jeremy Black, *The British Abroad: The Grand Tour in the Eighteenth Century* (Stroud, 1992), p. 139. Black's book provides much more information on the routes followed by British travellers.
29. Frances Acomb, *Anglophobia in France, 1763–1789* (Durham, NC, 1950).
30. McClelland, *German Historians*, citing Robert Elsasser, *Über die politischen Bildungsreisen der Deutschen nach England* (Heidelberg, 1917).
31. James Bradley, *Religion, Revolution and English Radicalism: Non-Conformity in Eighteenth-Century Politics and Society* (Cambridge, 1990), p. 410, argues that the unity the dissenters demonstrated on behalf of 'pro-Americanism' is striking.
32. Both quotations are cited in Michael Duffy, *The Younger Pitt* (London, 2000), p. 166.

Chapter 2

1. Cited by Mark Philp in Iain McCalman, *An Oxford Companion to the Romantic Age: British Culture 1776–1832* (Oxford, 1999).
2. Joseph Priestley, *Works*, 15, pp. 403–4.
3. R.R. Palmer, *The Age of the Democratic Revolution: A Political History of Europe and America, 1760–1800*, 2 vols (Princeton, 1959–64).
4. Simon Schama, *Patriots and Liberators: Revolution in the Netherlands, 1780–1813* (New York, 1977).
5. Simon Dixon, *The Modernisation of Russia 1676–1825* (Cambridge, 1999), p. 161.
6. It has been pointed out, however, that the encouragement of a creative literature in local vernaculars was, in part at least, designed to limit cultural dependence on the French. The Swedish Academy, for example, was founded in 1786. T. Munck, *The Enlightenment: A Comparative Social History 1721–1794* (London, 2000), p. 201.
7. David Bindman, *The Shadow of the Guillotine: Britain and the French Revolution* (London, 1989) – a volume compiled to accompany an exhibition in the British Museum.
8. René Pillorget, 'The Cultural Programmes of the 1789 Revolution', *History* Vol. 70 No. 230, October, 1985, p. 396.
9. Marie Peters, *The Elder Pitt* (London, 1998), p. 114.
10. Peters, *Elder Pitt*, p. 246.
11. Oscar Browning (ed.), *The Despatches of Earl Gower, English Ambassador at Paris, from June 1790 to August 1792* (Cambridge, 1885), ii, p. 243.
12. L. Colley, *Britons*, pp. 207–14.

13. J. Steven Watson, *The Reign of George III* (Oxford, 1960), p. 72.

14. Fortescue (ed.), *Letters of George III*, vi, p. 183, 11 December 1782.

15. This duality was, of course, not without its complications. It did mean that, on occasion, the king could bypass Parliament and pursue an independent foreign policy. T.C.W. Blanning, '"That Horrid Electorate" or "Ma Patrie Germanique"? George III, Hanover, and the Fürstenbund of 1785', *Historical Journal* Vol. 20 No. 2 (1977), pp. 311–44.

16. Stanley Ayling, *George the Third* (London, 1972), p. 205.

17. The debate can be followed, among others, in the following works: I.R. Christie, *Stress and Stability in Late Eighteenth Century Britain: Reflections on the Avoidance of Revolution* (Oxford, 1982); C. Emsley, *British Society and the French Wars 1783–1815* (London, 1979): C. Jones (ed.), *Britain and Revolutionary France: Conflict, Subversion and Propaganda* (Exeter, 1983); A. Goodwin, *The Friends of Liberty: The English Democratic Movement and the French Revolution* (London, 1979); G.A. Williams, *Artisans and Sans-Culottes: Popular Movements in England and France during the French Revolution* (London, 1968); H.T. Dickinson, *British Radicalism and the French Revolution 1785–1815* (Oxford, 1985); C. Worsley and I. Smith (eds), *The French Revolution and British Culture* (Oxford, 1989); Edward Royle, *Revolutionary Britannia: Reflections on the Threat of Revolution in Britain, 1789–1848* (Manchester, 2000).

18. Philp in Mark Philp (ed.), *The French Revolution and British Popular Politics* (Cambridge, 1991), p. 5.

19. Cited in David V. Erdman, *Commerce des Lumières: James Oswald and the British in Paris, 1790–1793* (Columbia, 1986), p. 104.

20. F.H. Hinsley, *Power and the Pursuit of Peace* (Cambridge, 1963), p. 177.

21. D. Hay, *Europe: The Emergence of an Idea* (Edinburgh, 1957), p. 123.

22. Norman Davies, '"The Languor of so Remote an Interest": British Attitudes to Poland, 1772–1832', *Oxford Slavonic Papers* 16 (1983), pp. 79-90.

23. See the introductory discussion in M. Ceadel, *The Origins of War Prevention: The British Peace Movement and International Relations, 1730–1854* (Oxford, 1996), pp. 4–14.

24. Cited in Ceadel, *Origins of War Prevention*, pp. 169–73.

25. T.C.W. Blanning, *The Origins of the French Revolutionary Wars* (London, 1986).

26. Jupp, *Grenville*, pp. 14–15, 298–9.

27. Jennifer Mori, *William Pitt and the French Revolution 1785–1795* (Keele, 1997), p. 109.

28. Jupp, *Grenville*, p. 147.

29. Michael Duffy, *The Englishman and the Foreigner* (Cambridge, 1986), pp. 284–8.

30. Paul W. Schroeder, *The Transformation of European Politics 1763–1848* (Oxford, 1996), p. 115.

31. J. Black, *A System of Ambition? British Foreign Policy 1660–1793* (London, 1991) and *British Foreign Policy in an Age of Revolutions* (Cambridge, 1994).

32. Cited in Emma Vincent, '"The Real Grounds of the Present War": John Bowles and the French Revolutionary Wars, 1792–1802', *History* Vol. 78 No. 254 (October 1993), p. 400.

33. Cited in Michael Howard, *War in European History* (Oxford, 1976), p. 88.

34. Geoffrey Best, *War and Society in Revolutionary Europe, 1770–1870* (London, 1982).

35. Howard, *War in European History*, p. 89.

36. David Geggus, 'The Anglo-French Conflict in the Caribbean in the 1790s', in C. Jones (ed.), *Britain and Revolutionary France*, pp. 27–39; Michael Duffy, *Soldiers, Sugar and Seapower: The British Expeditions to the West Indies and the War against Revolutionary France* (London, 1987).

37. J. Black, *Natural and Necessary Enemies: Anglo-French Relations in the Eighteenth Century* (London, 1986).

38. R.W. Seton-Watson, *Britain in Europe, 1789–1914* (Cambridge, 1937), p. 13.

39. Schroeder, *Transformation of European Politics*, p. 115.

40. Cited by Jeremy Black in his essay 'Gibbon and International Relations', in R. McKitterick and R. Quinault (eds), *Edward Gibbon and Empire* (Cambridge, 1997), p. 229.

41. Schroeder, *Transformation*, p. 194.

42. Black in McKitterick and Quinault, *Edward Gibbon and Empire*, pp. 236–7.

43. J. Black, *Maps and History: Constructing Images of the Past* (New Haven and London, 1997), pp. 25–6.

44. Norman Davies, *The Isles: A History* (London, 1999), pp. 778–81.

45. Black, *Maps and Politics*, pp. 126–9.

46. Nicholas Hope, 'Johann Gottfried Herder: the Lutheran Clergyman', in Keith Robbins (ed.), *Protestant Evangelicalism: Britain, Ireland, Germany and America c.1750–c.1950* (Oxford, 1990), p. 132.

47. Hagen Schulze, *States, Nations and Nationalism: From the Middle Ages to the Present* (Oxford, 1996), pp. 155–60.

48. Marianne Elliott, *Partners in Revolution: The United Irishmen and France* (New Haven, 1982).

49. R.F. Foster, *Modern Ireland, 1600–1972* (Harmondsworth, 1989), p. 269.

50. Nicholas Canny, 'Irish Resistance to Empire?', in Lawrence Stone (ed.), *An Imperial State at War: Britain from 1689 to 1815* (London and New York, 1994), p. 314.

51. T. Devine, *Scotland's Empire, 1600–1815* (London, 2003).

52. Prys Morgan, *Iolo Morganwg* (Cardiff, 1975), p. 39.

53. David Thomas and Prys Morgan, *Wales: The Shaping of a Nation* (Newton Abbot, 1984), p. 186.

54. Sabine Volk-Birke, 'Shakespeare in Germany in the 19th Century', in F. Bosbach, W. Filmer-Sankey and H. Hiery, *Prince Albert and the Development of Education in England and Germany in the 19th Century* (Munich, 2000), pp. 199–201.

55. Marcia Pointon, 'Shakespeare, Portraiture and National Identity', *Shakespeare Jahrbuch* Band 133/197, pp. 38–9; M. Dobson, *The Making of a National Poet: Shakespeare, Adaptation and Authorship 1660–1769* (Oxford, 1992).

56. Cited in A. Hastings, *The Construction of Nationhood: Ethnicity, Religion and Nationalism* (Cambridge, 1997), pp. 104–5.

57. Rosemary Ashton, *The German Idea: Four English Writers and the Reception of German Thought 1800–1860* (Cambridge, 1980), pp. 9, 31.

Chapter 3

1. Nigel Aston, *Religion and Revolution in France 1780–1804* (London, 2000), pp. 336–8.

2. Martyn Lyons, *Napoleon and the Legacy of the French Revolution* (London, 1994), pp. 82–7.

3. Philip G. Dwyer, *Talleyrand* (London, 2002), pp. 96–7.

4. Lyons, *Napoleon and the Legacy*, p. 178.

5. Cited in Geoffrey Ellis, *Napoleon* (London, 1997), p. 171.

6. F.J. Maccunn, *The Contemporary English View of Napoleon* (London, 1914) still has valuable material, but Stuart Semmel, *Napoleon and the British* (London, 2004) has a wider canvas.

7. Michael Duffy, *The Englishman and the Foreigner* (Cambridge, 1986), pp. 318–19.

8. See the discussion of these matters in Ellis, *Napoleon*, pp. 208–12.

9. Cited in Clive Emsley, *British Society in the French Wars 1793–1815* (London and Basingstoke, 1979), p. 135.

10. William Hazlitt, *The Life of Napoleon* (London, 1830).

11. Linda Colley, *Britons: Forging the Nation 1707–1837* (London, 1992), p. 408 n. 70.

12. Colley, *Britons*, pp. 306–10; See also the observations of E.P. Thompson in his essay 'Which Britons?', in *Persons and Polemics* (London, 1994).

13. Philip Ziegler, *Addington* (London, 1965), pp. 200–1.

14. Lawrence Stone observes that volunteers and militiamen were loyal, notwithstanding fears that they might turn their weapons on their betters, but highlights the number of middle-class men who bought themselves out of the militia – an indication, he thinks, of 'widespread lack of nationalist zeal among the middling sort'. He is commenting (p. 25) on Linda Colley's contribution (pp. 165–84) in L. Stone (ed.), *An Imperial State at War: Britain from 1689 to 1815* (London, 1994).

15. One such was Lord Grenville. Peter Jupp, *Lord Grenville 1759–1834* (Oxford, 1985), p. 310.

16. Cited in Seton-Watson, *Britain in Europe*, p. 19.

17.   C. Northcote Parkinson, *Britannia Rules: The Classic Age of Naval History 1793–1815* (Stroud, 1994 edn), p. 88.

18.   Cited and commented on in John Clarke, *British Diplomacy and Foreign Policy, 1782–1865: The National Interest* (London, 1989), p. 109.

19.   Ziegler, *Addington*, pp. 142–3.

20.   A.D. Harvey, *Britain in the Early Nineteenth Century* (London, 1978), p. 304.

21.   P.J. Cain and A.G. Hopkins, *British Imperialism: Innovation and Expansion 1688–1914* (London, 1993), p. 64.

22.   Eric Robinson, 'The Transference of British Technology to Russia', in B.M. Ratcliffe (ed.), *Great Britain and her World, 1750–1914: Essays in Honour of W.O. Henderson* (Manchester, 1975), p. 3.

23.   P.N. Stearns, 'Britain and the Spread of the Industrial Revolution', in C.J. Bartlett (ed.), *Britain Pre-Eminent: Studies in British World Influence in the Nineteenth Century* (London, 1969), pp. 12, 20.

24.   Jerome Blum, *The End of the Old Order in Rural Europe* (Princeton, 1978), p. 3.

25.   In 'Society and the Economy in the Eighteenth Century', Sir Tony Wrigley summarizes a lifetime's reflections on these matters. Stone (ed.), *An Imperial State*, pp. 72–91.

26.   T.M. Devine, *The Scottish Nation 1700–2000* (London, 1991), p. 106ff.

27.   P. Schroeder, *Transformation of European Politics*, pp. 392–3.

28.   Dwyer, *Talleyrand*, pp. 98–9.

29.   S. Woolf, *Napoleon's Integration of Europe* (London, 1991); G. Ellis, *The Napoleonic Empire* (Basingstoke and London, 1991); Philip G. Dwyer (ed.), *Napoleon and Europe* (London, 2001).

30.   S. Woolf, 'French Civilization and Ethnicity in the Napoleonic Empire', *Past & Present* No. 124 (August 1989) and 'The Construction of a European World-View in the Revolutionary-Napoleonic Years', *Past & Present* No. 136 (November 1992).

31.   A. Franklin and M. Philp, *Napoleon and the Invasion of Britain* (Oxford, 2003).

32.   Frank McLynn, *Invasion: From the Armada to Hitler, 1588–1945* (London, 1987), p. 112; R. Glover, *Britain at Bay* (London, 1973), pp. 77–102 gives a more detailed assessment of the 'Boulogne Flotilla'; Holland Rose's 'Did Napoleon Intend to Invade England?' in his *Pitt and Napoleon: Essays and Letters* (London, 1912), pp. 114–46 remains a classic essay. Two years later, in 1914, lecturing in Cambridge on the origins of the war that had just broken out, a war that might, in turn, lead to another invasion, Holland Rose condemned the apparent German need to 'hack their way through'. He recognized, however, that 'behind the lust of conquest there was an elemental force impelling the German people forward'. He hoped, therefore, that 'the fiat of mankind' would go forth that the Germans 'shall acquire, if need be, parts of Asia Minor, Mesopotamia, and South Brazil'. J. Holland Rose, *The Origins of the War* (Cambridge, 1914), p. 188. He does not seem to have believed that 'the fiat of mankind' should have been extended, in a comparably generous manner, to the elemental force that was Napoleon.

33.   Christopher D. Hall, *British Strategy in the Napoleonic War: 1803–15* (Manchester, 1992), pp. 5–6; John R. Elting, *Swords around the Throne: Napoleon's Grande Armée* (London, 1988), pp. 59–60.

34.   D. Winterbottom, *Henry Newbolt and the Spirit of Clifton* (Bristol, 1986), pp. 42–5, 57–8.

35.   Keith Robbins, *Sir Edward Grey* (London, 1971), p. 131.

36.   Hall, *British Strategy*, pp. 124–6.

37.   Janet M. Hartley, *Alexander I* (London, 1994), p. 60.

38.   This conclusion, reached by Dr Blanchard, is cited and discussed by Simon Dixon, *The Modernisation of Russia 1676–1825* (Cambridge, 1999), pp. 236–7.

39.   Cited in Vera Tolz, *Russia* (London, 2001), p. 75.

40.   H.H. Kaplan, *Russian Overseas Commerce with Great Britain during the Reign of Catherine II* (Philadelphia, 1995).

41.   Hartley, *Alexander*, p. 62.

42.   The text is printed in James Joll (ed.), *Britain and Europe: Pitt to Churchill 1793–1940* (London, 1967), pp. 48–50.

43.   Schroeder, *Transformation of European Politics*, p. 262 (and the discussion in surrounding pages).

44.   Schroeder, *Transformation of European Politics*, p. 297.

45.   Cited in Holland Rose, *Pitt and Napoleon*, p. 308.

46. Hall, *British Strategy*, p. 13.
47. Hall, *British Strategy*, p. 126.
48. Schroeder, *Transformation of European Politics*, p. 298.
49. W. Hinde, *George Canning* (London, 1975), pp. 21–2.
50. Schroeder, *Transformation of European Politics*, p. 384.
51. H.A. Winkler, *The Long Shadow of the Reich: Weighing Up German History* (London, 2002), p. 7.
52. James Bryce, *The Holy Roman Empire* (Oxford, 1864). It was a book (originally an Oxford Prize Essay) that laid the foundations of his distinguished career. Its impact can be judged by the fact that in a much-expanded version it reached an eighth edition in 1886. Thomas Kleinknecht, *Imperiale und internationale Ordnung: Eine Untersuchung zum anglo-amerikanischen Gelehrtenliberalismus am Beispiel von James Bryce (1838–1922)* (Göttingen, 1985).
53. Lyons, *Napoleon Bonaparte*, p. 275.
54. Schroeder, however, argues that 'the Continental System at its heart was a grandiose attempt to force economic behaviour to follow other than economic rules', *Transformation of European Politics*, p. 391.
55. Lyons, *Napoleon Bonaparte*, pp. 266–8.
56. Ellis, *Napoleon*, pp. 104–12.
57. Hinde, *Canning*, p. 186.
58. Glover, *Britain at Bay*, p. 147.
59. [Robert Southey] *Letters from England: by Don Manuel Alvarez Espriella. Translated from the Spanish* (London, 1807).
60. John W. Derry, *Castlereagh* (London, 1976), p. 118; Hinde, *Canning*, pp. 195–6.
61. A. Roberts, *Napoleon and Wellington* (London, 2001) charts and reflects on the views the two commanders held about one another.
62. Iain Pears, 'The Gentleman and the Hero: Wellington and Napoleon in the Nineteenth Century', in Roy Porter (ed.), *Myths of the English* (Oxford, 1992), pp. 216–36; P. Jupp, *The First Duke of Wellington in an Irish Context* (Southampton, 1997); quotation cited in A. Murdoch, *British History 1660–1832: National Identity and Local Culture* (London, 1998), p. 131.
63. Lyons, *Napoleon Bonaparte*, p. 245.
64. Charles Esdaile, *The Peninsular War* (London, 2002) is the best recent account.
65. Alberto Gil Novales, *The Image of Wellington and Britain in Spain after 1815* (Southampton, 1991).
66. William Bradford, *Sketches of the Country Character and Costume in Portugal and Spain made During the Campaign and on the Route of the British Army in 1808 and 1809* (London, 1809). Bradford's observations are in Lady Londonderry and H.M. Hyde (eds), *More Letters from Martha Wilmot: Impressions of Vienna, 1819–1829* (London, 1935), pp. xxvii–xxix.
67. Edited and introduced by Jack Simmons, *Robert Southey's Letters from England* (London, 1951), p. xiv.
68. M.J. Thornton, *Napoleon after Waterloo: England and the St Helena Decision* (Stanford, 1968).
69. Emsley, *British Society and the French Wars*, p. 177.
70. Some 200 years later, Marianne Elliott's *Robert Emmet: The Making of a Myth* (London, 2003) is an exemplary examination.
71. C. Bayly, *Imperial Meridian: The British Empire and the World, 1780–1830* (London, 1989), p. 127.
72. H.M. Hyde, *The Rise of Castlereagh* (London, 1933) gives a sympathetic account of his career in Ireland.

Chapter 4

1. David Gates, *Napoleonic Wars* (London, 1997).
2. Cited and discussed in S. Avineri, *Hegel's Theory of the Modern State* (Cambridge, 1972), pp. 196–7.

3. P.G. Dwyer, *Talleyrand* (London, 2002), p. 146.

4. D.R. Watson, 'The British Parliamentary System and the Growth of Constitutional Government in Western Europe', in C.J. Bartlett (ed.), *Britain Pre-Eminent: Studies in British World Influence in the Nineteenth Century* (London, 1969), pp. 106–7.

5. Cited in D. Armitage, 'The British Conception of Empire in the Eighteenth Century', in F. Bosbach and H. Hiery with C. Kampmann, *Imperium/Empire/Reich* (Munich, 1999), p. 98.

6. David Fitzpatrick, 'Ireland and the Empire', in A. Porter (ed.), *The Oxford History of the British Empire: The Nineteenth Century* (Oxford, 1999), p. 495.

7. Thomas O'Connor (ed.), *The Irish in Europe 1580–1815* (Dublin, 2001).

8. The Scottish case is examined in Charles W.J. Withers, *Urban Highlanders: Highland–Lowland Migration and Urban Gaelic Culture 1700–1900* (Edinburgh, 1998); another 'split' is examined in Krisztina Fenyo, *Contempt, Sympathy and Romance: Lowland Perceptions of the Highlands and the Clearances during the Famine Years, 1845–1855* (Edinburgh, 2000).

9. But, as Colin Kidd notes, despite his public image as a maker of national myths, Scott subscribed to the 'Anglo-British', interpretation of the history of liberty. C. Kidd, *Subverting Scotland's Past: Scottish Whig Historians and the Creation of an Anglo-British Identity, 1689–c.1830* (Cambridge, 1993), p. 270: Scott's trip produced a series of letters home, *Paul's Letters to his Kinsfolk* (London/Edinburgh, 1816), which were thinly disguised autobiography.

10. The college was, George thought, a 'most laudable effort'. Keith Robbins and John Morgan-Guy (eds), *A Bold Imagining: The University of Wales, Lampeter: Glimpses of an Unfolding Vision, 1827–2002* (Lampeter, 2002); R.J.W. Evans 'Was there a Welsh Enlightenment?', in R.R. Davies and Geraint H. Jenkins, *From Medieval to Modern Wales: Historical Essays in Honour of Kenneth O. Morgan and Ralph A. Griffiths* (Cardiff, 2004), pp. 142–59. We are, however, largely speaking of parallels (and divergencies) rather than contacts.

11. Cited in Anna Agnarsdóttir, 'Sir Joseph Banks and the Exploration of Iceland', in R.E.R. Banks *et al.* (eds), *Sir Joseph Banks: A Global Perspective* (Kew, 1994), p. 42. It was an island, however, that attracted literary Englishmen, in both subsequent centuries (William Morris in the early 1870s and W.H. Auden in the mid-1930s). Iceland kept its distance (under Denmark) both from Britain and Europe – G. Karlsson, *Iceland's 1100 Years: The History of a Marginal Society* (London, 2001).

12. G.W.F. Hegel, *Lectures on the Philosophy of World History: Introduction: Reason in History*, translated from the German edition of Johannes Hoffmeister by H.B. Nisbet (Cambridge, 1975), pp. 16, 102–3, 160–1. The superiority of maritime powers over land-based powers is a theme developed by Peter Padfield, *Maritime Supremacy and the Opening of the Western Mind* (London, 1999).

13. Geoffrey Jones, *Merchants to Multinationals: British Trading Companies in the Nineteenth and Twentieth Centuries* (London, 2002).

14. There was a ready readership for accounts of naval heroism, whether published or unpublished. See Dean King and John B. Hattendorf, *Every Man Will Do His Duty: An Anthology of First Hand Accounts from the Age of Nelson, 1793–1815* (London, 1997). The novels of C.S. Forester and Patrick O'Brian brought this era back to life in the twentieth century.

15. Henry Kissinger uses this term in his otherwise perceptive comments on 'The Insular Statesman', in his *The World Restored* (London, 1977 edn), p. 29.

16. J.E. Cookson, *Lord Liverpool's Administration: The Crucial Years, 1815–1822* (Edinburgh and London, 1975), p. 15.

17. Joll, *Britain and Europe*, pp. 54–6.

18. Earlier, in his *Campaigns in Poland in the years 1806 and 1807* (London, 1810), Wilson had provided an eye-witness scrutiny of the Russian army's composition and strategies.

19. M.E. Chamberlain, *Lord Aberdeen* (London, 1983), p. 63.

20. Watson, 'The British Parliamentary System', pp. 114–15.

21. Chamberlain, *Aberdeen*, pp. 163, 167.

22. Over 100,000 French prisoners of war were held captive in Britain – the traditional prisoner exchange system between Britain and France having been abandoned. Gavin Daly, 'Napoleon's Lost Legions: French Prisoners of War in Britain, 1803–1814', *History* Vol. 89 No. 295 (July 2004), pp. 361–80.

23. E.H. Kossmann, *The Low Countries 1780–1940* (Oxford, 1978), pp. 110–13.

24. H. Schulze, *Germany: A New History* (London, 1998), p. 110.

25. Sabine Freitag and Peter Wende (eds), *British Envoys to Germany 1816–1866 Vol. 1: 1816–1829* (Cambridge, 2000), pp. ix–xvii.

26. In a letter of 9 April 1814, cited in Kissinger, *World Restored*, pp. 142–3.

27. Professor Peter Marshall used this term in relation to the British and Asia in the eighteenth century in his 1983 inaugural lecture at King's College, London.

28. Schroeder, *Transformation of European Politics*, p. 575.

29. Sir Charles Webster, *The Congress of Vienna* (London, 1934, 1963) and Sir Harold Nicolson, *The Congress of Vienna* (London, 1945) are now almost themselves period pieces but still provide useful accounts. D. Dakin, 'The Congress of Vienna, 1814–15, and its Antecedents', in Alan Sked (ed.), *Europe's Balance of Power* (London, 1979), is a more recent sketch.

30. Kissinger, *A World Restored*, p. 182.

31. Schroeder, *Transformation of European Politics*, p. 578.

32. Joll, *Britain and Europe*, pp. 60–8.

33. Claus Bjørn, 'From Danish Patriot to Patriotic Dane: C.D.F. Reventlow and the Development of Danishness in the Early Nineteenth Century', in C. Bjørn, Alexander Grant and Keith J. Stringer (eds), *Social and Political Identities in Western Europe* (Copenhagen, 1994), pp. 179–92.

34. Jens Rahbek Rasmussen, 'Patriotic Perceptions: Denmark and Sweden, 1450—1850', in C. Bjørn, Alexander Grant and Keith J. Stringer, *Nations, Nationalism and Patriotism in the European Past* (Copenhagen, 1994), p. 173.

35. N. Hope, *German and Scandinavian Protestantism 1700 to 1918* (Oxford, 1995), p. 196.

36. Torsten Gunnarsson, *Nordic Landscape Painting in the Nineteenth Century* (London and New Haven, 1998) illustrates the extent to which the magnificent wilderness of the northern countries was consciously contrasted with the urban cultures deemed characteristic of 'Europe'. Later in the century , ancient 'filial' ties between Britain and Norway were rediscovered. It was, however, the contrast rather than the similarity that increasingly struck the British as they struggled with their global destiny and the ramifications of urbanization and industrialization. See Peter Fjågesund and Ruth A. Symes, *The Northern Utopia: British Perceptions of Norway in the Nineteenth Century* (Amsterdam/New York, 2003); T.K. Derry, *A History of Scandinavia* (London, 1979) and *A History of Modern Norway 1814–1972* (Oxford, 1973).

37. B. Seebohm (ed.), *Memoirs of the Life and Gospel Labours of Stephen Grellet* (London, 1870), pp. 150–1.

38. The text is quoted in G.A. Kertesz (ed.), *Documents in the Political History of the European Continent 1815–1939* (Oxford, 1968), pp. 8–9.

39. Cited in Derry, *Castlereagh*, p. 187.

40. For example by H.W.V. Temperley and C.K. Webster, 'The Congress of Vienna 1814–15 and the Conference of Paris 1919', in W.N. Medlicott (ed.), *From Metternich to Hitler: Aspects of British and Foreign History 1814–1939* (London, 1963), p. 15.

41. Hinsley, *Power and the Pursuit of Peace* (Cambridge, 1963), p. 196.

42. Schroeder, *Transformation of European Politics*, p. 577.

43. W.R. Ward, *The Protestant Evangelical Awakening* (Cambridge, 1992).

44. Hope, *German and Scandinavian Protestantism*, pp. 356, 364.

45. Owen Chadwick, *The Popes and European Revolution* (Oxford, 1981).

46. Joll, *Britain and Europe*, pp. 57–9. Similarly, although the House of Commons did accept the treaties in February 1816 (by 240 votes to 77), some speakers expressed alarm at the extent to which, having overthrown one military despot, Britain was now apparently aligning itself with three others.

47. Derry, *Castlereagh*, p. 198.

48. The 'State Paper' of 5 May 1820 is reproduced in Joll, *Britain and Europe*, pp. 69–82.

49. Citations in Carsten Holbraad, *The Concert of Europe* (London, 1970), pp. 126–30.

50. Cited in Hartley, *Alexander I*, p. 157.

51. Maria Todorovna, *Imagining the Balkans* (New York, 1997) naturally discusses the perceptions of the region in more detail than is possible in this brief summary.

52. Richard Clogg, *A Concise History of Greece* (Cambridge, 1992) provides a guide to these questions.

53. Sydney Checkland, *The Elgins 1766–1917* (Aberdeen, 1988), pp. 47–94.
54. Gallant, *Experiencing Dominion*, p. 18. During a later period of occupation (1945–47), the British were perceived by the islanders as lacking in human qualities, just another enemy occupying force. Nicholas Doumanis, *Myth and Memory in the Mediterranean: Remembering Fascism and Empire* (London, 1997), p. 195.
55. Fiona McCarthy, *Byron: Life and Legend* (London, 2000).
56. Charles A. Frazee, *Catholics and Sultans: The Church and the Ottoman Empire, 1453–1923* (Cambridge, 1983), p. 249.
57. Sir Richard Church, although of Irish Quaker stock, was one of the most conspicuous of these men. E.M. Church, *Chapters in an Adventurous Life in Italy and Greece* (Edinburgh and London, 1885).
58. John Rosselli, *Lord William Bentinck and the British Occupation of Sicily, 1811–14* (Cambridge, 1956).
59. S. and R. Percy, *The Percy Histories and Interesting Memorial on the Rise, Progress and Present State of all the Capitals of Europe* (London, 1823), cited in D. Arnold, *The Duke of Wellington and London* (Southampton, 2002), p. 12. I am indebted to Professor Arnold for material in these two paragraphs.
60. Yvonne Whelan, *Re-inventing Modern Dublin: Streetscape, Iconography and the Politics of Identity* (Dublin, 2003), pp. 44–51.
61. Cited in C. Hibbert, *George IV: Regent and King* (London, 1973), p. 268.
62. These comments, by Edouard de Montulé and Baron de Staël-Holstein respectively, are cited in Paul Langford, *Englishness Identified: Manners and Character 1650–1850* (Oxford, 2000), p. 6.
63. Charles E. McClelland, *The German Historians and England: A Study in Nineteenth-Century Views* (Cambridge, 1971), pp. 56–7: Hegel is cited in Shlomo Avineri, *Hegels's Theory of the Modern State*, p. 210; Hans-Christof Krause, 'Die deutsche Rezeption und Darstellung der englischen Verfassung im neunzehnten Jahrhundert', in R. Muhs, J. Paulmann and W. Steinmetz (eds), *Aneigung und Abwehr: Interkultureller Transfer zwischen Deutschland und Grossbritannien im 19 Jahrhundert* (Bodenheim, 1998).
64. J. Press, *Lord John Russell* (London, 1972), pp. 21–2.
65. Hegel, *Lectures on the Philosophy of World History*, pp. 166, 215.
66. A. Hennessy and J. King (eds), *The Land that England Lost: Argentina and Britain, a Special Relationship* (London, 1992).
67. Cited in W. Hinde, *George Canning* (London, 1973), p. 345.

Chapter 5

1. Recent studies of the 'inventing' of these nations include Nicholas Doumanis, *Italy* (London, 2001) and Stefan Berger, *Germany* (London, 2004). An older consideration of 1848 as a whole is P.N. Stearns, *The Revolutions of 1848* (London, 1974); R.J.W. Evans and Hartmut Pogge von Strandmann (eds), *The Revolutions in Europe 1848–1849: From Reform to Reaction* (Oxford, 2000) is a good recent collection of essays. There are many summary treatments in general texts, perhaps the most useful recent one being Robert Gildea, *Barricades and Borders: Europe 1800–1914* (Oxford, 1987), pp. 83–103. The place of 1848 within the study of nationalism can be approached through John Breuilly, *Nationalism and the State* (Manchester, 1985) and Peter Alter, *Nationalism* (London, 1989).
2. Leslie Mitchell, 'Britain's Reactions to the Revolutions', in Evans and Pogge von Strandmann (eds), *Revolutions in Europe*, pp. 83–98; I.M. Taylor, '1848 and the British Empire', *Past & Present* (February, 2000).
3. Mack Walker (ed.), *Metternich's Europe, 1813–1848* (New York, 1968) is only one of a number of authors to use such a term.
4. W. Roberts, *Prophet in Exile: Joseph Mazzini in England, 1837–1868* (New York, 1989).
5. Cited in Rosemary Ashton, *Little Germany: Exile and Asylum in Victorian Germany* (Oxford, 1986) p. 141; The general issues posed by the arrival of exiles are discussed in Bernard Porter, *The Refugee Question in Mid-Victorian Politics* (Cambridge, 1979).

6. Bolton King, *The Life of Mazzini* (London, 1911), pp. 73–99, 139–53. There were considerable numbers of 'foreigners' for whom, in time, Britain became their first country. Such 'accommodation' accorded with a notion that Britain was the 'land of sanctuary' for disaffected Europeans. Such 'transfers' made it increasingly important for states to try to define just who 'nationals' and 'foreigners' were. Andreas Fahrmeier, *Citizens and Aliens: Foreigners and the Law in Britain and the German States, 1789–1870* (New York, 2000); J.A. Garrard, *The English and Immigration, 1880–1910* (London, 1971); P. Panayi (ed.), *Germans in Britain since 1500* (London, 1996).
7. P. Morrell (ed.), *Leaves from the Greville Diary* (London, 1929), p. 572.
8. M.C.M. Simpson (ed.), *Correspondence and Conversations of Alexis de Tocqueville with Nassau Senior, 1834–59*, 2 vols (London, 1872), and M.C.M. Simpson (ed.), *Nassau Senior: Conversations with M. Thiers, M. Guizot etc*, 2 vols (London, 1878).
9. Fabrice Bensimon, *Les Britanniques face à la revolution française de 1848* (Paris, 2000). Earlier pieces include J.P.T. Bury, 'Great Britain and the Revolution of 1848', in Ferenc Fetjö, *Le Printemps des peuples* Vol. 1 (Paris, 1948), pp. 401–46; J.H. Grainger, 'The View from Britain II: The Moralizing Island', in E. Kamenka and F.B. Smith (eds), *Intellectuals and Revolution: Socialism and the Experience of 1848* (London, 1979); A.M. Birke, 'Die Revolution von 1848 und England', in his *Deutschland und Grossbritannien* (Munich, 1999), pp. 44–56.
10. Henry Weisser, *April 10: Challenge and Response in England in 1848* (London, 1983).
11. François Guizot, *Historical Essays and Lectures*, ed. Stanley Mellon (Chicago, 1972), pp. 246–8.
12. Ceri Crossley, 'History as a Principle of Legitimation in France (1820–48)', in Stefan Berger and Mark Donovan with Kevin Passmore, *Writing National Histories: Western Europe since 1800* (London, 1999), pp. 52–3.
13. Douglas Johnson, *Guizot: Aspects of French History 1787–1874* (London, 1964).
14. Donald Southgate, *The Most English Minister: The Policies and Politics of Palmerston* (London, 1966).
15. Leslie Mitchell, *Holland House* (London, 1980) shows how the wisdom offered by the Hollands was not confined to Spain, in his chapter 'The Hollands and Europe, 1789–1830', pp. 196–216.
16. Kenneth Bourne, *Palmerston: The Early Years, 1784–1841* (London, 1982).
17. K.H.D. Haley, *The British and the Dutch: Political and Cultural Relations through the Ages* (London, 1988) has comparatively little to say on the nineteenth century.
18. Kenneth Bourne (ed.), *The Letters of the Third Viscount Palmerston to Laurence and Elizabeth Sulivan 1804–1863* (London, 1979), pp. 128, 163, 289–90.
19. Patrick Bahners, 'Ranke's *History of the Popes*', in Benedikt Stuchtey and Peter Wende (eds), *British and German Historiography 1750–1950* (Oxford, 2000), pp. 123–57.
20. Cited in Holbraad, *Concert of Europe*, p. 140 n.
21. Jasper Ridley, *Lord Palmerston* (London, 1970), p. 148. Material in the preceding paragraph also owes much to Ridley's biography.
22. Muriel Chamberlain, *Lord Aberdeen* (London, 1983), p. 254.
23. A fact first noted by Professor Derek Beales. Boyd Hilton, 'The Gallows and Mr Peel', in T.C.W. Blanning and David Cannadine (eds), *History and Biography: Essays in Honour of Derek Beales* (Cambridge, 1996), p. 88.
24. Roland Quinault, 'The French Revolution of 1830 and Parliamentary Reform', *History* Vol. 79 No. 257 (October 1994), pp. 377–93 reviews previous writing on the subject and reaches this conclusion; Wolf D. Gruner, 'Grossbritannien und die Julirevolution von 1830: zwischen Legitimätsprinzip und nationalen Interesse', *Francia* 9 (1981), pp. 369–411.
25. Roger Magraw, *France 1815–1914: The Bourgeois Century* (London, 1983), pp. 68–9.
26. Cited in Roger Bullen, *Palmerston, Guizot and the Collapse of the Entente Cordiale* (London, 1974), p. 4.
27. P. Deloge, 'Petit pays et grandes puissances en Europe: le cas belgo-britannique, 1830–1950', *European Review of History* Vol. 10 No. 1 (Spring, 2003) is a useful summary.
28. A.D. Kriegel (ed.), *The Holland House Diaries 1831–1840* (London, 1977), p. 40.
29. Marian Kukiel, *Czartoryski and European Unity, 1770–1861* (Princeton, 1955); Lloyd S. Kramer, *Threshold of a New World: Intellectuals and the Exile Experience in Paris, 1830–1848* (Ithaca and London, 1998).

30. Peter Brock, 'Polish democrats and English radicals, 1832–1862: a chapter in the history of Anglo-Polish Relations', *Journal of Modern History* Vol. 25, No. 2 (June 1953), pp. 139–56.

31. J.H. Gleason, *The Genesis of Russophobia in Great Britain* (Cambridge, Mass., 1950), pp. 120–3.

32. Cited in H. Weisser, *British Working-Class Movements and Europe 1815–48* (Manchester, 1975), p. 51.

33. Cited in A.J.P. Taylor, *The Troublemakers: Dissent over Foreign Policy 1792–1939* (London, 1957), p. 43.

34. These matters are illuminatingly discussed in Bullen, *Palmerston, Guizot*, pp. 16–24.

35. P.J. Vatikiotis, *The History of Egypt from Muhammad Ali to Mubarak* (London, 1983), pp. 49–67.

36. Urquhart's extraordinary career is considered in Gertrude Robinson, *David Urquhart: Some Chapters in the Life of a Victorian Knight-Errant of Justice and Liberty* (Oxford, 1920).

37. Susan Chitty, *That Singular Person Called Lear: A Biography* (London, 1988), p. 106.

38. Tolz, *Russia*, pp. 80–4.

39. Chitty, *That Singular Person*, p. 170.

40. Donald Read, *Peel and the Victorians* (Oxford, 1987) considers the admiration for Peel in England.

41. Harry Hearder, *Cavour* (London, 1994), pp. 20–3.

42. Cited in Asa Briggs, 'Sir Robert Peel', in H. van Thal (ed.), *The Prime Ministers* I (London, 1974), p. 374.

43. The 'Spanish marriages' and related matters are dealt with in detail in Bullen, *Palmerston, Guizot*, pp. 282–92, and British–French relations at this time generally assessed on pp. 332–8. Aberdeen's approach can be seen through his biographer, Chamberlain, *Aberdeen*, pp. 297–388. Schroeder, *Transformation of European Politics*, p. 773, claims that a comparison of Britain's dealings with France over Spain and Russia's dealings with Austria and Prussia over Poland in 1846 demonstrated that 'the Russians understood how to manage their hegemonic sphere and preserve their leadership in it better than the British did'.

44. C.I. Hamilton, *Anglo-French Naval Rivalry, 1840–1870* (Oxford, 1993), pp. 18–22.

45. C.R. Middleton, *The Administration of British Foreign Policy, 1782–1846* (Durham, NC, 1977) provides a valuable appendix on the personnel of the Foreign Office.

46. Donald Read, *Press and People 1790–1850: Opinion in Three English Cities* (London, 1961), p. 68.

47. Mack Walker (ed.), *Metternich's Europe*, pp. 65–6.

48. Ivon Asquith, 'The Structure, Ownership and Control of the Press, 1780–1815', in G. Boyce, J. Curran and P. Wingate (eds), *Newspaper History from the 17th Century to the Present Day* (London, 1978).

49. Raymond Postgate and Aylmer Vallance, *Those Foreigners: The English People's Opinions on Foreign Affairs as Reflected in their Newspapers since Waterloo* (London, 1937).

50. David Brown, 'Compelling but not Controlling? Palmerston and the Press, 1846–1855', *History* Vol. 86 No. 281 (January 2001), pp. 41–61.

51. T. Morley, '"The Arcana of that Great Machine": Politicians and *The Times* in the Late 1840s', *History* Vol. 73 No. 237 (February 1988), pp. 38–54.

52. F.S.L. Lyons, *Internationalism in Europe, 1815–1914* (Leyden, 1963) is a general account of various manifestations of this 'internationalism'.

53. Piers Brendon, *Thomas Cook. 150 Years of Popular Tourism* (London, 1991).

54. Marjorie Morgan, *National Identities and Travel in Victorian Britain* (Basingstoke, 2001), pp. 14–16.

55. Thomas Pinney (ed.), *Selected Letters of Thomas Babington Macaulay* (Cambridge, 1982), pp. 198–9.

56. Alan Sillitoe, *Leading the Blind: A Century of Guidebook Travel 1815–1911* (Basingstoke, 1996), p. 10.

57. Messrs Jennings and Chaplin, for example, produced volumes of the *Landscape Annual*. Thomas Roscoe's *The Tourist in France* (London, 1834), p. vi, endeavoured to instruct 'on this noble and important portion of civilized Europe'.

58. Sillitoe, *Leading the Blind*, pp. 118–19.

59. Hugh Trevor-Roper (ed.), *Macaulay's Essays* (London, 1963), p. 275.
60. Benedikt Stuchtey, 'Literature, Liberty and Life of the Nation: British Historiography from Macaulay to Trevelyan', in Stefan Berger, Mark Donovan and Kevin Passmore (eds), *Writing National Histories: Western Europe since 1800* (London, 1999), pp. 30–3.
61. Its translation, which occurred in 1875, was the labour of eight historians from the infant Modern History Faculty at Oxford. Ranke, who endeavoured to write history as he found it, rather than to sustain any particular dogma, had visited archives across Europe. He married, in 1840, Clara Graves, a Protestant Irishwoman whom he had met in Paris.
62. Cited in Sillitoe, *Leading the Blind*, p. 3; Bernard Porter, '"Bureau and Barrack": Early Victorian Attitudes towards the Continent', *Victorian Studies* 27 (1984), pp. 407–33, and 'The Victorians and Europe', *History Today* 42 (January 1992), pp. 16–22.
63. Laurent Tissot, *Naissance d'une industrie touristique: Les Anglais et la Suisse au XIXe. siècle* (Lausanne, 2000).
64. Christophe Léribault, *Les Anglais à Paris* (Paris, 1994).
65. R.W. Jelf, *Sermons, Doctrinal and Practical Preached Abroad* (London, 1835), pp. xi–xii, 11.
66. Cited in B.I. Coleman (ed.), *The Idea of the City in Nineteenth-Century Britain* (London, 1973), p. 88; Tristram Hunt, *Building Jerusalem: The Rise and Fall of the Victorian City* (London, 2004) stresses the importance of Italian architecture and art as a model in the thinking of England's mercantile elite.
67. E.E. Lampard, 'The Urbanizing World', in H.J. Dyos and Michael Wolff (eds), *The Victorian City: Vol. 1* (London, 1976), p. 4.
68. P.J. Waller, *Town, City and Nation: England 1850–1914* (Oxford, 1983).
69. L.D. Bradshaw, *Visitors to Manchester* (Manchester, 1986).
70. Cited in Coleman, *Idea of the City*, pp. 106–7.
71. Or so Cooke Taylor reported in 1842, cited in Coleman, *Idea of the City*, p. 83.
72. Cited in Coleman, *Idea of the City*, p. 104.
73. A. Redford, *Manchester Merchants and Foreign Trade, 1794–1858* (Manchester, 1934), p. 199.
74. Asa Briggs, 'The Language of "Class"', in *The Collected Essays of Asa Briggs: Volume One: Words, Numbers, Places, People* (Brighton, 1985), pp. 3–33.
75. Cited in Weisser, *British Working-Class Movements*, pp. 54–6.
76. Alfred Plummer, *Bronterre: A Political Biography of Bronterre O'Brien, 1804–1864* (London, 1971).
77. A.R. Schoyen, *The Chartist Challenge: A Portrait of George Julian Harney* (London, 1958) is the standard life.
78. Margaret C.W. Wicks, *The Italian Exiles in London, 1816–48* (Manchester, 1937); Lucio Sponza, *Italian Immigrants in Nineteenth-Century Britain: Realities and Images* (Leicester, 1988).
79. Max Berger, *The British Traveller in America, 1836–60* (New York, 1943); Jane Louise Mesick, *The English Traveller in America: 1785–1835* (New York, 1922).
80. Cited and discussed in Christopher Mulvey, *Transatlantic Manners: Social Patterns in Nineteenth-Century Anglo-American Travel Literature* (Cambridge, 1990), pp. 118–19. The general issues discussed in this paragraph are considered more comprehensively in this book.
81. W. Hinde, *Richard Cobden: A Victorian Outsider* (London, 1987), p. 54; Weisser, *British Working-Class Movements*, p. 74.
82. Hinde, *Cobden*, p. 28. Other material in this paragraph is derived from this book and from Nicholas Edsall, *Richard Cobden: Independent Radical* (London and Cambridge, Mass., 1986), pp. 14–24.
83. Keith Robbins, *John Bright* (London, 1979), pp. 12–13.
84. Cited in Edsall, *Cobden*, p. 176.
85. Miles Taylor, *The European Diaries of Richard Cobden, 1846–1849* (Aldershot, 1994). The journeys are discussed in Edsall, *Cobden*, pp. 180–8, and Hinde, *Cobden*, pp. 172–82; the 'free trade' gospel is considered in A.C. Howe, *Free Trade and Liberal England, 1846–1946* (Oxford, 1997); Kenneth Fielden, 'The Rise and Fall of Free Trade', in Bartlett, *Britain Pre-Eminent*, pp. 76–100; Patrick O'Brien and Geoffrey Allen Pigman, 'Free Trade, British Hegemony and the International Economic Order in

the Nineteenth Century', *Review of International Studies*, Vol. 18/2 (April, 1992), pp. 89–114.

86. Pamela M. Pilbeam, *The Middle Classes in Europe 1789–1914: France, Germany, Italy and Russia* (Basingstoke, 1990); John Breuilly, *Labour and Liberalism in Nineteenth-Century Europe* (Manchester, 1994) and his 'Variations in Liberalism: Britain and Europe in the Mid-Nineteenth Century', *Diplomacy and Statecraft* Vol. 8 No. 3 (1997), pp. 91–123; J.R. Davis, *Britain and the German Zollverein, 1848–1866* (London, 1997).

87. Bolton King, *Mazzini*, p. 151. Rosario Romeo, 'Mazzinis Program und sein revolutionärer Einfluss in Europa', in A.M. Birke and G. Heydemann, *Die Herausforderung des europäischen Staatensystems; Nationale Ideologie und staatliches Interesse zwischen Restauration und Imperialismus* (Göttingen/Zürich, 1989), pp. 15–30.

88. These issues are comprehensively discussed in Ceadel, *Origins of War Prevention*.

89. Hinsley, *Power and the Pursuit of Peace*, p. 101.

90. Hinsley draws attention to Pierre Leroux's, *Organon des vollkommen Friedens* (1837), Gustav d'Eichthal's *De l'Unité Européenne (1840)*, Victor Considérant's *De la Politique générale et du role de la France en Europe (1840)* and Constantin Pecquer's *De la Paix* (1841) as examples of European peace plans that all envisaged the creation of a federation, a single government for Europe. Hinsley, *Power and the Pursuit of Peace*, p. 103.

91. Cited in W.H. van der Linden, *The International Peace Movement 1815–1874* (Amsterdam, 1987), pp. 379–80.

92. Hinsley, *Power and the Pursuit of Peace*, pp. 105–6.

93. L. O'Boyle, 'The Problem of an Excess of Educated Men in Western Europe, 1800–1850', *Journal of Modern History* Vol. xlii No. 4 (December 1970), pp. 471–95; William Thomas, The *Philosophic Radicals: Nine Studies in Theory and Practice, 1817–1841* (Oxford, 1979), pp. 450–1.

94. Nicholas Murray, *A Life of Matthew Arnold* (London, 1996), p. 75.

95. A.P. Stanley, *The Life and Correspondence of Thomas Arnold, D.D.* (London, 1845) II, pp. 380–1.

96. Cecilia Powell, *Italy in the Age of Turner 'The Garden of the World'* (London, 1998); Michael Liversidge (ed.), *Imagining Rome: British Artists and Rome in the Nineteenth Century* (London, 1996); C. Brand, *Italy and the English Romantics: The Italianate Fashion in Early Nineteenth-Century England* (Cambridge, 1957).

97. Keith Robbins, *Protestant Germany through British Eyes: A Complex Victorian Encounter* (London, 1993); Horton Harris, *David Friedrich Strauss and His Theology* (Cambridge, 1973); Owen Chadwick, *The Secularization of the European Mind in the 19th Century* (Cambridge, 1990), pp. 223–6.

98. Pinney, *Selected Letters*, p. 232.

99. Cited in Weisser, *British Working-Class Movements*, p. 90.

100. Stanley Weintraub, *Albert: Uncrowned King* (London, 1997), p. 124. It is only fair to add that they also discussed Dutch painting and the state of the arts in England.

101. Markus Mösslang, Sabine Freitag and Peter Wende (eds), *British Envoys to Germany, 1816–1866 II: 1830–1847* (Cambridge, 2002), pp. xvii–xxi. The volume gives a wide-ranging insight into perspectives held within the various territories. Frank Lorenz Müller, *Britain and the German Question: Perceptions of Nationalism and Political Reform, 1830–83* (Basingstoke, 2002).

102. Susanne Stark, *Translation and Anglo-German Cultural Relations in the Nineteenth Century* (Clevedon, 1999). The extent of translation, and the consequential cultural implications across Europe, has yet to be comprehensively studied.

103. Bolton King, *Mazzini*, p. 107. For a recent assessment of the 'Irish national question' see Vincent Comerford, *Ireland* (London, 2003).

104. Asa Briggs, 'Saxons, Normans and Victorians', in his *Collected Essays: Vol. II Images, Problems, Standpoints, Forecasts* (Brighton, 1985), pp. 215–35.

105. Keith Robbins, *Nineteenth Century Britain: Integration and Diversity* (Oxford, 1988). Palmerston, with an estate of 10,000 acres in Sligo in which he had a real interest, and which he visited often, together with slate business interests in North Wales, which he also visited, and as an Irish peer himself, was more aware of this diversity than many other English politicians. Keith Robbins, 'Palmerston, Bright and Gladstone in North Wales', in his *Politicians, Diplomacy and War in Modern British History* (London, 1994), pp. 37–52.

106. Cited in Hinsley, *Power and the Pursuit of Peace*, p. 101.

Chapter 6

1. Z. Steiner, *The Foreign Office and Foreign Policy 1898–1914* (Cambridge, 1969), pp. 16–17; J.P.C. Roach, *Public Examinations in England, 1850–1900* (Cambridge, 1971), p. 203.
2. J.A.S. Grenville, *Europe Reshaped 1848–1878* (London, 1976).
3. Bernard Porter, *Britain, Europe and the World 1850–1982; Delusions of Grandeur* (London, 1983), p. 32.
4. Citations and material in this paragraph are drawn from John Wolffe 'Burying the Duke of Wellington', in his *Great Deaths: Grieving, Religion, and Nationhood in Victorian and Edwardian Britain* (Oxford, 2000), pp. 28–55, and also his *God and Greater Britain: Religion and National Life in Britain and Ireland 1843–1945* (London, 1994), pp. 116–18.
5. David Brown, *Palmerston and the Politics of Foreign Policy, 1846–55* (Manchester, 2002) is the best recent assessment.
6. Saho Matsomoto-Best, *Britain and the Papacy in the Age of Revolution* (Woodbridge, 2003) is the most recent consideration of another aspect of 'the Italian question'.
7. Clarke, *British Diplomacy and Foreign Policy*, p. 237.
8. G.F.A. Best, *Mid-Victorian Britain 1851–75* (London, 1971), p. 3.
9. Porter, *Britain, Europe and the World*, p. 16.
10. K. Theodore Hoppen, *The Mid-Victorian Generation* (Oxford, 1998), pp. 302–3 and surrounding discussion.
11. Weintraub, *Albert*, pp. 250–1.
12. Barton Benedict, 'Ethnic Identities', in F. Bosbach and J.R. Davis (eds), *Die Weltausstellung von 1851 und ihre Folgen/The Great Exhibition and its Legacy* (Munich, 2002), p. 83.
13. Abigail Green, 'The Representation of the German States at the Great Exhibition', in Bosbach and Davis, *Great Exhibition*, pp. 267–77.
14. Cited in John Davis, 'The International Legacy', in Bosbach and Davis, *Great Exhibition*, pp. 338–9.
15. Mark Finlay, 'German–British Relations in the History of Nineteenth-Century Chemistry', in Bosbach, Filmer-Sankey and Hiery, *Prince Albert and the Development of Education*, pp. 190–4: W.H. Brock, *Justus von Liebig: The Chemical Gatekeeper* (Cambridge, 1997).
16. R. Lawton and R. Lee (eds), *Urban Population Development in Western Europe from the Late Eighteenth to the Early Twentieth Century* (Liverpool, 1989).
17. Marcia Pointon, '"From the Midst of Warfare and its Incidents to the Peaceful Scenes of Home"; The Exposition Universelle of 1855', *Journal of European Studies* xi (1981), pp. 233–61.
18. Patricia Mainardi, *Art and Politics of the Second Empire: The Universal Expositions of 1855 and 1867* (New Haven and London, 1989).
19. Peter T. Marsh, 'The Mid-Nineteenth Century British and French World's Fairs: A Paradoxical Comparison', in Bosbach and Davis, *Great Exhibition*, pp. 359–67.
20. Robert Tombs, *The Paris Commune 1871* (London, 1999), pp. 20–7.
21. Claire Driver, '*Capitale du Plaisir*: The Remaking of Imperial Paris', in Felix Driver and David Gilbert (eds), *Imperial Cities*, (Manchester, 1999), p. 73. More general aspects of the relationship between France and Britain at this juncture can be seen in F.C. Green, *French and British Civilization, 1850–1870* (London, 1965); C. Campos, *The View of France: From Arnold to Bloomsbury* (London, 1965); Sylvaine Marandon, *L'image de la France dans l'Angleterre Victorienne* (Paris, 1967); C. Crossley and I. Smith (eds), *Studies in Anglo-French Cultural Relations: Imagining France* (Basingstoke, 1988).
22. Cited in Brian Fothergill, *Nicholas Wiseman* (London, 1963), pp. 158–9.
23. Fisher, *Bryce* I, p. 121.
24. E.R. Norman, *Anti-Catholicism in Victorian England* (London, 1968) provides relevant documents and commentary.

25. Cited in Denis Gwynn, *Father Dominic Barberi* (London, 1947), p. 197.
26. Pinney (ed.), *Selected Letters*, p. 172.
27. J. Powell (ed.), *Liberal by Principle* (London, 1996), p. 57.
28. G.E. Marindin (ed.), *Letters of Frederic Rogers, Lord Blatchford* (London, 1896), p. 78.
29. A.L. Drummond, *The Kirk and the Continent* (Edinburgh, 1956), pp. 172–3; Fisher, *Bryce* I, p. 76.
30. So Stewart J. Brown, *The National Churches of England, Ireland and Scotland 1801–46* (Oxford, 2001), p. 410, concludes.
31. H. McLeod in H. McLeod (ed.), *European Religion in the Age of Great Cities 1830–1930* (London, 1995), pp. 13–17.
32. Rainer Liedtke and Stephen Wendehorst (eds), *The Emancipation of Catholics, Jews and Protestants: Minorities and the Nation-state in Nineteenth-Century Europe* (Manchester, 1999).
33. Cited in P. Butler, *Gladstone: Church, State and Tractarianism* (Oxford, 1982), pp. 122–3. This book expounds the evolution of Gladstone's religious ideas and attitudes up to 1859.
34. K.A.P. Sandiford, 'Gladstone and Europe', in Bruce L. Kinzler, *The Gladstonian Turn of Mind* (Toronto, 1985), pp. 177–96, which in turn draws on reflections in J.L. Hammond, *Gladstone and the Irish Nation* (London, 1938), pp. 49–66 and D.M. Schreuder, *Gladstone and Kruger* (London, 1969), pp. 37–97.
35. Owen Chadwick, 'Young Gladstone and Italy', in P.J. Jagger (ed.), *Gladstone, Politics and Religion* (London, 1985), pp. 82–3.
36. Cited in Derek Beales, *England and Italy 1859–60* (London, 1961), p. 168.
37. Derek Beales, 'Gladstone and Garibaldi', in P.J. Jagger (ed.), *Gladstone* (London, 1998), p. 153. See also Denis Mack Smith, *Garibaldi* (London, 1957), pp. 137–48.
38. An allegation made in a pamphlet cited by Richard Shannon, *Gladstone* I (London, 1982), p. 368.
39. Richard Jenkyns, *The Victorians and Ancient Greece* (Oxford, 1980), pp. 199–200.
40. A guide to the complex diplomacy that lies behind these simple statements is Norman Rich, *Why the Crimean War? A Cautionary Tale* (Hanover and London, 1985).
41. Cited in W. Baumgart, *The Peace of Paris 1856: Studies in War, Diplomacy and Peacemaking* (Santa Barbara/Oxford, 1981), p. 104. Comments on the conference/congress in this section are indebted to the insights in this volume.
42. Cited in Ceadel, *Origins of War Prevention*, p. 515.
43. Martin Ceadel, *Semi-Detached Idealists: The British Peace Movement and International Relations, 1854–1945* (Oxford, 2000), pp. 33–58.
44. Robbins, *Bright*, pp. 94–107; A. Howe, 'Richard Cobden and the Crimean War', *History Today* (June, 2004), pp. 46–51.
45. For visits of Russian novelists to Britain see Patrick Waddington (ed.), *Ivan Turgenev and Britain* (Oxford, 1995) and W.J. Leathbarrow (ed.), *Dostoevskii and Britain* (Oxford, 1995).
46. Richard Congreve, 'The West', in *International Policy: Essays on the Foreign Relations of England* (London, 1884, first published in 1866), pp. 9–13; Terence R. Wright, *The Religion of Humanity: the Impact of Comtean Positivism on Victorian Britain* (Cambridge, 1986) provides a broad context.
47. Mark Mazower, 'Travellers and the Oriental City *c.*1840–1920', *Transactions of the Royal Historical Society* Sixth ser. XII (2002), pp. 59–112. A.L. Macfie, *Orientalism* (London, 2002).
48. Leighton was writing in 1857. Mrs Russell Barrington, *The Life, Letters and Work of Frederic Leighton, Baron of Stretton* I (London, 1906), pp. 298–9.
49. Frederic Harrison, 'England and France', in *International Policy*, pp. 37–102.
50. G.M. Trevelyan, *Sir George Otto Trevelyan* (London, 1932), p. 64.
51. Green, *French and British Civilization*, p. 10.
52. Hamilton, *Anglo-French Naval Rivalry*, Chaper 6.
53. These issues are discussed in J.P. Parry, 'The Impact of Napoleon III on British Politics, 1851–1880', *Transactions of the Royal Historical Society* Sixth Ser. XI (2001), pp. 147–75.
54. Beales, *England and Italy*, pp. 166–70; C.T. McIntire, *England against the Papacy 1858–1861* (Cambridge, 1983); Matthias Buschkühl, *Great Britain and the Holy See 1746–1870* (Blackrock, 1982), pp. 96–9.

55. Chamberlain, *Aberdeen*, p. 525.
56. Clogg, *Concise History of Greece*, p. 66: C.M. Woodhouse, *Modern Greece: A Short History* (London, 1984), pp. 177–8.
57. Congreve, *International Policy*, p. 19.
58. Olive Anderson, *A Liberal State at War: English Politics and Economics during the Crimean War* (London, 1967), p. 283.
59. G. Grote, *Seven Letters on the Recent Politics of Switzerland* (London, 1947), p. iv; Oliver Zimmer, *A Contested Nation: History, Memory and Nationalism in Switzerland, 1781–1891* (Cambridge, 2003) provides an assessment of some of the issues that concerned Grote.
60. David Bebbington, 'Gladstone and Grote', in Peter J. Jagger (ed.), *Gladstone* (London, 1998), pp. 157–78.
61. McClelland, *The German Historians*, pp. 94–5.
62. Citations in W.A. van't Padje, 'Sir Alexander Malet and Prince Otto von Bismarck: An Almost Forgotten Anglo-German Friendship', *Historical Research* Vol. 72, No. 179 (October, 1999), pp. 285–8. I am also indebted to this article for other observations on Bismarck's perspectives. See also Lothar Gall, 'Bismarck und England', in Paul Kluke and Peter Alter (eds), *Aspekte der deutsch-britischen Beziehungen im Laufe der Jahrhunderte* (Stuttgart, 1978).
63. A.J.P. Taylor, *Bismarck: The Man and the Statesman* (London, 1955), pp. 15–20.
64. A.E.M. Ashley, *The Life of Henry John Temple, Viscount Palmerston* ii (London, 1876), p. 446: Ridley, *Palmerston*, p. 582.
65. The two most thorough examinations of British attitudes to German questions in mid-century are John Davis, *Britain and the German Zollverein, 1846–1866* (London, 1997) and Frank Müller, *Britain and the German Question: Perceptions of Nationalism and Political Reform, 1830–1883* (Basingstoke, 2002).
66. The most recent assessment in English is Katharine Anne Lerman, *Bismarck* (London, 2004), pp. 114–56.
67. Detailed studies are to be found in R. Millman, *British Foreign Policy and the Coming of the Franco-Prussian War* (Oxford, 1965). Longer-term aspects can be studied in books by Klaus Hildebrand, *Grossbritannien und die deutsche Reichsgründung. Preussen-Deutschland in der Sicht der grossen europäischen Mächte* (Munich, 1980) and *No Intervention. Die Pax Britannica und Preussen 1865/66–1866/70. Einer Untersuchung zur englischen Weltpolitik im 19. Jahrhundert* (Munich, 1997) and in contributions to the volume *Das Deutsche Reich im Urteil der Grossen Mächte und europäischen Nachbarn (1871–1945)* (Munich, 1995).
68. Cited in Matthew, *Gladstone*, pp. 181–2.
69. Congreve, *International Policy*, p. 13.
70. Ashton, *The German Idea*, p. 177.
71. Maurice Cowling, *Religion and Public Doctrine in Modern England: Vol. III Accommodations* (Cambridge, 2001), pp. 47–51.
72. Cited and discussed in Keith Robbins 'The Monarch's Concept of Foreign Policy: Victoria and Edward VII', in Adolf M. Birke, Magnus Brechtken and Alaric Searle (eds), *An Anglo-German Dialogue: The Munich Lectures on the History of International Relations* (Munich, 2000), p. 120.
73. See Günther Grüthal, 'Eine "englische Partei" in Berlin? Sir Robert Morier und die Neue Ära in Preussen', in Gerhard A. Ritter and Peter Wende (eds), *Rivalität und Partnerschaft: Studien zu den deutsch-britischen Beziehungen im 19. und 20. Jahrhundert* (Paderborn, 1999), pp. 29–52.
74. Schulze, *Germany*, p. 153.
75. Günther Hollenberg, *Englisches Interesse am Kaiserreich. Die Attraktivität Preussen-Deutschlands für konservative und liberale Kreise in Grossbritannien, 1860–1914* (Wiesbaden, 1974).
76. Arnold Haulltain, *A Selection from Goldwin Smith's Correspondence* (London, n.d.), p. 11; N.C. Chaudury, *Scholar Extraordinary: The Life of Professor the Rt. Hon. Friedrich Max Müller* (London, 1974).
77. Cited and discussed in James Campbell, 'Stubbs, Maitland and Constitutional History', in Stuchtey and Wende (eds), *British and German Historiography, 1750–1950*, p. 113.
78. Murray, *Matthew Arnold*, pp. 228–31; Rachel Bromwich, *Matthew Arnold and Celtic Literature* (Oxford, 1965).

79. L.P. Curtis, *Anglo-Saxons and Celts: A Study of Anti-Irish Prejudice in Victorian England* (Bridgeport, Conn., 1968).
80. George Borrow published his *Wild Wales* in 1862. Unlike his work in Spain, he had no need to distribute bibles in his travels through Wales in 1854. Julius Rodenberg, *An Autumn in Wales (1856)*, translated and edited by William Linnard (Cowbridge, 1985), recounts Welsh life near Llanfairfechan. It happens that the farm on which he stayed lies directly opposite a house in which this author once lived. J.A. Froude, however, spent the early 1850s at Plas Gwynant in the heart of Snowdonia looking at mountains, fishing, shooting and preparing, inter alia, a defence of the English Reformation. 'Wales' does not seem to have impinged. W.H. Dunn, *James Anthony Froude: A Biography, 1818–1856* (Oxford, 1961), pp. 168–9.
81. A succinct summary, 'Britain: A Lop-sided Affair' is in Hoppen, *The Mid-Victorian Generation*, pp. 513–23.
82. Cited in Murray, *Matthew Arnold*, p. 231.
83. R.H. Super (ed.), *Matthew Arnold. Schools and Universities on the Continent* (Michigan, 1964).
84. J.A. Froude, 'England and her Colonies', in *Short Studies on Great Subjects Second Series* (London, 1871), p. 176.
85. E.V. Quinn and J.M. Prest, *Dear Miss Nightingale: A Selection of Benjamin Jowett's Letters, 1860–1893* (Oxford, 1987), p. 195.

Chapter 7

1. K. Hildebrand, *Preussen-Deutschland in der Sicht der grossen europäischen Machte, 1860–1880* (Munich, 1980).
2. Angus Hawkins and John Powell, *The Diary of John Woodhouse, First Earl of Kimberley for 1862–1902*, Camden Fifth Series, Vol. 9 (London, 1997), p. 252.
3. Cited in Duroselle, *Europe: A History of its Peoples* (London, 1990), p. 333.
4. James Rennell Rodd, *Social and Diplomatic Memories 1884–1893* (London, 1922), p. 44; British ambassadors in Berlin were in no doubt that they were at the hub of Europe and that their own role was of great importance. Agatha Ramm, *Sir Robert Morier: Envoy and Ambassador in the Age of Imperialism, 1876–1893* (Oxford, 1973); Karina Urbach, *Bismarck's Favourite Englishman: Lord Odo Russell's Mission to Berlin* (London and New York, 1999). Edward Goschen, mainly of non-British descent and married to an American, was ambassador in Berlin, 1908–14. C.H.D. Howard (ed.), *The Diary of Edward Goschen, 1900–1914*, Camden Fourth Series, Vol. 25 (London, 1980).
5. Eric Storm, 'The Problems of the Spanish Nation-Building Process around 1900', *National Identities*, Vol. 6 No. 2 (2004), pp. 143–56.
6. David Atkinson, Denis Cosgrove and Anna Notaro, 'Empire in Modern Rome: Shaping and Remembering an Imperial City 1870–1911', in Driver and Gilbert, *Imperial Cities*, p. 44.
7. John Breuilly, 'Sovereignty and Boundaries: Modern State Formation and National Identity in Germany', in Mary Fulbrook (ed.), *National Histories and European History* (London, 1993); Heinrich August Winkler, *Der lange Weg nach Westen: Deutsche Geschichte von Ende des Alten Reiches bis zum Untergang der Weimarer Republik* (Munich, 2001), pp. 213–16.
8. Theodore R. Weeks, *Nation and State in Late Imperial Russia: Nationalism and Russification on the Western Frontier, 1863–1914* (DeKalb, Ill., 1996).
9. Robin Okey, 'Central Europe/Eastern Europe', *Past & Present* No. 137 (November, 1992), pp. 102–33, for an assessment of the various definitions that have been offered since the mid-nineteenth century.
10. Rennell Rodd, *Social and Diplomatic Memories*, p. 213.
11. Material in this paragraph is drawn from Morgan, *National Identities and Travel* and Sillitoe, *Leading the Blind*. George Gissing published his *By the Ionian Sea: Notes of a Ramble in Southern Italy* in 1901.

12. Fisher, *Bryce* I, p. 125.
13. G.R. de Beer, *Travellers in Switzerland* (Oxford, 1949); John Premble, *The Mediterranean Passion: Victorians and Edwardians in the South* (Oxford, 1987).
14. James Bryce, *Memories of Travel* (London, 1923), p. 141; P. Arengo-Jones, *Queen Victoria in Switzerland* (London, 1995).
15. Maura O'Connor, *The Romance of Italy and the English Political Imagination* (New York, 1998).
16. John Pemble, *Venice Rediscovered* (Oxford, 1995).
17. Pemble, *Mediterranean Passion*, p. 274.
18. Judith Champ, *The English Pilgrimage to Rome: A Dwelling for the Soul* (Leominster, 2000) examines the attractions of the city over a long period.
19. Rennell Rodd, *Social and Diplomatic Memories*, p. 251.
20. A. Lyall, *The Life of the Marquis of Dufferin and Ava* II (London, 1905), p. 243.
21. Rennell Rodd, *Social and Political Memories*, p. 89.
22. Bryce, *Memories of Travel*, p. 141.
23. H.D. Lloyd, *The Swiss Democracy: The Study of a Sovereign People* (London, 1908). Lloyd, an American, did not live to complete the work begun in two visits to Switzerland in 1901 and 1902. Hobson edited and completed the task.
24. E.M. Hogg, *Quintin Hogg* (London, 1904), p. 232.
25. H.C.G. Matthew (ed.), *The Gladstone Diaries XI 31 July 1883–December 1886* (Oxford, 1990), pp. 28–9.
26. Roundell Palmer, Earl of Selborne, *Memorials Part II: Personal and Political, 1865–1895* II (London, 1898), p. 231.
27. Paul Smith, *Lord Salisbury on Politics* (Cambridge, 1965), pp. 363–76. Of course, Salisbury made many other points in this article. He lamented that England lacked the 'faculty of assimilation', whereas France had achieved the nationalization of the Flemings of the Pas de Calais and the Celts of Brittany.
28. Lord E. Fitzmaurice, *The Life of Granville George Leveson Gower, Second Lord Granville* (London, 1905), p. 23.
29. Fitzmaurice, *Granville*, pp. 188, 217.
30. Roland Hill, *Lord Acton* (New Haven and London, 2000), pp. 171–2.
31. Shannon, *Gladstone* II, p. 90.
32. Paul Smith, *Disraeli* (Cambridge, 1996), p. 221.
33. This paragraph is indebted to the introduction by John Vincent to his edition of *The Diaries of Edward Henry Stanley, 15th Earl of Derby (1826–93) between September 1869 and March 1878* (London, 1994), pp. 1–31.
34. Keith Robbins, '"Experiencing the Foreign": British Foreign Policy Makers and the Delights of Travel', in Michael Dockrill and Brian McKercher (eds), *Diplomacy and World Power: Studies in British Foreign Policy, 1890–1950* (Cambridge, 1996), pp. 19–22.
35. Andrew Roberts, *Salisbury, Victorian Titan* (London, 1999), p. 29.
36. Roberts, *Salisbury*, p. 114.
37. M. Pinto-Duschinsky, *The Political Thought of Lord Salisbury* (London, 1967), pp. 12, 42.
38. Cited in Smith, *Salisbury on Politics*, p. 55.
39. Cited in Joll, *Britain and Europe*, pp. 160–2.
40. Robert Rhodes James, *Rosebery* (London, 1963), p. 49.
41. Rhodes James, *Rosebery*, p. 71.
42. Rhodes James, *Rosebery*, p. 158, speaks of Rosebery's friendships 'with the members of many leading families and officials in almost every European country', but this estimate may be exaggerated.
43. Angus Hawkins and John Powell, *Journals of John Wodehouse*, pp. 55–9.
44. C.H.D. Howard, *Splendid Isolation* (London, 1967) and *Britain and the Casus Belli 1822–1902* (London, 1974).
45. C.J. Lowe, *Salisbury and the Mediterranean 1886–1896* (London, 1965), p. 118.
46. Cited in Bernard Semmel, *Liberalism and Naval Strategy: Ideology, Interest and Sea Power during the Pax Britannica* (London, 1986), p. 125.
47. P.M. Kennedy, *The Rise and Fall of British Naval Mastery* (London, 1976); J.T. Sumida, *In Defence of Naval Supremacy: Finance, Technology and British Naval Policy 1889–1914* (London, 1989).

48. W. Baumgart, *Imperialism: The Idea and Reality of British and French Colonial Expansion, 1880–1914* (Oxford, 1982); P. Gifford and W.R. Louis, *Britain and Germany in Africa* (New Haven, 1967).
49. E.F. Penrose (ed.), *European Imperialism and the Partition of Africa* (London, 1975).
50. Hinsley, *Power and the Pursuit of Peace*, pp. 284–6.
51. R.T. Shannon, *Gladstone and the Bulgarian Atrocities* (London, 1983), pp. 26–7.
52. J.O. Johnston, *The Life of Henry Parry Liddon* (London, 1904), pp. 183–9.
53. Robert Eisner, *Travellers to an Antique Land: The History and Literature of Travel to Greece* (Ann Arbor, 1993) looks back over the nineteenth century; Rodanthi Tzanelli, 'Experiments on Puerile Nations, or the Impossibility of Surpassing your Father: The Case of the Anglo-Greek Dialogue', *National Identities* Vol. 6 No. 2 (2004), pp. 107–21.
54. Lady Grogan, *The Life of J.D. Bourchier* (London, n.d.), p. 29.
55. Grogan, p. 215.
56. Lord Howard of Penrith, *Theatre of Life* (London, 1936), p. 17.
57. Johnston, *Liddon*, pp. 208–14; for more general reflections on Turkey and Europe at this juncture see Herbert Butterfield and M. Wight (eds), *Diplomatic Investigations* (London, 1966), pp. 189–90 and M.E. Yapp, 'Europe in the Turkish Mirror', in *Past & Present* No. 137 (November 1992), pp. 134–55.
58. Cited in I.B. Neumann and Jennifer M. Welsh, 'The Other in European Self-Definition: An Addendum to the Literature on International Society', in *Review of International Studies* Vol. 17 No. 1 (October, 1991), p. 345.
59. Wardman, *Renan*, pp. 117–19; Harris, *David Friedrich Srauss*, pp. 235–7.
60. Matthew, *Gladstone*, pp. 236–7.
61. Premble, *Venice Rediscovered*, pp. 7–9, 108–9.
62. Johnston, *Liddon*, p. 103.
63. Raymond Pearson, 'Fact, Fantasy, Fraud: Perceptions and Projections of National Revival', *Ethnic Studies* Vol. 10 (1993), pp. 43–64.
64. Cited in J.A.S. Grenville, *Lord Salisbury and Foreign Policy: The Close of the Nineteenth Century* (London, 1970), p. 21.
65. V.G. Kiernan, *The Lords of Human Kind: European Attitudes towards the Outside World in the Imperial Age* (London, 1969).
66. T. Raychauduri, 'Europe in India's Xenology: The Nineteenth-Century Record', *Past & Present* No. 137 (November 1992), p. 158.
67. B. Semmel, *The Governor Eyre Controversy* (London, 1962); D.A. Lorimer, *Colour, Class and the Victorians: English Attitudes to the Negro in the Mid-Nineteenth Century* (Leicester, 1978).
68. Catherine Hall, *Civilising Subjects: Metropole and Colony in the English Imagination 1830–1867* (Cambridge, 2002), pp. 380–433.
69. This case, and cognate matters, are discussed in Niall Ferguson, *Empire: How Britain made the modern world* (London, 2004), pp. 198–205.
70. Peter Mandler, '"Race" and "Nation" in Mid-Victorian Thought', in S. Collini, R. Whatmore and B. Young (eds), *History, Religion, Culture: British Intellectual History 1750–1950* (Cambridge, 2000), pp. 224–44; Mark Lee, 'The Story of Greater Britain. What Lessons does it Teach?', *National Identities* Vol. 6 No. 2 (July 2004), pp. 123–42.
71. Cited and discussed by A. Porter in the 'Introduction' to A. Porter, *Oxford History of the British Empire*, pp. 22–4; A.P. Thornton, *The Imperial Idea and its Enemies* (London, 1959) remains a classic exposition.
72. R. Horsman, *Race and Manifest Destiny: The Origins of American Racial Anglo-Saxonism* (Cambridge, Mass., 1981).
73. This paragraph draws on Anne Orde, *The Eclipse of Great Britain: The United States and British Imperial Decline, 1895–1956* (London, 1996), pp. 9–19; Donald Cameron Watt, *Succeeding John Bull: America in Britain's Place 1900–1975* (Cambridge, 1986), pp. 26–8.
74. P.R.H. Slee, *Learning and a Liberal Education: The Study of Modern History in the Universities of Oxford, Cambridge and Manchester* (Manchester, 1986); R.N. Soffer, 'Nation, Duty, Character and Confidence: History at Oxford', *The Historical Journal* Vol. XXX No. 1 (1987), pp. 77–104; T.W. Heyck, *The Transformation of Intellectual Life in Victorian England* (London, 1982), pp. 139–50.
75. Margaret Lodge, *Sir Richard Lodge: A Biography* (London, 1946), pp. 23, 47, 52–3.

76. C.G. Coulton, *Fourscore Years* (London, 1945), pp. 186–99.
77. J.W. Burrow, *A Liberal Descent: Victorian Historians and the English Past* (Cambridge, 1983), pp. 178–201; James Bryce, *Studies in Contemporary Biography* (London, 1903), pp. 262–92.
78. Benedikt Stuchtey, 'Imperialism and the Frontier', in Stuchtey and Wende (eds), *British and German Historiography*, pp. 299–305.
79. Stuchtey, in Stuchtey and Wende, *British and German Historiography*, pp. 295–305; Deborah Wormell, *Sir John Seeley and the Use of History* (Cambridge, 1980).
80. John Burrow, 'Historicism and Social Evolution', in Stuchtey and Wende (eds), *British and German Historiography*, pp. 255–58.
81. Accessible in Homi Bhabha (ed.), *Nation and Narration* (London, 1990), pp. 8–22. Reflecting on Renan a century later, Ernest Gellner commented that 'will' or 'consent' was indeed an important factor in the formation of most human groups, but willed adherence also had to be matched by extraneous incentives, positive and negative, and on hopes and fears, if groups were to persist. E. Gellner, *Nations and Nationalism* (Oxford, 1983), p. 53. See also Anthony D. Smith, *The Nation in History: Historiographical Debates about Ethnicity and Nationalism* (Cambridge, 2000), pp. 11–12, and R. Young, *Colonial Desire: Hybridity in Theory, Culture and Race* (London, 1995), pp. 68–72.
82. J. Paulmann, 'Searching for a "Royal International": The Mechanics of Monarchical Relations in Nineteenth-Century Europe', in Geyer and Paulmann, *Mechanics of Internationalism*, p. 175.
83. Richard Williams, *The Contentious Crown: Public Discussion of the Monarchy in the Reign of Queen Victoria* (Aldershot, 1997), p. 169.
84. Robbins in Birke, Brechtgen and Searle, *An Anglo-German Dialogue*, pp. 115–29.
85. R. McLean, 'Kaiser Wilhelm II and the British Royal Family: Anglo-German Relations in Political Context, 1890–1914', *History* Vol. 86 No. 284 (October, 2001), pp. 478–502. MacLean looks at these issues more widely in *Royalty and Diplomacy in Europe, 1890–1914* (Cambridge, 2000).
86. John C.G. Röhl, 'The Kaiser and England', in Birke, Brechtgen and Searle, *An Anglo-German Dialogue*, p. 190; Lothar Reinemann, *Der Kaiser in England: Wilhelm II und sein Bild in der britischen Öffentlichkeit* (Paderborn, 2001).
87. B.H. Harrison, *The Transformation of British Politics 1860–1995* (Oxford, 1996), p. 89.
88. Hawkins and Powell, *The Wodehouse Diaries*, p. 387.
89. K. Newton, *British Labour, European Socialism and the Struggle for Peace, 1889–1914* (Oxford, 1985), p. 18; M. Donald, 'Workers of the World Unite? Exploring the Enigma of the Second International', in Geyer and Paulmann, *Mechanics of Internationalism*, pp. 182–5, 202.
90. Kertesz, *Documents*, pp. 233–41.
91. Owen Chadwick, *A History of the Popes, 1830–1914* (Oxford, 1998), pp. 161–214.
92. Norman, *English Catholic Church*, p. 266.
93. Chadwick, 'At the First Vatican Council', in *Acton and History*, pp. 76–102.
94. Gladstone to Granville, 2 November 1874 in Ramm, *Political Correspondence of Gladstone and Granville, II 1871–76*, p. 458; E.R. Norman, *Anti-Catholicism in Victorian England* (London, 1968), pp. 80–104.
95. Cited in Seton Watson, *Britain in Europe*, p. 544.

Chapter 8

1. Lord Vansittart, *The Mist Procession* (London, 1958) p. 29.
2. P.M.H. Bell, *France and Britain 1900–1940: Entente and Estrangement* (London, 1996), pp. 9–12.
3. Pascale Venier, 'French Foreign Policy and the Boer War', in Keith Wilson (ed.), *The International Impact of the Boer War* (Chesham, 2001), reverts to this view and takes issue with the revision that Christopher M. Andrew suggested in *Théophile Delcassé and the Making of the Entente Cordiale* (London, 1968). See also Venier's essay 'Théophile Delcassé and the Question of Intervention in the Anglo-Boer War, October

1899–March 1900', in Philippe Chassaigne and Michael Dockrill (eds), *Anglo-French Relations, 1898–1998: From Fashoda to Jospin* (London, 2002), pp. 44–55.

4. Cited in Reinermann, *Der Kaiser in England*, p. 177. The author, in the surrounding pages, discusses press reaction.

5. Cited in Christopher Clark, *Kaiser Wilhelm II* (London, 2000), p. 137.

6. Sir Charles Hardinge, councillor at the embassy, found the hostility of the Russian press and society 'quite phenomenal'. Sir Charles Hardinge, *Old Diplomacy* (London, 1947), p. 74; Derek Spring, 'Russian Foreign Policy and the Boer War', in Wilson (ed.), *International Impact*, pp. 56–9.

7. Gilles Farragu, 'Italy and the Boer War', in Wilson (ed.), *International Impact of the Boer War*, pp. 104–5.

8. Francis Bertie, cited in Keith Hamilton, *Bertie of Thame: Edwardian Ambassador* (Woodbridge, 1990), p. 30.

9. J. Wolffe, *Great Deaths*, pp. 229–39.

10. John Charmley, *Splendid Isolation: Britain and the Balance of Power 1874–1914* (London, 1999), pp. 261–93, is one recent discussion of a question that has been widely argued over in Britain and Germany for a century.

11. Cited and discussed by Benedikt Stuchtey in Benedikt Stuchtey and Eckhardt Fuchs (eds), *Writing World History 1800–2000* (Oxford, 2003), pp. 231–4.

12. Hugh Carey, *Duet for Two Voices* (Cambridge, 1979), p. 53. This volume, revolving around the career of Edward J. Dent, gives a picture of the lively musical interaction between England and the continent at this time.

13. Cited in David Gilmour, *Curzon* (London, 1994), p. 65.

14. Cited in Boyce, *Decolonisation*, pp. 67–8.

15. J. Eddy and D. Schreuder (eds), *The Rise of Colonial Nationalism: Australia, New Zealand, Canada and South Africa first assert their Nationalities, 1880–1914* (Sydney, 1988).

16. Cited in Boyce, *Decolonisation*, p. 57.

17. See the succinct survey by Ronald Hyam, 'The British Empire in the Edwardian Era', in Judith M. Brown and Wm Roger Louis (eds), *The Oxford History of the British Empire: The Twentieth Century* (Oxford, 1999), pp. 47–63.

18. P.T. Marsh, *Bargaining on Europe: Britain and the First Common Market, 1860–1892* (London, 1999). See also his essay 'The End of the Anglo-French Commercial Alliance, 1860–1894', in Chassaigne and Dockrill (eds), *Anglo-French Relations*, pp. 34–43.

19. Peter Cain, 'Political Economy in Edwardian England: The Tariff-Reform Controversy; in Alan O'Day, *The Edwardian Age: Conflict and Stability 1900–1914* (London, 1979), pp. 35–59, remains a useful assessment.

20. J.E. Kendle, *The Round Table Movement and Imperial Union* (Toronto, 1975); Ged Martin, 'The Idea of "Imperial Federation"', in R. Hyam and G. Martin (eds), *Reappraisals in British Imperial History* (London, 1975), pp. 121–38.

21. Kelly Boyd, *Manliness and the Boys' Story Paper in Britain:' A Cultural History, 1855–1940* (Basingstoke, 2003), pp. 130–1.

22. Jeremy Crump, 'The Identity of English Music: The Reception of Elgar', in Robert Colls and Philip Dodd (eds), *Englishness: Politics and Culture 1880–1920* (London, 1986), p. 171.

23. Robert Stradling and Meirion Hughes, *The English Musical Renaissance 1860–1940: Construction and Deconstruction* (London, 1993), pp. 50–3; Jerrold Northrop Moore, *Edward Elgar: A Creative Life* (Oxford, 1984), pp. 424–35.

24. John M. Mackenzie, *Orientalism: History, Theory and the Arts* (Manchester, 1995), p. 138.

25. Emma Letley, *Maurice Baring: A Citizen of Europe* (London, 1991), p. 114. It was Edmund Gosse who bestowed this 'citizenship' upon Baring.

26. Hamilton, *Bertie*, p. 22.

27. Keith Neilson, 'Only a D...d Marionette'? The Influence of Ambassadors on British Foreign Policy, 1904–1914', in Dockrill and McKercher (eds), *Diplomacy and World Power*, pp. 56–78 reflects on particular 'matches'.

28. Keith Robbins, *Present and Past: British Images of Germany in the First Half of the Twentieth Century and their Historical Legacy* (Göttingen, 1999).

29. Stephen Graham, *The Way of Martha and the Way of Mary* (London, 1915), p. 4. Eastern Christianity was 'Mary' and western 'Martha'.

30. Cited by H. Butterfield in 'Sir Edward Grey in July 1914', *Historical Studies* v (1965), pp. 1–25. See also my 'Britain in the Summer of 1914', in Keith Robbins, *Politicians, Diplomacy and War in Modern British History* (London, 1994), pp. 175–88.

31. Lord Zetland, *Lord Cromer* (London, 1932), p. 343.

32. D.F. Macdonald, 'The Great Migration', in Bartlett, *Britain Pre-Eminent*, p. 55.

33. Geoffrey Alderman, *Modern British Jewry* (Oxford, 1998), pp. 119–20, 210–11. To speak of a 'community', of course, greatly simplifies the clashes and cleavages within it.

34. G.K. Chesterton could not define a nation but in his *Irish Impressions* he felt that in Ireland an Englishman could 'only see it, smell it, hear it, handle it, bump into it, fall over it, kill it, be killed for it, or be damned for doing it wrong'. Maisie Ward, *Gilbert Keith Chesterton* (London, 1944), p. 343.

35. These matters are discussed more fully in Keith Robbins, *Great Britain: Identities, Institutions and the Idea of Britishness* (London, 1998), pp. 213–14.

36. James Loughlin, *Ulster Unionism and British National Identity since 1885* (London, 1995), pp. 30–1 for pertinent discussion.

37. Cited in Keith Robbins, *History, Religion and Identity in Modern Britain* (London, 1993), p. 287 and surrounding discussion.

38. J.E. Kendle, *Federal Britain: A History* (London, 1997).

39. Ronald G. Asch (ed.), *Three Nations – A Common History? England, Scotland, Ireland and British History* c.1600–1920 (Bochum, 1993) contains a paper on the home rule crisis by Sabine Krumwiede and a response by R.F. Foster, pp. 229–71.

40. Paul Ward, *Britishness since 1870* (London, 2004) pertinently discusses these issues.

41. Edward W. Said, *Orientalism* (London, 1995). This edition contains an 'Afterword', in response to the varied critical and political response to the book since its first appearance in 1978.

42. Gilmour, *Curzon*, p. 68.

43. Cited in Hyam in Brown and Louis, *The Twentieth Century*, p. 47.

44. Lord Newton, *Lord Lansdowne* (London, 1929) remains the only published biography. There is a sketch by P.J.V. Rolo in K. Wilson (ed.), *British Foreign Secretaries*, pp. 159–71.

45. Cited in Charmley, *Splendid Isolation*, p. 283.

46. Indeed, as Ian Nish states in *The Origins of the Russo-Japanese War* (London, 1985), p. 256 it can be argued that the alliance limited the scope of any war.

47. Gordon Daniel, 'The Anglo-Japanese Alliance and the British Press', in *Studies in the Anglo-Japanese Alliance (1902–1923)*, Suntory Centre, London School of Economics and Political Science Discussion Paper, January 2003.

48. Bell, *France and Britain*, pp. 28–33.

49. Charmley, *Splendid Isolation*, p. 322, believes that Lansdowne's eyes remained firmly fixed on 'British' rather than 'Franco-British interests'.

50. Peter Buitenhuis, *The Great War of Words: Literature as Propaganda 1914–18 and After* (London, 1987), pp. 142–3.

51. E.W. Edwards, 'The Prime Minister and Foreign Policy: The Balfour Government 1902–1905', in H. Hearder and H.R. Loyn (eds), *British Government and Administration: Studies presented to S.B. Chrimes* (Cardiff, 1974).

52. A.J. Balfour, *Nationality and Home Rule* (London, 1913), pp. 30–1; Jason Tomes, *Balfour and Foreign Policy: The International Thought of a Conservative Statesman* (Cambridge, 1997).

53. These details have been gleaned from J.A. Spender's *Life of Sir Henry Campbell-Bannerman* 2 vols (London, 1923).

54. These travels have been gleaned from Roy Jenkins, *Asquith* (London, 1964).

55. These travels have been gleaned from John Grigg, *Lloyd George: The People's Champion 1902–1911* (London, 1978) and *Lloyd George: From Peace to War 1912–1916* (London, 1985).

56. S. Gwynn (ed.), *The Letters and Friendships of Sir Cecil Spring-Rice* ii (London, 1929), pp. 159–60. See also Keith Robbins, 'Core and Periphery in Modern British History', in *History, Religion and Identity in Modern Britain*, pp. 248–51.

57. Keith Robbins, *Sir Edward Grey: A Biography of Lord Grey of Fallodon* (London, 1971).

58. Keith Robbins, 'Sir Edward Grey and the British Empire', reprinted in *Politicians, Diplomacy and War in Modern British History*, pp. 165–74.

59. Keith Wilson, 'Grey', in *British Foreign Secretaries*, p. 192; Charmley, *Splendid Isolation*, pp. 341–5.
60. The issues, summarily treated here, have been mulled over by many historians and can be pursued additionally in F.H. Hinsley (ed.), *British Foreign Policy under Sir Edward Grey* (Cambridge, 1977); Keith Wilson, *The Policy of the Entente: Essays on the Determinants of British Foreign Policy 1904–1914* (Cambridge, 1985).
61. Niall Ferguson, *The Pity of War* (London, 1999), pp. 61–2; Michael Hughes, 'Bernard Pares, Russian Studies and the Promotion of Anglo-Russian Friendship, 1907–14', *Slavonic and East European Review* No. 78 (2000), pp. 510–35.
62. Ferguson, *Pity of War*, p. 444.
63. Ferguson, *Pity of War*, p. 460.
64. See the essays in Keith Wilson (ed.), *Decisions for War, 1914* (London, 1995), and in R.J.W. Evans and Hartmut Pogge von Strandmann (eds), *The Coming of the First World War* (Oxford, 1988); J.W. Langdon, *July 1914: The Long Debate, 1918–1990* (Oxford, 1991); M. Hewitson, 'Germany and France before the First World War: A Reassessment of Wilhelmine Foreign Policy', *English Historical Review* Vol. CXV No. 462 (June 2000), pp. 570–606; M. Seligmann, '"A Barometer of National Confidence": a British Assessment of the Role of Insecurity in the Formulation of German Military Policy before the First World War', *English Historical Review* Vol. CXVII No. 471 (April 2002), pp. 333–55.
65. T.K. Derry, *A History of Scandinavia* (Minneapolis, 1979), pp. 268–79; Tony Griffiths, *Scandinavia* (Kent Town, 1991), p. 85.
66. Tage Kaarsted, *Great Britain and Denmark 1914–1920* (Odense, 1979). Denmark was 'of limited interest' to Britain but Britain was an important complementary factor in Denmark's relations with its neighbour, Germany. Essays in J. Sevaldsen, *Britain and Denmark: Political, Economic and Cultural Relations of the 19th and 20th Centuries* (Copenhagen, 2003) concentrate on Danish perceptions of Britain.
67. J.D. Gregory, *On the Edge of Diplomacy: Rambles and Reflections, 1902–1928* (London, n.d.), pp. 40–52.
68. F.R. Bridge, *Great Britain and Austria-Hungary 1906–1914: A Diplomatic History* (London, 1972), pp. 118–19.
69. Hugh and Christopher Seton-Watson, *The Making of a New Europe: R.W. Seton-Watson and the Last Years of Austria-Hungary* (London, 1981).
70. Frank Eyck, *G.P. Gooch: A Study in History and Politics* (London, 1982), p. 238.
71. H.N. Brailsford, *Macedonia* (London, 1906); the novelist Joyce Cary described his experiences of the Balkan War in *Memoir of the Bobotes* (London, 1965); the range of Brailsford's Balkan activities can be traced in F.M. Leventhal, *The Last Dissenter: H.N. Brailsford and his World* (Oxford, 1985).
72. R.J. Crampton, *The Hollow Detente: Anglo-German Relations in the Balkans 1911–1914* (London, n.d.), p. 19.
73. Joseph Heller, *British Policy towards the Ottoman Empire 1908–1914* (London, 1983).
74. Robbins, *Grey*, pp. 256–7.
75. Mosa Anderson, *Noel Buxton: A Life* (London, 1952), p. 56. The many complexities of Macedonia are explored in Peter Mackridge and Eleni Yannakakis, *Ourselves and Others: The Development of a Greek Macedonian Cultural Identity since 1912* (Oxford, 1997).
76. Erik J. Zürcher, *Turkey: A Modern History* (London, 1997), pp. 113–14.
77. However, according to the Edinburgh geographer 'Europe stops, not at Constantinople, but in the steppe region behind it, for the city itself has but little relation to the northern part of the peninsula on which it stands'. Marion I. Newbigin, *Geographical Aspects of Balkan Problems* (London, 1915), p. 16.
78. Hartmut Pogge von Strandmann, 'British and German Historians in 1914', in Stuchtey and Wende, *British and German Historiography*, pp. 335–72; Stuart Wallace, *War and the Image of Germany: British Academics 1914–1918* (Edinburgh, 1988); Keith Robbins, 'Britain in the Summer of 1914', in Robbins, *Politicians, Diplomacy and War in Modern British History*, pp. 175–88.
79. Keith Robbins, '*History*, the Historical Association and the "National Past"', in Robbins, *History, Religion and Identity in Modern Britain*, pp. 1–14.
80. Cited in Hyam, 'The British Empire in the Edwardian Era', in Brown and Louis, *The Oxford History of the British Empire*, p. 55.
81. H.G. Wells, *An Englishman Looks at the World* (London, 1916), pp. 334–5.

82. Richard Langhorne, 'Arbitration: The First Phase, 1870–1914', in Dockrill and McKercher (eds), *Diplomacy and World Power*, p. 51.
83. A.J.A. Morris, *The Scaremongers: The Advocacy of War and Rearmament 1896–1914* (London, 1984).
84. Martin Ceadel, *Semi-detached Idealists: The British Peace Movement and International Relations, 1854–1945* (Oxford, 2000), pp. 164–86 considers the various strands of opinion.
85. N. Angell, *Europe's Optical Illusion* (London, 1909).
86. Hinsley, *Power and the Pursuit of Peace*, pp. 141–2.
87. Hardinge, *Old Diplomacy*, p. 132.
88. James Bryce, *University and Historical Addresses* (London, 1913).
89. Kenneth Bourne, *Britain and the Balance of Power in North America, 1815–1908* (London, 1967), p. 410.
90. The Earl of Cromer, *Political and Literary Essays: Third Series* (London, 1916), p. 122.
91. Newton, *British Labour, European Socialism and the Struggle for Peace*, pp. 324–31.
92. Not for the first, nor for the last time, foreign policy might be said to be too serious a business even to have been left to the full cabinet, though some of its members found it quite convenient not to know fully what the foreign secretary had in mind. Keith Robbins, 'The Foreign Secretary, the Cabinet, Parliament and the Parties' and 'Public Opinion, the Press and Pressure Groups', reprinted in *Politicians, Diplomacy and War in Modern British History*, pp. 101–64. See also the chapter on the impact of the war in Keith Robbins, *The Abolition of War: The 'Peace Movement' in Britain, 1914–1919* (Cardiff, 1976), pp. 27–47.
93. David Stevenson, *The First World War and International Politics* (Oxford, 1988), p. 40, and *Armaments and the Coming of War: Europe 1904–1914* (Oxford, 1996), p. 419.
94. As A.J.P. Taylor, *The Struggle for Mastery in Europe 1848–1918* (Oxford, 1954), pp. 532–3, stressed.
95. A.J. Balfour, *Essays Speculative and Political* (London, 1920), p. 48.
96. Cited in Kendle, *Federal Britain*, p. 34.
97. Cited and discussed in Hinsley, *Power and the Pursuit of Peace*, pp. 140–1.
98. Dr Michael Sadler on 'The Universities and the War', in A.P. Newton (ed.), *The Empire and the Future* (London, 1916), pp. 8–9; George Robb, *British Culture and the First World War* (Basingstoke, 2002); John Cruickshank, *Variations on Catastrophe: Some French Responses to the Great War* (Oxford, 1982); Frank Field, *Three French Writers and the Great War* (Cambridge, 1975); Roland N. Stromberg, *Redemption by War: The Intellectuals and 1914* (Lawrence, 1982); and M. Eksteins, *Rites of Spring: The Great War and the Birth of the Modern Age* (London, 1989), offer other perspectives on the crisis.
99. Cited in Roberts, *Salisbury*, p. 692.
100. Cited in Holbraad, *Concert of Europe*, p. 180.
101. Cited in Paul Laity, *The British Peace Movement, 1870–1914* (Oxford, 2001), p. 225.
102. Robbins, *Abolition of War*, p. 18; Gerhard Besier, *Die protestantischen Kirchen Europas im Ersten Weltkrieg* (Göttingen, 1984) publishes a useful collection of documents. Introducing *The Russian Church* (London, 1916), the bishop of London commented that the war had brought together in bonds that, 'please God', would never be broken, the great nations of Russia and Great Britain. It was for that reason that the two churches, the 'souls' of the respective nations, should understand each other better and, if possible, draw closer together.
103. Leila J. Rupp, 'The Making of Women's International Organizations', in Geyer and Paulmann, *Mechanics of Internationalism*, pp. 224–5. The veteran world-famous Austrian peace activist Bertha von Suttner, however, insisted that opposition to war should be grounded in a rationality that women shared with men. Dorothy Grey, cited in Robbins, 'Sir Edward Grey and the British Empire', in Robbins, *Politicians, Diplomacy and War in Modern British History*, p. 170.

Chapter 9

1. Roger Eatwell, *Fascism: A History* (London, 1995); R.J. Overy, *The Dictators: Hitler's Germany and Stalin's Russia* (London, 2004).

2.   E.H. Carr, *International Relations since the Peace Treaties* (London, 1937), pp. 258–9.
3.   Donald Cameron Watt has an illuminating discussion of 'The European Civil War', in Wolfgang J. Mommsen and Lothar Kettenacker (eds), *The Fascist Challenge and the Policy of Appeasement* (London, 1983), pp. 3–21.
4.   Donald Cameron Watt, *How the War Came; The Immediate Origins of the Second World War* (London, 1989), p. 595.
5.   André Siegfried, *England's Story* (London, 1931), p. 231. Siegfried's book, and the views of other French writers, are discussed in Bell, *France and Britain*, pp. 198–200.
6.   Hew Strachan, *The First World War: Vol. 1 The Call to Arms* (Oxford, 2001), p. 98.
7.   Hagen Schulze, *Staat und Nation in der Europäischen Geschichte* (Munich, 1994), pp. 283–9, reflects on the relationship between 'Total War' and 'Total State'.
8.   Ian Clark, *Reform and Resistance in the International Order* (Cambridge, 1980) p. 121.
9.   The three most recent treatments are: Margaret Macmillan, *The Paris Peace Conference of 1919: The Attempt to End War* (London, 2001); Michael Dockrill and John Fisher (eds), *The Paris Peace Conference, 1919: Peace Without Victory?* (Basingstoke, 2001); Manfred P. Boemeke, Gerald D. Feldman and Elisabeth Glaser (eds), *The Treaty of Versailles: A Reassessment after 75 Years* (Cambridge, 1998).
10. There were also treaties at Saint Germain with Austria, at Trianon with Hungary, and at Neuilly with Bulgaria. The Sèvres Treaty, with the Ottoman Empire, was overtaken by events and was replaced in 1923 by the Treaty of Lausanne.
11. Cited in Robert Skidelsky, *John Maynard Keynes: Hopes Betrayed 1883–1920* (London, 1982), pp. 246–65.
12. Michael Howard, 'War in the Making and Unmaking of Europe', in *The Causes of Wars* (London, 1983), p. 164.
13. D. Cameron Watt, *Succeeding John Bull*, pp. 34–40, and Anne Orde, *Eclipse of Great Britain*, pp. 56–66, elaborate on points of British-American agreement and disagreement at this juncture.
14. Cited in V.H. Rothwell, *British War Aims and Peace Diplomacy 1914–1918* (Oxford, 1971), pp. 253–4.
15. M.L. Sanders and Philip M. Taylor, *British Propaganda during the First World War* (London, 1982), pp. 246–65. The view was subsequently taken that claims of German atrocities in 1914 in Belgium were 'propaganda'. John Horne and Alan Kramer, *German Atrocities, 1914: A History of Denial* (New Haven, 2001) in turn uncover 'denial'.
16. B.C. Busch, *Hardinge of Penshurst: A Study in the Old Diplomacy* (Hamden, 1980), p. 291.
17. Sybil Crowe and Edward Corp, *Our Ablest Public Servant: Sir Eyre Crowe 1864–1925* (Braunton, 1993), p. 322.
18. Sally Harris, *Out of Control: British Foreign Policy and the Union of Democratic Control, 1914–1918* (Hull, 1996); Arthur Ponsonby, *Democracy and Diplomacy* (London, 1915).
19. '1918–19: From War to Peace', *Journal of Contemporary History* Vol. 3 No. 4 (1968).
20. M.J. Daunton, 'How to Pay for the War: State, Society and Taxation in Britain, 1917–24', *English Historical Review* Vol. CXI No. 443 (September 1996), pp. 882–919.
21. Bruce Kent, *The Spoils of War: The Politics, Economic and Diplomacy of Reparations 1918–1932* (Oxford, 1991), pp. 373–90; Marc Trachtenberg, *Reparations in World Politics; France and European Economic Diplomacy, 1918–1923* (New York, 1980) are only two of many volumes on this subject.
22. Anne Orde, *British Policy and European Reconstruction after the First World War* (Cambridge, 1990). The author provides a summary contribution in Peter Catterall and C.J. Morris (eds), *Britain and the Threat to Stability in Europe, 1918–45* (London, 1993), pp. 8–15.
23. Jay Winter, *Sites of Memory, Sites of Mourning* (Cambridge, 1995), pp. 6, 227.
24. Keith Robbins, 'European Peace Movements and their Influence on Policy after the First World War', in R. Ahmann, A.M. Birke and M. Howard, *The Quest for Stability: Problems of West European Security 1918–1957* (Oxford, 1993), pp. 73–86; Peter Brock and Thomas P. Socknat, *Challenge to Mars: Essays on Pacifism from 1918 to 1945* (Toronto, 1999); Norman Ingram, *The Politics of Dissent: Pacifism in France, 1919–1939* (Oxford, 1991); K. Holl and W. Wette (eds), *Pazifismus in der Weimarer Republik* (Paderborn, 1981).

25. Keith Robbins, 'Protestant Churches and Peace', in Maurice Vaïsse, *Le Pacifisme en Europe des années 1920 aux années 1950* (Brussels, 1993), pp. 223–35.

26. Martin Ceadel, *Pacifism in Britain, 1914–1945: The Defining of a Faith* (Oxford, 1980) and *Semi-Detached Idealists: The British Peace Movement and International Relations, 1854–1945* (Oxford, 2000), pp. 239–434.

27. Arno J. Mayer, *The Persistence of the Old Regime: Europe to the Great War* (London, 1981); Keith Robbins, *The First World War* (Oxford, 1984).

28. 'The Contraction of England' and 'India and Britain: the climactic years, 1917–1947', in D.A. Low, *Eclipse of Empire* (Cambridge, 1993).

29. P.J. Cain and A.G. Hopkins, *British Imperialism: Crisis and Deconstruction 1914–1990* (London, 1993); Judith M. Brown and Wm Roger Louis, *The Oxford History of the British Empire: The Twentieth Century* (Oxford, 1999).

30. Mervyn O'Driscoll, '"To Bring Light Unto the Germans": Irish Recognition-seeking, the Weimar Republic and the British Commonwealth, 1930–2', *European History Quarterly* Vol. 33 No. 1 (January 2003), pp. 65–100.

31. Michael Howard, *The Continental Commitment* (London, 1972); Brian Bond, *British Military Policy between the Two World Wars* (Oxford, 1980).

32. Cited in P. Haggie, *Britannia at Bay: The Defence of the British Empire against Japan, 1931–1941* (Oxford, 1981), p. 73.

33. 'Failure to understand and deal with continental Europe' is the central thesis of Sir Roy Denman's *Missed Chances*, resulting in a situation, he supposed in 1996, in which Britain would end the century 'little more important than Switzerland', p. 1.

34. J.M. Keynes, *The Economic Consequences of the Peace* (London, 1919), p. 3.

35. Robert Skidelsky, *Keynes: Hopes Betrayed 1883–1920* (London, 1983), p. 122. Keynes had subsequently visited her in Germany. An 'Association of German Governesses in England' had 720 members in 1894. See Irene Hardach-Pinke, 'German Governesses in England', in Franz Bosbach, William Filmer-Sankey and Hermann Hiery, *Prince Albert and the Development of Education in England and Germany in the 19th Century* (Munich, 2000), pp. 23–31.

36. Frank Trentmann, 'Beyond Consumerism: New Historical Perspectives on Consumption', *Journal of Contemporary History* Vol. 39 No. 3 (2004), pp. 380–1. Trentmann draws here on the work of H.-G. Haupt, *Konsum und Handel: Europa im 19. und 20. Jahrhundert* (Göttingen, 2002).

37. A recent discussion of President Wilson's understanding is Allen Lynch, 'Woodrow Wilson and the principle of 'national self-determination'; a reconsideration', in *Review of International Studies* Vol. 28 (2002), pp. 419–36.

38. Agnes Headlam-Morley, *The New Constitutions of Europe* (Oxford, 1929). The author subsequently became professor of international relations at Oxford. She edited her father's *A Memoir of the Paris Peace Conference 1919* (London, 1972). See also Alan Sharp 'James Headlam-Morley: Creating International History', *Diplomacy and Statecraft* Vol. 9 No. 3 (November 1998), pp. 266–83.

39. R.L. Buell (ed.), *New Governments in Europe: The Trend toward Dictatorship* (New York, 1934), p. iv.

40. Richard Lamb, *Mussolini and the British* (London, 1997).

41. Headlam-Morley, p. 9; Buell, p. vii; Robert Skidelsky, *Oswald Mosley* (London, 1981); Keith Robbins, 'Stafford Cripps', in K. Jefferys (ed.), *Labour Forces: From Ernest Bevin to Gordon Brown* (London, 2002), pp. 63–80.

42. John Stevenson, 'Communism and the Failure of Fascism in Interwar Britain', in Martin Blinkhorn (ed.), *Fascists and Communists: The Radical Right and the Establishment in Twentieth-Century Europe* (London, 1990), pp. 284–92.

43. David Jarvis, 'British Conservatism and Class Politics in the 1920s', *English Historical Review* Vol. CXI No. 440 (February 1996), pp. 59–84; N.J. Crowson, *Facing Fascism: The Conservative Party and the European Dictators 1935–1940* (London, 1997).

44. Keith Robbins 'The British Way and Purpose', in Keith Robbins (ed.), *The British Isles, 1901–1951* (Oxford, 2002), pp. 73–100, reflects more extensively on these matters. See essays in the same volume by Duncan Tanner, pp. 43–67, W.R. Garside, pp. 163–92, and Rodney Lowe, pp. 197–226, on political, economic and social issues.

45. E. Barker, *National Character and the Factors in its Formation* (London, 1927).

46. Andrew Thorpe, *The Failure of Extremism in Inter-War Britain* (Exeter, 1989); Paul Ward, *Britishness since 1870* (London, 2004), pp. 103–4; Philip Williamson, *National*

Crisis and National Government: British Politics, the Economy and Empire, 1926–1932 (Cambridge, 1992) and *Stanley Baldwin. Conservative Leadership and National Values* (Cambridge, 1999); Stanley Baldwin, *On England* (London, 1926); Martin Pugh, 'The Rise of Labour and the Political Culture of Conservatism, 1890–1945', *History* Vol. 87 No. 288 (October 2002), pp. 514–37, and his *Hurrah for the Blackshirts! Fascists and Fascism in Britain between the Wars* (London, 2005); Richard Griffiths, *Patriotism Perverted: Captain Ramsay, the Right Club and British Anti-Semitism, 1939–40* (London, 1998).

47. Tom Buchanan, *Britain and the Spanish Civil War* (Cambridge, 1997); Contrasts can be seen in Hywel Francis, 'Welsh Miners and the Spanish Civil War', *Journal of Contemporary History* Vol. 5 No. 3 (1970), pp. 177–91; James Flint, '"Must God go Fascist?": English Catholic opinion and the Spanish Civil War', *Church History* LVI (1987), pp. 364–74; James E. Hopkins, *Into the Heart of Fire: The British in the Spanish Civil War* (Stanford, 2000). Glyn Stone, *The Oldest Ally: Britain and the Portuguese Connection, 1936–1941* (Woodbridge, 1994).

48. D.C. Watt, 'America and the British Foreign-Policy-Making Elite, from Joseph Chamberlain to Anthony Eden, 1895–1956', in his *Personalities and Policies: Studies in the Formulation of British Foreign Policy in the Twentieth Century* (London, 1985), pp. 19–52, looks at 'the other side' of this particular coin.

49. F.M. Leventhal, *Arthur Henderson* (Manchester, 1989).

50. Peter Edwards, 'The Austen Chamberlain–Mussolini Meetings', *Historical Journal* XIV, 1 (1971), pp. 153–64.

51. A. Schwarz, *Die Reise ins Dritte Reich: Britische Augenzeugen im nationalistischen Deutschland (1933–39)* (Göttingen, 1993).

52. Gordon Martel (ed.), *The Times and Appeasement: The Journals of A.L. Kennedy*, Camden Fifth Series (London, 2000), p. 88.

53. Skidelsky, *Keynes*, p. 189.

54. Norman Rose, *Vansittart: Study of a Diplomat* (London, 1978); so concludes Brian McKercher, 'Old Diplomacy and New: The Foreign Office and Foreign Policy, 1919–1939', in Dockrill and McKercher, *Diplomacy and World Power*, pp. 79–114; see also, in the same volume, Donald Cameron Watt, 'Chamberlain's Ambassadors', pp. 136–70.

55. C.R. Buxton in C.R. Buxton (ed.), *Towards a Lasting Settlement* (London, 1915), p. 58.

56. Keith Robbins, 'British Diplomacy and Bulgaria, 1914–15', in *Politicians, Diplomacy and War*, pp. 221–2.

57. Robert T. Nightingale, *The Personnel of the British Foreign Office and Diplomatic Service, 1851–1929* (London, 1930).

58. Greenwood in A.J. Grant *et al.*, *An Introduction to the Study of International Relations* (London, 1916).

59. Erik Goldstein, *Winning the Peace: British Diplomatic Strategy, Peace Planning and the Paris Peace Conference, 1916–1920* (Oxford, 1991), p. 282. The handbooks were subsequently published.

60. A.J. Pollard, *The League of Nations in History* (Oxford, 1918), p. 12.

61. Eileen Power, 'History and World Peace', in F.S. Marvin (ed.), *The Evolution of World Peace* (London, 1921), pp. 182–5; Maxine Berg, *Eileen Power: A Woman in History 1889–1940* (Cambridge, 1996), pp. 83–109. Power travelled extensively in the Far East and thought in 'world' rather than 'European' terms.

62. D.J. Markwell, 'Sir Alfred Zimmern Revisited 50 Years On', *Review of International Studies*, Vol. 12 No. 4 (Oct. 1986), pp. 279–92; G.K. Peatling, 'Globalism, Hegemonism and British Power: J.A. Hobson and Alfred Zimmern Reconsidered', *History* Vol. 89, 3, No. 295 (July 2004), pp. 381–98.

63. W.H. McNeill, *Arnold J. Toynbee: A Life* (Oxford, 1989): Christopher Brewin, 'Research in a Global Context: A Discussion of Toynbee's Legacy', *Review of International Studies* Vol. 18 No. 2 (April, 1992), pp. 115–30.

64. James Bryce, *International Relations* (London, 1922) p. 364.

65. Sir John Wheeler-Bennett, *Knaves, Fools and Heroes in Europe between the Wars* (London, 1974).

66. G.M. Trevelyan, *Reminiscences of an Historian* (London, 1919), pp. 240–2; G.M. Trevelyan, *Scenes from Italy's War* (London, 1919).

67. A.E. Zimmern, *Europe in Convalescence* (London, 1922), p. 22.

68. F.S. Oliver, *The Endless Adventure* (London, 1930) ii, pp. 119–20. Baldwin was a great admirer of Oliver's writings. See also, on the general theme, Peter Mandler, *History and National Life* (London, 2002).

69. Viscount Grey of Fallodon, *The League of Nations* (Oxford, 1918), pp. 8–9.

70. George W. Egerton, *Great Britain and the Creation of the League of Nations: Strategy, Politics and International Organization, 1914–1919* (Chapel Hill, 1978); Robbins, *Abolition of War*; and 'Lord Bryce and the First World War', in Robbins, *Politicians, Diplomacy and War*, pp. 189–214; League to Enforce Peace, *Enforced Peace* (New York, 1916).

71. J.P.D. Dunbabin, 'The League of Nations' Place in the International System', *History* Vol. 78 No. 254 (October, 1993), pp. 421–42.

72. The British engineer Allan Young, *Forward from Chaos* (London, 1933) cited in Jo-Anne Pemberton, 'New Worlds for Old: The League of Nations in the Age of Electricity', *Review of International Studies* Vol. 28 No. 2 (April, 2002), pp. 327–8.

73. Arthur Salter, *Memoirs of a Public Servant*, p. 160.

74. James Barros, *Betrayal from Within: Joseph Avenol, Secretary-General of the League of Nations, 1933–1940* (New Haven and London, 1969), p. 8.

75. Butler, *Confident Morning* (London, 1950), pp. 161–2.

76. Donald S. Birn, *The League of Nations Union 1918–1945* (Oxford, 1981).

77. Hinsley, *Power and the Pursuit of Peace*, p. 315.

78. Martel (ed.), *The Times and Appeasement*, p. 7.

79. James Barros, *Office without Power: Secretary-General Sir Eric Drummond 1919–1933* (London, 1979); A.C. Temperley, *The Whispering Gallery of Europe* (London, 1939), p. 45.

80. C.K. Webster and Sydney Herbert, *The League of Nations in Theory and Practice* (London, 1933), p. 304.

81. Christopher Thorne, *The Limits of Foreign Policy: The West, the League and the Far Eastern Crisis of 1931–1933* (London, 1972); Daniel P. Waley, *British Public Opinion and the Abyssinian War, 1935–36* (London, 1975).

82. Cited in Douglas Johnson, 'Britain and France in 1940', *Transactions of the Royal Historical Society Fifth Series* Vol. 22 (1972), p. 149.

83. Butler, *Confident Morning*, pp. 42–3.

84. Georges Bernanos, 'Letters to the English', in *Plea for Liberty* (London, 1945), p. 28.

85. James Munson (ed.), *Echoes of the Great War: The Diary of the Reverend Andrew Clark 1914–1919* (Oxford, 1985), p. 199.

86. Robert Graves, *Goodbye to All That* (London, 1929), p. 259.

87. Harry Lauder, *A Minstrel in France* (New York, 1918), p. 134.

88. Sir David Kelly, *The Ruling Few* (London, 1952), p. 20. The author, a British diplomat of Irish Protestant background, like Sir Henry, thought that the divided mentality of their background (or was it schizophrenia?) helped them cope when they encountered different cultures.

89. C.E. Callwell, *Field Marshal Sir Henry Wilson, his Life and Diaries* ii (London, 1927), p. 99; Milner is cited in David R. Woodward, *Lloyd George and the Generals* (London, 1983), p. 312.

90. Clemenceau's encounter is put in a broader context in Jacques Fortes, *Fascination and Misgivings: the United States in French Opinion, 1870–1914* (Cambridge, 2000).

91. Jean-Baptiste Duroselle, *Clemenceau* (Paris, 1988), pp. 68–88; Robert K. Hanks, 'Georges Clemenceau and the English', *Historical Journal* Vol. 45, No. 1 (2002), pp. 53–77. One of his contacts was the socialist H.M. Hyndman, who wrote an admiring biography, *Clemenceau: The Man and his Time* (London, 1919). Hyndman found in the London Library the copy of the translation of Mill's work that Clemenceau had himself presented to Mill. Mill himself, who died in Avignon, loved France and many other French Radicals admired him. For his own views on international relations see K.E. Miller, 'John Stuart Mill's Theory of International Relations', *Journal of the History of Ideas* 22 (1961), pp. 493–514.

92. David Stevenson, *French War Aims against Germany 1914–1919* (Oxford, 1982), pp. 76–80, 100–2; cf. Rothwell, *British War Aims*, and Goldstein, *Winning the Peace*.

93. Bell, *France and Britain 1900–1940*, pp. 94–112, explores contrasting perceptions.

94. A. Lentin, '"Appeasement" at the Paris Peace Conference', in Dockrill and Fisher (eds), *The Paris Peace Conference, 1919*, pp. 60–1; A. Lentin, *Guilt at Versailles: Lloyd George and the Pre-History of Appeasement* (London, 1985); Douglas Newton, *British Policy and the Weimar Republic, 1918–1919* (Oxford, 1997).

95. Anthony Adamthwaite, *Grandeur and Misery: France's Bid for Power in Europe, 1914–1940* (London, 1995).
96. Dockrill and Goold, *Peace without Promise*, p. 86.
97. Goldstein, *Winning the Peace*, p. 276.
98. Keith Wilson, *Channel Tunnel Vision, 1850–1945: Dreams and Nightmares* (London, 1995) Chapter 5.
99. Cited in Alan Sharp, 'British Perceptions of France', in David Dutton (ed.), *Statecraft and Diplomacy in the Twentieth Century* (Liverpool, 1995), p. 64.
100. E. O'Riordan, *British Foreign Policy and the Ruhr Occupation Crisis, 1922–24* (Basingstoke, 2000).
101. Angela Kaiser, *Lord D'Abernon und die englische Deutschland-politik 1920–1926* (Frankfurt-am-Main, 1989) is a full study of the influential role played by the British ambassador in Berlin.
102. C. Maier, *Recasting Bourgeois Europe* (Princeton, 1975); Gaynor Johnson (ed.), *Locarno Revisited: European Diplomacy, 1920–1929* (London, 2004).
103. Bell, *France and Britain*, p. 151.
104. David Dutton, *Austen Chamberlain: Gentleman in Politics* (Bolton, 1985), p. 259.
105. Sir Austen Chamberlain, *Down the Years* (London, 1935), pp. 151–71; R. Grayson, *Austen Chamberlain and the Commitment to Europe: British Foreign Policy, 1924–1929* (London, 1997) takes a more 'positive' view.
106. Sir Austen Chamberlain, 'Great Britain as a European Power', *Journal of the Royal Institute of International Affairs* Vol. 9 (1930), pp. 180–8.
107. Wm Roger Louis, *Great Britain and Germany's Lost Colonies, 1914–1919* (Oxford, 1987).
108. Philip Noel-Baker, *The First World Disarmament Conference, 1932–33 and Why it Failed* (Oxford, 1979), p. 118, continued to argue that if British ministers 'had really tried' a treaty could have been obtained and the Second World War avoided.
109. Cited in R.A.C. Parker, 'Probleme britischer Aussenpolitik während der Weltwirtschaftskrise', in Josef Becker/Klaus Hildebrand (eds), *Internationale Beziehungen in der Weltwirtschaftskrise 1929–1933* (Munich, 1980), p. 13.
110. Dell provided a foreword to the English translation of Léon Blum's *Peace and Disarmament* (London, 1932), pp. 15–16.
111. Cited in Reynolds, *Britannia Overruled*, p. 118.
112. Klaus Jaitner, 'Aspekte britischer Deutschlandpolitik 1930–1932', in Becker/Hildebrand, *Internationale Beziehungen* quotes the memorandum in full on pp. 31–8.
113. Dick Richardson and Carolyn Kitching, 'Britain and the World Disarmament Conference', in Catterall and Morris (eds), *Britain and the Threat to Stability*, pp. 35–56.
114. These issues are examined in Nicholas Rostow, *Anglo-French Relations 1934–36* (Basingstoke, 1984) and Martin Thomas, *Britain, France and Appeasement: Anglo-French Relations in the Popular Front Era* (Leamington Spa, 1996).
115. See the general discussion in Keith Robbins, *Appeasement* (Oxford, 1997).
116. Michael Dockrill, *British Establishment Perspectives on France, 1936–40* (Basingstoke, 1999) and his summary 'British Official Perceptions of France and the French, 1936–1940', in Chassaigne and Dockrill, *Anglo-French Relations 1898–1998*, pp. 94–108.
117. Winston S. Churchill, *The Second World War: The Gathering Storm* (London, 1950 Reprint Society), pp. 178–9.
118. Cited in David Ayerst, *Garvin of the Observer* (London, 1985), p. 176.
119. Robbins, *Present and Past*, p. 34.
120. David G. Williamson, *The British in Germany 1918–1930: The Reluctant Occupiers* (Oxford, 1991), p. 347; G.H. Bennett, *British Foreign Policy during the Curzon Period, 1919–24* (Basingstoke, 1995).
121. Stephanie Salzmann, *Great Britain, Germany and the Soviet Union: Rapallo and After, 1922–1934* (Woodbridge, 2003) is the most thorough recent treatment of this question.
122. Strachan, *The First World War*, pp. 1130–4 cites various German authors on these themes.
123. Hans-George Drescher, *Ernst Troeltsch: His Life and Work* (London, 1992), pp. 314–15. Troeltsch's *Deutscher Geist und Westeuropa* was published posthumously in 1925.

124. Cited in S. Wallace, *War and the Image of Germany: British Academics 1914–1918* (Edinburgh, 1988), pp. 193–7.
125. C.H. Herford, *The Mind of Post-War Germany* (Oxford, 1927), p. 25.
126. R. Gardiner and H. Rocholl (eds), *Britain and Germany: A Frank Discussion Instigated by Members of the Younger Generation* (London, 1928); F.L. Carsten, *Britain and the Weimar Republic: The British Documents* (London, 1984; M. Gilbert, *Britain and Germany between the Wars* (London, 1964).
127. W.H. Auden, *The Orators* (London, 1932), p. 83.
128. D. Clemens, *Herr Hitler in Germany. Wahrnehmugen und Deutungen des Nationalsozialismus in Grossbritannien 1920 bis 1939* (Göttingen, 1996); Josef Henke, *England in Hitler's politischem Kalkül* (Boppard am Rhein, 1973) examines the reverse calculation; G. Strobl, *The Germanic Isle: Nazi Perceptions of Britain* (Cambridge, 2000) broadens the canvas. See also G.T. Waddington, '*Hassgegner*: German Views of Great Britain in the Later 1930s', *History* Vol. 81 No. 261 (January, 1996), pp. 22–39.
129. Cited in Donald McLachlan, *In the Chair: Barrington-Ward of* The Times (London, 1971), p. 110.
130. See essays on Martin Niemöller and the German church struggle, as interpreted in Britain, in Robbins, *History, Religion and Identity*, pp. 161–94; Alan Wilkinson, 'Bishop Bell and Germany', in Catterall and Morris (eds), *Britain and the Threat to Stability*, pp. 74–93.
131. Richard Griffiths, *Fellow Travellers of the Right; British Enthusiasts for Nazi Germany, 1933–39* (London, 1980).
132. Giles MacDonagh, *A Good German: Adam von Trott zu Solz* (London, 1989); that there were and remain differences of view can be seen in Silvia Daniel, '"Troubled Loyalty": Britische-deutsche Debatten um Adam von Trott zu Solz 1933–1969', *Vierteljahreshefte für Zeitgeschichte* (July, 2004), pp. 409–40.
133. There is now a considerable literature on the refugees: G. Hirschfeld (ed.), *Exile in Great Britain* (Leamington Spa, 1984), p. 2. A.J. Sherman, *Island Refuge: Britain and Refugees from the Third Reich 1933–1939* (London, 1973); Marion Berghahn, *Continental Britons: German-Jewish Refugees from Nazi Germany* (Oxford, 1988); Bernard Wasserstein, *Britain and the Jews of Europe, 1939–45* (Oxford, 1979); Louise London, 'British Reactions to the Jewish Flight from Europe', in Catterall and Morris (eds), *Britain and the Threat to Stability*, pp. 57–73 and her book *Whitehall and the Jews: British Immigration Policy, Jewish Refugees and the Holocaust* (Cambridge, 2000). German law faculties lost about a quarter of their staff as a result of the Nazi regime. The work of those who came to Britain is examined in Jack Beatson and Reinhard Zimmermann (eds), *Jurists Uprooted: German-Speaking Emigré Lawyers in Twentieth Century Britain* (Oxford, 2004); Daniel Snowman, *The Hitler Emigrés: the Cultural Impact on Britain of Refugees from Nazism* (London, 2002); Anthony Grenville, *Refugees from the Third Reich in Britain* (Amsterdam, 2002).
134. The statements, respectively, of John Charmley, *Chamberlain and the Last Peace* (London, 1989), p. 212, and R.A.C. Parker, *Chamberlain and Appeasement: British Policy and the Coming of the Second World War* (Basingstoke, 1993), p. 347.
135. A compelling picture of its wartime condition is presented in Maureen Healy, *Vienna and the Fall of the Habsburg Empire: Total War and Everyday Life in World War I* (Cambridge, 2004).
136. See the essay 'Imperial Hangovers: The Case of Austria', in Robert A. Kann, *Dynasty, Politics and Culture* (Boulder, Colorado, 1991), pp. 335–52.
137. Lord Salter, *Memoirs of a Public Servant* (London, 1961), p. 176.
138. Michael Stewart, *Life and Labour* (London, 1980), p. 35.
139. *Naomi Mitchison's Vienna Diary* (London, 1934).
140. Wheeler-Bennett, *Knaves, Fools and Heroes*, p. 120.
141. Sir Walford Selby, *Diplomatic Twilight 1930–1940* (London, 1953), pp. 9–82; Lindsay W. Michie, *Robert Hadow: First Secretary in the British Foreign Office, 1931–1939* (Westport, 1996), pp. 9–27.
142. G.E.R. Gedye, *Fallen Bastions* (London, 1939).
143. Dutton, *Austen Chamberlain*, pp. 250–1.
144. Julia Namier, *Lewis Namier* (Oxford, 1971), pp. 136–52; S. Collini, 'Idealizing England: Élie Halévy and Lewis Namier', in *English Pasts* (Oxford, 1999), pp. 67–84.
145. Herbert Olbrich, '"Our role should be that of a disinterested amicus curiae" – Great

Britain and Eastern Europe in the 1920s', in Hans-Heinrich Jansen and Ursula Lehmkuhl, *Grossbritannien, das Empire und die Welt* (Bochum, 1995), pp. 105–24.

146. Norman Davies, *Europe*, pp. 934–6. His book is *White Eagle, Red Star; The Polish-Soviet War, 1919–20* (London, 1972).

147. Alan J. Foster, 'Britain and East Central Europe 1918–1948', in Peter Stirk (ed.), *Mitteleuropa: History and Prospects* (Edinburgh, 1994), pp. 118–19.

148. Cited in Keith Feiling, *The Life of Neville Chamberlain* (London, 1946), p. 472.

149. R.H. Bruce Lockhart, *Retreat from Glory* (London, 1934), p. 56.

150. Its head was Béla Kun, a Jewish ex-prisoner of war who had just returned from Russia. There was alarm, occasionally, even on the part of Sir Eyre Crowe, that 'the heart and soul of all revolutionary and terroristic movements have invariably been Jews'.

151. N.J. Crowson (ed.), *Fleet Street, Press Barons and Politics: The Journals of Collin Brooks, 1932–1940*. Roual Historical Society, Camden Fifth Series Vol. 11 (London, 1998), pp. 289–90.

152. 'Ruritania' is considered in V. Goldsworthy, *Inventing Ruritania: The Imperialism of the Imagination* (London, 1998).

153. Emil Nagy in Count Albert Apponyi *et al.*, *Justice for Hungary* (London, 1929), pp. 366–7.

154. Viscount Rothermere, *Warnings and Predictions* (London, 1939), pp. 123–4.

155. His foreword to C.A. Macartney, *Hungary* (London, 1934) a volume in a series of national histories that Fisher edited designed to illuminate the 'historical forces' at work in the contemporary world. Macartney agreed that it would be ludicrous to pretend that Hungary bore any resemblance to what Britons understood by democracy but he thought that 'the millennial endurance of the oligarchic system in Hungary cannot be explained on any other assumption than that it is peculiarly adapted to Magyar psychology', pp. 355–6. In 1939, Owen O'Malley, newly appointed British minister in Budapest, thought that the Foreign Office and ministers in London knew nothing of Hungary and did not wish to learn anything. Owen O'Malley, *The Phantom Caravan* (London, 1954), p. 202.

156. M.-L. Recker, *England in der Donauraum 1919–1929. Probleme einer europäischen Nachkriegsordnung* (Stuttgart, 1976). The author has also edited a useful volume in which contributors look at the British-German relationships in the Baltic and in the Balkans in *Von der Konkurrenz zur Rivalität. Das britisch-deutsche Verhältnis in den Ländern der europäischen Peripherie 1919–39* (Stuttgart, 1986); a more recent interpretation is G. Bátonyi, *Britain and Central Europe, 1918–1933* (Oxford, 1999).

157. Alan Sharp, 'Britain and the protection of minorities at the Paris Peace Conference, 1919', in A.C. Hepburn (ed.), *Minorities in History* (London, 1978), pp. 170–88.

158. Hugh and Christopher Seton-Watson, *The Making of a New Europe: R.W. Seton-Watson and the Last Years of Austria-Hungary* (London, 1981), p. 355.

159. Sydney Herbert, *Nationality and its Problems* (London, 1920), p. 170.

160. See various articles by Mark Cornwell, 'The Rise and Fall of a "Special Relationship": Britain and Czechoslovakia 1930–1948', in Brian Brivati and Harriet Jones (eds), *What Difference did the War Make?* (Leicester, 1993), pp. 131–50; 'A Fluctuating Barometer: British Diplomatic Views of the Czech-German Relationship in Czechoslovakia, 1918–1938', in Eva Schmidt-Hartmann and Stanley B. Winters (eds), *Great Britain, the United States and the Bohemian Lands, 1848–1938* (Munich, 1991); 'The Struggle on the Czech-German Language Border, 1880–1940' *English Historical Review* Vol. CIX No. 433 (September, 1994), pp. 914–51. Keith Robbins, 'Konrad Henlein, the Sudeten Question and British Foreign policy', in Robbins, *Politicians, Diplomacy and War*, pp. 273–98.

161. R.B. Mowat, *Nineteenth-Century Europe* (London, 1928), p. 190; Sir Henry Wilson, speaking in Belfast in 1920, upset the Foreign Office by saying that he 'liked to see a small state as part of a great empire'. Cited in Sharp, 'Minorities', p. 184.

162. Sir Harry Brittain, *Happy Pilgrimage* (London, n.d.), pp. 212–16.

163. John Hiden and Patrick Salmon, *The Baltic States and Europe: Estonia, Latvia and Lithuania in the Twentieth Century* (London, 1991), p. 74. The book also has further information on British policy and interests.

164. E.D. Simon, *The Smaller Democracies* (London, 1939).

165. Lord Strang, *Home and Abroad* (London, 1956), pp. 52–3.

166. Rebecca West, *Black Lamb and Grey Falcon* (London, 1942).

167. Cited in Patrick Finney, 'Raising Frankenstein: Great Britain, "Balkanism" and the Search for a Balkan Locarno in the 1920s', *European History Quarterly* Vol. 33 No. 3 (July, 2003), p. 333.
168. Dimitri Pentzopoulos, *The Balkan Exchange of Minorities and its Impact on Greece* (London, 2002).
169. William Teeling, *Why Britain Prospers* (London, 1938), pp. 284–5.
170. Halford Mackinder, *Democratic Ideals and Reality* (London, 1919), pp. 214–15.
171. Cited in Sharp, 'British Perceptions of France', in Dutton (ed.), *Statecraft and Diplomacy*, p. 73.
172. Winfried Baumgart and Konrad Repgen (eds), *Brest-Litovsk* (Göttingen, 1989).
173. Keith Neilson, *Strategy and Supply: The Anglo-Russian Alliance 1914–17* (London, 1984), p. 312.
174. The three volumes of Richard H. Ullman, *Anglo-Soviet Relations, 1917–1921* (Princeton, 1961, 1967 and 1972) examine these matters thoroughly.
175. Cited in Stephen White, *Britain and the Bolshevik Revolution: A Study in the Politics of Diplomacy 1920–1924* (London, 1979), p. 114; Stuart Macintyre, *A Proletarian Science* (Cambridge, 1980).
176. Taylor, *Struggle for Mastery*, p. 568.
177. Norman Davies, *Europe*, p. 932, exempts himself from this failure.
178. Cited in Hiden and Salmon, *Baltic Nations and Europe*, p. 84.
179. James Flint, 'English Catholics and the Proposed Soviet Alliance, 1939', *Journal of Ecclesiastical History* Vol. 48 No. 3 (July, 1997), pp. 468–84.
180. *Labour and the Peace Treaty* (London, 1919), p. 64.
181. Stephen White, 'British Labour in Soviet Russia, 1920', *English Historical Review* Vol. CIX No. 432 (June, 1994), pp. 621–40.
182. Andrew Thorpe, *The British Communist Party and Moscow, 1920–43* (Manchester, 2000); T. Rees and A. Thorpe (eds), *International Communism and the Communist International* (Manchester, 1998). Even so, the extent to which the CPGB had some 'autonomy' remains a subject of debate.
183. C. Delisle Burns, *International Politics* (London, 1920), p. 172.
184. Stephen Howe, 'Labour and International Affairs', in Duncan Tanner, Pat Thane and Nick Tiratsoo (eds), *Labour's First Century* (Cambridge, 2000), p. 124.
185. Paul Ward, *Red Flag and Union Jack: Englishness, Patriotism and the British Left, 1881–1924* (Woodbridge, 1998); F.M. Leventhal, *Arthur Henderson* (Manchester, 1989), pp. 85–6; Keith Robbins, 'Labour Foreign Policy and International Socialism: MacDonald and the League of Nations', in Robbins, *Politicians, Diplomacy and War*, pp. 239–71.
186. Stefan Berger, *The British Labour Party and the German Social Democrats, 1900–1951: A Comparative Study* (Oxford, 1994); Christine Collette, *The International Faith: Labour's Attitudes to European Socialism, 1918–1939* (Aldershot, 1998); Donald Sassoon, *One Hundred Years of Socialism: The West European Left in the Twentieth Century* (London, 1998).
187. N. Wood, *Communism and the British Intellectuals* (London, 1959); F.S. Northedge and Audrey Wells, *Britain and Soviet Communism: The Impact of a Revolution* (London, 1982).
188. Walter Citrine, *I Search for Truth in Russia* (London, 1936).
189. Keith Robbins, 'Britain, 1940 and Christian Civilization', in Robbins, *History, Religion and Identity*, pp. 195–214.
190. Pegg, *Evolution of the European Idea*, describes the activities of individuals and societies.
191. Cornelia Navari, 'The Origins of the Briand Plan', in A. Bosco (ed.), *The Federal Idea: the History of Federation from Enlightenment to 1945* (London, 1991), pp. 211–36; Ralph White, '"Through a Glass, Darkly": The Foreign Office Investigation of French Federalism, January–May 1930', in Dutton (ed.), *Statecraft and Diplomacy*; Robert Boyce, 'Britain's First No to Europe: Britain and the Briand Plan, 1929–1930', *European Studies Review* 10 (1980), pp. 17–45, and 'Was there a "British" Alternative to the Briand Plan?', in Catterall and Morris (eds), *Britain and the Threat to Stability*, pp. 17–34 offer diverging reflections.
192. Siân Nicholas, 'Being British: Creeds and Cultures', in Robbins, *The British Isles*, p. 128.

193. See the discussion both of Briand and of Coudenhove-Kalergi in Wilson and van der
      Dussen (eds), *The History of the Idea of Europe*, pp. 98–106.
194. Julian Huxley and A.C. Haddon, *We Europeans* (London, 1935 [1938 edn]), pp.
      286–7.
195. H.A.L. Fisher, *A History of Europe* (London, 1936), pp. 6–7.

Chapter 10

1.   Anthony Eden, *Days for Decision* (London, 1949), p. 145.
2.   J.G.A. Pocock, 'The New British History in Atlantic Perspective', *American Historical
      Review* Vol. 104 (1999), pp. 492–3; J.G.A. Pocock, 'British History: A Plea for a New
      Subject', *New Zealand Journal of History* 8 (1974), pp. 3–21; J.G.A. Pocock, 'History
      and Sovereignty: The Historiographical Response to Europeanization in Two British
      Cultures', *Journal of British Studies* 31 (1992), pp. 358–89; C. Bridge and K.
      Federorovich (eds), *The British World: Diaspora, Culture and Identity* (London, 2003).
3.   J.G.A. Pocock, 'Deconstructing Europe' (1991) reprinted in P. Gowan and P. Anderson
      (eds), *The Question of Europe* (London, 1997), pp. 297–317.
4.   Christopher Lord, *British Entry into the European Community under the Heath
      Government of 1970–1974* (Aldershot, 1993).
5.   Edward Heath, *The Course of My Life* (London, 1998), pp. 105–6. His pre-war travels
      had taken him to Germany, Poland and Spain. William Whitelaw, another prominent
      Tory who had seen service in Belgium, the Netherlands and Germany in 1944–45, was
      'desperately keen' that another world war would never again start in western Europe.
      W. Whitelaw, *The Whitelaw Memoirs* (London, 1989), p. 74.
6.   N.J. Crowson, 'The Conservatives and Europe since 1945', in R. Broad and V. Preston
      (eds), *Moored to the Continent? Britain and European Integration* (London, 2001), pp.
      173–92.
7.   Uwe Kitzinger, *Diplomacy and Persuasion. How Britain Joined the Common Market*
      (London, 1973).
8.   David Butler and Uwe Kitzinger, *The 1975 Referendum* (London, 1976); Philip
      Goodhart, *Fullhearted Consent: The Story of the Referendum Campaign – and the
      Campaign for the Referendum* (London, 1976); Douglas Jay, *After the Common
      Market: A Better Alternative for Britain* (London, 1968), p. 13.
9.   Cited in Vaughan, *Post-War Integration in Europe*, p. 203.
10.   David Sanders, *Losing an Empire, Finding a Role: British Foreign Policy since 1945*
      (Basingstoke, 1990); Michael Dockrill and John W. Young (eds), *British Foreign Policy,
      1945–56* (Basingstoke, 1989); Stephen George, *Britain and European Integration since
      1945* (Oxford, 1991); Michael Charlton, *The Price of Victory* (London, 1983); Ritchie
      Ovendale (ed.), *The Foreign Policy of the British Labour Governments, 1945–51*
      (Leicester, 1984); P.M.R. Stirk and Dick Willis (eds), *Shaping Postwar Europe.
      European Unity and Disunity 1945–1957* (London, 1991); Wolfram Kaiser, *Using
      Europe, Abusing the Europeans* (London, 1996); Dominik Geppert (ed.), *The Postwar
      Challenge, 1945–1958* (Oxford, 2003).
11.   General accounts have frequently been written more from a desire to explain 'what went
      wrong' and to point 'the way forward' than to understand the complexity of the issues.
      G. Radice, *Offshore: Britain and the European Idea* (London, 1992); H. Young, *This
      Blessed Plot: Britain and Europe from Churchill to Blair* (London, 1998).
12.   René Girault and Gérard Bossuat (eds), *Les Europe des Européens* (Paris, 1993);
      Elisabeth du Réau, *L'Idée de l'Europe au Xxième siècle* (Paris, 1996); R. Brubaker,
      Nationalism Reframed: Nationhood and the National Question in the New Europe
      (Cambridge, 1996); B. Jenkins and S. Sofos (eds), *Nation and Identity in Contemporary
      Europe* (London, 1996); N. Piers Ludlow, 'Us or Them? Europe in British Political
      Discourse', in Bo Strath and Mikael af Malmborg (eds), *The Meanings of Europe*
      (Oxford, 2002).
13.   C. Harvie, 'The Moment of British Nationalism 1939–1970', *Political Quarterly* 71
      (2000), pp. 328–40; Keith Robbins, 'State and Nation in the United Kingdom since
      1945', in *History, Religion and Identity*, pp. 227–38.

14. Stuart Ward, 'The End of Empire and the Fate of Britishness', in *History, Nationhood and the Question of Britain* (Basingstoke, 2004), pp. 242–58.
15. The phrase is that of the writer on the British Empire (and on Wales) Jan Morris. See Keith Robbins '"This Grubby Wreck of Old Glories": The United Kingdom and the End of the British Empire', in *History, Religion and Identity*, pp. 281–92.
16. Hugh Seton-Watson concluded in his *Nations and States* (London, 1976), p. 42, that the United Kingdom was no longer united and that the centuries-long process of union into one kingdom, which had appeared successful in the first half of the twentieth century, appeared so no longer.
17. Keith Robbins, 'Cultural Independence and Political Devolution in Wales', in H.T. Dickinson, *The Challenge to Westminster: Sovereignty, Devolution and Independence* (East Linton, 2000), pp. 81–90. The volume contains other essays on cognate themes.
18. T. Nairn, *The Break-Up of Britain: Crisis and Neo-Nationalism* (London, 1977).
19. C. Harvie, *The Rise of Regional Europe* (London, 1994); Barry Jones and Michael Keating (eds), *The European Union and the Regions* (Oxford, 1995).
20. The argument against any such glib acceptance is strongly put by N. Piers Ludlow, 'Postwar Britain and Ideas of National Independence', in Geppert, *Postwar Challenge*, pp. 259–72.
21. David Reynolds, '1940: Fulcrum of the Twentieth Century?' *International Affairs* Vol. 66 No. 2 (1990), pp. 325–50, and his 'Churchill and the "Decision" to Fight on in 1940: Right Policy, Wrong Reasons', in Richard Langhorne (ed.), *Diplomacy and Intelligence during the Second World War: Essays in Honour of F.H. Hinsley* (Cambridge, 1985), pp. 147–67.
22. Alan Milward, *The New Order and the French Economy* (London, 1970); Christian Leitz, *Nazi Germany and Neutral Europe during the Second World War* (Manchester, 2001).
23. P.M.H. Bell, *France and Britain, 1940–1994: The Long Separation* (London, 1997), pp. 13–21.
24. Peter Davies, *Dangerous Liaisons: Collaboration and World War Two* (London, 2004).
25. Keith Robbins, '1945: British Victory?', *History* Vol. 71 No. 231 (February 1986), pp. 61–6.
26. Martin Conway and José Gotovich, *European Exile Communities in Britain 1940–45* (New York and Oxford, 2001) focuses on the Belgian experience particularly, but also has material on the Norwegians, the Poles, the Czechoslovaks, the French, the Dutch and the Socialist International; W. Röder, *Die deutschen sozialistischen Exilgruppen in Grossbritannien, 1940–1945* (Hanover, 1968).
27. D. Cesarani and T. Kushner (eds), *The Internment of Aliens in Twentieth Century Britain* (London, 1993); Walter Tschuppik, *Quislings: Hitler's Trojan Horses* (London, 1940). Tschuppik was a Czechoslovak newspaper man.
28. Nicholas Atkin, *The Forgotten French: Exiles in the British Isles, 1940–44* (Manchester, 2003).
29. A contemporary account, E. Tangye Lean, *Voices in the Darkness: The Story of the European Radio War* (London, 1943), may be compared with A. Briggs, *The War of Words: The History of Broadcasting in the United Kingdom, Vol. 3* (Oxford, 1995).
30. Michael Balfour, *Propaganda in War, 1939–45: Organisation, Policies and Publics in Britain* (London, 1979).
31. Essays in M. Smith and P. Stirk (eds), *Making the New Europe – European Unity and the Second World War* (London, 1990). British writers likewise speculated on what wartime experiences would mean for post-war relationships – for example, Rowland Kenney, *The Northern Triangle* (London, 1946).
32. For example, E.N. van Kleffens, *The Rape of the Netherlands* (London, 1940); L. de Jong, *Holland Fights the Nazis* (London, 1940?); Halvdan Koht and Sigmund Skard, *The Voice of Norway* (London, 1940?); Dik Lehmkuhl, *Journey to London: The Story of the Norwegian Government at War* (London, 1945); P. Salmon (ed.), *Britain and Norway in the Second World War* (London, 1995) contains pertinent essays.
33. Michael Bratby and Ernest Watkins, *Iceland Presents* (Reykjavik, 1941).
34. Ritchie Calder, *Carry On London* (London, 1941); Jean R. Freedman, *Whistling in the Dark: Memory and Culture in Wartime London* (Lexington, 1999); Susan Briggs, *The Home Front: War Years in Britain 1939–1945* (London, 1975); Mark Connelly, *We Can Take It! Britain and the Memory of the Second World War* (London, 2004); Maureen Waller, *London 1945* (London, 2004).

35. Sonya O. Rose, *Which People's War? National Identity and Citizenship in Wartime Britain, 1939–1945* (Oxford, 2004): S.P. MacKenzie, *Politics and Military Morale: Current-Affairs and Citizenship Education in the British Army, 1914–1950* (Oxford, 1992).

36. Asa Briggs, 'Britain and Europe after 1945', in Birke, Brechtken and Searle, *An Anglo-German Dialogue*, p. 244.

37. Pierre Maillaud, *The English Way* (Oxford, 1945), p. 266. Mortimer's comments are on p. 9.

38. The handbook to accompany the series was written by J. Hampden Jackson, pp. 28–30.

39. G.D.H. Cole, *Great Britain in the Post-War World* (London, 1942), pp. 161–2.

40. E.H. Carr, *Conditions of Peace*, p. 209.

41. Anthony J. Nicholls, 'The German "National Character" in British Perspective', in Jordan, *Conditions of Surrender*, pp. 26–39; Aubrey Douglas Smith, *Guilty Germans?* (London, 1942).

42. Curt Geyer and Walter Loeb, *Gollancz in German Wonderland* (London, 1944), p. 88; Curt Geyer, *Hitler's New, Kaiser's Old* (London, 1944); Heinrich Fraenkel, *Help Us Germans to Beat the Nazis* (London, 1941).

43. A.J.P. Taylor, *The Course of German History* (London, 1951), p. 7.

44. Royal Institute of International Affairs, *The Problem of Germany* (London, 1943), p. 11. Lothar Kettenacker, *Krieg zur Friedenssicherung. Deutschlandplanung der britischen Regierung während des Zweiten Weltkriegs* (Göttingen, 1989) and his sketch 'British Post-War Planning for Germany: Haunted by the Past', in Jordan (ed.), *Conditions of Surrender*, pp. 13–25; Carl-Christoph Schweitzer, 'Britische Deutschlandbilder im Zweiten Weltkrieg', in Ritter and Wende, *Rivalität und Partnerschaft*, pp. 203–25.

45. Richard Vaughan, *Post-War Integration in Europe* (London, 1976), pp. 16–20. W. Lipgens (ed.), *Europa-Föderationspläne der Widerstandsbewegungen, 1940–1945* (Munich, 1968); W. Lipgens (ed.), *Documents on the History of European Integration Vol. 2, Plans for European Union in Great Britain and in Exile, 1939–45* (Berlin, 1986); Keith Robbins, 'The Treaty of Versailles, "Never Again" and Appeasement', in Michael Dockrill and John Fisher (eds), *The Paris Peace Conference, 1919: Peace without Victory?* (Basingstoke, 2001), pp. 103–14.

46. G.D.H. Cole, *Europe, Russia and the Future* (London, 1941), pp. 14–15, 153.

47. M. Chaning-Pearce (ed.), *Federal Union: A Symposium* (London, 1940); John S. Hoyland, *Federate or Perish* (London, 1944); Duncan and Elizabeth Wilson, *Federation and World Order* (London, 1940); W. Ivor Jennings, *A Federation for Western Europe* (Cambridge, 1940); Sir Charles Kimber, 'Federal Union', in Catterall and Morris, *Britain and the Threat to Stability*, pp. 105–11; Richard Mayne and John Pinder, *Federal Union: The Pioneers* (London, 1990); Peter Wilson, 'The New Europe Debate in Wartime Britain', in P. Murray and P. Rich (eds), *Visions of European Unity* (Boulder, Colorado, 1996).

48. E.H. Carr, *Conditions of Peace* (London, 1942), pp. 205–9; Michael Cox (ed.), *E.H. Carr: A Critical Appreciation* (Basingstoke, 2000) examines various facets of Carr's thought and activity. Jonathan Haslam, *The Voice of Integrity: E.H. Carr* (London, 1999).

49. Streit's *Union Now* had gone through many impressions when it was published in 1939. *Union Now with Britain* (London, 1941) was its sequel.

50. 'The Hope of Federation', in Philip Gibbs, *Bridging the Atlantic: Anglo-American Fellowship as the Way to World Peace* (London, 1944?).

51. Harold James, *Europe Reborn: A History, 1914–2000* (London, 2003), p. 195.

52. Alfred M. de Zayas, *Nemesis at Potsdam: The Anglo-Americans and the Expulsion of the Germans: Background, Execution, Consequences* (London, 1977); P. Ahonen, *After the Expulsion: West Germany and Eastern Europe 1945–1990* (Oxford, 2003) looks at the long-term consequences of this 'ethnic cleansing'.

53. David Vital, *A People Apart: A Political History of the Jews in Europe, 1789–1939* (Oxford, 1999) gives a picture of life as it had been. Mark Mazower, *Dark Continent: Europe's Twentieth Century* (London, 1998), pp. 215–24.

54. P. Stachura (ed.), *The Poles in Britain, 1940–2000: From Betrayal to Assimilation* (London, 2004); Sheila Patterson, 'The Polish Exile Community in Britain', *Polish Rev* 6 (1961), pp. 69–97; Maud Bulbring, 'Post-War Refugees in Great Britain', *Population Studies* 8 (1954), pp. 99–112.

55. Patrick Gordon Walker, *The Lid Lifts* (London, 1945), pp. 69–71. Walker had been an Oxford don.

56. Ulrike Jordan (ed.), *Conditions of Surrender: Britons and Germans Witness the End of the War* (London, 1997), p. 90.

57. Robert Pearce (ed.), *Patrick Gordon Walker: Political Diaries 1932–1971* (London, 1991), p. 161.

58. David Williamson, *A Most Diplomatic General: The Life of General Lord Robertson of Oakridge* (London, 1996). Robertson was a Scot born in India. Most of his career, before the war, had been spent in India and South Africa.

59. For comments on the attitudes of other historians see Philip Bell, 'A Historical Cast of Mind: Some Eminent English Historians and their Attitudes to Continental Europe in the Middle of the Twentieth Century', *Journal of European Integration History* Vol. 2 No. 2 (1996), pp. 5–19.

60. Karl Jaspers, *The European Spirit* (London, 1948). The essay was written in German in 1946.

61. Karl Spiecker, *Germany from Defeat to Defeat* (London, 1943), p. 154.

62. All that the victors could do would be 'to provide the environment'. H.N. Brailsford, *The German Problem* (London n.d. [1944?]), p. 15.

63. Tony Sharp, *The Wartime Alliance and the Zonal Division of Germany* (Oxford, 1975).

64. Arthur Hearnden, *Red Robert; A Life of Robert Birley* (London, 1984), pp. 141–2.

65. Kurt Jürgensen, 'British Occupation Policy after 1945 and the Problem of "Re-educating Germany"', *History* Vol. 68, No. 223 (June, 1983), pp. 225–43; Nicholas Pronay and Keith Wilson (eds), *The Political Re-Education of Germany and Her Allies* (London, 1985); David Phillips (ed.), *German Universities after the Surrender: British Occupation Policy and the Control of Higher Education* (Oxford, 1983); Arthur Hearnden, *The British in Germany: Educational Reconstruction after 1945* (London, 1978).

66. Johannes-Dieter Steinert and Inge Weber-Newth, *Labour and Love: Deutsche in Grossbritannien nach dem Zweiten Weltkrieg* (Osnabrück, 2000).

67. Raymond Ebsworth, *Restoring Democracy in Germany* (London, 1960); W. Rudzio, 'Export englischer Demokratie? Zur Konzeption der britischen Besatzungspolitik in Deutschland', *Vierteljahreshefte für Zeitgeschichte* 17 (1969), pp. 219–36.

68. Alec Cairncross, *The Price of War: British Policy on German Reparations 1941–49* (Oxford, 1986); Alan Kramer, *Die britische Demontagepolitik am Beispiel Hamburgs 1945–1950* (Hamburg, 1991).

69. Patricia Meehan, *A Strange Enemy People: Germans under the British, 1945–1950* (London, 2001) is the most recent treatment in English; Ian D. Turner (ed.), *Reconstruction in Post-War Germany. British Occupation Policy and the Western Zones* (Oxford, 1989); Kurt Jürgensen, *Die Briten in Schleswig-Holstein 1945–49* (Neumünster, 1989); D.C. Watt, *Britain looks to Germany: British Opinion and Policy towards Germany since 1945* (London, 1965); K. Larres and E. Meehan (eds), *Uneasy Allies: British-German Relations and European Integration since 1945* (Oxford, 2000).

70. A.G. Dickens, *Lübeck Diary* (London, 1947), pp. 210–11.

71. Marie-Luise Recker, 'Westminster als Modell? Der Deutsche Bundestag und das britische Regierungssystem', in Ritter and Wende (eds), *Rivalität und Partnerschaft*, pp. 313–35.

72. J. Noakes, P. Wende and J. Wright, *Britain and Germany in Europe 1949–1990* (Oxford, 2002) explores the relationship at various levels of interaction.

73. Erich Meissner, *Germany in Peril* (London, 1942).

74. Jaspers, *European Spirit*, p. 15.

75. Ernest Barker, George Clark, Paul Vaucher, *The European Inheritance* Vol. III (Oxford, 1954), p. 354. This work was originally planned in connection with the Conference of Allied Ministers of Education during the years 1943–45. The volumes were stated to be written by European scholars, from a European point of view and for the use of European readers. The 'European scholars' were British, French and Belgian. Geoffrey Barraclough, *European Unity in Thought and Action* (Oxford, 1963), p. 4, pointed out the extent to which 'inheritance' could be interpreted one-sidedly.

76. Keith Robbins, 'Social and Political Ideas in Europe, 1939–70', in *Conflict and Stability in the Development of Modern Europe, 1789–1970* (Milton Keynes, 1980), pp. 77–104, sketches these cross-currents of opinion. More detailed accounts are naturally available in the histories of individual countries. Standard accounts, with varying

'European' emphases, are to be found in Peter Calvocoressi, *Resilient Europe 1870–2000* (London, 1991); D.W. Urwin, *Western Europe since 1945* (London, 1981).

77. David Reynolds, 'Britain and the New Europe: The Search for Identity since 1940', *The Historical Journal* Vol. 31 No. 1 (1988), pp. 223–39, is a useful review of publications appearing in that era. It drew the conclusion (p. 239) that 'Britain is now part of Europe: the referendum debate of the mid-1970s and the rows over the budget have been settled'.

78. Stephen Spender, *European Witness* (London, 1946).

79. Introduction to Jaspers, *European Spirit*, p. 11.

80. E.P. Thompson, *Beyond the Cold War* (London, 1982), p. 2. E.P. Thompson was quoting his own brother.

81. M. Cole (ed.), *Our Soviet Ally: Essays* (London, 1943), p. vii.

82. K. Gibberd, *Soviet Russia* (London, 1942), pp. 74–5.

83. Hewlett Johnson, *The Socialist Sixth of the World* (London, 1939), p. 18; *Soviet Strength* (1943); *Soviet Success* (London, n.d. [1946?]).

84. Hewlett Johnson, *Soviet Strength*, p. 123.

85. Bernard Pares, *Russia and the Peace* (Harmondsworth, 1944), p. 193; relations between the two allies at different levels can be seen in K. Graham Ross (ed.), *The Foreign Office and the Kremlin: British Documents on Anglo-Soviet Relations, 1941–1945* (Cambridge, 1984); Martin Kitchen, *British Policy towards the Soviet Union during the Second World War* (Basingstoke, 1986); Joan Beaumont, *Comrades in Arms: British Aid to Russia, 1941–1945* (London, 1980).

86. Walter Elliot, 'What is the difference?', *Russian Review* No. 2, March 1946.

87. Jennie Lee, *Our Ally Russia – the Truth* (London, 1941), pp. 63–4; Walter Citrine stressed that refusal to collaborate with the Communist Party did not mean that there was any doubt about British Labour doing its utmost to support the valiant Russians. W. Citrine, *In Russia Now* (London, 1942), p. 10. Victor Gollancz believed that, in cooperation, Britain and the Soviet Union could solve 'the problem of the modern world' – the reconciliation of an economy centrally planned for the common good, with personal freedom. Victor Gollancz, *Russia and Ourselves* (London, 1941), pp. 57–8.

88. A. Sisman, *A.J.P. Taylor: A Biography* (London, 1995), p. 187.

89. D.W. Brogan, *The Free State* (London, 1945); F. von Hayek, *The Road to Serfdom* (London, 1944) offered the conclusions of an Austro-Briton.

90. Churchill was speaking at Fulton, Missouri, in March 1946. David Carlton, *Churchill and the Soviet Union* (Manchester, 1999).

91. Peter J. Taylor, *Britain and the Cold War: 1945 as Geopolitical Transition* (London, 1990).

92. Keith Robbins, *The World since 1945* (Oxford, 1998).

93. A continuing focus on 'the world' rather than on 'Europe' among British international historians can be seen in P.A. Reynolds and E.J. Hughes, *The Historian as Diplomat: Charles Kingsley Webster and the United Nations, 1939–46* (London, 1976) and John D. Fair, *Harold Temperley: A Scholar and Romantic in the Public Realm* (Newark, Del., 1992).

94. A.W. Porte, *Europe between the Superpowers: The Enduring Balance* (New Haven, 1979 [2nd edn, 1986)]; Elizabeth Barker in turn places *The British between the Superpowers, 1945–50* (London, 1983); C.S. Maier, 'The Presence of the Superpowers in Europe (1946–54): An Overview', in Antonio Varsori (ed.), *Europe 1945–1990s: The End of an Era* (London, 1994); David Reynolds (ed.), *The Origins of the Cold War in Europe* (New Haven, 1994); W. Loth, *The Division of the World* (London, 1988); Anne Deighton, 'The Cold War in Europe, 1945–1947: Three Approaches', in Ngaire Woods, *Explaining International Relations since 1945* (Oxford, 1996).

95. G. Lundestad, *Empire by Integration: The United States and European Integration, 1945–1997* (Oxford, 1998).

96. Curtis Keeble, *Britain, the Soviet Union and Russia* (London, 2000).

97. A. Bullock, *Ernest Bevin: Foreign Secretary* (London, 1983) presents the world scene in 1945 in his opening chapter. Two recent surveys of Labour's foreign policy covering this period are Rhiannon Vickers, *The Labour Party and the World: Vol. 1: The Evolution of Labour's Foreign Policy 1900–1951* (Manchester, 2003) and John W. Young, *The Labour Governments 1964–70: Vol. 2: International Policy* (Manchester, 2003).

98. Kenneth Harris, *Attlee* (London, 1982), p. 315.
99. Alan Bullock, *The Life and Times of Ernest Bevin Vol. 1* (London, 1960), pp. 370–1.
100. H. Morrison, *An Autobiography* (London, 1960), p. 279.
101. D.R. Thorpe, *Selwyn Lloyd* (London, 1989), pp. 93, 281.
102. Healey and Crossman were two other Labour figures of this generation in the cabinet who had travelled extensively in pre-war Europe. Crossman had unsuccessfully married a German Jewish woman he had met in Berlin. Healey had travelled in vacations from Oxford in Germany, France and Greece. His war service took him to North Africa and Italy. He met Poles and developed a lasting affection for a people he believed to have suffered as much as his own Irish ancestors. D. Healey, *The Time of My Life* (London, 1989), p. 61. His work as post-war international secretary of the Labour Party gave him a controversial knowledge of European socialist parties.
103. George Brown, *In My Way* (Harmondsworth, 1972), p. 119.
104. M. Stewart, *Life and Labour* (London, 1980). Although possessing 'social knowledge of French and German', he would only transact business in English, p. 145.
105. Ina Zeiniger-Bagielowska, *Austerity in Britain: Rationing, Controls, and Consumption 1939–1955* (Oxford, 2000); Keith Robbins, *The Eclipse of a Great Power: Modern Britain, 1870–1992* (London, 1994) provides a broader assessment of these developments than can be attempted here.
106. Arthur Marwick, *The Sixties: Cultural Revolution in Britain, France, Italy and the United States c.1958–c.1974* (Oxford, 1998).
107. David Reynolds, *Rich Relations: The American Occupation of Britain 1942–1945* (London, 1995); Keith Robbins, *Great Britain*, pp. 310–13. A rash of books appeared designed to increase understanding of the United States. Denis Brogan, who wrote with equally facility on France, was a notable interpreter. D.W. Brogan, *USA: An Outline of the Country, its People and Institutions* (Oxford, 1941). Even H.N. Brailsford had written with unusual warmth on the prospect of *America Our Ally* (London, 1940); John Baylis, *Anglo-American Defence Relations, 1939–1984* (London, 1984); T.J. Botti, *The Long Wait: The Forging of the Anglo-American Nuclear Alliance, 1945–1958* (New York, 1987); W.R. Louis and H. Bull (eds), *The 'Special Relationship': Anglo-American Relations since 1945* (Oxford, 1986); R.B. Manderson-Jones, *The Special Relationship: Anglo-American Relations and Western European Unity, 1947–1956* (London, 1972).
108. Cited in Brian McKercher, *Transition of Power: Britain's Loss of Global Pre-eminence to the United States 1930–1945* (Cambridge, 1999), p. 343; Orde, *Eclipse of Great Britain*, pp. 157–9; W.F. Kimball (ed.), *Churchill and Roosevelt: The Complete Correspondence* (Princeton, 1984).
109. R.M. Hathaway, *Ambiguous Partnership: Britain and America, 1944–1947* (London, 1981); C.J. Bartlett, *'The Special Relationship': A Political History of Anglo-American Relations since 1945* (London, 1992); R. Edmonds, *Setting the Mould: The United States and Britain 1945–1950* (Oxford, 1986).
110. Cited in Alan Dobson, 'Anglo-American Relations in the Second World War', in Catterall and Morris (eds), *Britain and the Threat to Stability*, p. 137.
111. Christopher Andrew, 'The British-American "Special Relationship" and Intelligence since the Second World War', in Birke, Brechtken and Searle (eds), *An Anglo-German Dialogue*, p. 238.
112. B. Heuser, *Nuclear Mentalities? Strategies and Beliefs in Britain, France and the FRG* (London, 1988).
113. P. Papastratis, *British Policy towards Greece during the Second World War 1941–1944* (Cambridge, 1984).
114. In *The Meaning of Berlin* (London 1962), p. 16, a British government publication reiterated that 'the Western Powers cannot contemplate that the division of Germany should be permanent'. Saki Dockrill, *Britain's Policy for West German Rearmament* (London, 1991); Beatrice Heuser, 'Britain and the Federal Republic of Germany in NATO, 1955–1990', in Noakes, Wende and Wright, *Britain and Germany in Europe*, pp. 141–62, examines this fluctuating relationship.
115. The Federal Republic of Germany tilted uneasily between Paris and Washington. On the one hand, the 1963 treaty with France promoted a reconciliation that was 'European' but on the other, security needs continued to point to the United States. In short, within the Europe of NATO each country had its own 'special relationship' with the United States. Hans W. Gatzke, *Germany and the United States: 'A Special Relationship?'*

(London, 1980, and Gustav Schmidt (ed.), *Zwischen Bündnissicherung und priv-iligierter Partnerschaft: Die deutsch-britischen Beziehungen und die Vereinigten Staaten von Amerika 1955–1963* (Bochum, 1995) examine this diplomatic triangle.

116. The Labour MP John Edwards was exceptional in his commitment to the work of the Council of Europe. He ruefully compared his behaviour with that of Labour MPs who allegedly sat around and did nothing. Tam Dalyell, *Dick Crossman: A Portrait* (London, 1989), pp. 219–20.

117. Keith Robbins, 'Winston Churchill und Europa', in Heinz Duchhardt (ed.), *Europäer des 20 Jahrhunderts* (Mainz, 2002), pp. 145–64: Max Beloff, 'Churchill and Europe', in Blake and Louis (eds), *Churchill* (Oxford, 1993); John W. Young, 'Churchill's "No" to Europe: the Rejection of European Union by Churchill's Post-War Government 1951–1952', *Historical Journal* 28 (1985), pp. 923–37; Winston S. Churchill, *Europe United: Speeches 1947 and 1948* (London, 1950).

118. Cited in R. Ben Jones, *The Making of Contemporary Europe* (London, 1980), p. 56.

119. Alan Milward, *The Reconstruction of Western Europe, 1945–51* (London, 1984) and *The European Rescue of the Nation-State* (London, 1992); Andrew Moravcsik, *The Choice of Europe: Social Purpose and State Power from Messina to Maastricht* (Ithaca, 1998); E. di Nolfo (ed.), *Power in Europe Vol. II: Great Britain, France, Germany and Italy and the Origins of the EEC, 1952–7* (Berlin, 1992); Anne Deighton (ed.), *Building Postwar Europe: National Decision-Makers and European Institutions, 1948–1963* (London, 1995).

120. James Ellison, 'Britain and the Treaties of Rome, 1955–1959', in Broad and Preston (eds), *Moored to the Continent? Britain and European Integration*, pp. 33–51, summa-rizes his longer *Threatening Europe: Britain and the Creation of the European Community, 1955–58* (London, 2000). Its title and that of Martin P.C. Schaad, *Bullying Bonn: Anglo-German Diplomacy on European Integration 1955–61* (London, 2000) emphasizes the strong pressure Britain tried to apply to achieve its kind of Europe.

121. Edmund Dell, 'Britain's Failure over the Schuman Plan', in Roger Broad and Virginia Preston (eds), *Moored to the Continent? Britain and European Integration* (London, 2001), p. 31. The full exposition of Dell's view is *The Schuman Plan and the British Abdication of Leadership in Europe* (Oxford, 1995). For ways in which Britain subse-quently sought 'association' see J.W. Young, 'The Schuman Plan and British Association', in J.W. Young (ed.), *The Foreign Policy of Churchill's Peacetime Administration, 1951–1955* (Leicester, 1988), pp. 109–34; Geoffrey Warner,' Die britische Labour-Regierung und die Einheit Westeuropas 1948-51', *Vierteljahreshefte für Zeitgeschichte* Vol. 28 No. 3 (1980), pp. 310–30.

122. Dean Acheson, *Present at the Creation* (London, 1970), p. 387.

123. Denman, *Missed Chances*, p. 201.

124. Wolfram Kaiser, *Using Europe, Abusing the Europeans: Britain and European Integration, 1945–1963* (Basingstoke, 1996) and, specifically on EFTA, his 'Challenge to the Community: The Creation, Crisis and Consolidation of the European Free Trade Association, 1958–1972', *Journal of European Integration History*, Vol. 3, No. 1 (1997), pp. 7–33; Jeremy Moon, *European Integration in British Politics, 1950–1963: A Study in Issue Change* (Aldershot, 1985).

125. Jacqueline Tratt, *The Macmillan Government and Europe: A Study in the Process of Policy Development* (London, 1996) considers the reasons fully.

126. P. Williams, *Hugh Gaitskell* (London, 1979), p. 729. Gaitskell, who had an eye for such things, thought that the women of Paris in 1950 were much less well dressed than he had expected and they seemed 'somehow more English than before the war', cited in P. Williams, *The Diary of Hugh Gaitskell* (London, 1983), p. 177.

127. David Dilks, *de Gaulle and the British* (Hull, 1996), p. 33.

128. F. Kersaudy, *Churchill and de Gaulle* (London, 1981).

129. N. Piers Ludlow, *Dealing with Britain: The Six and the First UK Application to the EEC* (Cambridge, 1997), p. 251. See also Richard Davis 'The "Problem of de Gaulle", 1958–1967', in Chassaigne and Dockrill (eds), *Anglo-French Relations*, pp. 161–73.

130. Pearce, *Gordon Walker Political Diaries*, p. 286.

131. William Pickles, *Not with Europe: The Political Case for Staying Out* (London, 1962).

132. The 'European Unity' considered admirably by John W. Young in *Britain and European Unity, 1945–1992* (Basingstoke, 1993), *Britain, France and the Unity of Europe*

(Leicester, 1984) and 'Towards a New View of British Policy and European Unity 1945–1957', in Ahmann, Birke and Howard, *The Quest for Stability*, pp. 435–62, relates to a confined Europe.

133. HMSO, *Background to the Negotiations: Britain and the European Communities* (London, 1962).

134. Avi Shlaim, *Britain and the Origins of European Unity 1940–1951* (Reading, 1978).

135. The closest approximation to British anxieties was to be found in northern Europe. See Thorsten B. Olesen (ed.), *Interdependence versus Integration: Denmark, Scandinavia and Western Europe, 1945–1960* (Odense, 1995).

136. Heinz Duchhardt and Andreas Kunz (eds), *'Europäisches Geschichte' als historiographisches Problem* (Mainz, 1997); S. Woolf, 'Europe and its Historians', *Contemporary European History* (August 2003), pp. 323–37; Derek Heater, *The Idea of European Unity* (Leicester, 1992).

137. Fernando Guirao, *Spain and the Reconstruction of Western Europe, 1945–57: Challenge and Response* (London, 1998) notes the adjustments the Franco regime had to make.

138. Joanna Dziechciowska, 'Anti-British Propaganda in Polish Newspapers of the Stalinist Period: On Relationships between Great Britain and the Countries of the Socialist Camp', *Polish-AngloSaxon Studies* Vol. 10/11 (Poznan, 2003), pp. 63–91.

139. D.W. Urwin, *Western Europe since 1945* (London, 1981 edn), pp. xi–xii. Urwin saw that there might be doubt about Italy.

140. Roger Morgan, *West European Politics since 1945* (London, 1972), pp. 2–3.

141. Walther L. Bernecker, 'Spanien. Zwischen Isolation und Integration', in M. Salewski (ed.), *Nationale Identität und Europäische Einigung* (Göttingen, 1991), pp. 125–68.

142. Philip de Zulueta cited in A. Horne, *Macmillan, 1894–1956* (London, 1988), p. 35.

143. See the essay by Niedhart in G. Niedhart (ed.), *Das kontinentale Europa und die britische Inseln* (Mannheim, 1993), pp. 205–13.

144. Beatrice Heuser, 'Alliance Bedevilled by History: Franks, Germanics and Anglo-Saxons in the Cold War', in Luciano Tosi, *Europe, its Borders and the Others* (Naples, 2000), pp. 313–49, perceptively explores European identities and transatlantic relations.

145. See the discussion in Douglas Johnson, *How European are the French?* (Reading, 1996); 'Nationale und europäische Momente bei der Formulierung der französischen Europapolitik nach 1945', in Salewski (ed.), *Nationale Identität*, pp. 73–86; S.J. Woolf (ed.), *The Rebirth of Italy, 1943–50* (London, 1972); R.J.B. Bosworth and P. Dogliani, *Italian Fascism: History, Memory and Representation* (Basingstoke, 1999).

146. Thanasis D. Sfikas, *The British Labour Government and the Greek Civil War: The Imperialism of 'Non-Intervention'* (Ryburn, 1994).

147. Edward Thompson and Christopher Hill being perhaps the most prominent. A.J.P. Taylor, though not a party member, thought the Soviet action 'shameful' but some 20 years later considered it a rising by 'all the most reactionary forces'. Sisman, *A.J.P. Taylor*, pp. 283–4.

148. Born in Prague, Z.A.B. Zeman interpreted events for British readers in *Prague Spring: A Report on Czechoslovakia, 1968* (Harmondsworth, 1989). Two years earlier, the Czech historian J.V. Polisensky had judged the moment right to produce a short study of the connections between the two countries – *Britain and Czechoslovakia* (Prague, 1966).

149. G. Niedhart, 'The British Reactions towards Ostpolitik: Anglo-West German Relations in the Era of Détente, 1967–71', in Christian Haase (ed.), *Debating Foreign Affairs: The Public and British Foreign Policy since 1867* (Berlin/Vienna, 2003), pp. 130–52; Roger Morgan, 'Willy Brandt's "Neue Ostpolitik": British Perceptions and Positions 1969–1975', in Birke, Brechtken and Searle, *An Anglo-German Dialogue*, pp. 179–202.

Chapter 11

1. M. Jebb (ed.), *The Diaries of Cynthia Gladwyn* (London, 1995), p. 211.

2. Lord Gladwyn, *Memoirs* (London, 1972).

3. Brown, *In My Way*, pp. 123–4.

4. Reprinted in his *Channels and Tunnels: Recollections on Britain and Abroad* (London, 1987), pp. 143–58. His *The Private Office: A Personal View of Five Foreign Secretaries and of Government from Inside* (London, 1984) reflects more generally on these issues.
5. *Daily Telegraph*, 25 September 2004.
6. R. Boardman and A.J.L. Groom (eds), *The Management of Britain's External Relations* (London, 1973); William Wallace, *The Foreign Policy Process in Britain* (London, 1976); Yoel Cohen, *Media Diplomacy: The Foreign Office in the Mass Communication Age* (London, 1986); Geoffrey Moorhouse, *The Diplomats: The Foreign Office Today* (London, 1977); Simon Jenkins and Anne Sloman, *With Respect Ambassador: An Inquiry into the Foreign Office* (London, 1985).
7. A. Horne, *Macmillan 1957–1986* (London, 1989), p. 357.
8. Roy Jenkins, *A Life at the Centre* (London, 1991), pp. 417–18. It was the contention of the Referendum Party, funded by Sir James Goldsmith, that fought the 1997 general election with little success, that British politicians had 'lied through their teeth' and had taken Britain into a federal Europe by deceit.
9. Denis Healey, *The Time of My Life* (London, 1989), pp. 115–16.
10. Jane Schneider (ed.), *Italy's 'Southern Question': Orientalism in One Country* (Oxford, 1998). Some interpretations placed southern Italy as the territorial watershed between 'Europeanized (or Americanized) Italy and 'African' Italy.
11. Roy Jenkins, *European Diary* (London, 1989), p. 2; Sir Crispin Tickell, who worked for him, assesses Jenkins as President of the European Commission in Anthony Adonis and Keith Thomas (eds), *Roy Jenkins: A Retrospective* (Oxford, 2004), pp. 179–202.
12. Roy Jenkins, *A Life at the Centre* (London, 1991), pp. 444–55, gives an account of his initial aspirations and impressions.
13. Jenkins, *Life at the Centre*, p. 484.
14. Peter Ludlow, *The Making of the European Monetary System: A Case Study in the Politics of the European Community* (London, 1982).
15. Mervyn Jones, *Michael Foot* (London, 1994), p. 378.
16. Geoffrey Rippon, who had led for Britain in the accession negotiations, became leader of the European Conservative Group in 1977, and was never afraid to advocate such new dimensions to European policy as could 'fully safeguard the civilisation we share together'. Geoffrey Rippon, *Our European Future* (London, 1978), p. 17.
17. Edward Heath, *The Course of My Life* (London, 1998), p. 696.
18. For example, by Keith Middlemas, *Orchestrating Europe: The Informal Politics of the European Union 1973–1995* (London, 1995), p. 354.
19. Margaret Thatcher, *The Path to Power* (London, 1995), pp. 344–7.
20. Horne, *Macmillan 1957–86*, p. 262.
21. Michael Bromley, 'The Media', in Jonathan Hollowell (ed.), *Britain since 1945* (Oxford, 2003), pp. 211–37; Christina Schäffner, 'The Concept of "Europe"', in the British Weekly *The Economist* over the years 1975–1988', in Christiane Villain-Gandossi and others, *Le Concept de l'Europe dans le Processus de la CSCE* (Tübingen, 1990).
22. Keith Dowding, 'The Civil Service', in Hollowell (ed.), *Britain since 1945*, pp. 184–7.
23. Denman, *Missed Chances*, p. 259.
24. She mentions reading Douglas Reed's *Insanity Fair* and R. Bruce Lockhart's *Guns or Butter*. She attended 'extension lectures' from the University of Nottingham on international affairs. She read the *Daily Telegraph* every day and ran home from school to make her first acquaintance with a wireless. Her sister had an Austrian Jewish pen friend who later came to Grantham. Margaret Thatcher, *The Path to Power* (London, 1995), pp. 22–31.
25. His father had been the director of finance to the high commission for the (occupied) Rhineland – where he was born. Roy Jenkins comments that, at her first meeting of the European Council, Margaret Thatcher was very oddly treated by Giscard, though he does not attribute this to 'simple anglophobia' since he considered Giscard to be 'semi-anglophile'. Jenkins, *Life at the Centre*, p. 494.
26. Cited in Bell, *France and Britain 1940–1994*, p. 245.
27. Lord Carrington, *Reflect on Things Past* (London, 1988), pp. 66, 310; W. Whitelaw, *The Whitelaw Memoirs* (London, 1989), p. 74.
28. Stephen George, *An Awkward Partner: Britain in the European Community* (Oxford, 1998), pp. 150–6.
29. There is, of course, a considerable literature on the 'Thatcher years' and no overall

assessment of her governments is attempted here. Eric Evans, *Thatcher and Thatcherism* (London, 1997) is a useful short study.

30. Clemens A Wurm, 'Sozialisten und europäische Integration. Die britische Labour Party 1945–1984', *Geschichte in Wissenschaft und Unterricht* (1987/5), pp. 280–95, summarizes the party's ragged course.

31. Geoffrey Howe, *Conflict of Loyalty* (London, 1994), p. 21.

32. Howe, *Conflict of Loyalty*, pp. 536–7.

33. Debman, *Missed Chances*, p. 169.

34. R. Harmsen and M. Spiering (eds), *Euroscepticism: Party Politics, National Identity and European Integration* (Amsterdam, 2004) does not confine itself to British Euroscepticism.

35. A.J. Nicholls, 'The Academic Community: Modern and Contemporary Historians', in Noakes, Wende and Wright, *Britain and Germany in Europe*, pp. 307–26; Mary Fulbrook (ed.), *National Histories and European History* (London, 1993).

36. Christhard Hoffmann cited in Peter Alter (ed.), *Out of the Third Reich: Refugee Historians in Post-war Britain* (London, 1998), p. xix; John Breuilly, 'Historians and the Nation', in P. Burke (ed.), *History and Historians in the Twentieth Century* (Oxford, 2002), pp. 55–87.

37. Robert Phillips, *History Teaching, Nationhood and the State* (London, 1998); Akira Iriye, 'The Internationalization of History', *American Historical Review* Vol. 94 No. 1 (February 1989), pp. 1–10; Helen Brocklehurst and Robert Phillips (eds), *History, Nationhood and the Question of Britain* (Basingstoke, 2004); Oliver J. Daddow, *Britain and Europe since 1945: Historiographical Perspectives on Integration* (Manchester, 2004); William Wallace, 'Foreign Policy and National Identity in the United Kingdom', *International Affairs* Vol. 67 No. 1 (1991), pp. 65–80; Kenneth Lunn, 'Reconsidering "Britishness": The Construction and Significance of National Identity in Twentieth Century Britain', in B. Jenkins and S. Sofos (eds), *Nation and Identity in Contemporary Europe* (London, 1996), pp. 83–100.

38. Keith Robbins, *Insular Outsider? 'British History' and European Integration* (Reading, 1990); T.J. Schulte, 'Europe in History Textbooks: Short Paper from Great Britain', in G. Renner (ed.), *Die Europäische Einigung im Schulbuch* (Bonn, 1992).

39. Alan Sked, an authority on the Habsburg monarchy and on twentieth-century Britain was for a time leader of the United Kingdom Independence Party. An intelligent person, he thought, would see that Britain had 'the most successful history of any country in the world' and would not want to be mired in the European Union. Alan Sked, *An Intelligent Person's Guide to Post-War Britain* (London, 1997), p. 177.

40. Cited in Bell, *France and Britain 1940–1994*, p. 295.

41. Michael Chisholm, *Britain on the Edge of Europe* (London, 1995), p. 166.

42. Anne Corbett and Hilary Footitt, *Crossing the Channel: Promoting Academic Mobility in Europe* (London, 2001).

43. The contributors to J.A. Mangan (ed.), *Tribal Identities: Nationalism, Europe and Sport* (Manchester, 1995) look at these issues on a broad front.

44. Douglas Hurd, *Memoirs* (London, 2003), pp. 432–5.

45. For useful essays see John O'Loughlin and Herman van der Wusten (eds), *The New Political Geography of Eastern Europe* (London, 1993).

46. The books of Hans Magnus Enzensberger and Edgar Morin, for example, are summarized and discussed in Wilson and van der Dussen, *History of the Idea of Europe*, pp. 178–80.

47. P. Katzenstein (ed.), *Mitteleuropa: Between Europe and Germany* (New York, 1998) has a revealing title.

48. Larry Siedentop, *Democracy in Europe* (New York, 2003), pointed to the plurality of understandings of the term 'democracy' – and that there had been a British special path.

49. Timothy Garton Ash, *The Magic Lantern: The Revolution of '89 Witnessed in Warsaw, Budapest, Berlin and Prague* (London, 1990) remains the best account by a British observer.

50. Martin McCauley, *Gorbachev* (London, 1998), p. 44; Alex Pravda and Peter Duncan (eds), *Soviet-British Relations since the 1970s* (London, 1990).

51. Philip Zelikow and Condoleeza Rice, *Germany Unified and Europe Transformed: A Study in Statecraft* (Harvard, 1995) is an analysis that gains particular interest in the light of the post occupied by the second author a decade later.

52.   Arnd Bauerkämper (ed.), *Britain and the GDR: Relations and Perceptions in a Divided World* (Berlin, 2002); John Peet had edited a journal, *Democratic German Report*, which was among the GDR's most effective propaganda in Britain. S. Berger and N. Laporte, 'John Peet (1915–1988): An Englishman in the GDR', *History* Vol. 89 No. 293 (January 2004), pp. 49–69.

53.   A.M. Birke, 'Britain and German Unity', in Birke, *Britain and Germany*, p. 291.

54.   Harold James and Marla Stone (eds), *When the Wall Came Down; Reactions to German Unification* (London, 1992).

55.   Simon Winchester, *The Fracture Zone: A Return to the Balkans* (London, 1999) is an account by a British journalist.

56.   Mazower, *Dark Continent*, p. 410.

57.   Grace Davie, *Religion in Modern Europe: A Memory Mutates* (Oxford, 2000); H. McLeod and W. Ustorf, *The Decline of Christendom in Western Europe, 1750–2000* (Cambridge, 2003).

58.   J.L. Esposito and F. Burgat (eds), *Modernising Islam: Religion and the Public Sphere in Europe and the Middle East* (London, 2003); H. Ansari, *The 'Infidel Within'; The History of Muslims in Britain from 1800 to the Present* (London, 2004).

59.   Keith Robbins, 'Location and Dislocation: Ireland, Scotland and Wales in their Insular Alignment', in J. Morrill (ed.), *The Promotion of Knowledge: Lectures to mark the Centenary of the British Academy 1902–2002* (Oxford, 2004), pp. 163–80; Paul Gillespie (ed.), *Britain's European Question: The Issues for Ireland* (Dublin, 1996) explores the triangular British/Irish/European relationship.

60.   Keith Robbins, *Britishness and British Foreign Policy: Foreign and Commonwealth Office Historians Occasional Papers No. 14* (London, 1997); and 'Devolution and "British" Foreign Policy', *International Affairs* Vol. 74 No. 1 (January 1998), pp. 105–17; A.D. Smith, 'National Identity and the Idea of European Unity, *International Affairs*, Vol. 68 No. 1 (January, 1992), pp. 55–76; Timothy Garton Ash, 'Is Britain European?', *International Affairs* Vol. 77 No. 1 (January, 2001), pp. 1–14.

61.   For a plausible, if fleeting, Franco-British 'third way' see F.-C. Mougel, 'Lionel Jospin–Tony Blair: Building a Comparison', in Chassaigne and Dockrill, *Anglo-French Relations*, pp. 189–202.

62.   Harold James notes that where German and French firms merged, the language of corporate communication was often English. James, *Europe Reborn*, p. 396. It was reported in April 2004 that more than 57 per cent of all Commission documents were drafted in English, compared to 29 per cent in French and 5 per cent in German. *Daily Telegraph*, 24 April 2004; M. Fettes, 'Europe's Babylon: Towards a Single European Language?', *History of European Ideas* 13 (1991).

63.   John Gillingham, *European Integration, 1950–2003: Superstate or New Market Economy* (Cambridge, 2003) is a stimulating overview; Frank Schimmelfennig, *The EU, NATO and the Integration of Europe: Rules and Rhetoric* (Cambridge, 2003).

64.   'We the people reject this wretched constitution', wrote William Rees-Mogg in *The Times* (21 June 2004). The prime minister was trying to defy 'the historic instincts of the British people'. A fellow columnist, Anatole Kaletsky, urged that France and Germany could build their superstate if they wanted to 'but leave us out of it' (24 June 2004).

65.   Andrew Gamble and Gavin Kelly, 'Britain and EMU', in Kenneth Dyson (ed.), *European States and the Euro: Europeanization, Variation and Convergence* (Oxford, 2002), pp. 97–119; Roy Jenkins had urged, though in vain, in relation to monetary union, that Britain 'should not be left waving from the railway platform for the fourth time'. Lord Jenkins of Hillhead, 'Britain in Europe: Left Behind Again?', *Royal Bank of Scotland Review* No. 162 (June 1989), pp. 3–8.

66.   As has been pointed out, the euro is in part an attempt to construct a European identity by making Europe a part of 'everyday life'. Matthias Kaelberer, 'The euro and European identity' *Review of International Studies* Vol. 30 No. 2 (April 2004), p. 177.

67.   *Daily Telegraph*, 15 May 2004.

68.   William Wallace, 'Governing without Statehood: the Unstable Equilibrium', in Helen Wallace and William Wallace, *Policy-Making in the European Union* (Oxford, 1996), p. 439.

69.   It is now a little odd to read confident assertion being made in 2001 that 'it is now clear that Britain has been displaced as America's principal ally in Europe by the reunited

Germany'. Ian Davidson 'Britain's Place in the World since 1945', in Broad and Preston (eds), *Moored to the Continent?*, p. 228.

70. Richard von Weizsäcker, 'Channel Crossing: Common European Tasks and Challenges', *Bulletin of the German Historical Institute, London* Vol. XXVI, No. 2 (November 2004), p. 10.

71. Contrary views on 'Europe and America' – and how Britain should 'place' itself – can be found in Stephen Haseler, *Super-State: The New Europe and its Challenge to America* (London, 2004) and Timothy Garton Ash, *Free World* (London, 2004).

72. Jean Guiffan, *Histoire de l'Anglophobie en France* (Rennes, 2004) reflects on the fact that 15 per cent of French people apparently declared that they did not like the English and a larger number still regarded them as 'hereditary enemies'.

Bibliography

The endnotes provide references to material cited in the text and offer detailed guidance to further reading. The following bibliography offers a selection of titles on a chapter-by-chapter basis, though some of the books consider matters across a wider timeframe.

General

Black, J., *Convergence or Divergence? Britain and the Continent* (Basingstoke, 1994).

Black, J., *Maps and History: Constructing Images of the Past* (New Haven and London, 1997).

Breuilly, J., *Nationalism and the State* (Manchester, 1982).

Davies, N., *Europe: A History* (Oxford, 1996).

Davies, N., *The Isles* (Basingstoke and Oxford, 1999).

Duroselle, J.-B., *Europe: A History of its Peoples* (London, 1990).

Hay, D., *Europe: The Emergence of an Idea* (Edinburgh, 1957).

Hinsley, F.H., *Power and the Pursuit of Peace* (Cambridge, 1963).

Joll, J. (ed.), *Britain and Europe: Pitt to Churchill, 1793–1940* (London, 1967).

Powell, D., *Nationhood and Identity: The British State since 1800* (London, 2002).

Robbins, K., *Great Britain: Identities, Institutions and the Idea of Britishness* (London, 1998).

Schroeder, P.W., *The Transformation of European Politics 1763–1848* (Oxford, 1996).

Seton-Watson, R.W., *Britain in Europe, 1789–1914* (Cambridge, 1937).

Taylor, A.J.P., *The Struggle for Mastery in Europe* (Oxford, 1954).

Tosi, L., *Europe, Its Borders and The Others* (Perugia, 2000).

Chapter 1

Brockliss, L. and Eastwood, D. (eds), *A Union of Multiple Identities: The British Isles c.1750–c.1850* (Manchester, 1997).

Foster, R.F., *Modern Ireland 1600–1792* (London, 1988).

Langford, P., *Englishmen Identified: Manners and Character 1650–1850* (Oxford, 2000).

McKay, D. and Scott, H., *The Rise of the Great Powers 1648–1815* (London, 1983).

Munck, T., *The Enlightenment: A Comparative Social History, 1721–1794* (London, 2000).

Schulze, H., *States, Nations and Nationalism from the Middle Ages to the Present* (Oxford, 1996).

Chapter 2

Best, G.F.A., *War and Society in Revolutionary Europe, 1770–1870* (London, 1982).

Black, J., *Natural and Necessary Enemies: Anglo-French Relations in the Eighteenth Century* (London, 1986).

Blanning, T.C.W., *The Origins of the French Revolutionary Wars* (London, 1986).

Ceadel, M., *The Origins of War Prevention: The British Peace Movement and International Relations, 1730–1854* (Oxford, 1996).

Colley, L., *Britons: Forging the Nation, 1707–1837* (London, 1996).

Dickinson, H.T., *British Radicalism and the French Revolution, 1785–1815* (Oxford, 1985).

Dixon, S., *The Modernisation of Russia 1676–1825* (Cambridge, 1999).

McCalman, I., *An Oxford Companion to the Romantic Age: British Culture 1776–1832* (Oxford, 1999).

Royle, E., *Revolutionary Britannia: Reflections on the Threat of Revolution in Britain, 1789–1848* (Manchester, 2000).

Stone, L. (ed.), *An Imperial State at War: Britain from 1689 to 1815* (London and New York, 1994).

Chapter 3

Bayly, C., *Imperial Meridian: The British Empire and the World, 1780–1830* (London, 1989).

Cain P.J. and Hopkins, A.G., *British Imperialism: Innovation and Expansion 1688–1914* (London, 1993).

Clarke, J., *British Diplomacy and Foreign Policy, 1782–1865: The National Interest* (London, 1989).

Duffy, M., *The Englishman and the Foreigner* (Cambridge, 1986).
Dwyer, P.G. (ed.), *Napoleon and Europe* (London, 2001).
Ellis, G., *Napoleon* (London, 1997).
Hall, C.D., *British Strategy in the Napoleonic War 1803–1815* (Manchester, 1992).
Lyons, M., *Napoleon and the Legacy of the French Revolution* (London, 1994).
Roberts, A., *Napoleon and Wellington* (London, 2001).
Semmel, S., *Napoleon and the British* (London, 2004).
Woolf, S., *Napoleon's Integration of Europe* (London, 1991).

Chapter 4

Cookson, J.E., *Lord Liverpool's Administration: The Crucial Years, 1815–1822* (Edinburgh and London, 1975).
Dwyer, P.G., *Talleyrand* (London, 2002).
Gates, D., *Napoleonic Wars* (London, 1997).
Holbraad, C., *The Concert of Europe* (London, 1970).
Kissinger, H., *A World Restored* (London, 1977).

Chapter 5

Berger, S., Donovan, M. with Passmore, K. (eds), *Writing National Histories: Western Europe since 1800* (London, 1999).
Edsall, N., *Richard Cobden: Independent Radical* (London, 1986).
Evans, R.J.W. and Pogge von Strandmann, H. (eds), *The Revolutions in Europe 1848–1849: From Reform to Reaction* (Oxford, 2000).
Howe, A.C., *Free Trade and Liberal England, 1846–1946* (Oxford, 1997).
Johnson, D., *Guizot: Aspects of French History, 1787–1874* (London, 1964).
Morgan, M., *National Identities and Travel in Victorian Britain* (Basingstoke, 2001).
Robbins, K., *Nineteenth-Century Britain: Integration and Diversity* (Oxford, 1988).

Chapter 6

Ceadel, M., *Semi-detached Idealists: The British Peace Movement and International Relations 1854–1945* (Oxford, 2000).
Grenville, J.A.S., *Europe Reshaped 1848–1878* (London, 1976).
Hoppen, K.T., *The Mid-Victorian Generation* (Oxford, 1998).
McLeod, H., *European Religion in the Age of Great Cities 1830–1930* (Oxford, 2001).

Porter, B., *Britain, Europe and the World 1850–1982: Delusions of Grandeur* (London, 1983).

Wolffe, J., *God and Greater Britain: Religion and National Life in Britain and Ireland 1843–1945* (London, 1994).

Chapter 7

Burrow, J.W., *A Liberal Descent: Victorian Historians and the English Past* (Cambridge, 1983).

Chadwick, O., *A History of the Popes, 1830–1914* (Oxford, 1998).

Fulbrook, M., *National Histories and European History* (London, 1993).

Grenville, J.A.S., *Lord Salisbury and Foreign Policy: The Close of the Nineteenth Century* (London, 1970).

Howard, C.H.D., *Splendid Isolation* (London, 1967).

Chapter 8

Bell, P.M.H., *France and Britain 1900–1940: Entente and Estrangement* (London, 1996).

Charmley, J., *Splendid Isolation: Britain and the Balance of Power 1874–1914* (London, 1999).

Hinsley, F.H. (ed.), *British Foreign Policy under Sir Edward Grey* (Cambridge, 1977).

Kendle, J.E., *Federal Britain* (London, 1997).

Marsh, P.T., *Bargaining on Europe: Britain and the First Common Market, 1860–1892* (London, 1999).

Robbins, K., *The First World War* (Oxford, 1984).

Stevenson, D., *The First World War and International Politics* (Oxford, 1988).

Wilson, K. (ed.), *Decisions for War, 1914* (London, 1995).

Chapter 9

Berger, S., *The British Labour Party and the German Social Democrats, 1900–1951: A Comparative Study* (Oxford, 1994).

Catterall, P. and Morris, C.J. (eds), *Britain and the Threat to Stability in Europe 1918–45* (London, 1993).

Fisher, H.A.L., *A History of Europe* (London, 1936).

Goldstein, E., *Winning the Peace: British Diplomatic Strategy: Peace Planning and the Paris Peace Conference, 1916–1920* (Oxford, 1991).

Macmillan, M., *The Paris Peace Conference of 1919: The Attempt to End War* (London, 2001).

Robbins, K., *Appeasement* (Oxford, 1997).

Watt, D.C., *How the War Came: The Immediate Origins of the Second World War* (London, 1989).

Chapter 10

Bell, P.M.H., *France and Britain, 1940–1994: The Long Separation* (London, 1997).

Conway, M. and Gotovich J., *European Exile Communities in Britain 1940–45* (Oxford, 2001).

James, H., *Europe Reborn: A History, 1914–2000* (London, 2003).

Kaiser, W., *Using Europe, Abusing the Europeans* (London, 1996).

Mazower, M., *Dark Continent: Europe's Twentieth Century* (London, 1998).

Radice, G., *Offshore: Britain and the European Idea* (London, 1992).

Reynolds, D. (ed.), *The Origins of the Cold War in Europe* (New Haven, 1994).

Young, H., *This Blessed Plot; Britain and Europe from Churchill to Blair* (London, 1998).

Chapter 11

Chisholm, M., *Britain on the Edge of Europe* (London, 1995).

Dyson, K. (ed.), *European States and the Euro: Europeanization, Variation and Convergence* (Oxford, 2002).

Gillingham, J., *European Integration 1950–2003: Superstate or New Market Economy* (Cambridge, 2003).

Jenkins, R., *A Life at the Centre* (London, 1991).

Ludlow, P., *The Making of the European Monetary System: A Case Study in the Politics of the European Community* (London, 1982).

Middlemas, K., *Orchestrating Europe: The Informal Politics of the European Union, 1973–1995* (London, 1995).

Ward, P., *Britishness since 1870* (London, 2004).

Weight, R., *Patriots: National Identity in Britain 1940–2000* (Basingstoke, 2002).

Index